Empowering Digital Sovereignty:

Balancing Privacy and Global Connectivity

Sanjay Misra
Institute for Energy Technology, Norway

Petter Kvalvik
Institute for Energy Technology, Norway

Kai Morgan Kjølerbakken
Institute for Energy Technology, Norway

Per-Arne Jørgensen
Institute for Energy Technology, Norway

IGI Global
Scientific Publishing
Publishing Tomorrow's Research Today

Vice President of Editorial Melissa Wagner
Director of Acquisitions Mikaela Felty
Director of Book Development Jocelynn Hessler
Production Manager Mike Brehm
Cover Design Jose Rosado

Published in the United States of America by
IGI Global Scientific Publishing
701 East Chocolate Avenue
Hershey, PA, 17033, USA
Tel: 717-533-8845
Fax: 717-533-7115
Website: https://www.igi-global.com E-mail: cust@igi-global.com

Library of Congress Cataloging-in-Publication Data

LCCN: 2024056720 (CIP Data Pending)
ISBN13: 9798369391372
Isbn13Softcover: 9798369391389
EISBN13: 9798369391396

British Cataloguing in Publication Data
A Cataloguing in Publication record for this book is available from the British Library.

Table of Contents

Detailed Table of Contents

As subset of digital sovereignty, data sovereignty characterizes data sharing in modern data ecosystems. The main goal is to preserve the interest of the data rights holder using different technical approaches, such as policy management and usage control, to establish transparency and trust. At first glance, many of the characteristics of data sovereignty align with privacy. This chapter per the authors discusses the delimitation of both concepts. This elaboration is prepared by first analyzing data sovereignty from an economic, organizational, regulatory, and technical perspective using a systematic literature review (SLR) presenting 38 relevant articles. The subsequent comparison according to selected properties highlights many similarities and significant differences. This chapter per the authors emphasizes the importance of clearly distinguishing data sovereignty and privacy in theory and practice. However, it indicates that many privacy-preserving software engineering approaches, e.g., concerning requirements engineering (RE), can be transferred to the data sovereignty domain.

As smart cities evolve with advanced surveillance systems, the balance between public safety and citizens' digital sovereignty has emerged as a critical concern. This paper presents a qualitative study that explores how modern observation techniques, such as AI-powered cameras, facial recognition, and real-time monitoring, enhance urban security while simultaneously threatening individual privacy. Through an interdisciplinary analysis of surveillance technologies, legal frameworks, and governance models, the study highlights the growing risks of mass surveillance, data misuse, and erosion of personal freedoms. The proposed framework is illustrated through the example of Delhi's smart city development, revealing systemic gaps in transparency, consent, and accountability. The paper further examines regulatory and technological strategies that can mitigate privacy invasions without undermining security goals.

The proposed system was evaluated using the widely recognized NSL-KDD and CIC-IDS-2017 datasets. The results from these evaluations highlighted several qualitative benefits, including improved detection accuracy, greater processing efficiency, and better alignment with Digital Sovereignty principles. Moreover, the real-time processing capabilities of the system contributed to reduced data storage requirements, as the need for long-term data retention was minimized. The system's adaptability to local data laws further ensures that it can be deployed across various regions, complying with local regulations without sacrificing performance. Overall, the experimental results demonstrated significant advancements in both the accuracy and efficiency of intrusion detection, making this approach a promising solution for modern network security challenges.

Digital sovereignty has become a vital concern in an era marked by complex cyber threats and growing demands for data protection, transparency, and ethical governance. This study aims to develop a structured framework that enhances digital sovereignty by integrating security, privacy, and trust indicators. Using the MICMAC methodology, supported by expert consensus through the Delphi technique, we identified and analyzed 33 governance indicators to understand their influence and interdependencies. The analysis revealed ten key drivers, including financial transparency, ethical use of AI, and privacy by design, which exert the highest direct and indirect impacts on digital governance. These findings offer actionable insights for policymakers and organizations seeking to build resilient, user-focused, and ethically grounded digital governance systems.

The increasing demand for efficient energy management and privacy concerns poses challenges for smart grids in developing regions. This study introduces a Federated AIoT Framework integrating Federated Learning (FL) with IoT, leveraging a Federated Graph Attention Network (FeGAN) to enhance Nigeria's smart grid. The framework decentralizes model training, improving grid efficiency while ensuring data privacy. Results show a 92% accuracy in grid optimization, 89% accuracy in energy theft detection, and a 15% reduction in energy losses. Additionally, it demonstrated superior scalability and privacy-preserving mechanisms, achieving an F1 score of 0.91 for grid efficiency and 0.86 for theft detection. The Matthews Correlation Coefficient (MCC) for privacy reached 0.95, underscoring robust security. Federated Learning creates an opportunity for conducting secure smart grid management with scalability together with privacy compliance in resource-limited settings. Research expansion will target wider implementation within various power systems to integrate renewable power generation.

In the evolving landscape of cybercrime in the financial sector, criminals exploit modern technology for fraudulent activities, particularly on the dark web, necessitating robust cybersecurity measures. This study explores cybersecurity threats on the Dark Web and proposes protective measures for FinTech users using the Multilayer Perceptron (MLP) technique. The research addresses digital sovereignty (DS) by investigating how MLP-based threat detection can empower users and institutions to reclaim control over their data, ensuring privacy and autonomy in decentralized financial ecosystems. The MLP model, trained on Kaggle-sourced data, achieved 97% accuracy in identifying vulnerabilities such as social engineering, phishing, and malware. Key findings reveal that user behaviors like accessing hacked websites, leaving digital footprints, and reusing passwords significantly increase exposure to threats.

The integration of Artificial Intelligence (AI) and Internet of Things (IoT) technologies is transforming precision agriculture by enabling accurate, real-time detection of crop diseases while ensuring data sovereignty. The Federated AIoT framework, combined with Graph Attention Networks (GATs), processes decentralized sensor and image data locally, addressing privacy concerns and supporting sustainable practices. Using federated learning, the model aggregates local updates from each farm to build a global model that benefits from diverse environments without compromising individual data ownership. Evaluated on the PlantVillage dataset and synthetic data, the framework achieved 90% accuracy, 90% precision, 75% recall, an F1-score of 81%, and a Matthews Correlation Coefficient (MCC) of 67%, indicating strong early disease detection performance. This approach empowers farmers with data control and offers scalability across varied agricultural contexts, with future research focused on improving real-time scalability in resource-limited settings.

The rapid digitalisation of financial services has increased financial crime risks. This necessitates robust AML and CTF frameworks that respect DS and privacy. This chapter investigates how DS can strengthen AML/CTF compliance while balancing national autonomy with global cooperation. We evaluate their DS implications through

This chapter explores synthetic data's transformative role in computer vision model training, emphasizing privacy and responsible AI in the context of digital sovereignty. Starting with an overview of computer vision and deep learning, the chapter explains how these technologies enable machines to interpret visual data. Synthetic data, created to mirror real-world scenarios, emerges as a solution for protecting privacy, enabling training without exposing sensitive information. Through diverse case studies, it demonstrates how synthetic data can eliminate identifiable features, supporting privacy-centric, ethical AI. Readers gain a comprehensive understanding of the technical and accountable frameworks that make synthetic data crucial in advancing responsible AI while safeguarding digital privacy and fostering innovation.

Artificial intelligence has become a foundational pillar of digital sovereignty by reinforcing data privacy, infrastructure autonomy, and ethical oversight. This chapter explores how AI can be strategically leveraged to enhance national control through responsible innovation, data localization, and accountable governance. Drawing on a multidisciplinary literature review and comparative analysis of Estonia, the EU, Singapore, and South Korea, the study identifies critical enablers of digital sovereignty. Estonia has implemented over 80 AI-powered public services; the EU's Digital Compass targets 75% enterprise adoption of AI, big data, or cloud by 2030; Singapore's 100E programme has supported more than 38 industry-focused AI deployments; and South Korea has invested $2 billion in AI R&D to boost domestic innovation. Findings highlight that AI-driven innovation, strong regulatory frameworks, SME empowerment, and privacy-first policies are vital for digital autonomy. The chapter concludes that achieving digital sovereignty requires a balanced approach—combining technological leadership

Artificial intelligence (AI) integration in healthcare has generated fierce debate between healthcare workers, policymakers, and patients. AI can transform healthcare by increasing accuracy in diagnoses, automating clinical workflows, and achieving better outcomes for patients; but it has also sparked a host of ethical challenges relating to patient privacy or data security, and the potential use of biased decision-making. This chapter investigates how AI impacts the healthcare sector, providing both a pro and con analysis of its adoption. AI has the potential to improve diagnosis accuracy, clinical workflows and patient outcomes. Despite this, reliance on AI continue to rise in the healthcare sector but also worrying about patient confidentiality, data security and making wrong decisions based on bias. To leverage the opportunities but also prevent the pitfalls of AI, responsible development and deployment are required by healthcare organisations and policymakers.

The growing adoption of cloud services in business operations has introduced new security challenges for compliance management. This chapter aims to present a structured approach to evaluating the security risks associated with business process compliance requirements. A fuzzy logic-based framework is developed using the ISO 27001 standard to assess the risk levels of compliance requirements extracted from regulatory documents. The results show that the framework enables accurate classification of requirements into low, medium, or high risk, enhancing decision-making in compliance budgeting. This approach supports effective compliance management, improves information security, and can be adapted across various industries.

Preface

INTRODUCTION

In the age of ubiquitous connectivity and relentless digital transformation, the question of who controls data—and how that control is exercised—has become one of the defining challenges of our time. With data flowing freely across borders and technologies evolving faster than regulatory frameworks, the concept of *digital sovereignty* has emerged as a critical focal point for governments, businesses, and individuals alike. It is against this backdrop that we present *Empowering Digital Sovereignty: Balancing Privacy and Global Connectivity*, a comprehensive and timely reference volume designed to navigate the tensions between privacy, innovation, and geopolitical realities in the digital domain.

This book explores the intricate landscape of digital sovereignty through a multidisciplinary lens, bringing together expert perspectives from law, technology, policy, and ethics. As editors, we have aimed to curate a balanced dialogue that acknowledges both the promises and perils of an increasingly interconnected world. From the development of legal frameworks and privacy regulations to the deployment of AI-enabled cybersecurity tools and the strategic management of cross-border data flows, this volume provides a nuanced understanding of the tools, challenges, and responsibilities involved in asserting digital control.

One of the distinguishing features of this work is its commitment to real-world application. Through a diverse range of case studies, the book explores how various nations are approaching digital sovereignty—some with success, others facing obstacles that offer critical lessons. These examples serve not only as informative snapshots but also as prompts for broader reflection on the ethical dilemmas and strategic decisions that define this evolving field.

We also pay close attention to the dual role of artificial intelligence: as both an enabler and a potential threat to digital sovereignty. The chapters critically examine how AI technologies can support autonomy and resilience, while also highlighting the new vulnerabilities they introduce—especially in the context of surveillance, algorithmic bias, and platform dominance.

Our goal in compiling this volume is threefold. First, we aim to bridge gaps between disciplines, encouraging holistic and collaborative approaches to complex digital challenges. Second, we seek to provide actionable insights for policymakers, technologists, and industry leaders striving to craft responsible and future-ready data governance models. Third, we hope to spark continued academic research and global dialogue around the essential balance between open data ecosystems and the protection of individual and national rights.

This book is intended for a wide and diverse readership. Policymakers and government officials will find critical analysis of current trends and technologies impacting data regulation. IT professionals and business executives will gain clarity on the operational implications of digital sovereignty in a global economy. Scholars and students will benefit from an integrated view of the legal, technical, and philosophical dimensions of this field.

As editors, we are deeply grateful to the contributors who brought this project to life. Their insights, rigor, and forward-thinking perspectives have shaped a publication that we believe will serve as a vital resource for anyone navigating the shifting terrain of digital sovereignty.

ORGANIZATION OF THE BOOK

Chapter 1: A Delimitation of Data Sovereignty from Privacy

In this foundational chapter, the authors explore the nuanced distinctions between data sovereignty and privacy—two closely linked yet conceptually distinct components of digital sovereignty. Through a systematic literature review spanning economic, organizational, regulatory, and technical lenses, the chapter synthesizes insights from 38 scholarly works to present a comparative analysis of the two concepts. The authors argue that while overlapping in intent and application, data sovereignty and privacy diverge in scope and implementation, particularly in how they define ownership, control, and responsibility over data. This distinction is not just theoretical—it carries practical implications for software engineering, regulatory compliance, and policy development. The chapter also emphasizes how privacy-preserving techniques, especially in requirements engineering, can be adapted to bolster data sovereignty frameworks. This critical reflection sets the stage for the book's broader examination of digital autonomy and rights.

Chapter 2: Smart City Surveillance Governance Challenges in Balancing Privacy, Security, and Digital Sovereignty

As urban centers embrace smart city innovations, surveillance technologies pose significant challenges to digital sovereignty. This chapter presents a qualitative analysis of the governance tensions that arise when public safety goals intersect with the rights to privacy and data autonomy. Drawing on the case of Delhi's smart city development, the authors critically assess AI-driven surveillance mechanisms, including facial recognition and real-time monitoring systems. The findings reveal deep-seated governance gaps—particularly in transparency, consent, and accountability—highlighting the risks of mass surveillance and data misuse. The authors propose a regulatory and technological framework that aims to reconcile these tensions, advocating for policy instruments that preserve citizen rights without compromising urban security. This chapter offers a timely exploration of how democratic values can be upheld in data-driven urban environments.

Chapter 3: Automated Intrusion Detection in Streaming Data: A Sovereignty-Aware Approach with Machine Learning and Semantic Insights

With data security emerging as a linchpin of digital sovereignty, this chapter introduces a sovereignty-aware intrusion detection system designed for real-time data streams. Leveraging machine learning and semantic modeling, the system demonstrates high accuracy and processing efficiency using benchmark datasets like NSL-KDD and CIC-IDS-2017. Importantly, it aligns with regional data sovereignty requirements by minimizing long-term data storage and adapting to local legal frameworks. The chapter illustrates how such systems can simultaneously enhance network security and uphold jurisdictional data autonomy. This practical and scalable approach positions itself as a viable solution for organizations seeking to reinforce cybersecurity while adhering to national and regional data governance standards.

Chapter 4: Strengthening Digital Sovereignty: A Structural Analysis of Digital Governance Indicators

Recognizing the complexity of digital governance, this chapter provides a robust structural analysis of the key indicators influencing digital sovereignty. Using the MICMAC methodology and insights from the Delphi technique, the authors identify 33 governance indicators and analyze their interrelationships. Among them, ten drivers—such as financial transparency, ethical AI use, and privacy by design—emerge as pivotal to building ethical, secure, and resilient digital ecosystems. The chapter offers a valuable framework for policymakers and institutional leaders to evaluate and enhance their governance strategies. By translating theoretical constructs into actionable guidance, the study reinforces the centrality of trust, transparency, and ethics in the digital age.

Chapter 5: Federated AIoT Framework for Privacy-Preserving Smart Grid Management

This chapter addresses the dual imperatives of energy efficiency and data privacy in smart grid management, especially in developing countries. Introducing a Federated AIoT Framework, the authors combine Federated Learning and IoT technologies through a Graph Attention Network (FeGAN) to optimize Nigeria's power grid. The decentralized nature of the system ensures privacy compliance while delivering high performance—achieving 92% grid optimization accuracy and 89% in energy theft detection. With strong scalability and privacy metrics, this approach demonstrates how digital sovereignty can be upheld even in resource-constrained environments. The framework also offers a template for broader application across global energy infrastructures, particularly as nations seek to integrate renewable energy within secure, sovereign digital systems.

Chapter 6: Preserving Digital Sovereignty in FinTech: A Multilayer Perceptron Approach to Dark Web Threat Detection and Privacy-Centric Cybersecurity

Digital sovereignty in the FinTech landscape faces growing threats from cybercriminals operating in the shadows of the dark web. In this chapter, the authors present a machine learning-based cybersecurity model utilizing Multilayer Perceptrons (MLP) to detect and mitigate threats such as phishing, malware, and social engineering. Trained on real-world data from Kaggle, the model achieves 97% accuracy, offering a robust solution for protecting decentralized financial systems. The authors emphasize how this approach empowers users and institutions to maintain control over their digital assets and identities. By aligning advanced threat detection with privacy principles, the chapter makes a compelling case for integrating sovereignty-oriented cybersecurity in financial ecosystems.

Chapter 7: Federated Graph Attention Neural Networks (FeGAN) for Privacy-Preserving Crop Disease Detection

In a compelling intersection of agriculture, AI, and digital sovereignty, this chapter proposes a privacy-preserving framework for early crop disease detection.

Utilizing Federated Learning and Graph Attention Networks, the model processes decentralized farm data without compromising ownership or privacy. Evaluated on both real and synthetic agricultural datasets, the framework achieves strong performance metrics, including 90% precision and an MCC of 67%. The chapter highlights how this model empowers farmers with control over their data while enhancing food security and sustainability. Scalable across varied agricultural settings, the approach exemplifies how sovereignty-preserving technologies can serve rural and resource-limited populations, opening new pathways for ethical innovation in precision agriculture.

Chapter 8: Strengthening Digital Sovereignty in the Fight Against Money Laundering and Terrorism Financing: Balancing Privacy, Security, and Global Cooperation

The digitalization of financial services has undoubtedly enhanced operational efficiency but has also heightened risks related to money laundering and terrorism financing. In this chapter, the authors address these challenges by examining how digital sovereignty (DS) can bolster anti-money laundering (AML) and counter-terrorist financing (CTF) frameworks without compromising individual privacy or national autonomy. Through case studies and analysis of evolving regulatory mechanisms, including AI and blockchain technologies, the chapter illustrates how privacy-preserving solutions and collaborative international models can enhance compliance. The authors advocate for a scalable, DS-centric approach that not only respects jurisdictional integrity but also strengthens global cooperation in financial crime prevention—underscoring the need for balance between security, privacy, and sovereignty in financial systems.

Chapter 9: Face Morphing Attack Detection: Privacy and Digital Sovereignty Issues, Methods and Future Direction

Face morphing presents a significant challenge to biometric authentication systems, threatening both individual privacy and institutional control over digital identities. This chapter investigates face morphing attack detection through the lens of privacy and digital sovereignty, using the LINDUUN framework as a methodological anchor. The authors introduce a taxonomy of detection approaches and critically evaluate the implications these methods have on sovereignty and user privacy. With actionable recommendations for addressing vulnerabilities, the chapter urges policymakers, researchers, and system designers to prioritize privacy-centric design and governance. The findings push forward the discourse on safeguarding identity systems in an era where facial recognition is increasingly embedded into public and private infrastructures.

Chapter 10: AI-Powered Synthetic Data Generation for Training Vision Models Ensuring Privacy, Good Governance and Responsible AI in the Era of Digital Sovereignty

This chapter explores the rising importance of synthetic data in training AI vision models, particularly in preserving privacy and reinforcing ethical AI practices under the framework of digital sovereignty. As real data becomes increasingly restricted due to privacy concerns, synthetic data offers a compelling alternative for building high-performing models without compromising personal information. The authors detail technical mechanisms and case studies that demonstrate how synthetic datasets can replicate real-world diversity while maintaining anonymization. This privacy-first, innovation-enabling approach aligns with principles of responsible AI and good governance, providing a viable path forward for data-driven development that respects both human rights and national interests.

Chapter 11: Securing Digital Sovereignty Through AI: Balancing Innovation, Ethics, and Data Protection

Artificial Intelligence is not just a technological asset—it is a strategic pillar for securing digital sovereignty. This chapter provides a comparative analysis of national AI strategies, focusing on Estonia, the EU, Singapore, and South Korea, to illustrate how AI can reinforce sovereign control over digital infrastructure, data governance, and innovation pathways. Through a comprehensive literature review, the authors highlight key enablers such as ethical oversight, SME support, and regulatory clarity. The chapter argues that responsible innovation must be anchored in privacy-first policies and long-term investment in domestic technological capacity. It offers a roadmap for nations seeking to balance rapid digital advancement with ethical safeguards and public accountability.

Chapter 12: Role of AI in the Healthcare Industry: Revolutionizing Healthcare or Threatening Privacy?

AI's growing presence in healthcare is transforming diagnosis, treatment, and operational efficiency—but not without trade-offs. This chapter engages with the critical tension between innovation and privacy in the healthcare sector. Through a balanced analysis of both benefits and drawbacks, the authors reveal how AI enhances diagnostic accuracy and patient care while simultaneously introducing concerns around bias, confidentiality, and data misuse. The chapter calls for healthcare providers and policymakers to adopt responsible development frameworks that embed data protection and ethical AI into every layer of implementation. It contributes to the broader discourse on maintaining patient trust in an increasingly automated healthcare landscape.

Chapter 13: A Framework for Assessing the Security Risk of Requirements: Towards an Improved Business Processes Compliance Management

In the age of digital business transformation, regulatory compliance must evolve to keep pace with complex cloud-based architectures. This chapter introduces a fuzzy logic-driven framework for assessing the security risks of compliance requirements, grounded in ISO 27001 standards. By classifying requirements into risk levels, the approach enables informed decision-making on resource allocation and threat mitigation. The authors highlight the adaptability of this method across various sectors and underscore its relevance to improving information security and digital sovereignty. This structured, risk-based model empowers organizations to maintain compliance while reinforcing autonomy over their data processes and systems.

Chapter 14: Security and Privacy Control Architecture for Outlier Hunting on Network Traffic in Higher Education

Higher education institutions, increasingly reliant on digital infrastructure, face distinct cybersecurity challenges. This chapter proposes an advanced control architecture for monitoring and protecting network traffic using deep learning models. By leveraging recurrent neural networks and autoencoders, the system accurately detects anomalies that may signal security threats or performance failures. The findings underscore the importance of precision, recall, and F1-score metrics in evaluating real-time responsiveness. The chapter provides a scalable privacy-enhancing framework specifically tailored for educational environments, ensuring that academic institutions can safeguard sensitive data while aligning with broader principles of digital sovereignty.

CONCLUSION

As we conclude this volume, *Empowering Digital Sovereignty: Balancing Privacy and Global Connectivity*, it is clear that digital sovereignty is no longer a theoretical aspiration—it is a pressing, multidimensional imperative. Across the chapters in this book, contributors from diverse academic, technical, and policy backgrounds have explored how digital sovereignty intersects with global trends in artificial intelligence, financial security, data governance, smart infrastructure, healthcare innovation, and more. While the challenges vary across sectors and regions, a common thread emerges: the urgent need to reimagine governance frameworks, technologies, and ethical standards that preserve autonomy without stifling innovation.

This collection has demonstrated that protecting digital sovereignty does not necessitate isolation or rigidity. Rather, it calls for strategic collaboration, responsible innovation, and adaptive regulation that empowers individuals, institutions, and nations to retain meaningful control over their digital assets, identities, and infrastructure. The integration of privacy-by-design principles, federated learning models, synthetic data techniques, and sovereignty-aware AI systems showcases the breadth of viable solutions already in development—and the potential for these approaches to scale.

We hope this book encourages dialogue, drives research, and informs policy at a critical juncture where data localization debates, AI governance, and global digital dependencies are rapidly evolving. As editors, we believe that fostering digital sovereignty is essential not only for protecting rights and values, but also for building resilient and equitable digital ecosystems for the future.

It is our sincere wish that the insights, frameworks, and innovations presented in these chapters will serve as a valuable resource for scholars, technologists, decision-makers, and practitioners alike—guiding the way toward a digitally sovereign world where privacy, innovation, and global cooperation are not mutually exclusive, but mutually reinforcing.

Chapter 1
A Delimitation of Data Sovereignty From Privacy

Julia Pampus
https://orcid.org/0000-0003-2309-6183
Fraunhofer Institute for Software and Systems Engineering ISST, Germany

Maritta Heisel
University of Duisburg-Essen, Germany

ABSTRACT

As subset of digital sovereignty, data sovereignty characterizes data sharing in modern data ecosystems. The main goal is to preserve the interest of the data rights holder using different technical approaches, such as policy management and usage control, to establish transparency and trust. At first glance, many of the characteristics of data sovereignty align with privacy. This chapter per the authors discusses the delimitation of both concepts. This elaboration is prepared by first analyzing data sovereignty from an economic, organizational, regulatory, and technical perspective using a systematic literature review (SLR) presenting 38 relevant articles. The subsequent comparison according to selected properties highlights many similarities and significant differences. This chapter per the authors emphasizes the importance of clearly distinguishing data sovereignty and privacy in theory and practice. However, it indicates that many privacy-preserving software engineering approaches, e.g., concerning requirements engineering (RE), can be transferred to the data sovereignty domain.

DOI: 10.4018/979-8-3693-9137-2.ch001

INTRODUCTION

Nowadays, organizations collect and store massive amounts of data. However, their value generation suffers from barriers to sharing data with other organizations, mainly due to market dynamics and the fear of losing competitive advantages. Data breaches and misuses may be so harmful to businesses that companies prefer not to share their data at all instead of taking a mostly unknown risk. By establishing an environment for business-to-business data sharing, dataspaces aim for shared governance, trust models, and technical interoperability to address the aforementioned issues and enable new business models (Otto, 2022).

Industrial data sharing within dataspaces involves multiple actors, primarily the *data provider* that provides the data transfer and publishes the data offering and the *data consumer* that consumes the data and uses it. The data provider may be the data rights holder or an entity that represents the data rights holder (Pettenpohl et al., 2022). Within dataspaces, during data sharing, the concept of *data sovereignty* is addressed. Overall, data sovereignty describes the "self-determination [and autonomy] of individuals and organizations with regard to the use of their data" (Jarke et al., 2019, p.550). It is a subset of digital sovereignty, which, in turn, is a subset of technical sovereignty (Calzada, 2021).

Some dataspaces operate in domains involving personal data, e.g., in healthcare, thereby raising the question of how data sovereignty and privacy relate to each other and how they differ. So far, to the best of our knowledge, no research deals with the distinction between data sovereignty and privacy in detail (cf. Section "Related Work"). Therefore, we pose the following research questions (RQs):

- RQ1: How is data sovereignty defined in the scientific literature?
- RQ2: How can data sovereignty be delimited from privacy?

We address the RQs by performing an SLR and considering different perspectives of data sovereignty. Just as the data economy encompasses regulatory, economic, organizational, and technical aspects, we elaborate on data sovereignty at these levels. We compare it to the idea of privacy using a model that structures privacy enhancing technologies (PETs). Using six dimensions, we can identify many differences and similarities that help develop industrial data sharing with and without focusing on personal data. In summary, we present the following contributions in this chapter:

- We elaborate on the current definitions and concepts of data sovereignty as part of digital sovereignty in scientific literature.
- We compare the concepts of data sovereignty to the concept of privacy.

- We derive theoretical and practical implications for further research in the area of digital sovereignty.

The remainder of this paper is structured as follows: Section "Background" introduces the subjects of privacy and PETs and presents related work. Then, Section "Methodology" outlines our research method. In Section "Results", we describe the concept and definitions of data sovereignty. Based on this elaboration, we compare different aspects of data sovereignty with privacy to derive theoretical and practical implications and answer the RQs in Section "Discussion". Finally, in Section "Conclusions", we summarize our work.

BACKGROUND

This section introduces concepts and works we use as a basis for this paper. We briefly outline the concept of privacy, followed by a taxonomy for PET. Subsequently, we present an earlier work that deals with a comparison of data sovereignty and privacy.

Privacy

Research in privacy has evolved significantly over time, particularly in response to technological advancements and the increasing collection of personal data.

> *"At the broadest level [...], privacy is a fundamental human right that encompasses the right to be left alone. In the commercial, consumer context, privacy entails the protection and appropriate use of the personal information of customers, and the meeting of expectations of customers about its use. For organizations, privacy entails the application of laws, policies, standards and processes by which Personally Identifiable Information (PII) of individuals is managed" (Pearson & Benameur, 2010, p.693).*

It involves complying with the European Union's applicable privacy laws and regulations, such as the General Data Protection Regulation (GDPR) (European Parliament & Council, 2016). Scientific research in the field of privacy aims to develop and improve techniques and frameworks for ensuring the privacy and protection of personal data in various contexts. Technical or non-technical implementations focus primarily on protecting personal information from unauthorized access, disclosure, or misuse. One approach to this is granting individuals rights and transparency about their data and using authentication and access control strategies (Sun et al., 2014).

Privacy-enhancing Technologies

Figure 1. Dimensions of PETs (Heurix et al., 2015)

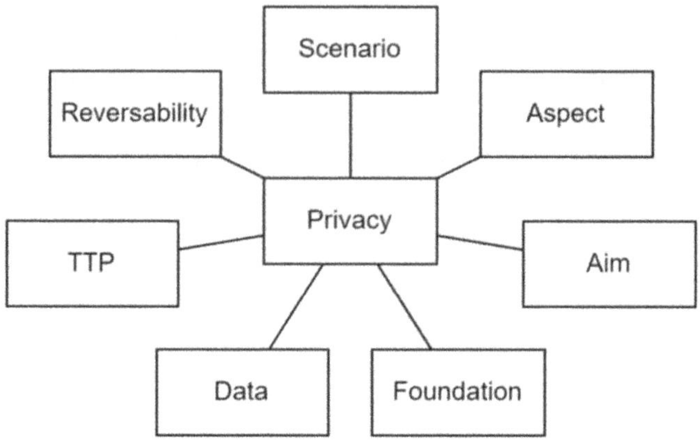

Note. Overview of dimensions from the taxonomy for PETs by Heurix et al. (2015).

In 2015, Heurix et al. (2015) presented a taxonomy for PETs. This taxonomy comprises seven dimensions considered when developing PETs, depicted in Figure 1. The first dimension *scenario* refers to the actors involved in the data sharing scenario and what threat they pose in data usage. The *aspect* considers the identity, content (data), and behavior (metadata) targeted by a PET. The *aim* deals with achieving privacy by following indistinguishability, unlinkability, deniability, and confidentiality. Next, the *foundation* describes the conceptual basis building on security mechanisms such as cryptography. *Data* describes two types of information that are handled by PETs, data-in-motion and data-in-transit. The *trusted third party* (TTP) is a trusted entity that may be involved in the operation or usage of PETs. Heurix et al. (2015) distinguish a set of sub-dimensions describing the frequency of interactions with such a TTP (frequent, in phases, task-specific). Last, the dimension *reversibility* states the ability to reverse an operation, to what extent (e.g., partial or full) this is done, and with what degree of involvement of the data originator.

We do not consider the last dimension relevant for data sovereignty and, therefore, do not include it in the delimitation in Section "Delimitation from Privacy".

Related Work

Hummel et al. (2018) first compared data sovereignty and privacy in 2018. The authors consider both concepts interrelated, while data sovereignty goes beyond privacy. According to their elaboration, privacy focuses on enforcing individual rights and protecting against data misuse. At the same time, data sovereignty does not restrict data use above the right to share data. Hummel et al. (2018) distinguish the protection of personal data from the promotion of solidarity and the everyday use of data. Thus, the primary motivation behind data sovereignty is sharing data to establish information linkage for data value creation. At the same time, privacy primarily aims to keep as much data as possible. The authors claim that there are also differences in the freedom of action since individuals can only choose between sharing or not sharing data. In contrast, the concept and technical approaches behind data sovereignty allow users to define and customize data usage conditions by design. In general, privacy refers to personal information, while data sovereignty refers to data sharing in a social or industrial context. Thus, the contextual focus is different. Using the following research and comparison of both concepts in Section "Results", we expand this comparison to a more technical level.

METHODOLOGY

Figure 2. SLR process

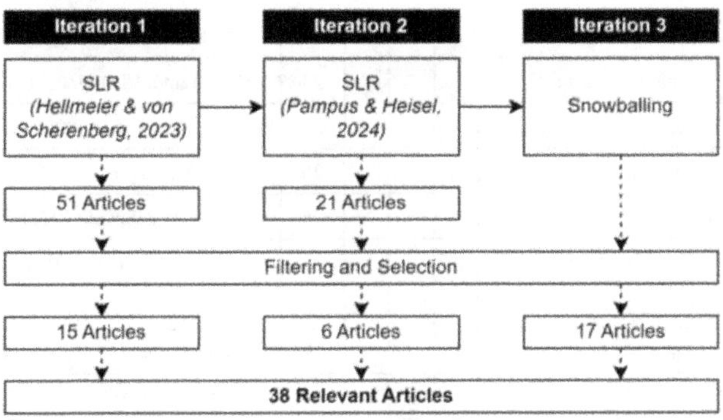

Note. Overview of SLR process that has been conducted as part of this research

To answer the RQs, we need to understand how the term data sovereignty is defined in the literature. For this, we conduct an SLR, following the guidelines by Kitchenham (2007). We divide our research into three phases, respectively, iterations, as depicted in Figure 2. The first iteration relies on the SLR conducted by Hellmeier and von Scherenberg (2023). We adopt their inclusion and exclusion criteria and review the result set by scanning the abstracts and searching for publications that formulate their definition of data sovereignty or elaborate on its core principles. Out of the original 51 articles that focus on data sovereignty provided by Hellmeier and von Scherenberg (2023), we reduce the result set to 15 articles.

Next, in the second iteration, we renew the first SLR by consulting the work of Pampus and Heisel (2024). They have extended the SLR by Hellmeier and von Scherenberg (2023) with newer articles. Reviewing their additional result set of 21 articles, we extract six and add them to our final literature set, listed in Table 1. Finally, in the third iteration, we apply the snowballing technique of Wohlin et al. (2020) by forward and backward searching through cited or citing articles. With this, we identify another 17 articles that either define data sovereignty or explain relevant concepts that we reference in Section "Concept of Data Sovereignty". Overall, our final literature set contains 38 articles.

Table 1. Final literature set

No.	Definition	Iteration			No.	Definition	Iteration		
		1	2	3			1	2	3
1	Alsamhi et al. (2024)			X	20	Irion, (2012)	X		
2	Bader et al., (2020)			X	21	Jarke et al. (2019)	X		
3	Bartsch et al. (2022)			X	22	Khatri & Brown (2010)			X
4	Bruckner & Jahnke (2021)			X	23	Landolfi et al. (2019)			X
5	Cappiello et al. (2020)			X	24	Lauf et al. (2022)		X	
6	Calzada (2021)	X			25	Mackey et al. (2022)		X	
7	Cheong & Chang (2007)			X	26	Nagel et al (2021)	X		
8	Couture & Toupin (2019)	X			27	Otto et al. (2018)	X		
9	Cuno et al. (2019)	X			28	Oliveira & Lóscio (2018)			X
10	Drees et al. (2021)			X	29	Pampus & Heisel (2024)			X
11	Falcão et al. (2023)		X		30	Palanisamy & Verhaart (2014)			X
12	De Filippi & McCarthy (2012)	X			31	Pedreira et al. (2021)	X		
13	Firdausy et al. (2022b)		X		32	Peterson et al. (2011)	X		
14	Franklin et al. (2005)			X	33	Polatin-Reuben & Wright (2014)	X		
15	Giese & Anderl (2022)		X		34	Sarabia-Jácome et al. (2019)			X
16	Gil et al. (2022)			X	35	Schmidt et al. (2022)		X	
17	Hellmeier & von Scherenberg (2023)			X	36	Schuette & Brost (2018)			X
18	Hummel et al. (2018)	X			37	Zieglmeier & Pretschner (2021)	X		
19	Hummel et al. (2021)	X			38	Zrenner et al. (2019)	X		

Note. The data has been collected conducting an SLR (more in Section "Methodology").

RESULTS

We present the results of our research as descriptive and interpretive findings. By doing so, we define the concept of data sovereignty from multiple perspectives (economic, organizational, legal, technical) and, subsequently, present a delimitation from privacy.

Descriptive Findings

Data sovereignty is a relatively young term in research, mainly being discussed since 2018 in the domain of information systems (ISs) (Hellmeier & von Scherenberg, 2023). Having strong inter-dependencies with digital sovereignty, technological sovereignty, and cyber sovereignty, some researchers have focused on the delimitation of those terms in their work (Couture & Toupin, 2019; Hellmeier & von Scherenberg, 2023; Hummel et al., 2021; Firdausy et al., 2022b; Pedreira et al., 2021). While many works consider the concept of data sovereignty and technical approaches for its establishment, only a few concentrate on defining data sovereignty as a term. Table 2 shows a list of primary definitions of data sovereignty in the literature, sorted by frequency of citations (as of February 2025). We discuss some of these in the following subsections.

Table 2. Definitions of the term data sovereignty

No.	Definition	Source	Num. of Citations
D1	"establishing data location at a granularity sufficient for placing it within the borders of a particular nation-state. We call this notion data sovereignty." (p.1)	Peterson et al. (2011)	154
D2	"data sovereignty combines principles of IT management, information assurance, and data protection, with means to address new legal risks arising from transborder transfers and the new intermediary involved, that is, the cloud service provider." (p.65)	Irion (2012)	140
D3	"Data sovereignty refers to the self-determination of individuals and organizations with regard to the use of their data." (p.550)	Jarke et al. (2019)	113
D4	"The term 'data sovereignty', […], refers to a spectrum of approaches adopted by different states to control data generated in or passing through national internet infrastructure. It can be understood as a subset of cyber sovereignty, defined as the subjugation of the cyber domain to local jurisdictions." (p.1)	Polatin-Reuben & Wright (2014)	80
D5	"the capability of a natural person or corporate entity for exclusive self determination with regard to its economic data goods." (p.27)	Nagel et al (2021)	70
D6	"Data sovereignty means protecting the digital assets which an organization or individual controls and which have been sold or shared willingly with another entity." (p.115)	Cappiello et al. (2020)	70

continued on following page

Table 2. Continued

No.	Definition	Source	Num. of Citations
D7	"data sovereignty [...] as a digital right for communities/citizens" (p.1158)	Calzada (2021)	68
D8	"is defined as the ability of the data owner to decide itself how to share and use its data." (p.101)	Sarabia-Jacome et al. (2020)	53
D9	"we define data sovereignty as the ability to decide in a self-determined way, at any time, and by means of preferences, which entity can use one's own (personal) data for selected purposes." (p.3)	Lauf et al. (2022)	35
D10	"Concepts of self-determination and the capability of a data provider to keep control over their own data assets form the term data sovereignty." (p.8)	Hellmeier & von Scherenberg (2023)	31
D11	"as the right of a [...] nation to govern the collection, ownership, and application of data generated by its members." (p.2627)	Mackey et al. (2022)	22
D12	"digital sovereignty subsumes data sovereignty [...], standing for a company's autonomy to use its digital assets to share private and sensitive data." (p.118)	Firdausy et al. (2022b)	19
D13	"data sovereignty, i.e., the self-determination over accessing, processing, managing, or securing their data." (p.51)	Schmidt et al. (2022)	12
D14	"data sovereignty as consumers' ability to determine what information is and is not shared, influence the flow of their data/information, trace data flows across the involved platforms, and check for compliance with their preferences." (p.453)	Bartsch et al. (2022)	5
D15	"Data sovereignty is the right that individuals and organizations own to control the access to and the disclosure of their private and sensitive data." (p.1)	Firdausy et al. (2022a)	4

Note. The data has been extracted from the results set presented in Table 1.

Concept of Data Sovereignty

Initially, the definition of data sovereignty was mainly shaped by socioeconomic and sociopolitical views (Calzada, 2021; Couture & Toupin, 2019; Polatin-Reuben & Wright, 2014). Following the definitions D04, D07, and D11 (cf. Table 2), the sovereign over the data under protection is described as a citizen, a community, or a nation, a state, or a country (Calzada, 2021; Irion, 2012; Polatin-Reuben & Wright, 2014). In this context, a distinction is made between week and strong sovereignty, depending on whether it concerns digital rights aspects in the private sector or the preservation of national security (Polatin-Reuben & Wright, 2014). In relation to this, the subject of data sovereignty evolved in the direction of cloud services (Irion, 2012; Palanisamy & Verhaart, 2014) and, thus, also towards policy enforcement in distributed infrastructures (Gil et al., 2022). Considering D01 and D02 (cf. Table 2), the definition and implementation of usage conditions in the context of this mainly focus on the localization of data and corresponding restrictions (Peterson et al., 2011; Irion, 2012).

Over time, examining data sovereignty in the literature has moved into a more technical realm (Bartsch et al., 2022) and has been particularly shaped by the domain of data economics (Zrenner et al., 2019). The statements in D03, D06, D05, D08 to D10, and D12 to D15 (cf. Table 2) represent corresponding definitions related to ISs. In this context, data sovereignty is often seen in conjunction with data protection or privacy, implying that data is a kind of property (Cuno et al., 2019). The data sovereign, who is usually an individual or an organization (Cappiello et al., 2020; Firdausy et al., 2022a; Hellmeier & von Scherenberg, 2023; Jarke et al., 2019), has the ability to make independent and self-determined decisions about the use of their data (Bruckner & Jahnke, 2021; Firdausy et al., 2022a; Hellmeier & von Scherenberg, 2023; Jarke et al., 2019; Lauf et al., 2022; Sarabia-Jácome et al., 2019; Schmidt et al., 2022). To this end, they can define and, if necessary, restrict the use of the data (Bruckner & Jahnke, 2021). Thereby, the ability to define, monitor, and enforce data usage (Hummel et al., 2018) gives the data sovereign control over the entire data flow (Bartsch et al., 2022; Couture & Toupin, 2019). This policy enforcement implies that data handling must comply with legal regulations and the provider's requirements at the time of the data request and sharing and, afterwards, in a potentially different spatial and temporal context (Gil et al., 2020).

Considering existing definitions, we conclude that the concept of data sovereignty "cannot be limited to one research domain" (Hellmeier & von Scherenberg, 2023, p.10). Especially data ecosystems, data governance, and usage control are predominantly mentioned in literature dealing with data sovereignty. This overlap with other research fields motivates us to explain the economic, organizational, regulatory, and technical perspectives on data sovereignty in the following subsections.

Economic Context

From an economic point of view, research refers to data as asset (Bruckner & Jahnke, 2021; Hellmeier & von Scherenberg, 2023). As mentioned before, the subject of data sovereignty, especially in recent years, is often considered in relation to the term *data ecosystem*, "a complex socio-technical network that enables collaboration between autonomous actors in order to explore data" (Oliveira & Lóscio, 2018, p.590). The instantiation of a data ecosystem is also called *dataspace*. According to the definition of Franklin et al. (2005), dataspaces are "a new abstraction for data management" (p. 27) with the primary goal to allow the integration of distributed and heterogeneous data sources. Their designs and implementations primarily comprise data sovereignty, interoperability, and trust (Gil et al., 2022). Following Hummel et al. (2018), in the context of the market economy, it is especially relevant "that policy and lawmakers find ways to uphold competition and ensure that the market offers a plurality of data-intensive services from providers with different privacy and control mixes" (p.6) for the successful implementation of data sovereignty.

As part of the dataspace movement, the International Data Spaces Association[1] provides key concepts and technologies for networks that allow data sharing concerning data sovereignty (Otto, 2019). These include business, functional, process, information, and system layers. As a central technical component in this regard, the dataspace connector, i.e., a data sharing system, is responsible for the communication processes of dataspace participants and forms the foundation for the technical implementation of data sovereignty. It provides interfaces to enable (and require) the implementation of data sovereignty to be further addressed in backend systems and the overall infrastructure of the individual organizations.

Organizational Context

Critical voices state that "data sovereignty is not more than a new label for an existing information management practice" (Irion, 2012, p.51). To a certain extent, this is true, as the underlying concepts rely on classic *data governance* (Cuno et al., 2019). Data governance aims to maximize the value of data as an asset in organizations (Otto, 2011) by defining data principles, processes, and standards for data management, data access, and the data life cycle (Cheong & Chang, 2007; Khatri & Brown, 2010). In this context, data sovereignty enables the optimization of data usage and maximization of its value.

From a business perspective, data sovereignty offers the opportunity for new business models and sets "incentives for responsible innovation" (Hummel et al., 2018, p.7). As organizations operate in various jurisdictions with different data protection and privacy regulations, by adhering to data sovereignty principles, they can avoid/mitigate legal complications, financial penalties, and reputational damage associated with non-compliance.

Regulatory Context

As there is an economic and organizational context, also regulatory aspects are of significant importance when it comes to data sovereignty (Hellmeier & von Scherenberg, 2023). Depending on the data and sharing context, "intellectual property law, data protection law, and laws protecting confidentiality and trade secrets may apply" (Irion, 2012, p.50), while the definition of property rights in the sense of ownership, which is mainly used as a non-legalistic term, has not yet been finalized (Irion, 2012).

Research considers the role of data sovereignty in the regulatory context in two different ways: some define data sovereignty solely as an implementation and form of regulations (Cappiello et al., 2020) such as the GDPR and the Data Act (European Parliament & Council, 2023). In contrast, others see data sovereignty as something that applies where data handling is "not already covered by existing regulations" (Cuno et al., 2019, p.9).

Technical Context

The first crucial aspect of an approach for the (semi-automated) implementation of data sovereignty is the use of policies, which allow the definition and processing of declarative and machine-readable data usage conditions (Bader et al., 2020; Bartsch et al., 2022). In this sense, policies usually consist of predefined actions, prohibitions, and permissions, in the context of Open Data Rights Language (ODRL) (W3C, 2018) also grouped as 'rules'. Giese and Anderl (2022) consider them as sovereignty criteria. The technical enforcement of policies is called *usage control*. Usage control is an extension of access control and means the "ability to continuously monitor and control the usage of resources such as files or services" (Schuette & Brost, 2018, p.289). Thereby, the implementation of policies is subsequently monitored (Jarke et al., 2019), e.g., by auditing mechanism to trace the data provenance (Bartsch et al., 2022). This field of research has recently been expanded, i.e., in the direction of distributed usage control (Gil et al., 2022).

The second part of (technically) implementing data sovereignty focuses on creating a *trustworthy* and *secure* environment in which data sharing and usage can be enabled. This approach is justified because data sovereignty concerns more than just the data itself, e.g., the data infrastructure (Hummel et al., 2021) and other non-technical factors (Hummel et al., 2018).

- *Security*: The terms data sovereignty and security are frequently linked in research (Landolfi et al., 2019; Otto et al., 2019). Implementing security is one aspect of successfully establishing data sovereignty (Gil et al., 2022; Pampus & Heisel, 2024). While the concept of data sovereignty generally does not require security, many usage control approaches incorporate security mechanisms and techniques and thus thrive for the higher trustworthiness of the system.
- *Trust*: The concept of trust is omnipresent when dealing with confidential or valuable data. The assumption is that trust in the other party and their systems and the willingness to share data increases with the implementation of data

sovereignty. In the same way, trust is important in the actual implementation of data sovereignty since non-technical processes must take over where technologies are not effective (Pampus & Heisel, 2024). For example, compliance processes that involve human decision-making may complement technical processes. Ultimately, this ends with the required trust in the counter-party and the confidence that this party will follow the usage guidelines and make their handling of the data transparent in order to support the trust technically (Zieglmeier & Pretschner, 2021).

A somewhat outdated but ubiquitous approach to preserving data sovereignty is storing data in- house, in fully controlled environments, and only making public or open data available in public cloud environments (De Filippi & McCarthy, 2012). The implementation of data sovereignty using security and trust "requires a highly flexible framework which must combine usage control, access control, data provenance, and further means to enforce data protection" (Cappiello et al., 2020, p.101), e.g., following the Extensible Access Control Markup Language (OASIS, 2013) standard's architecture. Therefore, the first approaches have concentrated on implementing usage control in isolated and controlled services (Drees et al., 2021). Following this, the trend in research towards decentralized implementation of data sharing and processing systems (Alsamhi et al., 2024) leads to the assumption that many different technologies will be integrated to detect and mitigate malicious behavior (Peterson et al., 2011) and to make the data life cycle transparent in the first place (Falcão et al., 2023).

Delimitation From Privacy

Data sovereignty and privacy are often mentioned in the same context (Cappiello et al., 2020). This reference exists not only because of the terminological similarities but also because of the strong interconnection of the representing concepts. Overall, our research fits the elaboration by Hummel et al. (2018): Data sovereignty is based on the idea that data is an economic and commercial good and subject to jurisdiction-specific rules and regulations. In the context of privacy, data is treated as an individual's property that needs to be protected. Thus, privacy focuses more on the personal perspective and the implementation of laws protecting individuals' privacy rights covering data collection, usage, and sharing (cf. Section "Related Work").

While many fundamental motivations and technical approaches are more or less similar, we consider the dimensions of Heurix et al. (2015) (cf. Section "Privacy-enhancing Technologies") for a comparison of both concepts in the following.

Scenario

To clarify terminologies, first, we must consider the different entities involved in a data sharing process. In privacy scenarios, the data provider, a person, acts as the *client* using a data consuming service, the *server*. In industrial data sharing, the *data provider*, usually, is an organization providing data for data usage (processing, distribution) out of their scope of action (cf. Section "Introduction"). Thus, the *data consumer* is the requesting entity, not the data provider. The client and server roles are switching depending on the communication flow (request of data offerings, negotiation of policies, initiation of transfer processes).

In terms of privacy, Heurix et al. (2015) differentiate two threat scenarios: (1) an *untrusted client* (person, data provider) tries to find out more information by using a service than they should have access to and/or (2) an *untrusted server* (service, data consumer) collects more information from a person than necessary. In sovereign data sharing, neither scenario poses any actual threats. First, it is irrelevant if a data sharing participant can draw connections between data. Second, a data consumer's motivation is not to collect data about other data sharing participants. However, the mutual scenario described by Heurix et al. (2015) is given: We can assume that both data sharing participants do not trust each other. In addition, external actors, probably intercepting communication flows, threaten the sovereignty of both data sharing participants (provider and consumer).

Aspect

Following Heurix et al. (2015), the dimensions of aspects targeted by PETs are three-fold, focusing on identity, content, and behavior.

- *Identity*: Taking the definition of Article 4 from the GDPR, "'personal data' means any information relating to an identified or identifiable natural person ('data subject'); an identifiable natural person is one who can be identified, directly or indirectly, in particular by reference to an identifier such as a name, an identification number, location data, an online identifier or to one or more factors specific to the physical, physiological, genetic, mental, economic, cultural or social identity of that natural person" (European Parliament & Council, 2016, Art.4). The goal of PETs is hiding or masking the identity of persons by enforcing data handling in a privacy-preserving way, e.g., by enforcing pseudo- or anonymization. Data sovereignty, in contrast, encompasses more than just personal data. The data in focus can be generated by applications, machines, processes, or similar. The ownership then belongs to the organization as a data rights holder. Following this, the identity of the data origin is not necessarily a person and, therefore, must not be hidden. Pseudo- or anonymization would be a requirement for data usage conditions for specific use cases.

- *Content*: The target of both concepts is the shared and/or collected data. Privacy focuses on the data and its life cycle (i.e., collection, processing, storage (Wing, 2019)). As part of the six privacy protection goals by Hansen (2015), privacy requires the confidentiality of data. Following this, PETs must restrict granting data access to any unallowed third party. The same applies to data sovereignty, provided the consumed data should not be shared. For example, a data rights holder could state public usage of data as part of their usage conditions. Even in that case, data sovereignty would be respected. Regarding data sovereignty, data confidentiality prevents data misuse and positively impacts the building of trust (Pampus & Heisel, 2024).
- *Behavior*: According to Heurix et al. (2015), PETs should prevent deriving behavioral information from user interactions. This prevention focuses on the data records, i.e., the metadata of data. Considering personal information, it is possible that metadata could provide information about the data subject. The derivation of behavioral information is not of any relevance to the establishment of data sovereignty. Nevertheless, some data sharing system architectures may require transaction data collection to enable subsequent verification of the data flow or enforcement of data usage policies. Here, too, it should be ensured that transaction data do not end up in the wrong hands.

Aim

The aim describes how PETs achieve privacy (cf. Section "Privacy-enhancing Technologies"). One primary requirement is the impossibility of distinguishing one data subject (person) from another. Therefore, the collected data must not be linkable or relatable to other data (targeting unlinkability (Hansen et al., 2015)). A common approach to address this requirement and to take preventive action in case of unintended disclosure is the addition of 'noise', i.e., untrue information, to obscure data. This unlinkability does not influence (weaken or strengthen) the assessment of data sovereignty, in contrast to all other privacy protection goals (confidentiality, integrity, availability, unlinkability, intervenability, transparency) (Pampus & Heisel, 2024).

Data sovereignty focuses on the data sovereign, i.e., the subject who owns the data, respectively, holds the rights to a dataset. The reviewed literature predominantly defines data sovereignty as the 'ability' or 'right' of a data rights holder (cf. Table 2). The technical implementation is concerned with defining, negotiating, and implementing data usage conditions. Here, the essential goal is to design the transparency and trust along the data value chain (acquisition, analysis, curation, storage, usage (Curry, 2016)) and included processes (cf. Section “Technical Context”).

Foundation

The foundation of preserving privacy is implementing security. Security is not a primary aspect of data sovereignty; in this context, security methods merely increase trust in a system (cf. Section “Technical Context”). Policies play an important role in the technical implementation of both concepts. As part of privacy and digital rights management, privacy policies describe how data may be processed. The GDPR define the following operations: “collection, recording, organization, structuring, storage, adaptation or alteration, retrieval, consultation, use, disclosure by transmission, dissemination or otherwise making available, alignment or combination, restriction, erasure or destruction” (European Parliament & Council, 2016, Art.4(2)). A typical example is the agreement to cookies. Here, the data consumer (the website operator) provides information about the use of the data and a certain number of choices that the data provider (website visitor) can agree to. The choices align with the requirements of the GDPR. For example, Articles 5 and 15 describe principles for processing personal data or access rights after data sharing (European Parliament & Council, 2016). This interaction pattern follows the principle of consent to (restricted) data usage as part of a protective and constraining concept (Hummel et al., 2018).

In the context of data sovereignty, approaches such as usage control and policy definition languages such as ODRL are commonly used. In a respective data sharing scenario, the data provider (usually an organization) defines how the data may and should be used. ODRL defines a set of allowed operations (actions), such as use, anonymize, or distribute. By using data sharing systems that establish data sovereignty, the very passive role of consent transforms into an active role of choice without categorically prioritizing the maximization of restrictiveness over the sharing of data (Hummel et al., 2018). Moreover, the data provider and consumer here are not obliged to consent to the default but can negotiate the terms of use and actively make counter-proposals (Firdausy et al., 2022a; Jarke et al., 2019). This freedom allows for greater flexibility and integration into business processes.

Data

The focus of PETs is data-in-motion and data-at-rest. The same applies to technologies ensuring data sovereignty. In both cases, the negotiated data usage policies must be enforced throughout the entire data life cycle.

Trusted Third Party

The concept of privacy often requires a third party acting as a broker or mediator between two or more parties to provide functions supporting the implementation of security and privacy (e.g., user registration). In sovereign data sharing, another party than the two data sharing participants is generally not foreseen. Both parties directly interact with each other and can respect and enforce the requirements related to data usage. Again, the comparison between consent and free choice can be drawn (cf. Section "Foundation"): While users of PETs are usually confronted with the given technical conditions, in sovereign data sharing, e.g., within dataspaces, both data sharing participants agree upon trusted third parties. These third parties can be identity provisioning or auditing services, serving as trust anchors (cf. Section "Technical Context").

DISCUSSION

In summary, data sovereignty in data sharing can be examined from different perspectives at different levels. Generally, it can be characterized primarily by the self-determination of both data sharing participants: they can choose which data is shared, under which usage conditions this sharing happens, and whether they accept these conditions or negotiate different conditions. Naturally, in the context of industrial data sharing, this has only limited effect since, in most cases, market power dictates which of the two data sharing participants is in the stronger position (Pampus & Heisel, 2024). For example, if a regulation forces organizations to share specific data, then self-determination is limited.

Answer to RQ1

As a summary of our research, data sovereignty describes the ability of a data sharing participant (individual or organization) to take actions in the data sharing process autonomously and self-determined. The data rights holder has a unique role, being a data sharing participant that produces data and can assert access and usage conditions to the shared data. These data usage conditions must be respected and implemented throughout the entire data value chain (discovery, curation, interpretation, distribution, exploitation), whether within or outside the scope of action of the data rights holder. This requirement applies (1) regardless of what and how many other stakeholders are involved in the data value chain, organizationally or technically, and (2) regardless of whether the context in which the data is located at any point in its life cycle changes. In this context, we define data as intangible information or representations of tangible objects or a defined collection of them, which are the subject of data sovereignty.

Answer to RQ2

We regard the concept of privacy as a subset of data sovereignty. Privacy primarily applies when the data sovereign's data relates to an individual, regardless of whether the data sovereign is the actual provider of the data or not. Essentially, the motivations and principles behind data sovereignty and privacy are the same; the aim is to establish confidential and trusted data usage and to ensure compliance with data usage conditions (policies). However, the focus of the implementation of privacy strongly relies on the security domain, and the data subject plays only a passive role in the data collection process. However, data sovereignty emphasizes the autonomy and self-determination of both data sharing participants, while there are fewer technical restrictions than in privacy-relevant scenarios. In addition, trusted third parties play an essential role in privacy, specified by the service provider (data consumer), whereas data sovereignty aims for the free choice of trust anchors.

Implications

The delimitation of data sovereignty from privacy has theoretical and practical implications. On the one hand, our research has strengthened and expanded on the position of Hummel et al. (2018). We have achieved this primarily by consulting more recent literature and considering various aspects (economic, organizational, regulatory, technical). While privacy is a much older field of research, we have highlighted the benefits of learning from privacy and PETs both conceptually and technically when addressing data sovereignty by identifying similarities and differences. Our observations are particularly relevant for the domains that (must) combine both concepts. Especially in the healthcare domain, there are recent approaches for bridging both concepts in human-centric data ecosystems (Scheider et al., 2023a; Scheider et al., 2023b; Horgan et al., 2022). We have highlighted that the two concepts are not mutually exclusive, allowing architectural approaches to consider both but without mixing the concepts. This differentiation is particularly relevant within the context of RE.

Limitations & Future Work

Our research also shows some limitations. First, the SLR is not entirely up to date but stagnates in autumn 2023. We assume that the basic definitions and concepts have not changed since then. However, this would need to be verified. Second, we have not considered the technologies in detail. Although we based our comparison of the two concepts on the dimensions of PETs, examining the technologies that enforce data sovereignty and privacy in more detail and comparing their mechanisms to derive more specific implications for practice would be beneficial. During this examination, it would also be interesting to explore whether the data sovereignty domain could adopt RE methods from the privacy domain. One aspect of this would be comparing data usage policies in industrial data sharing and privacy policies regarding definition and enforcement.

CONCLUSIONS

We investigated how data sovereignty is defined in the literature and how it can be delimited from privacy. We addressed the questions using an SLR with a total set of 89 articles and examined the concept of data sovereignty from different perspectives, as well as contrasting multiple aspects of privacy and PETs. Essentially, we explained the difference and the importance of understanding it to accurately classify the legal context, conduct an appropriate risk assessment, and consider the results during the software engineering process. With this, we have contributed to knowledge building in a young research area and advanced the practical implementation of digital sovereignty.

DECLARATION OF GENERATIVE AI AND AI-ASSISTED TECHNOLOGIES

During the preparation of this work, the authors utilized AI-assisted tools such as DeepL and Grammarly to enhance English language accuracy, including spelling, grammar, and punctuation. The content generated or corrected by these tools was thoroughly reviewed, revised, and edited by the authors to ensure accuracy and originality. The authors accept full responsibility for the originality of the final content of this publication.

REFERENCES

Alsamhi, S. H., Hawbani, A., Kumar, S., Timilsina, M., Al-Qatf, M., Haque, R., Nashwan, F. M. A., Zhao, L., & Curry, E. (2024). Empowering Dataspace 4.0: Unveiling Promise of Decentralized Data-Sharing. *IEEE Access : Practical Innovations, Open Solutions*, *12*, 112637–112658. DOI: 10.1109/ACCESS.2024.3442968

Bader, S., Pullmann, J., Mader, C., Tramp, S., Quix, C., Müller, A. W., & Lange, C. (2020). The international data spaces information model–an ontology for sovereign exchange of digital content. In *International Semantic Web Conference* (pp. 176-192). Cham: Springer International Publishing. DOI: 10.1007/978-3-030-62466-8_12

Bartsch, J., Dehling, T., Lauf, F., Meister, S., & Sunyaev, A. (2022). Let the computer say NO! The neglected potential of policy definition languages for data sovereignty. In *Selbstbestimmung, Privatheit und Datenschutz: Gestaltungsoptionen für einen europäischen Weg* (pp. 449–468). Springer Fachmedien Wiesbaden. DOI: 10.1007/978-3-658-33306-5_22

Bruckner, F., & Jahnke, N. (2021). Datenschutz und Datensicherheit in Datenökosystemen - IIP-Ecosphere Whitepaper (1.0). *Zenodo*. DOI: 10.5281/zenodo.4588330

Calzada, I. (2021). Data co-operatives through data sovereignty. *Smart Cities*, *4*(3), 1158–1172. DOI: 10.3390/smartcities4030062

Cappiello, C., Gal, A., Jarke, M., & Rehof, J. (2020). Data ecosystems: Sovereign data exchange among organizations (Dagstuhl Seminar 19391). *Dagstuhl Reports*, *9*(9), 66–134.

Cheong, L. K., & Chang, V. (2007). The need for data governance: a case study. *ACIS 2007 proceedings*, 100.

Couture, S., & Toupin, S. (2019). What does the notion of "sovereignty" mean when referring to the digital? *New Media & Society*, *21*(10), 2305–2322. DOI: 10.1177/1461444819865984

Cuno, S., Bruns, L., Tcholtchev, N., Lämmel, P., & Schieferdecker, I. (2019). Data governance and sovereignty in urban data spaces based on standardized ICT reference architectures. *Data*, *4*(1), 16. DOI: 10.3390/data4010016

Curry, E. (2016). The big data value chain: definitions, concepts, and theoretical approaches. *New horizons for a data-driven economy: A roadmap for usage and exploitation of big data in Europe*, 29-37.

De Filippi, P., & McCarthy, S. (2012). Cloud computing: Centralization and data sovereignty. *European Journal of Law and Technology, 3*(2).

Drees, H., Kubitza, D. O., Lipp, J., Pretzsch, S., & Langdon, C. S. (2021). Mobility data space – first implementation and business opportunities. In *ITS World Congress*.

European Parliament & Council. (2016). Regulation (EU) 2016/679 of the European Parliament and of the Council of 27 April 2016 on the protection of natural persons with regard to the processing of personal data and on the free movement of such data (General Data Protection Regulation). *Official Journal of the European Union, L, 119*, 1–88.

European Parliament & Council. (2023). Regulation (EU) 2023/2854 of the European Parliament and of the Council of 13 December 2023 on harmonised rules on fair access to and use of data and amending Regulation (EU) 2017/2394 and Directive (EU) 2020/1828 (Data Act). *Official Journal of the European Union, L, 151*, 1–16.

Falcão, R., Matar, R., Rauch, B., Elberzhager, F., & Koch, M. (2023). A reference architecture for enabling interoperability and data sovereignty in the Agricultural Data Space. *Information (Basel), 14*(3), 197. DOI: 10.3390/info14030197

Firdausy, D., Silva, P. D. A., van Sinderen, M. J., & Iacob, M. E. (2022a). Semantic discovery and selection of data connectors in international data spaces. In *Interoperability for Enterprise Systems and Applications*. I-ESA.

Firdausy, D. R., Silva, P. D. A., Van Sinderen, M., & Iacob, M. E. (2022b). Towards a reference enterprise architecture to enforce digital sovereignty in international data spaces. In *2022 IEEE 24th Conference on Business Informatics (CBI)* (Vol. 1, pp. 117-125). IEEE. DOI: 10.1109/CBI54897.2022.00020

Franklin, M., Halevy, A., & Maier, D. (2005). From databases to dataspaces: A new abstraction for information management. *SIGMOD Record, 34*(4), 27–33. DOI: 10.1145/1107499.1107502

Giese, T., & Anderl, R. (2022, November). Maintaining Control over Distributed Data Through a Data Sovereignty Model. In *2022 IEEE 7th International Conference on Information Technology and Digital Applications (ICITDA)* (pp. 1-7). IEEE. DOI: 10.1109/ICITDA55840.2022.9971218

Gil, G., Arnaiz, A., Diez, F. J., & Higuero, M. V. (2020, June). *Evaluation methodology for distributed data usage control solutions. In 2020 Global Internet of Things Summit (GIoTS)*. IEEE.

Gil, G., Arnaiz, A., Higuero, M., Diez, F. J., & Jacob, E. (2022). Context-Aware Policy Analysis for Distributed Usage Control. *Energies, 15*(19), 7113. DOI: 10.3390/en15197113

Hansen, M., Jensen, M., & Rost, M. (2015, May). *Protection goals for privacy engineering. In 2015 IEEE security and privacy workshops*. IEEE.

Hellmeier, M., & von Scherenberg, F. (2023). A Delimitation of Data Sovereignty from Digital and Technological Sovereignty. In *ECIS*.

Heurix, J., Zimmermann, P., Neubauer, T., & Fenz, S. (2015). A taxonomy for privacy enhancing technologies. *Computers & Security*, *53*, 1–17. DOI: 10.1016/j.cose.2015.05.002

Horgan, D., Hajduch, M., Vrana, M., Soderberg, J., Hughes, N., Omar, M. I., & Sky Gross, E. (2022, August). European health data space—An opportunity now to grasp the future of data-driven healthcare. [). MDPI.]. *Health Care*, *10*(9), 1629. PMID: 36141241

Hummel, P., Braun, M., Augsberg, S., & Dabrock, P. (2018). Sovereignty and data sharing. *ITU Journal on Future and Evolving Technologies, 1*(2).

Hummel, P., Braun, M., Tretter, M., & Dabrock, P. (2021). Data sovereignty: A review. *Big Data & Society*, *8*(1), 205395172098201. DOI: 10.1177/2053951720982012

Irion, K. (2012). Government cloud computing and national data sovereignty. *Policy and Internet*, *4*(3-4), 40–71. DOI: 10.1002/poi3.10

Jarke, M., Otto, B., & Ram, S. (2019). Data sovereignty and data space ecosystems. *Business & Information Systems Engineering*, *61*(5), 549–550. DOI: 10.1007/s12599-019-00614-2

Khatri, V., & Brown, C. V. (2010). Designing data governance. *Communications of the ACM*, *53*(1), 148–152. DOI: 10.1145/1629175.1629210

Kitchenham, B. (2007). *Guidelines for performing systematic literature reviews in software engineering* (Vol. 5). Technical report, ver. 2.3 ebse technical report. ebse.

Lauf, F., Scheider, S., Bartsch, J., Herrmann, P., Radic, M., Rebbert, M., ... & Meister, S. (2022). Linking data sovereignty and data economy: arising areas of tension.

Mackey, T. K., Calac, A. J., Keshava, B. C., Yracheta, J., Tsosie, K. S., & Fox, K. (2022). Establishing a blockchain-enabled Indigenous data sovereignty framework for genomic data. *Cell*, *185*(15), 2626–2631. DOI: 10.1016/j.cell.2022.06.030 PMID: 35868267

Nagel, L., Hierro, J. J., Perea, E., Lycklama, D., Mertens, C., Taillandier, A. S., . . . Grguric, A. (2021). *Design principles for data spaces: position paper* (No. RWTH-2022-09082). E. ON Energy Research Center.

OASIS. (2013). extensible access control markup language (xacml) version 3.0. *A:(22 January 2013). URl:* http://docs. oasis-open. org/xacml/3.0/xacml-3.0-core-spec-os-en. html

Oliveira, M. I. S., & Lóscio, B. F. (2018). What is a data ecosystem? In *Proceedings of the 19th Annual International Conference on Digital Government Research: Governance in the Data Age* (Article No. 74, pp. 1-9). Association for Computing Machinery.

Otto, B. (2011). A morphology of the organisation of data governance.

Otto, B. (2019). Interview with Reinhold Achatz on "data sovereignty and data ecosystems". *Business & Information Systems Engineering*, *61*(5), 635–636. DOI: 10.1007/s12599-019-00609-z

Otto, B., Hompel, M. T., & Wrobel, S. (2019). International Data Spaces: Reference architecture for the digitization of industries. *Digital transformation*, 109-128.

Otto, B., Lohmann, S., Steinbuß, S., Teuscher, A., Auer, S., Boehmer, M., ... & Hierro, J. (2018). Ids reference architecture model. industrial data space. version 2.0.

Otto, B., Ten Hompel, M., & Wrobel, S. (2022). *Designing data spaces: The ecosystem approach to competitive advantage*. Springer Nature. DOI: 10.1007/978-3-030-93975-5

Palanisamy, V., & Verhaart, M. (2014). Compliance and Data Sovereignty Issues on Cloud Technology.

Pampus, J., & Heisel, M. (2024). An Empirical Examination of the Technical Aspects of Data Sovereignty. In *Proceedings of the 19th International Conference on Software Technologies* (pp. 112-122). DOI: 10.5220/0012760600003753

Pearson, S., & Benameur, A. (2010, November). Privacy, security and trust issues arising from cloud computing. In *2010 IEEE Second International Conference on Cloud Computing Technology and Science* (pp. 693-702). IEEE. DOI: 10.1109/CloudCom.2010.66

Pedreira, V., Barros, D., & Pinto, P. (2021). A review of attacks, vulnerabilities, and defenses in industry 4.0 with new challenges on data sovereignty ahead. *Sensors (Basel)*, *21*(15), 5189. DOI: 10.3390/s21155189 PMID: 34372425

Peterson, Z. N., Gondree, M., & Beverly, R. (2011). A position paper on data sovereignty: The importance of geolocating data in the cloud. In *3rd USENIX Workshop on Hot Topics in Cloud Computing (HotCloud 11).*

Pettenpohl, H., Spiekermann, M., & Both, J. R. (2022). International Data Spaces in a Nutshell.

Polatin-Reuben, D., & Wright, J. (2014). An internet with BRICS characteristics: Data sovereignty and the balkanisation of the internet. In *4th USENIX Workshop on Free and Open Communications on the Internet (FOCI 14).*

Sarabia-Jácome, D., Palau, C. E., Esteve, M., & Boronat, F. (2019). Seaport data space for improving logistic maritime operations. *IEEE Access : Practical Innovations, Open Solutions*, *8*, 4372–4382. DOI: 10.1109/ACCESS.2019.2963283

Scheider, S., Lauf, F., & Geller, S. (2023a). Data sovereign humans and the information economy: towards design principles for human centric B2C data ecosystems.

Scheider, S., Lauf, F., Möller, F., & Otto, B. (2023). A reference system architecture with data sovereignty for human-centric data ecosystems. *Business & Information Systems Engineering*, *65*(5), 577–595. DOI: 10.1007/s12599-023-00816-9

Schmidt, K., Munilla Garrido, G., Mühle, A., & Meinel, C. (2022, August). Mitigating sovereign data exchange challenges: A mapping to apply privacy-and authenticity-enhancing technologies. In *International Conference on Trust and Privacy in Digital Business* (pp. 50-65). Cham: Springer International Publishing. DOI: 10.1007/978-3-031-17926-6_4

Sun, Y., Zhang, J., Xiong, Y., & Zhu, G. (2014). Data security and privacy in cloud computing. *International Journal of Distributed Sensor Networks*, *10*(7), 190903. DOI: 10.1155/2014/190903

W3C (2018). ODRL vocabulary & expression 2.2. https://www.w3.org/TR/odrl-vocab/

Wing, J. M. (2019). The Data Life Cycle. *Harvard Data Science Review*, *1*(1). Advance online publication. DOI: 10.1162/99608f92.e26845b4

Wohlin, C., Mendes, E., Felizardo, K. R., & Kalinowski, M. (2020). Guidelines for the search strategy to update systematic literature reviews in software engineering. *Information and Software Technology*, *127*, 106366. DOI: 10.1016/j.infsof.2020.106366

Zieglmeier, V., & Pretschner, A. (2021). Trustworthy transparency by design. *arXiv preprint arXiv:2103.10769.*

Zrenner, J., Möller, F. O., Jung, C., Eitel, A., & Otto, B. (2019). Usage control architecture options for data sovereignty in business ecosystems. *Journal of Enterprise Information Management*, *32*(3), 477–495. DOI: 10.1108/JEIM-03-2018-0058

ENDNOTES

1 https://internationaldataspaces.org/ (accessed on 2025-03-08)

Chapter 2
Smart City Surveillance: Governance Challenges in Balancing Privacy, Security, and Digital Sovereignty

Sanjay Misra
https://orcid.org/0000-0002-3556-9331
Institute for Energy Technology, Halden, Norway

Kousik Barik
https://orcid.org/0000-0001-9296-9561
Universidad de Alcalá, Madrid, Spain

Petter Kvalvik
Institute for Energy Technology, Halden, Norway.

Per-Arne Jørgensen
https://orcid.org/0000-0001-9480-738X
Institute for Energy Technology, Halden, Norway

ABSTRACT

As smart cities evolve with advanced surveillance systems, the balance between public safety and citizens' digital sovereignty has emerged as a critical concern. This paper presents a qualitative study that explores how modern observation techniques, such as AI-powered cameras, facial recognition, and real-time monitoring, enhance urban security while simultaneously threatening individual privacy. Through an

DOI: 10.4018/979-8-3693-9137-2.ch002

interdisciplinary analysis of surveillance technologies, legal frameworks, and governance models, the study highlights the growing risks of mass surveillance, data misuse, and erosion of personal freedoms. The proposed framework is illustrated through the example of Delhi's smart city development, revealing systemic gaps in transparency, consent, and accountability. The paper further examines regulatory and technological strategies that can mitigate privacy invasions without undermining security goals.

INTRODUCTION

The rapid advancement of smart city technologies has revolutionized urban management, enhancing efficiency, security, and connectivity. Governments and city planners increasingly deploy surveillance systems equipped with AI-powered cameras, biometric recognition, and data analytics to monitor public spaces and prevent crime (Braun et al., 2018; Singh, 2023). While these technologies improve security, they also raise serious privacy concerns, as vast amounts of personal data are collected, stored, and analyzed without citizens' full awareness or consent (Nandy, 2023; Mosa et al., 2024). The concept of digital sovereignty, which refers to individuals' control over their personal data in the digital domain, is now at risk as mass surveillance systems expand globally (Zatarain, 2019; Dubey & Sharma, 2024). Furthermore, regulatory frameworks often struggle to keep pace with the rapid evolution of surveillance technologies, creating legal and ethical challenges (Edwards, 2016; Losavio et al., 2018).

Several studies have explored the implications of surveillance in smart cities, focusing on privacy threats and regulatory frameworks. For example, Braun et al. (2018) analyzed how AI-based surveillance compromises anonymity in public spaces, highlighting concerns over facial recognition and behavioral tracking. Similarly, Singh (2023) examined the broader impact of mass surveillance on civil liberties and digital rights, emphasizing the risks of centralized data control. From a legal perspective, Edwards (2016) discussed the challenges of regulating AI-driven surveillance, emphasizing gaps in current data protection laws. Additionally, reports from organizations such as the European Data Protection Board (EDPB, 2022) and the United Nations Human Rights Office (OHCHR, 2021) have addressed the increasing need for stricter regulations to balance security and privacy. While these studies provide valuable insights, there is limited discussion on how digital sovereignty is specifically challenged within smart city ecosystems, especially in the context of real-time surveillance and government-controlled data processing (Mosa et al., 2024).

Despite extensive research on smart city surveillance, existing studies often emphasize either technological advancements or legal perspectives without integrating a comprehensive analysis of digital sovereignty (Nandy, 2023). There is a lack of detailed investigation into how modern observation techniques, such as AI-powered facial recognition and behavioral analytics, affect personal freedoms at both legal and societal levels (Singh, 2023; Fan et al., 2025). Moreover, current regulatory measures struggle to keep pace with rapidly evolving surveillance technologies, leaving citizens vulnerable to privacy intrusions (EDPB, 2022; OHCHR, 2021). This gap highlights the urgent need for a framework that ensures both security and digital sovereignty within smart cities (Losavio et al., 2018; Raghav et al., 2025).

Major Contribution

This paper aims to address the identified research gap by providing the following key contributions:

- Analyzing how modern smart city surveillance techniques impact digital sovereignty and citizen privacy.
- Investigating the shortcomings of existing privacy regulations in mitigating mass surveillance threats.
- Proposing a balanced approach that integrates security needs with privacy-preserving mechanisms.
- Outlining potential policy recommendations and technological solutions to protect citizens' rights.

Research Problems and Questions

The rapid integration of AI surveillance, biometric systems, and IoT networks into smart city infrastructures—while beneficial for urban security and efficiency—has introduced complex privacy challenges. Each of these technologies presents unique risks to citizen privacy, autonomy, and data protection, and these risks are often exacerbated by fragmented legal frameworks and insufficient regulatory oversight. Despite growing academic attention, there remains a significant gap in evaluating these technologies under a unified lens of digital sovereignty and governance accountability. This section articulates the core research questions that guide this study.

RQ1: How do AI-powered surveillance systems in smart cities impact citizen privacy and digital sovereignty?

Rationale: Increasing use of facial recognition and behavioral tracking without transparency and lack of comprehensive analysis on how AI surveillance challenges personal freedoms.

RQ2: What are the privacy and ethical risks associated with the deployment of biometric identification systems in public smart city infrastructures?

Rationale: Biometric data is unique and irreplaceable, raising concerns after breaches and limited research on long-term privacy consequences and ethical handling of biometric data.

RQ3: In what ways do IoT-enabled sensor networks contribute to mass data collection, and what are the potential implications for user consent and data security?

Rationale: IoT devices often operate passively, collecting data without informed consent and absence of standard privacy-preserving protocols and public engagement mechanisms.

RQ4: What regulatory and technological frameworks can effectively balance urban security needs with the protection of digital rights in smart cities?

Rationale: Regulatory bodies are struggling to catch up with rapidly evolving surveillance technologies and fragmented or outdated data protection laws, especially in developing regions.

RQ5: How can transparency, accountability, and citizen participation be integrated into smart surveillance governance models?

Rationale: Citizens often remain unaware of data collection practices in public spaces and limited research on participatory governance and trust-building in smart surveillance systems.

Table 1 presents the alignment of research questions with technology domains and governance

Table 1. Alignment of research questions with technology domains and governance

Research Question	Relevant Domain	Governance Focus
RQ1	AI-Powered Surveillance	Ethical AI use, transparency, algorithmic audits
RQ2	Biometric Systems	Consent, data permanence, legal protections
RQ3	IoT & Sensor Networks	Passive data collection, informed consent
RQ4	Cross-cutting (All domains)	Legal frameworks, regulatory alignment
RQ5	Cross-cutting (All domains)	Citizen engagement, participatory governance

Structure of the Paper

The remainder of this paper is structured as follows: Section 2 provides an overview of smart city surveillance technologies and their privacy implications. Section 3 reviews existing legal frameworks and regulatory challenges. The proposed conceptual framework to balance governance for privacy and security in smart cities is presented in Section 4. The results and discussion are illustrated in Section 5. Finally, Section 6 concludes the paper with key insights and future research directions.

SMART CITY SURVEILLANCE TECHNOLOGIES AND THEIR PRIVACY IMPLICATIONS

As smart cities increasingly embrace digital transformation, surveillance technologies have become central to urban security, governance, and data-driven decision-making. However, the rapid deployment of these systems has introduced complex privacy, ethical, and legal challenges. This section categorizes the major surveillance technologies into three core domains (Table 1): AI-powered surveillance systems, biometric identification technologies, and Internet of Things (IoT) sensor networks. Each domain plays a pivotal role in enhancing operational efficiency and public safety, yet also raises pressing concerns about mass surveillance, data breaches, and loss of individual autonomy. The section also highlights that governance and policy frameworks intersect all these domains (Figure 1), influencing how these technologies are deployed, regulated, and received by the public. Figure 2 outlines the detailed taxonomy of privacy and security-related challenges. It consists of three categories: AI-powered surveillance, biometric surveillance systems, and IoT and sensor networks. The details are outlined in terms of privacy, security, and an application perspective. Table 2 presents major categories for smart city surveillance, privacy & security.

Table 2. Suggested major categories for smart city surveillance privacy & security

Category	Focus Area
1. **AI-Powered Surveillance**	Facial recognition, behavior analysis, predictive policing
2. **Biometric Identification Systems**	Fingerprint, iris, gait, voice – permanent, sensitive personal data
3. **IoT and Sensor Networks**	Traffic, environmental, location-based data – often passively collected

Figure 1. Overview of privacy and security concerns in smart city surveillance

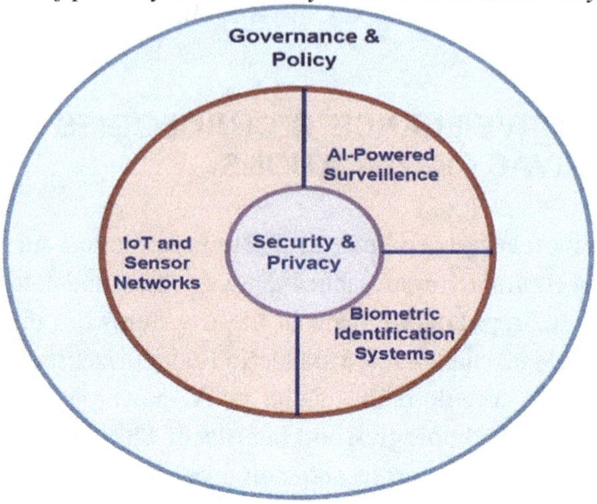

Figure 2. Taxonomy of privacy and security concerns in smart city surveillance

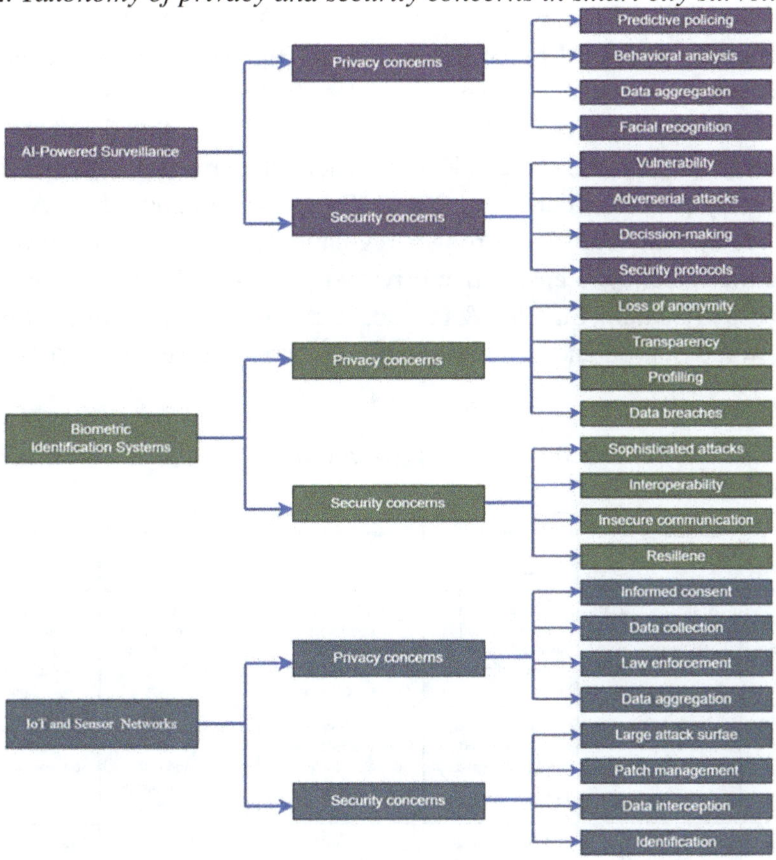

AI-Powered Surveillance Cameras

One of the most widely used surveillance technologies in smart cities is AI-enhanced camera systems that leverage facial recognition, object detection, and behaviour analysis (Gautam, Sunidhi, & Prasad, 2025). These systems can detect anomalies, track individuals, and identify suspicious activities in real-time, making them essential tools for urban security and law enforcement (Haleem, 2023). China's extensive surveillance network, equipped with AI-powered cameras, has been reported to monitor and identify individuals across cities, raising concerns about the global expansion of AI surveillance (Feldstein, 2019). Similarly, cities like London and

New York use facial recognition technology to assist in law enforcement operations, integrating AI into public safety initiatives (Jain & Mitra, 2025).

However, the use of AI in surveillance raises significant privacy concerns regarding constant monitoring, potential misidentification, and mass data collection without consent (Bhagat et al., 2025). Studies have shown that facial recognition systems are prone to racial and gender bias, leading to wrongful identifications and discriminatory policing (Feldstein, 2019). The growing adoption of AI-powered surveillance systems calls for stronger regulations, ethical AI frameworks, and increased transparency to ensure that privacy rights are upheld while maintaining urban security (Gautam, Sunidhi, & Prasad, 2025). The summary of existing works on AI-Powered Surveillance Cameras in Smart Cities is given in Table 3.

Table 3. Summary of existing works on AI-powered surveillance cameras in smart cities

Reference	Technology Used	Major Problem Addressed	Identified Gap	Recommendations	Other Insights
Gautam, Sunidhi, & Prasad (2025)	AI-powered facial recognition, object detection, behavior analysis	Privacy risks due to constant surveillance and data collection	Lack of clear regulatory frameworks to govern AI-based surveillance	Implement ethical AI governance and privacy-centric regulations	Discusses how AI-enhanced surveillance can improve security while raising ethical concerns
Haleem (2023)	AI-powered surveillance for drones and vehicles	Unauthorized tracking and invasion of privacy	Insufficient safeguards for AI-driven vehicle and drone surveillance	Introduce strict data protection laws and real-time monitoring frameworks	Focuses on AI-based surveillance in transportation systems
Jain & Mitra (2025)	AI applications in secure 6G-enabled smart city infrastructure	Risks of facial recognition bias and wrongful identification	Lack of AI model fairness and transparency in surveillance decisions	Enhance algorithmic transparency and bias mitigation strategies	Examines the role of 6G in improving AI-driven surveillance accuracy
Bhagat et al. (2025)	AI and machine learning for predictive surveillance	Ethical concerns about mass surveillance and civil liberties	Absence of standardized policies for AI-powered behavior analysis	Develop ethical AI policies balancing security and privacy	Highlights future trends in AI-driven predictive surveillance systems
Feldstein (2019)	Global AI Surveillance Expansion Case Studies	Government overreach and mass data collection risks	Limited international frameworks to regulate AI surveillance expansion	Promote international cooperation on AI surveillance policies	Provides global insights into AI surveillance deployment across different regions

Biometric-based Authentication System

Smart cities are increasingly deploying biometric-based authentication for security and access control in public spaces, airports, and transportation hubs (Farazdaghi, Eslahi, & El Meouche, 2021). Technologies such as fingerprint scanning, iris recognition, and gait analysis provide seamless identification, reducing the need for traditional ID verification while enhancing urban security (Ross, Banerjee, & Chowdhury, 2020). Additionally, voice biometric technology is gaining traction as a method for enhancing public safety and security, particularly in sectors such as law enforcement and transportation (Ouahab et al., 2024). However, despite these advancements, the widespread collection and storage of biometric data present significant privacy risks.

Key concerns associated with biometric surveillance include data breaches, unauthorized tracking, and the loss of anonymity (Sedik et al., 2021). Unlike passwords, biometric data is permanent—once compromised, it cannot be changed, making it an attractive target for cybercriminals. Several high-profile breaches, such as the hacking of India's Aadhaar biometric database, have demonstrated the vulnerabilities of centralized biometric systems, raising questions about the security of such infrastructures (Fawzy, 2024). Moreover, biometric-based privacy preservation protocols have been proposed to address security gaps in smart city applications, yet challenges remain in implementing robust data protection measures (Nyangaresi et al., 2024). These issues highlight the need for improved encryption, decentralized storage, and stronger legal frameworks to ensure that biometric technologies do not compromise citizens' fundamental privacy rights. Table 4 provides a summary of existing works.

Table 4. Summary of existing works on biometric identification systems in smart cities

Reference	Technology Used	Major Problem Addressed	Identified Gap	Recommendations	Other Insights
Ross, Banerjee, & Chowdhury (2020)	Biometric data forensic techniques	Security vulnerabilities in biometric databases	Lack of robust forensic mechanisms for biometric data breaches	Implement stronger forensic tools and encryption methods for biometric data security	Highlights the role of digital forensic schemes in protecting biometric data
Farazdaghi, Eslahi, & El Meouche (2021)	Fingerprint, iris recognition, gait analysis	Challenges in biometric authentication adoption in smart cities	Insufficient standardization and interoperability of biometric systems	Establish universal biometric standards and improve integration with existing infrastructure	Focuses on the deployment challenges of biometric systems in urban settings
Sedik et al. (2021)	Deep learning for biometric alteration detection	Risk of biometric spoofing and identity fraud	Lack of AI-based solutions to detect fake biometric identities	Use AI and machine learning to detect manipulated biometric data	Explores the role of deep learning in preventing biometric forgery

continued on following page

Table 4. Continued

Reference	Technology Used	Major Problem Addressed	Identified Gap	Recommendations	Other Insights
Fawzy (2024)	Policy analysis of biometric citizen data	Ethical and privacy concerns in biometric surveillance	Limited public discourse on biometric citizens and their rights	Re-evaluate the legal and ethical implications of biometric policies	Introduces the concept of "biometric citizens" in governance policies
Ouahab et al. (2024)	Voice biometric authentication	Security and usability of voice biometrics in public safety applications	Concerns about the accuracy and reliability of voice authentication	Enhance voice recognition algorithms and implement multi-factor authentication	Discusses the role of voice biometrics in urban security
Nyangaresi et al. (2024)	Biometric privacy preservation protocols	Data privacy risks in biometric smart city applications	Limited research on privacy-enhancing biometric authentication	Develop privacy-preserving techniques like fuzzy commitment schemes	Proposes a novel protocol for securing biometric data in smart cities

Internet of Things (IoT) and Sensor Networks

Smart cities rely on IoT-enabled devices, such as traffic sensors, environmental monitors, and smart streetlights, to collect data for efficient urban management (Cui et al., 2018). These devices play a critical role in real-time data collection to improve traffic flow, air quality monitoring, and energy conservation (Ghazal et al., 2023). However, they also gather vast amounts of personal and behavioral data, often without explicit user consent, raising concerns about citizen privacy and data security (Al-Turjman, Zahmatkesh, & Shahroze, 2022).

For instance, smart traffic cameras do more than detect traffic violations—they also track vehicle movements and monitor real-time location data, leading to concerns over continuous surveillance and potential misuse by authorities (Cottrill et al., 2020). Similarly, IoT-based environmental sensors can monitor crowd density, air pollution, and even individuals' movements in public spaces, creating a pervasive surveillance ecosystem (Bohli, Langendörfer, & Skarmeta, 2022). While these technologies offer improved urban efficiency, they also blur the boundaries between public security and mass surveillance, raising ethical and legal challenges.

Furthermore, IoT networks remain highly vulnerable to cyberattacks, as weak security protocols often expose them to unauthorized access and data breaches (Rao & Deebak, 2023). Past cyber incidents have demonstrated how hackers exploit insecure IoT infrastructures, compromising smart city control systems and citizen data (Pramanik et al., 2023). For example, large-scale IoT botnet attacks have shown how compromised IoT devices can be weaponized to disrupt city operations (Cui et al., 2018). Addressing these vulnerabilities requires stronger encryption techniques, decentralized data management, and regulatory policies that safeguard user privacy while maintaining smart city functionality (Bohli, Langendörfer, & Skarmeta, 2022). Table 5 provides a summary of existing works.

Table 5. Summary of existing works on IoT and sensor networks in smart cities

Reference	Technology Used	Major Problem Addressed	Identified Gap	Recommendations	Other Insights
Cui et al. (2018)	IoT-enabled smart city infrastructure	Security vulnerabilities in IoT-based smart city applications	Lack of robust security mechanisms for IoT networks	Develop encryption and authentication techniques to protect IoT data	Discusses challenges and opportunities in IoT security
Bohli, Langendörfer,& Skarmeta (2022)	Data aggregation in IoT systems	Privacy risks in large-scale IoT data collection	Insufficient privacy-preserving data aggregation methods	Implement decentralized and secure data aggregation frameworks	Focuses on protecting personal data in IoT-driven smart cities
Al-Turjman, Zahmatkesh, & Shahroze (2022)	IoT communications and privacy protection	Lack of consent in personal data collection from smart city sensors	Absence of standardized privacy laws for IoT applications	Establish unified global privacy regulations for IoT devices	Provides a comprehensive overview of privacy issues in IoT networks
Cottrill et al. (2020)	IoT-based environmental sensors	Trust and transparency issues in IoT surveillance systems	Lack of citizen awareness and informed consent mechanisms	Improve public engagement and transparency in IoT data collection	Examines design strategies for privacy-conscious IoT applications
Rao & Deebak (2023)	IoT security technologies in smart cities	Cybersecurity threats targeting IoT networks	Weak security protocols and authentication mechanisms	Strengthen security frameworks using AI and blockchain for IoT protection	Highlights security risks associated with IoT in industries and cities
Ghazal et al. (2023)	IoT-connected wireless sensor networks (WSNs)	Unauthorized access and data breaches in smart city IoT systems	Limited adoption of advanced encryption techniques for WSNs	Use machine learning-based intrusion detection systems	Proposes security solutions for IoT-driven smart city infrastructures
Pramanik et al. (2023)	IoT privacy and security frameworks	Growing risk of IoT-based mass surveillance	Inadequate legal enforcement on IoT privacy violations	Strengthen data protection laws and ethical AI use in IoT monitoring	Analyzes privacy risks related to IoT deployments in urban spaces

GOVERNANCE AND POLICY AND PROPOSED FRAMEWORK

As smart city technologies rapidly expand, the governance and policy frameworks that underpin their ethical deployment have struggled to keep pace. Surveillance practices involving AI-powered monitoring, biometric identification, and IoT sensor networks often outpace legal reforms, leaving significant gaps in how citizen rights, data ownership, and privacy are protected. Governance, therefore, plays a critical cross-cutting role in ensuring transparency, accountability, and inclusiveness in surveillance operations. This section examines the existing literature on smart city governance, with a focus on data protection, institutional frameworks, ethical oversight, and citizen participation in surveillance-related decision-making.

While several smart city projects advocate for enhanced digital services and public safety, critics argue that these systems often adopt a top-down, technocratic model, which may marginalize vulnerable groups or overlook civil liberties (Galič, 2022; Bergsrud & Vaseeharanathan, 2024). Others, however, demonstrate how inclusive governance models and participatory design can empower citizens and improve public trust in surveillance infrastructure (Khanna & Khanra, 2023). Moreover, the lack of standardized data governance frameworks leads to inconsistent practices in data collection, access, sharing, and deletion across different city departments and stakeholders (Johnson et al., 2022; Karbassi et al., 2022).

The role of policy instruments—such as privacy impact assessments, ethical audits, public engagement mechanisms, and institutional coordination—is increasingly seen as essential to navigating the complex relationship between innovation and human rights (El-Sherif & Khalil, 2022; Estevez et al., 2021). However, fragmented regulatory approaches, especially in developing regions, result in weak enforcement, limited legal recourse for citizens, and unchecked surveillance by both state and private actors (Ahmad & Dethy, 2019; Yang et al., 2019). A shift toward adaptive, transparent, and multi-stakeholder governance is critical to aligning technological advancement with democratic accountability.

The summary of relevant works for governance and policy for smart city surveillance is given in Table 6.

Table 6. Summary of existing works on governance & policy in smart city surveillance

Reference	Focus Area	Key Contribution	Main Gap	Recommendation
Ahmad & Dethy (2019)	Privacy provisions	Proposed foundational privacy principles	Weak legal enforcement	Constitutional digital rights protection
Khanna & Khanra (2023)	Citizen empowerment	Linked inclusive governance to citizen trust	Inconsistent engagement methods	Community-driven data governance
Galiè (2022)	Ethical critique	Critiqued mass surveillance culture	Overlooking individual privacy	Rebalancing surveillance with civil liberties
Bergsrud & Vaseeharanathan (2024)	Vulnerable groups	Exposed ethical risks for marginalized populations	Underrepresented in policy	Include equity-focused policy evaluations
Johnson et al. (2022)	Data governance	Defined components of smart city data governance	Institutional misalignment	Unified governance protocols
Karbassi et al. (2022)	Governance models	Advocated for standardized data frameworks	Absence of universal models	Standardize urban data accountability
El-Sherif & Khalil (2022)	Policy instruments	Presented tools for effective smart city governance	Weak local policy adoption	Ethical audit and policy training
Estevez et al. (2021)	Smart governance vision	Conceptual model for future smart governance	Limited real-world roadmaps	Develop tech-governance integration plans

PROPOSED FRAMEWORK: LAYERED ARCHITECTURE FRAMEWORK FOR PRIVACY AND SECURITY IN SMART CITIES

Framework Overview

To provide a coherent structure for understanding the interaction between surveillance technologies, legal safeguards, citizen engagement, and governance outcomes a Layered Architecture Framework for privacy and security in smart cities is shown in Figure 3. The framework is organized into five interconnected layers, each building upon and supporting the other, forming a vertically integrated system that reflects real-world implementation logic.

At its foundation, the Technology Layer ensures that surveillance systems are designed with embedded privacy mechanisms, including edge computing and secure audit trails. The Policy & Legal Layer governs the use of these technologies through enforceable data protection laws and sectoral regulations. The Citizen Interface Layer translates these protections into user-facing controls such as consent management and transparency dashboards. Above this, the Governance Layer provides oversight and accountability mechanisms through multi-stakeholder councils and public grievance redressal. Finally, the Outcomes Layer captures the societal impacts of this ecosystem, emphasizing trust, digital sovereignty, and democratic accountability.

This five integrated layers, from technology and legal foundations to governance and outcomes, designed to ensure that urban surveillance systems protect citizen privacy, support accountability, and uphold digital sovereignty.

Figure 3. Layered architecture framework for privacy and security in smart cities

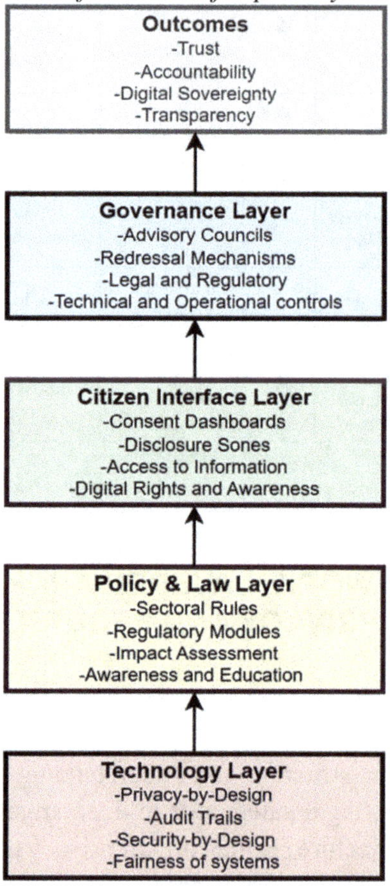

This framework is designed to help policymakers and urban planners evaluate and manage surveillance technologies in a manner that protects civil liberties while ensuring urban safety.

Table 7. Key components of the framework

Layer	Component	Function
Technology	Privacy-by-design (e.g., edge processing, data minimization)	Reduce data exposure and enable local anonymization before storage
	Interoperable data logs and audit trails	Ensure traceability and real-time alerts for data misuse
Policy & Law	Sector-specific privacy rules (e.g., transport, public health)	Prevent cross-domain misuse of citizen data
	Regulatory compliance modules (e.g., GDPR-inspired DPAs)	Embed accountability and independent audits
Citizen Interface	Digital consent dashboard (opt-in/opt-out)	Empower citizens to control their participation in smart services
	Surveillance disclosure zones (e.g., signage, mobile alerts)	Increase real-time awareness of surveillance presence
Governance	Stakeholder advisory councils (public–private–citizen)	Enable participatory governance and trust-building
	Redressal mechanisms (ombudsperson or smart city helpline)	Offer accessible complaint resolution for data misuse

Case Study: Application Example: Delhi Smart City

Delhi, as one of India's selected Smart Cities under the Smart Cities Mission (SCM), has undergone several technological upgrades since 2015, focusing on urban infrastructure, mobility, surveillance, and citizen services. Key interventions have included the installation of CCTV cameras, development of smart command and control centres (ICCC), air quality monitoring stations, integrated traffic systems, and digital access to services.

According to the ORF Evaluation Report by Aijaz (2020), Delhi's smart city strategy prioritized infrastructure and security through surveillance and e-governance, but suffered from limited community participation, incomplete policy guidelines, and weak implementation of data privacy protocols. For instance:

- Over 2,000 smart surveillance cameras were installed, but there is no formal privacy policy guiding how this data is used or stored.
- The ICCC in East Delhi was expected to integrate traffic, utility, and public safety data; however, inter-agency coordination remains weak, and citizen data protection is not standardized.
- The system lacks a public consent mechanism for use of facial recognition or environmental data.

- Projects were often implemented without citizen consultation, particularly in low-income and informal areas.

Current gaps in Delhi's smart surveillance strategy is given in Table 8

Table 8. Identified gaps and impact

Identified Gaps	Impact
Absence of a unified privacy framework	Citizens are unaware of when/how they are surveilled
No opt-in/opt-out for surveillance or digital services	Loss of control over personal data
Lack of transparency in public–private data handling	Reduced trust in government and civic systems
Weak grievance redressal and public accountability	Limited recourse in cases of data misuse or profiling
Underrepresentation of marginalized groups	Biased surveillance coverage and digital exclusion

Table 9 will demonstrate how our proposed framework improves Delhi's smart city.

Table 9. Framework implementation in Delhi

Framework Element	Application in Delhi
Citizen Interface Layer	Introduce a digital privacy dashboard for services like property tax, water, and transport; deploy surveillance signage and app alerts in monitored zones
Technology Layer	Require edge-based data processing in ICCCs to anonymize data at source; integrate automated audit logs for facial recognition access
Policy & Law Layer	Develop city-specific data privacy policy aligned with India's Digital Personal Data Protection Act (DPDP, 2023); mandate inter-agency data governance protocols
Governance Layer	Form a Smart Surveillance Advisory Council (SSAC) involving citizens, municipal reps, and civil society to oversee new surveillance projects
Redressal Mechanism	Set up a citizen grievance portal integrated with ICCC for real-time alerts and complaints on surveillance misuse

Novelty of the Proposed Framework

Unlike existing models that focus primarily on technology or policy in isolation, this framework is:

Holistic – Integrates legal, technical, participatory, and governance aspects
Actionable – Provides practical tools like consent dashboards and audit trails
Modular – Can be scaled across departments (traffic, health, utilities)

Citizen-Centric – Puts control back in the hands of users, with feedback loops and ethical safeguards

It shifts the paradigm from **"Surveillance-First Smart Cities"** to **"Rights-Respecting Smart Cities"**, where digital empowerment and data responsibility coexist.

What's Needed for Implementation?

Implementing this framework in Delhi would require:

1. **Policy Backing**: Enactment of municipal-level privacy legislation aligned with national data protection laws.
2. **Institutional Support**: Collaboration between the Delhi Smart City Limited (DSCL), Municipal Corporations, Delhi Police, and Delhi Government's IT Department.
3. **Funding & Capacity Building**: Dedicated funding for privacy infrastructure and training for civic employees and contractors.
4. **Civic Engagement Campaigns**: Raise public awareness about data rights, surveillance zones, and grievance channels.
5. **Tech-Industry Partnership**: Involve ethical AI and IoT firms to co-develop privacy-enhancing technologies.

RESULTS AND DISCUSSION

Addressing the RQs

RQ1: How do AI-powered surveillance systems in smart cities impact citizen privacy and digital sovereignty?

The analysis in Section 2.2.1 revealed that AI-powered surveillance systems—such as facial recognition, object detection, and predictive behaviour analysis—are increasingly integrated into smart city infrastructures to enhance urban security. However, their deployment often lacks adequate oversight, leading to significant challenges for individual privacy rights and the broader principle of digital sovereignty.

Key Findings

- Data Collection Without Consent: AI-driven video analytics continuously capture biometric and behavioral data from individuals in public spaces, often without explicit consent or awareness. This contributes to the erosion of anonymity in public life, a key component of digital freedom.

- Algorithmic Bias & Discrimination: Several referenced studies (e.g., Feldstein, 2019; Bhagat et al., 2025) indicate that facial recognition systems can identify individuals based on race or gender, raising concerns about discriminatory surveillance practices and inaccurate profiling.
- Mass Surveillance Infrastructure: The convergence of AI and high-resolution CCTV networks, as seen in cities like Beijing, London, and New York, illustrates how smart city security systems can evolve into tools of mass surveillance, posing a direct threat to digital sovereignty (Gautam et al., 2025; Jain & Mitra, 2025).
- Lack of Transparency and Accountability: Stakeholders (governments, private tech vendors) rarely disclose how AI surveillance data is processed, stored, or shared, which violates principles of data ownership, transparency, and informed decision-making—core aspects of digital sovereignty.

This study contributes to the ongoing discourse by synthesizing technological, ethical, and legal concerns around AI surveillance and highlighting two critical tensions:

1. The tension between urban safety and individual autonomy, where enhanced security often comes at the cost of diminished privacy.
2. The tension between technological capability and regulatory maturity, as AI outpaces current governance systems.

Our research also underscores the need for:

- Stricter legal frameworks governing AI surveillance deployments.
- Ethical AI guidelines ensuring algorithmic fairness and transparency.
- Public transparency mechanisms (e.g., signage, opt-out policies, algorithmic audits) to restore trust.

Table 10 demonstrates how RQ1 addresses AI-powered surveillance and its impact on privacy & digital sovereignty

Table 10. RQ1 focus area and discussion

Focus Area	Discussion
Technological Scope	Examines facial recognition, behavior tracking, and real-time video analytics in public spaces.
Privacy Implications	Highlights risks such as lack of consent, constant monitoring, and profiling biases.
Digital Sovereignty	Emphasizes citizen loss of data control, reduced anonymity, and lack of transparency in AI use.
Research Contribution	Synthesizes technical, ethical, and legal concerns; positions AI surveillance as a digital sovereignty challenge.
Policy Recommendations	Advocates for ethical AI guidelines, algorithmic audits, and transparent data governance frameworks.

RQ2: What are the privacy and ethical risks associated with the deployment of biometric identification systems in public smart city infrastructures?

Biometric systems are widely adopted in smart cities for identity verification and access control across various public infrastructures, including transportation hubs, government buildings, and surveillance networks. These systems leverage fingerprints, iris, facial, voice, and gait recognition technologies. While biometrics offer operational efficiency and enhanced security, they also introduce serious **privacy, ethical, and governance challenges**, especially when integrated into surveillance mechanisms.

Key Findings

- Permanence and Irreversibility of Biometric Data: Unlike passwords, biometric traits cannot be changed once compromised. Breaches such as the widely reported Aadhaar database incident in India underscore the irreplaceable nature of biometric identifiers (Ross et al., 2020; Fawzy, 2024).
- Massive Biometric Data Collection Without Consent: In many cases, biometric data is collected during registration or routine access to public services without full transparency or informed consent. This violates principles of autonomy and personal data control (Farazdaghi et al., 2021; Fawzy, 2024).
- Misuse and Function Creep: Once collected, biometric data is often used beyond its original purpose—a phenomenon known as function creep. This undermines trust and opens the door to unauthorized surveillance, profiling, and tracking (Sedik et al., 2021).
- Surveillance of Vulnerable Populations: Biometric surveillance can disproportionately affect vulnerable groups—such as migrants or individuals with

disabilities—by reinforcing systemic bias and reducing access to public services (Bergsrud & Vaseeharanathan, 2024).

This study highlights that biometric surveillance in smart cities challenges both privacy and ethical norms by removing the possibility of opt-out, limiting recourse after data compromise, and enabling covert population tracking. The research contributes by:

- Demonstrating that biometric privacy is fundamentally different from other digital privacy forms due to permanence.
- Emphasizing the ethical dilemma between security and bodily integrity in biometric data use.
- Recommending consent-based, purpose-limited deployment of biometric systems guided by transparent and auditable protocols.

The following Table 11 demonstrates how RQ2 is Addressed in this paper.

Table 11. RQ2 focus area and discussion

Focus Area	Discussion
Technology Scope	Explores fingerprint, iris, gait, and voice recognition used in public smart city services.
Privacy Risks	Emphasizes the irreversible nature of biometric data, potential for breaches, and lack of consent.
Ethical Concerns	Highlights risks of misuse, function creep, and discriminatory surveillance practices.
Research Contribution	Frames biometric privacy as a critical pillar of digital sovereignty and bodily autonomy.
Policy Recommendations	Advocates for consent-based data collection, data minimization, and ethical biometric governance frameworks.

RQ3: In what ways do IoT-enabled sensor networks contribute to mass data collection, and what are the potential implications for user consent and data security?

The integration of Internet of Things (IoT) devices in smart cities has introduced new efficiencies in urban management—monitoring traffic, environmental conditions, energy use, and public behavior in real-time. However, these connected sensor networks are often designed to collect data passively, raising significant concerns around privacy, consent, and data governance.

Key Findings

- Ubiquitous, Passive Surveillance: Smart city IoT systems often operate in the background—capturing user behaviors such as location patterns, dwell time, and mobility habits—without requiring active interaction or awareness from the citizen (Cui et al., 2018; Cottrill et al., 2020).
- Lack of Consent Mechanisms: Most IoT implementations in public spaces lack clear mechanisms for opting in or out of data collection. Citizens are rarely informed when and how their data is collected, stored, or used (Pramanik et al., 2023; Al-Turjman et al., 2022).
- Data Aggregation & Security Risks: IoT data is frequently aggregated and shared across systems (e.g., traffic, law enforcement, energy management) without transparency. This creates attack surfaces for hackers, as seen in past smart city cyberattacks, and increases the risk of re-identification from anonymized datasets (Rao & Deebak, 2023; Bohli et al., 2022).
- Governance Gaps: The rapid deployment of IoT infrastructures has outpaced legal and ethical frameworks. Many cities lack clear data retention policies, consent protocols, or citizen feedback channels (Yang et al., 2019; Johnson et al., 2022).

This study demonstrates that IoT surveillance in smart cities is uniquely problematic because of its invisibility—citizens often don't even know when they're being monitored. The paper contributes by:

- Highlighting the passive and persistent nature of IoT surveillance and its implications for personal autonomy.
- Identifying consent and transparency as critical but neglected elements in IoT governance.
- Emphasizing the urgency of data minimization, public signage, and multilayered cybersecurity strategies for public IoT systems.

The following Table 12 demonstrates how RQ3 is Addressed in this paper.

Table 12. RQ3 focus area and discussion

Focus Area	Discussion
Technology Scope	Reviews use of smart sensors in traffic, environment, lighting, and public monitoring.
Privacy Risks	Identifies passive data collection, location tracking, and user invisibility.
Consent & Autonomy	Explores absence of opt-in/opt-out mechanisms and user awareness.
Security Concerns	Notes risks of data aggregation, cyberattacks, and de-anonymization.
Policy Recommendations	Advocates for public signage, transparent data practices, consent layers, and stronger IoT governance.

RQ4: What regulatory and technological frameworks can effectively balance urban security needs with the protection of digital rights in smart cities?

The findings from previous sections demonstrate that AI surveillance, biometric systems, and IoT technologies all pose complex challenges to privacy and digital sovereignty in smart cities. While these technologies are often justified by their contribution to urban safety and operational efficiency, their unchecked deployment reveals a critical gap between innovation and regulation. RQ4 explores what kinds of frameworks—both regulatory and technological—can restore this balance.

Key Findings

- Fragmented and Outdated Legal Frameworks: Across many jurisdictions, current privacy laws are not designed to address the continuous, automated, and mass nature of smart city surveillance. For example, while the General Data Protection Regulation (GDPR) in the EU sets a strong standard, many regions lack equivalent protections (Yang et al., 2019; Johnson et al., 2022).
- Lack of Standardized Data Governance Models: Smart cities often involve multiple stakeholders—including municipal governments, private tech firms, and utility providers. Without unified data governance structures, personal data flows across entities with limited oversight or accountability (Karbassi et al., 2022; El-Sherif & Khalil, 2022).
- Insufficient Technical Safeguards: Despite advances in AI and encryption, many smart city systems lack privacy-by-design features, making them vulnerable to breaches, misuse, and unintended surveillance (Cui et al., 2018; Sedik et al., 2021).
- Reactive vs. Proactive Governance: Most legal responses to smart city surveillance are reactive—responding to breaches or public backlash—rather

than proactive, embedded in design and procurement stages (Ahmad & Dethy, 2019; Estevez et al., 2021).

Interpretation & Contribution of This Study

This research emphasizes the urgent need for a hybrid governance model—combining legal regulations with embedded technological safeguards—to ensure digital rights are not sacrificed for urban security. Key contributions include:

- Mapping where and how current regulations fall short in protecting digital sovereignty.
- Recommending multi-stakeholder data governance frameworks tailored to smart city complexity.
- Advocating for ethical AI guidelines, privacy impact assessments, and citizen feedback loops as part of surveillance system design.

Table 13 demonstrates how RQ4 is addressed in this paper.

Table 13. Addressing RQ4

Focus Area	Discussion
Legal Frameworks	Highlights regulatory gaps, lack of standardization, and outdated privacy laws.
Data Governance	Analyzes need for cross-sector data accountability and shared standards.
Technical Measures	Identifies absence of privacy-by-design and weak cybersecurity layers.
Research Contribution	Calls for hybrid frameworks integrating law, ethics, and engineering.
Policy Recommendations	Introduces governance models with embedded consent, audits, and transparency mechanisms.

RQ5: How can transparency, accountability, and citizen participation be integrated into smart surveillance governance models?

A recurring theme throughout the analysis of smart surveillance technologies is the disconnect between technology deployment and public engagement. In most cities, surveillance infrastructures are introduced as technical or administrative upgrades, without meaningful consultation, participatory planning, or transparency. RQ5 explores how governance models can evolve to actively include citizens and foster accountability.

Key Findings

- Limited Awareness and Informed Consent: Most citizens are unaware of when, how, or why they are being surveilled in smart cities. Public signage, open data policies, and community forums are rare or poorly implemented, which undermines trust and reinforces the "surveillance without representation" concern (Jameson et al., 2019; Galič, 2022).
- Lack of Participatory Governance Mechanisms: Current governance structures often lack formal avenues for residents to question, influence, or monitor surveillance decisions. This limits democratic oversight over technologies that directly affect civil liberties (Khanna & Khanra, 2023; Bokhari & SeungHwan, 2024).
- Transparency Gaps in Public-Private Collaborations: When private vendors deploy and manage surveillance systems, accountability becomes diffused, making it difficult for citizens to know who holds or uses their data (Johnson et al., 2022; El-Sherif & Khalil, 2022).
- Ethical Concerns Among Vulnerable Groups: Surveillance disproportionately affects marginalized populations who often have less voice in urban planning, increasing the risk of biased policing and algorithmic discrimination (Bergsrud & Vaseeharanathan, 2024).

This research emphasizes that technological legitimacy depends on procedural legitimacy. Integrating transparency and citizen participation is not only a democratic imperative but also a means to enhance system effectiveness, ethical alignment, and social acceptance. Contributions include:

- Identifying a framework for citizen-centred surveillance governance grounded in transparency, feedback, and shared accountability.
- Recommending public consultations, algorithmic transparency, civic tech tools, and local data stewardship as foundational principles.

Table 14 shows how RQ5 is addressed in this paper

Table 14. Addressing RQ5

Focus Area	Discussion
Citizen Awareness	Exposes low public visibility and lack of opt-in mechanisms.
Participatory Governance	Highlights the absence of citizen feedback or audit rights over surveillance tools.
Transparency Gaps	Explores opacity in public-private surveillance operations and procurement.

continued on following page

Table 14. Continued

Focus Area	Discussion
Research Contribution	Proposes participatory and equity-focused governance principles for smart city systems.
Policy Recommendations	Suggests citizen engagement protocols, transparent procurement, public dashboards, and ethical oversight boards.

Summary Discussion: Synthesis of Findings and Achievement of Research Objectives

This study set out to investigate the privacy challenges and governance implications of smart city surveillance technologies through the lens of digital sovereignty. Drawing from a multidimensional analysis of AI-powered surveillance, biometric identification systems, and IoT-enabled sensor networks, this paper examined the technological risks, societal impacts, and regulatory limitations embedded in modern urban surveillance.

Synthesis of Research Questions

Across the five research questions, several key themes emerged:

- RQ1 revealed that AI-powered surveillance systems, while efficient, present a high risk of behavioral profiling, algorithmic bias, and mass surveillance, which compromise citizen autonomy and transparency. These findings directly tie into concerns about digital sovereignty in public spaces.
- RQ2 explored biometric surveillance, uncovering deep concerns about data permanence, lack of consent, and the ethical use of bodily identifiers. Biometric technologies introduce risks that are not only technological but existential, raising fundamental questions about identity, consent, and irreversibility.
- RQ3 showed that IoT sensor networks often operate as invisible layers of surveillance, collecting behavioral and location data without citizen awareness. The passive nature of data collection, coupled with poor consent mechanisms and weak cybersecurity, further highlights the erosion of data ownership and personal control.
- RQ4 emphasized the regulatory vacuum in which these technologies operate. Fragmented legal protections, outdated privacy laws, and the lack of cross-sector data governance frameworks contribute to systemic vulnerabilities and unchecked power asymmetries between data controllers and citizens.

- RQ5 demonstrated that citizen participation and transparency are often absent in smart city surveillance planning and implementation. Without public consultation, algorithmic transparency, and inclusive governance mechanisms, the legitimacy and ethical standing of surveillance systems remain questionable.

Together, these findings reveal a complex and interdependent web of technological, legal, and ethical challenges that smart cities must confront in order to ensure that security does not come at the expense of civil liberties.

The following Table 15 demonstrates how objectives are fulfilled with RQs.

Table 15. Fulfillment of research objectives

Research Objective	How It Was Achieved
1. To analyze the impact of smart city surveillance technologies on citizen privacy	Addressed in RQ1–RQ3 by evaluating AI, biometric, and IoT systems and their privacy implications.
2. To explore the legal and ethical gaps in surveillance governance	Covered in RQ4 through analysis of fragmented policies, outdated laws, and lack of ethical guidelines.
3. To investigate how digital sovereignty is challenged by emerging surveillance practices	Synthesized across all RQs, especially RQ1 and RQ2, emphasizing data ownership, consent, and autonomy.
4. To recommend a governance framework that ensures accountability, transparency, and participation	Addressed in RQ4 and RQ5 with concrete policy and governance suggestions rooted in ethical and participatory design.

Overall Implication

The results demonstrate that smart city surveillance is not just a technical issue—it is a political and ethical one. Without robust governance, citizen engagement, and privacy-preserving technologies, smart cities risk transforming into surveillance states rather than sustainable, inclusive urban environments.

This study serves as a call to policymakers, technologists, and urban planners to embed transparency, accountability, and human rights into the DNA of smart city development.

CONCLUSION AND FUTURE WORK

This paper contributes to the discourse in four key areas:

1. Technological assessment of AI, biometrics, and IoT systems in smart cities.

2. Legal and ethical evaluation of privacy risks and regulatory shortcomings.
3. Framing surveillance as a challenge to digital sovereignty.
4. Policy recommendations to support transparency, ethical design, and participatory governance.

To move beyond, this study offers three specific pathways to advance **digital sovereignty** in smart city surveillance:

1. **Mandatory Citizen Data Control Interfaces**: Every public-facing smart city service that collects data - whether traffic cameras, biometric access, or IoT air sensors, must include a citizen-accessible portal or app that allows users to view, modify, or revoke consent in real time. This places **the agency directly in citizens' hands**, not just in policy documents.
2. **Decentralized Surveillance Logs with Public Access Rights**: Cities should adopt **blockchain-inspired audit trails** for surveillance systems where any citizen can check when and how their data was accessed, by which agency, and for what purpose—introducing **radical transparency** into a space traditionally opaque.
3. **Legal Requirement for Participatory Governance in Surveillance Deployment**: Before deploying any new surveillance tech, smart cities should be legally required to conduct **open consultations** with communities, publish privacy impact assessments, and obtain local citizen council approvals—making **collective sovereignty a prerequisite for digital control**.

These recommendations move beyond theoretical frameworks and into **tangible implementation models** that prioritize citizen self-determination. By embedding these ideas within Delhi's evolving smart city architecture, this paper proposes a realistic pathway to achieving **ethical, citizen-centric surveillance governance**.

Future Work

While this study offers a robust conceptual and analytical foundation, several avenues remain open for further exploration:

- Empirical Evaluation of Citizen Perceptions: Future research could include quantitative surveys or interviews with urban residents to measure awareness, trust, and attitudes toward surveillance systems. This would provide ground-level insights to complement the policy analysis.

- Comparative Policy Analysis: A cross-national study comparing how different cities (e.g., Amsterdam, Singapore, Delhi, Toronto) regulate surveillance could uncover best practices and governance gaps across legal cultures.
- Development of a Digital Sovereignty Index: A standardized index could be developed to evaluate how various smart cities protect or undermine digital sovereignty through their surveillance systems.
- Simulation and Technical Modeling: Simulating privacy-preserving surveillance architectures (e.g., federated learning, differential privacy) could help demonstrate how security and privacy can co-exist in technical deployments.
- Longitudinal Impact Study: Future longitudinal research should track how surveillance practices evolve post-implementation and what their social, legal, and psychological consequences are over time.

REFERENCES

Ahmad, W., & Dethy, E. (2019). Preventing surveillance cities: Developing a set of fundamental privacy provisions. *Journal of Science Policy & Governance*, *15*(1), 1–11.

Aijaz, R. (2020). *The Smart Cities Mission in Delhi, 2015–2019: An Evaluation*. ORF Report.

Al-Turjman, F., Zahmatkesh, H., & Shahroze, R. (2022). An overview of security and privacy in smart cities' IoT communications. *Transactions on Emerging Telecommunications Technologies*, *33*(3), e3677. DOI: 10.1002/ett.3677

Bergsrud, L. T., & Vaseeharanathan, A. (2024). Surveillance in Smart Cities: A Case Study of Ethical Implications for Vulnerable Groups (Master's thesis, NTNU).

Bhagat, D., Hanwate, A., Salunkhe, R. V., Jagyasi, T., Sardare, P., & Sahu, M. (2025). Future Perspectives on Surveillance Systems. In Modern Advancements in Surveillance Systems and Technologies (pp. 349-370). IGI Global Scientific Publishing.

Bohli, J. M., Langendörfer, P., & Skarmeta, A. F. (2022). Security and privacy challenge in data aggregation for the IoT in smart cities. In *Internet of Things* (pp. 225–244). River Publishers. DOI: 10.1201/9781003338659-5

Braun, T., Fung, B. C., Iqbal, F., & Shah, B. (2018). Security and privacy challenges in smart cities. *Sustainable Cities and Society*, *39*, 499–507. DOI: 10.1016/j.scs.2018.02.039

Cottrill, C. D., Jacobs, N., Markovic, M., & Edwards, P. (2020). Sensing the city: Designing for privacy and trust in the internet of things. *Sustainable Cities and Society*, *63*, 102453. DOI: 10.1016/j.scs.2020.102453

Cui, L., Xie, G., Qu, Y., Gao, L., & Yang, Y. (2018). Security and privacy in smart cities: Challenges and opportunities. *IEEE Access : Practical Innovations, Open Solutions*, *6*, 46134–46145. DOI: 10.1109/ACCESS.2018.2853985

Dubey, S., & Sharma, R. (2024). The Privacy Paradox: The Future of Personal Data Protection in the Big Data Age. Issue 6 Int'l JL Mgmt. &. *Human.*, *7*, 1647.

Edwards, L. (2016). Privacy, security and data protection in smart cities: A critical EU law perspective. *European Data Protection Law Review*, *2*(1), 28–58. DOI: 10.21552/EDPL/2016/1/6

El-Sherif, D. M., & Khalil, E. E. (2022). Policy instruments for facilitating smart city governance. In *Smart Cities Policies and Financing* (pp. 305–317). Elsevier. DOI: 10.1016/B978-0-12-819130-9.00052-8

Estevez, E., Pardo, T. A., & Scholl, H. J. (Eds.). (2021). *Smart cities and smart governance: Towards the 22nd century sustainable city* (Vol. 37). Springer Nature. DOI: 10.1007/978-3-030-61033-3_4

Fan, W. Q., Ismail, A. S., Mohammed, F., & Mukred, M. (2025). AI-Driven Smart City Security and Surveillance System: A Bibliometric Analysis. In *Current and Future Trends on AI Applications* (Vol. 1, pp. 305–328). Springer Nature Switzerland. DOI: 10.1007/978-3-031-75091-5_17

Farazdaghi, E., Eslahi, M., & El Meouche, R. (2021). An overview of the use of biometric techniques in smart cities. *The International Archives of the Photogrammetry, Remote Sensing and Spatial Information Sciences*, *44*, 41–45. DOI: 10.5194/isprs-archives-XLIV-2-W1-2021-41-2021

Fawzy, R. M. (2024). BIOMETRIC CITIZENS in smart cities: Re-evaluating citizens' conceptualizations in smart cities policies as extended metaphorical arguments. *Journal of Language and Politics*, *23*(2), 283–305. DOI: 10.1075/jlp.22097.faw

Feldstein, S. (2019). The Global Expansion of AI Surveillance: Vol. 17. *No. 9.* Carnegie Endowment for International Peace.

Galič, M. (2022). Smart cities as "big brother only to the masses": The limits of personal privacy and personal surveillance. *Surveillance & Society*, *20*(3), 306–311. DOI: 10.24908/ss.v20i3.15759

Gautam, V., Sunidhi, S., & Prasad, S. (2025). AI-Powered Surveillance for Smart Cities. In *Internet of Vehicles and Computer Vision Solutions for Smart City Transformations* (pp. 245–265). Springer Nature Switzerland. DOI: 10.1007/978-3-031-72959-1_11

Ghazal, T. M., Hasan, M. K., Alzoubi, H. M., Alshurideh, M., Ahmad, M., & Akbar, S. S. (2023). Internet of things connected wireless sensor networks for smart cities. In *The Effect of Information Technology on Business and Marketing Intelligence Systems* (pp. 1953–1968). Springer International Publishing. DOI: 10.1007/978-3-031-12382-5_107

Haleem, H. (2023). AI-powered Surveillance of Drones and Vehicles: A Step Towards Smart Cities.

Jain, V., & Mitra, A. (2025). AI Applications in Secure 6G-Enabled Smart City Infrastructure. In Building Tomorrow's Smart Cities With 6G Infrastructure Technology (pp. 175-198). IGI Global Scientific Publishing.

Johnson, J., Hevia, A., Yergin, R., Karbassi, S., Levine, A., & Ortiz, J. (2022). Data governance frameworks for smart cities: Key considerations for data management and use. Journal of Law & Mobility, 1.

Karbassi, S., Levine, A., & Ortiz, J. (2022). Data Governance Frameworks for Smart Cities.

Khanna, P., & Khanra, S. (2023). Citizen empowerment through smart surveillance: Evidence from Indian smart cities. Digital Policy. *Regulation & Governance*, *25*(4), 385–401. DOI: 10.1108/DPRG-11-2022-0141

Losavio, M. M., Chow, K. P., Koltay, A., & James, J. (2018). The Internet of Things and the Smart City: Legal challenges with digital forensics, privacy, and security. *Security and Privacy*, *1*(3), e23. DOI: 10.1002/spy2.23

Mosa, M. J., Barhoom, A. M., Alhabbash, M. I., Harara, F. E., Abu-Nasser, B. S., & Abu-Naser, S. S. (2024). AI and Ethics in Surveillance: Balancing Security and Privacy in a Digital World.

Nandy, D. (2023). Human rights in the era of surveillance: Balancing security and privacy concerns. *Journal of Current Social and Political Issues*, *1*(1), 13–17. DOI: 10.15575/jcspi.v1i1.442

Nyangaresi, V. O., Abduljabbar, Z. A., Mutlaq, K. A. A., Bulbul, S. S., Ma, J., Aldarwish, A. J., Honi, D. G., Al Sibahee, M. A., & Neamah, H. A. (2024). Smart city energy-efficient data privacy preservation protocol based on biometrics and fuzzy commitment scheme. *Scientific Reports*, *14*(1), 16223. DOI: 10.1038/s41598-024-67064-z PMID: 39003319

Ouahab, I. B. A., Elaachak, L., Bouhorma, M., Alluhaidan, Y. A., & Zafar, B. (2024, May). Voice Biometric Technology: Enhancing Public Safety and Security in Smart Cities. In *2024 Mediterranean Smart Cities Conference (MSCC)* (pp. 1-6). IEEE.

Pramanik, S., Pandey, D., Joardar, S., Niranjanamurthy, M., Pandey, B. K., & Kaur, J. (2023, October). An overview of IoT privacy and security in smart cities. In AIP Conference Proceedings (Vol. 2495, No. 1). AIP Publishing. DOI: 10.1063/5.0123511

Raghav, A., Singh, B., Raghav, R., & Edina, K. D. (2025). AI and Robotics in Smart City Governance: Ethical and Legal Pathways for Sustainable Urbanization. In Machine Learning and Robotics in Urban Planning and Management (pp. 1-24). IGI Global Scientific Publishing.

Rao, P. M., & Deebak, B. D. (2023). Security and privacy issues in smart cities/industries: Technologies, applications, and challenges. *Journal of Ambient Intelligence and Humanized Computing*, *14*(8), 10517–10553. DOI: 10.1007/s12652-022-03707-1

Ross, A., Banerjee, S., & Chowdhury, A. (2020). Security in smart cities: A brief review of digital forensic schemes for biometric data. *Pattern Recognition Letters*, *138*, 346–354. DOI: 10.1016/j.patrec.2020.07.009

Sedik, A., Tawalbeh, L. A., Hammad, M., Abd El-Latif, A. A., El-Banby, G. M., Khalaf, A. A., & Iliyasu, A. M. (2021). Deep learning modalities for biometric alteration detection in 5G networks-based secure smart cities. *IEEE Access : Practical Innovations, Open Solutions*, *9*, 94780–94788. DOI: 10.1109/ACCESS.2021.3088341

Singh, T. (2023, October). AI-Driven Surveillance Technologies and Human Rights: Balancing Security and Privacy. In International Conference on Smart Systems: Innovations in Computing (pp. 703-717). Singapore: Springer Nature Singapore.

Yang, L., Elisa, N., & Eliot, N. (2019). Privacy and security aspects of E-government in smart cities. In *Smart Cities Cybersecurity and Privacy* (pp. 89–102). Elsevier. DOI: 10.1016/B978-0-12-815032-0.00007-X

Zatarain, J. M. N. (2019). Smart cities and personal data: balancing innovation, technology and the law. Revista Direito, Estado e Sociedade, (54).

Chapter 3
Automated Intrusion Detection in Streaming Data:
A Sovereignty-Aware Approach With Machine Learning and Semantic Insights

Ayan Chatterjee
https://orcid.org/0000-0003-0407-7702
NILU, Norway

ABSTRACT

The proposed system was evaluated using the widely recognized NSL-KDD and CIC-IDS-2017 datasets. The results from these evaluations highlighted several qualitative benefits, including improved detection accuracy, greater processing efficiency, and better alignment with Digital Sovereignty principles. Moreover, the real-time processing capabilities of the system contributed to reduced data storage requirements, as the need for long-term data retention was minimized. The system's adaptability to local data laws further ensures that it can be deployed across various regions, complying with local regulations without sacrificing performance. Overall, the experimental results demonstrated significant advancements in both the accuracy and efficiency of intrusion detection, making this approach a promising solution for modern network security challenges.

DOI: 10.4018/979-8-3693-9137-2.ch003

INTRODUCTION

The rapid rise in cyber-attacks highlights the critical need for advanced Intrusion Detection Systems (IDS) in modern network defenses. Traditional IDS, which primarily use signature-based detection, struggle to identify novel or obfuscated threats. However, with the advent of machine learning and big data processing, more sophisticated IDS solutions have emerged, capable of real-time data analysis to detect anomalies and potential intrusions (Markevych and Dawson, 2023; Ali et al., 2024). As nations increasingly prioritize digital sovereignty—controlling their digital infrastructure and data—the importance of robust and adaptive IDS in safeguarding network security and data privacy has become paramount (Bellanova et al., 2022; Pedreira et al., 2021). IDS are a critical component of national cybersecurity strategies. With the rise of cloud services and globalized digital infrastructure, the data monitored by IDSs often crosses borders, leading to concerns over data sovereignty (Bellanova et al., 2022; Tan et al., 2023). Ensuring that an IDS adheres to the principles of Digital Sovereignty involves guaranteeing that data is processed, stored, and managed within the legal frameworks of the region or nation in which the IDS is deployed (Zinovieva and Shitkov, 2023; Wang et al., 2024).

Previous research has explored various approaches to IDS, including signature-based, anomaly-based, and hybrid models (Markevych and Dawson, 2023; Pedreira et al., 2021; Adiwal and Misbahuddin, 2023). While signature-based systems are efficient in detecting known attacks, they lack the capability to identify zero-day exploits. Anomaly-based systems, which utilize machine learning, can detect novel threats but often suffer from high false positive rates. To address existing challenges, researchers have proposed integrating machine learning with streaming data platforms to enhance detection accuracy and provide contextual understanding of network traffic. The primary aim of this study is to develop a real-time IDS that leverages automatic machine learning, streaming data, semantic knowledge representation and advanced reasoning. Incorporating streaming data and its semantic representation can enhance the context-awareness and real-time capabilities of IDS (Noor et al., 2023; El Barachi, 2009). Streaming data allows the IDS to process and analyze data in real-time, while semantic representation ensures a structured and meaningful understanding of the streaming data, facilitating more accurate and adaptive threat detection. Moreover, automatic machine learning models can learn from historical data and intricate knowledge to predict potential security threats or classify network activities as normal or malicious (Ahsan et al., 2022). The identified research questions for this study are:

- How can streaming data platforms be used for real-time intrusion detection?

- What is the impact of automated machine learning pipelines on streaming intrusion detection data?
- How can semantic thinking improve the contextual under- standing and reasoning of IDS?
- How does the proposed IDS consider Digital Sovereignty?

The study is structured as follows: Section 2 describes exis ing studies, and novelty of this work. Section 3 describes the proposed system, including its design, data flow in the system, semantic description, automatic machine learning pipeline, and proposed algorithm. Section 4 discusses the datasets used, evaluation metrics, and experimental setup. Section 5 presents experimental results and discussions. Finally, Section 6 concludes the study and suggests future work.

RELATED WORK

The literature search was systematically conducted across databases such as Google Scholar, IEEE Xplore, Springer- Link, ScienceDirect, and Google Scholar, using search strings, such as "Intrusion Detection Systems", "Digital Sovereignty", "Machine Learning", "Deep Learning", "Semantic Ontology", "Federated Learning", and "Edge Computing". Inclusion criteria focused on peer-reviewed research published within the last 6 years, emphasizing advanced technologies in IDS and Digital Sovereignty. Exclusion criteria included pre-2018 publications, studies focused solely on traditional IDS, and blockchain, non- English papers, and non-peer-reviewed content. The PRISMA framework (Page et al., 2021) guided the review, ensuring a systematic and transparent selection process. The relevant articles have been cited and their detailed elaboration is outside the scope of this study.

Intrusion Detection Methods and Techniques

Recent advancements in IDS technologies have focused on enhancing detection accuracy, efficiency, and adaptability by incorporating machine learning and deep learning techniques. Machine learning-based IDS, utilizing techniques such as Sup- port Vector Machines (SVM), Random Forests, and Neural Net- works, have significantly improved the detection of network intrusions, enhancing both accuracy and adaptability (Kocher and Kumar, 2021; Thakkar and Lohiya, 2021; Dang, 2022; Sowmya and Anita, 2023; Santhosh Kumar et al., 2023). Deep learning approaches, particularly those involving Convolutional Neural Networks (CNNs) and Recurrent Neural Networks (RNNs), are employed to detect more complex and subtle intrusion patterns, improving the detection of zero-day attacks and reducing false positives

(Qazi et al., 2023; Thakkar and Lohiya, 2023; Awajan, 2023). Semantics and Federated learning has emerged as a significant method for IDS, enabling learning from distributed data without centralizing it, thereby maintaining Digital Sovereignty by keeping data within its original jurisdiction while contributing to a global learning model (Ayo et al., 2024; Awajan, 2023; Agrawal et al., 2022). Moreover, integrating IDS with edge computing supports real-time detection and response at the network edge, closer to the data source, reducing latency and enhancing scalability, making it suitable for large-scale deployments while ensuring compliance with Digital Sovereignty principles (He et al., 2023; Abdulganiyu et al., 2023).

The role of Digital Sovereignty in these advancements is crucial, as it ensures that these technologies should be developed and deployed in ways that respect national control over data and cybersecurity infrastructure.

Digital Sovereignty and IDS

Digital sovereignty has become a key issue as countries seek greater control over their digital infrastructure, data, and cyber environments. The concept has been extensively studied in the context of data localization, regulatory frameworks, and the development of sovereign digital infrastructure. Studies have explored various aspects of Digital Sovereignty, including data localization, regulatory frameworks, and the development of sovereign infrastructures. Through the integration of novel elements from the existing set of studies, this work significantly advances the field of IDS and provides a robust solution that aligns with the growing demands for Digital Sovereignty in cybersecurity.

Various studies (Floridi, 2020; Roberts et al., 2021; Bellanova et al., 2022; Pohle, 2020) have highlighted the importance of data localization laws as a means of asserting Digital Sovereignty, allowing states to control data generated within their borders and ensuring compliance with national regulations. The European Union's General Data Protection Regulation (GDPR) (Goddard, 2017) exemplifies how regulatory frameworks can enforce Digital Sovereignty by mandating that the personal data of EU citizens be processed according to EU laws, even when handled by foreign entities. Additionally, countries are increasingly developing sovereign digital infrastructures, such as national cloud services and communication networks, to reduce dependence on foreign technology providers and maintain control over critical digital services.

Limited studies (Bellanova et al., 2022; Pedreira et al., 2021; Tan et al., 2023; Zinovieva and Shitkov, 2023; Wang et al., 2024; Ivic and Troitin˜o, 2022) have explored the development of IDS frameworks aligned with national Digital Sovereignty requirements, emphasizing the importance of integrating IDS with sovereign digital infrastructures to keep cybersecurity operations under national control. Implementing IDS in multinational organizations presents challenges, particularly in ensuring compliance with the diverse legal requirements across jurisdictions. This underscores the need for IDS that can adapt to local regulations. Integrating Digital Sovereignty into broader cybersecurity frameworks, including IDS, is crucial for ensuring data is monitored and processed in compliance with local laws, thereby enhancing national security and aligning IDS operations with sovereign interests.

Novel Contribution

The proposed work introduces several novel contributions to the intersection of Digital Sovereignty and IDS. Proposed system features an automated TPOT using genetic programming-based machine learning pipeline (Olson and Moore, 2016) that dynamically adapts to new threats, enabling continuous learning and improving detection capabilities. By integrating Apache Kafka (Garg, 2013) for real-time data processing, the IDS handles high-throughput network traffic and makes instantaneous decisions, crucial for modern cybersecurity. Addition- ally, a semantic ontology based on the Web Ontology Language (OWL) (Chatterjee et al., 2021b; Chatterjee and Prinz, 2022) enhances detection accuracy and ensures compliance with local regulations, aligning the system with Digital Sovereignty principles. The IDS is designed to fully comply with national and regional sovereignty laws, ensuring all data processing, storage, and decision-making occur within the boundaries of the sovereign state, thereby mitigating foreign influence and maintaining control over the nation's digital infrastructure. A qualitative comparison has been performed in Table 1 to show the novelty. The contributions are summarized as follows:

Table 1. Qualitative comparison of related works on digital sovereignty and IDS

Aspect	Digital Sovereignty (Without IDS)	Digital Sovereignty (With IDS)	Our Work
Focus frame-works	Data localization, regulatory, sovereign infrastructures	Integration of sovereignty in IDS, compliance with local regulations, national security Automated ML pipeline, real-time streaming data processing, and semantic ontology for enhanced detection and compliance	
Data Localization	Emphasizes the importance of storing and processing data within national borders	Applies data localization principles to IDS data monitoring and analysis	Ensures IDS data is processed locally with real-time decision-making
Regulatory Compliance	Discusses GDPR, local laws, and their impact on data sovereignty	Addresses the challenge of making IDS compliant with local laws and regulations	Integrates regulatory requirements directly into the IDS system design using semantic reasoning
Infrastructure Control	Development of national digital infrastructures like sovereign clouds and networks	Ensures IDS is part of a sovereign digital infrastructure	Uses local infrastructure and ensures that the IDS is not reliant on foreign-controlled platforms
Cybersecurity	General discussions on national cybersecurity strategies in relation to digital sovereignty	Focus on how IDS can enhance national security by aligning with sovereignty principles	Enhances IDS with automated, real-time ML-based detection while ensuring sovereignty compliance
Novelty	Regulatory analysis, theoretical frameworks for sovereignty	Practical implementation of IDS within sovereignty-compliant frameworks	A comprehensive, automated, and scalable IDS framework with se- mantic reasoning and real-time streaming capabilities

- Proposes a novel IDS framework that integrates AutoML (TPOT), semantic reasoning, and streaming data analytics.
- Ensures data localization and compliance with regional regulations, directly supporting digital sovereignty.
- Develops an OWL-based ontology to contextualize network traffic and support regulatory inference.
- Achieves high performance on benchmark datasets while maintaining DS-compliance in deployment.

PROPOSED WORK

The design and development of the proposed intrusion detection system involve following aspects.

System Design

The proposed IDS system is designed with Digital Sovereignty in mind. It ensures that all network traffic data and intrusion alerts are stored within the geographic boundaries of the nation or region. The system adheres to local laws, such as GDPR in the EU, particularly in data processing and machine learning contexts. Additionally, it leverages local data centers and cloud providers that comply with national sovereignty laws, avoiding reliance on foreign-controlled infrastructure. The proposed system consists of several key components (see Fig. 1). The **Data Sources** include network sensors and logs that generate raw traffic data. The **Kafka Producer** is responsible for ingesting this raw data and sending it to Kafka topics. The **Kafka Broker** manages these topics and distributes the data to consumers. The **Kafka Consumer** then consumes the data, classifies it using a machine learning model, and routes it to the appropriate topics. The **Machine Learning Model** plays a crucial role in classifying network traffic as either good or bad. To enhance classification accuracy and provide contextual understanding, a **Semantic Reasoner** is used, which leverages an OWL ontology. Once the data is classified, it is stored in **Data Storage** for further analysis. Finally, the **Monitoring System** continuously monitors Kafka topics and triggers alerts based on detected intrusions. Figure 1 also illustrates the interaction between the system components, from data ingestion to classification, semantic representation, and storage.

Predictive Analysis

TPOT automates the discovery of the most effective combinations of data preprocessing steps and machine learning models, enhancing both predictive accuracy and robustness (Olson and Moore, 2016). By leveraging genetic programming, TPOT efficiently explores and evaluates thousands of potential pipelines to identify the optimal model for a given dataset, including the fine-tuning of hyperparameters. The process begins with the generation of random pipelines, followed by an evaluation of their performance. Top-performing pipelines are then selected, and genetic operators like crossover and mutation are applied across generations to progressively refine the results. After a predetermined number of generations, the best pipeline is selected. TPOT is highly configurable, allowing customization of feature selection methods and the use of various sklearn classifiers such as RandomForest, Logistic

Regression, SVC, DecisionTree, KNN, and Naive Bayes (Olson and Moore, 2016). In this study, the TPOTClassifier is configured with 20 generations and a population size of 100, providing extensive exploration of the feature space. A high mutation rate of 0.9 is employed, with a crossover rate of 0.1, to prioritize the discovery of new solutions over the recombination of existing ones. The models are optimized for accuracy using 5-fold cross-validation with stratification, ensuring that the selected pipelines perform consistently across different data splits. Moreover, the used data has been split in 80:20 ratio with stratification and random state 42 to fit the TPOT classifier. Stratified K-folds ensure that each cross-validation fold contains a representative proportion of each class, thereby preserving the class distribution in the training and validation sets, which is especially important for imbalanced datasets.

Figure 1. The processes in the proposed IDS system. Arrows define the flow of data in the system

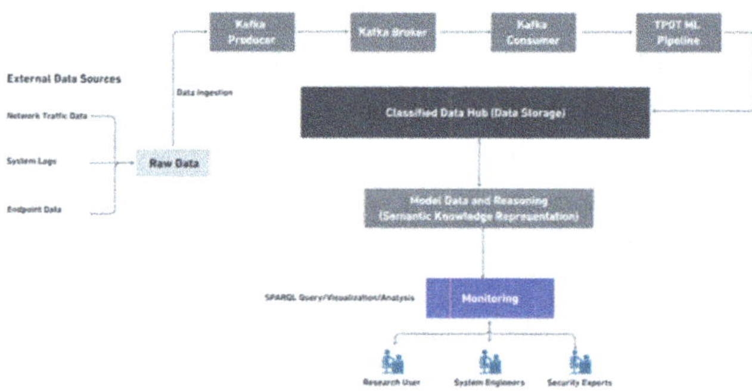

Semantic Description and Digital Sovereignty

`The semantic reasoning component of the IDS integrates knowledge of local regulations and compliance requirements by extending the OWL ontology to include classes and properties that represent regulatory constraints and data sovereignty mandates. While traditional databases excel in structured storage and data querying, they lack the capability for semantic reasoning and the integration of diverse data sources. Ontologies, on the other hand, provide a more dynamic and interconnected approach, enhancing the ability to offer personalized and contextual recommendations. Designing an OWL ontology for an IDS that utilizes machine learning, streaming data, and semantic knowledge representation requires the definition of various classes, properties, logical operators (such as AND, OR, NOT), inference rules, and axioms, using set theory or first-order predicate logic, to accurately capture the semantics of network traffic monitoring and intrusion detection. Let $G = (V, E)$ be a directed graph where V represents the set of all concepts and E represents the set of all relationships (Chatterjee et al., 2023, 2022). The relationships between these classes help to infer new knowledge about the network state, such as identifying potential threats based on anomalous traffic patterns.

$V = \{\text{System, Intrusion, NetworkTraffic, Alert, ...}\}$

$E = \{\text{subClassOf, hasFeature, detectedBy,)}\}$

SPARQL is a query language for handling RDF data, representing web information in a graph form (Chatterjee et al., 2021b). It is vital for extracting and using data from ontologies, particularly in retrieving and managing information from ontology-based knowledge graphs (Chatterjee and Prinz, 2022). A basic graph pattern in SPARQL can be represented as:

$\{?s\ P\ ?o\}$

where $?s$ is a subject variable, P is a predicate, and $?o$ is an object variable. A triple pattern is an RDF triple where each of the subject, predicate, and object may be a variable.

Let T represent the set of all triple patterns:

$\mathrm{T} = \{(?s, P, ?o) \mid ?s, ?o \in I \cup V \cup \mathrm{V} \text{ and } P \in R\}$

where V is the set of SPARQL variables. The further terminologies are depicted in Fig. 2.

Pipeline Algorithm

The following algorithm outlines the data processing pipeline implemented in the proposed system. The algorithm processes raw network traffic data in real time by extracting features and classifying the data as good or bad using a machine learning model. Based on the classification, the data is published to the corresponding Kafka topic (good or bad) and then stored in a database with a semantic structure for further evaluation. The system also monitors the data flow and generates alerts when necessary. The complexity analysis of the algorithm is as follows:

The Terminological Box (TBox) Defines the Vocabulary of the IDS Ontology

$\text{System}(x) \rightarrow \forall y\ (\text{hasModel}(x, y) \rightarrow \text{MachineLearningModel}(y))$

$\text{System}(x) \rightarrow \forall y\ (\text{monitors}(x, y) \rightarrow \text{NetworkTraffic}(y))$

$\text{NetworkTraffic}(x) \rightarrow \forall y\ (\text{hasFeature}(x, y) \rightarrow \text{Feature}(y))$

$\text{Intrusion}(x) \rightarrow \forall y\ (\text{detectedBy}(x, y) \rightarrow \text{MachineLearningModel}(y))$

$\text{Intrusion}(x) \rightarrow \forall y\ (\text{causedBy}(x, y) \rightarrow \text{NetworkTraffic}(y))$

$\text{Intrusion}(x) \rightarrow \forall y\ (\text{triggers}(x, y) \rightarrow \text{Alert}(y))$

$\text{Alert}(x) \rightarrow \forall y\ (\text{generatedFor}(x, y) \rightarrow \text{User}(y))$

$\text{Feature}(x) \rightarrow \forall y\ (\text{isDerivedFrom}(x, y) \rightarrow \text{NetworkTraffic}(y))$

$\text{Anomaly}(x) \rightarrow \exists y\ (\text{NetworkTraffic}(y) \wedge \text{isAnomalous}(x, y))$

The Assertional Box (ABox) Contains Assertions About Instances in the IDS Ontology

System(IDS1), hasModel(IDS1, MLModel1), monitors(IDS1, NetworkTraffic1) Intrusion(Intrusion1), detectedBy(Intrusion1, MLModel1), causedBy(Intrusion1, NetworkTraffic1) NetworkTraffic(NetworkTraffic1), hasFeature(NetworkTraffic1, Feature1)

Feature(Feature1), isDerivedFrom(Feature1, NetworkTraffic1) Alert(Alert1), triggers(Intrusion1, Alert1), generatedFor(Alert1, User1) User(User1)

Logical Rules to Infer New Knowledge Within the IDS

$\forall x(\text{NetworkTraffic}(x) \wedge \text{hasFeature}(x, y) \wedge \text{isAnomalous}(y) \rightarrow \text{Anomaly}(x))$

$\forall x(\text{Intrusion}(x) \wedge \text{detectedBy}(x, y) \rightarrow \text{triggersAlert}(x))$

$\forall x(\text{Alert}(x) \wedge \text{triggers}(y, x) \rightarrow \text{generatedFor}(x, z) \wedge \text{User}(z))$

Time Complexity Analysis: The time complexity of the algorithm can be summarized as follows: Initializing the Kafka producer, consumer, and machine learning model, as well as subscribing to the raw data topic, are constant time operations, $O(1)$. The main complexity arises in the loop that processes each of the n messages. Feature extraction takes $O(f)$ per message, and classifiction using a Random Forest with m trees and depth d is $O(m \cdot d)$. Publishing the result and storing the data are both $O(1)$ operations. Therefore, the total time complexity is $O(n \cdot (f + m \cdot d))$.

Space Complexity Analysis: The space complexity is determined by the storage requirements of the Kafka producer, consumer, and the machine learning model. Kafka components require $O(1)$ space. For a Random Forest with m trees of depth d, model storage is $O(m \cdot 2^d)$. Feature storage requires $O(f)$, and storing the classified data needs $O(n)$. Thus, the overall space complexity is $O(m \cdot 2^d + f + n)$.

Constraint Programming Formulation

Intrusion Detection Systems (IDS) can be modeled as a *Constraint Satisfaction Problem (CSP)* where the system must satisfy a set of logical, temporal, and semantic constraints based on streaming data. Formally, let a CSP be defined as a triple

CSP = (X, D, C), where:

- $X = \{x_1, x_2, \ldots, x_n\}$ is a finite set of variables.
- $D = \{D_1, D_2, \ldots, D_n\}$ where each D_i is a finite domain of values for variable x_i.
- $C = \{c_1, c_2, \ldots, c_m\}$ is a set of constraints restricting the values that the variables can simultaneously take.

For IDS, we define:

- Variables X as observed traffic features.
- Domains D as the possible values/features (e.g., protocol, source IP, packet size).

Algorithm 1 Data Processing Pipeline

```
Input: Raw network traffic data
Output: Classified data (good or bad)
Initialize Kafka producer and consumer
Initialize machine learning model
Subscribe to raw data topic
for each message in raw data topic do
Extract features from network traffic
Classify data using the machine learning model
if classification == 'good' then
Publish data to good data topic
else
Publish data to bad data topic
end if
end for
Store classified data in the database following a semantic structure for easy reasoning
Monitor topics and generate alerts if needed
```

- Constraints C as rules representing detection thresholds, semantic axioms, and regulatory policies (e.g., "packet rate $> \tau \Rightarrow$ possible DoS").

The goal is to assign values to all variables such that all constraints in C are satisfied. This forms the basis of real-time decision-making and anomaly detection.

Overall Complexity with Ontology and Machine Learning

Let n be the number of features, m be the number of rules/constraints, and k be the number of ontology axioms or logical conditions. The hybrid inference engine (semantic + ML pipeline) operates in two modes:

- **Rule-based Evaluation:** Each constraint $c_i \in C$ is checked in $O(1)$, for total complexity $O(m)$.
- **Machine Learning Prediction:** Using Random Forest with T trees and depth d, each prediction requires $O(T \cdot d)$.
- **Semantic Reasoning:** OWL reasoning (DL-Lite, SHOIN) has worst-case complexity of $O(2^k)$, but in practice Her- miT and ELK reduce reasoning to $O(k \cdot \log k)$ with optimization.

Hence, the worst-case end-to-end pipeline complexity is:

$$O(n \cdot T \cdot d + m + k \cdot \log k)$$

P vs NP-Completeness Analysis

Intrusion detection as a binary classification problem is in **P**, when using supervised learning. However, the general IDS configuration problem (e.g., optimizing detection over evolving constraints, streaming data, and rule sets) can be reduced to the Set Cover or 3-SAT problem, known to be **NP-Complete**. For instance, verifying whether there exists a combination of feature constraints that leads to a rule firing (attack detection) can be formulated as:

$$\exists x \in D^n \text{ s.t. } \forall c_i \in C, c_i(x) = \text{true}$$

This is equivalent to the Boolean Satisfiability Problem (SAT). Therefore, IDS rule satisfaction and semantic reasoning with open-world assumptions is NP-Complete in the general case.

Mathematical Foundations of Knowledge Representation

The formal semantics of the IDS ontology are grounded in Description Logic (DL), a subset of First Order Logic. Key operators:

- Concept inclusion: $A \sqsubseteq B$ (A is a subclass of B)
- Existential restriction: $\exists R.C$ (Some R to a C)
- Universal restriction: $\forall R.C$ (All R are C) Define the TBox T and ABox A:

T = {Intrusion ⊑ ∃detectedBy.MLModel} A = {detectedBy(Intrusion1, MLModel1)}

Reasoning involves checking whether $T \cup A \models \phi$, for a query ϕ, typically with tableau or resolution-based inference.

Reasoning and Inference Rules

Consider the inference rules used in semantic IDS:

IF $\text{Traffic}(x) \wedge \text{hasFeature}(x, y) \wedge \text{isAnomalous}(y) \Rightarrow \text{Anomaly}(x)$ IF $\text{Anomaly}(x) \wedge \text{causedBy}(x, z) \Rightarrow \text{Alert}(z)$

These are encoded as **Horn clauses**:

$\text{Anomaly}(x) \leftarrow \text{Traffic}(x), \text{hasFeature}(x, y), \text{isAnomalous}(y)$

Deductive Closure and Consistency

To ensure consistency:

$A \cup T \models \perp$

Where $\perp$ denotes contradiction. The reasoner must compute the deductive closure cl(A ∪ T), ensuring that all inferred facts are logically consistent.

Graph-Theoretic Knowledge Base Model

The ontology has been modeled as a labeled directed graph

$G = (V, E)$, where:

- V = Concepts and individuals.
- E = Object properties $R(x, y)$ represented as edges.

Let degree(v) define the number of inferred relations. A dense graph (high degree) implies high reasoning complexity. Graph traversal and inference (e.g., using SPARQL) becomes expensive in large-scale streaming settings unless optimized us- ing caching and materialization techniques.

MATERIALS AND METHODS

Datasets Used and Data Handling Policies

The study uses the NSL-KDD and CIC-IDS-2017 datasets (Thakkar and Lohiya, 2020), which are widely recognized benchmark datasets for evaluating IDS performance. These datasets provide labeled network traffic data that include va ious types of attacks and normal traffic. The datasets have been handled in compliance with data localization laws, ensuring that any personal or sensitive data is anonymized and that they are processed in a manner that respects the sovereignty of the data's origin.

Feature selection utilized the SelectKBest, which identifies statistically significant features, and the Variance Threshold, which removes low-variance features. Correlation analysis confirmed that features were not highly correlated. In addition to handling missing and NaN data with in-place value imputation, the RobustScaler from sklearn is highly effective for scaling data with outliers. Unlike StandardScaler, which uses the mean and standard deviation (and can be skewed by outliers), Ro- bustScaler leverages the interquartile range (IQR) and median. This approach makes it more resistant to the influence of extreme values, providing more reliable scaling for datasets that contain outliers. As a result, it's a better choice when outliers are present in the data. Furthermore, stratification has been used to add data fairness and avoid bias.

The ontology also integrates features from the NSL-KDD and CIC-IDS-2017 datasets to enable detailed analysis and reasoning. Moreover, certain parts of the datasets have been used in a simulated platform as real-time streaming data to verify the predictive analysis component of the proposed system as a proof of concept.

Validation of Sovereignty Compliance

Sovereign compliance validation involves a thorough process to ensure that machine learning models and data processing pipelines comply with sovereign requirements. This process includes verifying that all data is stored in approved geographic locations (known as data residency checks) to confirm compliance with local laws. In addition, regulatory compliance audits are performed regularly to ensure that data processing methods comply with relevant legal and regulatory frameworks.

Performance Metrics

To evaluate and select the best pipelines, TPOT uses several performance metrics, including Accuracy, Precision, Recall, F1-score, and Matthews Correlation Coefficient (MCC) (Chatterjee et al., 2020, 2021a, 2023, 2022). A stratification technique, employing a Stratified Split with 80% of the data for training and 20% for testing, ensures that the class pro- portions in both the training and test sets match those of the original dataset (Hutchinson, 1982). This approach minimizes bias and enhances the reliability of the training and evaluation process by maintaining consistent performance metrics across different dataset partitions. Furthermore, the performance of the IDS has been evaluated against (Fernandes, 2017; Killelea, 2002) – Throughput (TPS), Latency (ms), Scalability (%), CPU Utilization (%), Memory Utilization (%), Network Bandwidth Utilization (%), Accuracy (%), Error Rate (%), System Stabil- ity, and Response Time to Scaling (s).

Experimental Setup

This study used Python 3.9.15 with libraries like pandas (v. 1.5.2), NumPy (v. 1.22.4), SciPy (v. 1.7.3), Matplotlib (v. 3.6.2), Seaborn (v. 0.12.0), and scikit-learn (v. 1.1.3) for data processing and model development. For the streaming services, Apache Kafka 3.8.0 had been used. The environment was configured on Windows 10 using Anaconda and Jupyter Notebook

6.5.2. The system had 16 GB RAM and a 64-bit architecture, running models on the CPU due to the dataset's small size. Additionally, this study used OWL 2 Prote´ge´ in the Prote´ge´ editor to design the ontology model, with Hermit reasoner for consistency checking. Moreover, the experimental setup includes deploying the IDS in a controlled environment using Docker that simulates compliance with Digital Sovereignty principles. The Kafka infrastructure, automatic machine learning pipeline, semantic knowledge representation, and storage solutions are all hosted in a local data center that adheres to national sovereignty laws. Moreover, to capture the performance metrics of the proposed IDS and expose them through a Flask API, testing framework such as *pytest* with *psutil* have been used. For manual testing Postman (Desktop version 11.11.0) has been used. Moreover, SQLLite3 has been used for data persistence.

RESULTS

The experimental results consist of following sub-sections:

Performance of the Distributed System

The performance evaluation in a simulated environment with Python Flask API demonstrates that the IDS can efficiently handle high throughput with low latency and high accuracy under load (see Table 2). Moreover, the Apache Kafka provides high throughput and low latency, making it an ideal choice for real-time data streaming applications, even under heavy load. It efficiently handles large amounts of data through horizontal scalability, ensuring reliable messaging and fault tolerance in the proposed distributed IDS.

The prototype system demonstrates high performance in a local environment, deployed in Docker and tested using the Python psutil and pytest libraries. It processes approximately 1200 transactions per second with a latency of 120-130 ms, while maintaining detection accuracy under load. The system scales efficiently, achieving significant performance gains with optimal CPU and memory utilization. Future improvements will focus on optimizing resource usage, reducing response time to scaling, and deploying the application either in the cloud or on a dedicated VMware setup. Additionally, implementing throttling mechanisms to manage traffic spikes will ensure system stability and prevent resource exhaustion under extreme load conditions.

Table 2. Performance evaluation of IDS under load and high throughput

Metric	Description	Value
Throughput (TPS)	Transactions per second processed by the system	≈ 1200 TPS
Latency (ms)	Average time to process a packet	120-130 ms
Scalability (%)	Performance gain with added resources	94-96%
CPU Utilization (%)	Percentage of CPU used under load	70-75%
Memory Utilization (%)	Percentage of memory used under load	60-65%
Network Bandwidth Utilization (%)	Percentage of network bandwidth used	80-85%
Accuracy (%)	Detection accuracy under load	98.0%
Error Rate (%)	Percentage of packet loss or dropped connections	0.1%
System Stability	System uptime and error-free operation	Stable
Response Time to Scaling (s)	Time to adjust to load changes	2-3 s

Predictive Analysis Results

The acquired TPOT uses a genetic algorithm to optimize ma- chine learning pipelines and automatically searches for the best pipeline by looping through several generations of potential pipelines and evolving them to maximize performance based on a given metric. The predictive analysis consists of the evaluation of following datasets:

NSL-KDD Datasets

The NSL-KDD (NSL-KDD, accessed: 25.09.2024) provides a more balanced and realistic set of training and testing data for machine learning-based IDS research, which helps to perform performance evaluation against various types of attacks such as DoS, Probe, U2R (User to Root), and R2L (Remote to Local). The processed dataset contained 1,48,516 records with 42 features, including 77,054 Class:0 (None) and 71,463 Class:1 (Intrusion) entries after combining all different types of attacks. In this study, TPOT identified the best pipeline, which exclusively used the **VarianceThreshold + RandomForestClas- sifier(bootstrap=False, criterion=gini, max depth=None, max features=sqrt, min samples leaf=1, min samples split=13, estimators=250)**, achieving an accuracy of 99.17% (Precision: 99.17%, Recall: 99.17%, F1-score: 99.17%, MCC: 98.34%). This is the best performance achieved so far in the same datasets for a binary classification problem.

CIC-IDS-2017 Datasets

The CIC-IDS-2017 dataset (CIC-IDS-2017, accessed: 25.09.2024) contains real network traffic that includes normal activity, various attack types, packet captures, flow-based features, and labeled data, making it valuable for training machine learning models for intrusion detection. In this dataset, the classes for prediction analysis are represented by the following mapping using the Robust Scalar: label mapping = {'BENIGN': 0, 'DDoS': 1, 'PortScan': 2, 'Bot': 3, 'Infiltration': 4, 'Web Attack – Brute Force': 5, 'Web Attack – XSS': 6, 'Web Attack – Sql Injection': 7, 'FTP-Patator': 8, 'SSH-Patator': 9, 'DoS slowloris': 10, 'DoS Slowhttptest': 11, 'DoS Hulk': 12, 'DoS GoldenEye': 13, 'Heartbleed': 14}.

The combined and processed CIC-IDS-2017 dataset contained 2,830,743 records with 78 features, including entries for following classes: {'BENIGN': 2,273,097, 'DDoS': 1,28,027, 'PortScan': 1,58,930, 'Bot': 1966, 'Infiltration': 36, 'Web Attack – Brute Force': 1507, 'Web Attack – XSS': 652, 'Web At- tack – Sql Injection': 21, 'FTP-Patator': 7938, 'SSH-Patator': 5897, 'DoS slowloris': 5796, 'DoS Slowhttptest': 5499, 'DoS Hulk': 2,31,073, 'DoS GoldenEye': 10,293, 'Heartbleed': 11}.

In this study, TPOT identified the best pipeline, which exclusively used the **VarianceThreshold + RandomForestClassi- fier(bootstrap=True, criterion=gini, max depth=None, max features=auto, min samples leaf=1, min samples split=2, estimators=100)**, achieving an accuracy of 99.8% (Precision: 99.8%, Recall: 99.8%, F1-score: 99.8%, MCC: 99.6%). This is the best performance achieved so far in the same datasets with multi-class scenario as related works have focused on prediction analysis after converting the datasets into a binary classification problem.

In both datasets, despite its simplicity, RandomForestClassi- fier proved effective, likely due to the dataset's alignment with the model's assumption of normally distributed features. By combining **VarianceThreshold** for feature selection with **Ran- domForestClassifier**, the ensemble approach further enhances performance by filtering out low-variance features and improving the classifier's ability to generalize. Its fewer parameters and simplicity helped prevent overfitting, making it a robust choice for this dataset. The advantages stem from its appropriate assumption of feature distribution, effective feature selection, and probabilistic nature, supporting good generalization without overfitting.

Compliance to Ethical AI

The TPOT-based intrusion detection approach adheres to AI ethical principles by automating model selection and hyperparameter optimization, thereby reducing human bias in model development. It emphasizes transparency by providing an interpretable pipeline and revealing feature importance, which supports accountability in decision making. The use of stratified cross-validation ensures fairness by maintaining a balanced representation of all classes, thereby mitigating potential bias against minority classes. In addition, the focus on performance metrics such as precision, recall, and MCC emphasizes not only the accuracy of predictions but also the broader impact of predictions, thereby promoting responsible AI. Finally, by automating feature selection, unnecessary data usage is minimized and data minimization and data protection are promoted.

Semantic Knowledge Engineering

The key classes of OWL ontology are shown in Figure 2 (Ax- iom: 36, Logical axiom: 19, Declaration axiom: 17, Class: 8, object property: 8, data property: 1, individual count: 3, SubClassOf: 1). Using the Hermit reasoner in Prote´ge´, reasoning was completed in under 20 seconds with no inconsistencies. When loaded in Jena (TTL format, OWL full), reading time was 0.6-1.0 second, and queries for ontology elements executed in under 1.0 second. Each ontology model, as an RDF graph, links to a document manager (default: "OntDocumentManager") for document processing. In the ontology API, all ontology classes inherit from OntResource, sharing attributes (versionInfo, comment, label, seeAlso, isDefinedBy, sameAs, differentFrom) and methods (add, set, list, get, has, remove). These logical inferences, based on the ontology, ensure data consistency and va- validity as depicted in Figure 3. Moreover, feature relationship and reasoning capabilities are depicted in Fig. 5.

The ontology consists of several key classes representing the primary entities within the IDS framework. The *System* class represents the overall Intrusion Detection System responsible for monitoring and securing the network. The *Intrusion* class captures unauthorized access or attacks detected by the system, while *NetworkTraffic* represents the monitored data flows. The *MachineLearningModel* class denotes the algorithms used to analyze network traffic and detect intrusions, and *Feature* represents the attributes extracted from network data, crucial for intrusion detection. The *Alert* class signifies the notifications generated when an intrusion is detected, and *User* represents the individuals or entities interacting with the IDS, particularly in response to alerts. The *Anomaly* class, a subclass of *Intrusion*, identifies abnormal network activities that may indicate a security threat.

The ontology defines several object properties to describe the relationships between these classes. The *hasModel* property links a *System* to a *MachineLearningModel*, indicating the model used for detection. The *monitors* property connects a *System* to *NetworkTraffic*, reflecting active monitoring. The *hasFeature* property associates *NetworkTraffic* with *Feature*, denoting the extraction of relevant data attributes. The *triggers* property relates an *Intrusion* to an *Alert*, while *detectedBy* links an *Intrusion* to the *MachineLearningModel* that identified it. The *causedBy* property connects an *Intrusion* to the specific *NetworkTraffic* that triggered the detection, and *generatedFor* associates an *Alert* with the *User* notified of the intrusion. Lastly, *isDerivedFrom* links a *Feature* to its source *NetworkTraffic*. The ontology also includes the data property *isAnomalous*, a Boolean attribute that indicates whether a *Feature* is anomalous, aiding in classifying network traffic as normal or suspicious. The following SPARQL queries provide comprehensive insights into the functioning of the IDS, combining detection, feature analysis, and alert generation in a concise manner:

```
Query 1: Retrieve All Intrusions Detected by a Specific Machine Learning Model and Their Associated Alerts

SELECT ?intrusion ?alert

WHERE {
```

```
?intrusion rdf:type ids:Intrusion .

?intrusion ids:detectedBy ids:MLModel1 .

?intrusion ids:triggers ?alert .

}
```

Query 2: List All Features Derived from a Specific Network Traffic Instance and Indicate if They Are Anomalous

```
SELECT ?feature ?isAnomalous

WHERE {

ids:NetworkTraffic1 ids:hasFeature ?feature .

?feature ids:isAnomalous ?isAnomalous .

}
```

Query 3: Retrieve All Network Traffic Monitored by a Specific IDS System Along with Any Generated Alerts and Associated Users

```
SELECT ?networkTraffic ?alert ?user

WHERE {
```

```
ids:IDS1 ids:monitors ?networkTraffic .

?networkTraffic ids:hasFeature ?feature .

?feature ids:isAnomalous true .

?networkTraffic ids:causedBy ?intrusion .

?intrusion ids:triggers ?alert .

?alert ids:generatedFor ?user .

}
```

Digital Sovereignty Related to Intrusion Detection

The proposed IDS approach complies with the principle of digital sovereignty by ensuring that all data processing and storage occurs within national borders, thereby complying with data localization laws and protecting sensitive information from foreign access. By leveraging local infrastructure and complying with national regulations, the system prevents external interference and ensures that the state maintains full control over its cybersecurity operations. In addition, the integration of semantic reasoning based on locally managed ontologies improves the contextual understanding of network traffic within national legal and regulatory frameworks and strengthens the system's alignment with digital sovereignty.

Discussion

The processing of streaming data for predictive analysis before storage in the proposed IDS ensures real-time detection of threats and decisions to act upon them, hence reducing the response time to likely intrusions while also reducing storage of irrelevant or benign data This proactive approach also enhances both efficiency and effective way of safeguarding the network.

The proposed IDS approach demonstrates **compliance with Digital Sovereignty** by ensuring that all data processing and storage activities occur within the national borders, adhering to data localization laws and safeguarding sensitive information from foreign interference. By utilizing local infrastructure and maintaining strict compliance with national regulations, the system ensures that the state's cybersecurity operations remain fully under its control, free from external influence. Furthermore, the integration of semantic reasoning based on locally governed ontologies enhances the system's ability to contextualize network traffic within the bounds of national legal and regulatory frameworks, thereby reinforcing its alignment with the principles of Digital Sovereignty. This comprehensive ap- approach addresses the research questions by illustrating the effectiveness of streaming data platforms for real-time intrusion detection, the impact of automated machine learning pipelines on handling streaming data, the role of semantic reasoning in improving IDS's contextual understanding, and how the proposed system aligns with Digital Sovereignty.

Figure 2. The structure of the proposed IDS ontology in Prote´ge´

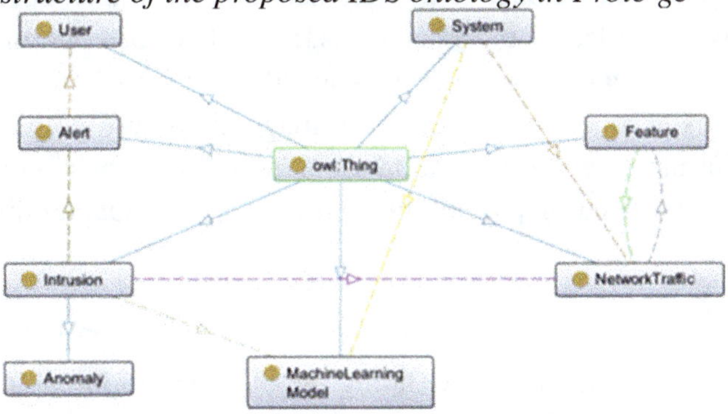

Figure 3. Logical expressions representing relationships between features and intrusion detection

$$\forall x, y(\text{NetworkTraffic}(x) \wedge \text{hasFeature}(x, y) \rightarrow \text{Feature}(y))$$
$$\forall x, y(\text{Feature}(y) \wedge \text{isAnomalous}(y) \rightarrow \text{Anomaly}(x))$$
$$\forall x(\text{Intrusion}(x) \wedge \text{detectedBy}(x, \text{MLModel1}) \rightarrow \text{triggers}(x, \text{Alert1}))$$
$$\forall x(\text{Alert}(\text{Alert1}) \rightarrow \text{generatedFor}(\text{Alert1}, \text{User1}))$$
$$\forall x(\text{System}(\text{IDS1}) \wedge \text{monitors}(\text{IDS1}, \text{NetworkTraffic1}))$$

Limitations

Although the proposed IDS exhibits strong real-time detection capabilities and complies with digital sovereignty, some limitations still exist. First, the current implementation is tested in a controlled local environment; large-scale deployment in practice may cause additional delays and network variations. Second, while the ontology supports regulatory considerations, it needs to be continuously updated to reflect changes in data protection laws in different jurisdictions. Third, while TPOT can automate model optimization, it may not capture domain-specific nuances without human intervention. Addressing these limitations in future work will further improve the scalability, compliance accuracy, and adaptability of the IDS.

Future Work

Future research will focus on extending the ontology to integrate with distributed triple stores such as GraphDB to enable federated queries across sovereign nodes. In addition, we aim to integrate federated learning techniques to ensure data privacy during collaborative IDS training. Other improvements include optimizing the AutoML pipeline for edge environments and ex-expanding regulatory reasoning capabilities using a rule-based engine. These improvements support dynamic compliance across jurisdictions while strengthening the real-time capabilities of sovereign digital infrastructure.

CONCLUSIONS

This paper proposes a novel attack detection approach that not only leverages machine learning pipeline, streaming data, and semantic reasoning, but also strictly adheres to the principles of digital sovereignty. The proposed system demonstrates high accuracy and efficiency in detecting intrusions in real-time, making it a promising solution for modern network security challenges. By ensuring that data processing and storage comply with local regulations, the proposed IDS can improve national cybersecurity while respecting the sovereignty of the country or region where it is deployed. Future work will focus on extending the ontology with augmented concepts in GraphDB for clustering, and scalability, improving predictive model robustness, scaling the system for larger network environments, optimizing the system's compliance mechanisms and exploring how digital sovereignty can be further integrated into other cybersecurity frameworks.

Figure 4. Ontology-based feature relationship and reasoning

$$\forall x(\text{System}(x) \rightarrow \exists y(\text{hasModel}(x, y) \land \text{MachineLearningModel}(y)))$$
$$\forall x(\text{System}(x) \rightarrow \exists y(\text{monitors}(x, y) \land \text{NetworkTraffic}(y)))$$
$$\forall x(\text{NetworkTraffic}(x) \rightarrow \exists y(\text{hasFeature}(x, y) \land \text{Feature}(y)))$$
$$\forall x(\text{Intrusion}(x) \rightarrow \exists y(\text{detectedBy}(x, y) \land \text{MachineLearningModel}(y)))$$
$$\forall x(\text{Intrusion}(x) \rightarrow \exists y(\text{causedBy}(x, y) \land \text{NetworkTraffic}(y)))$$
$$\forall x(\text{Intrusion}(x) \rightarrow \exists y(\text{triggers}(x, y) \land \text{Alert}(y)))$$
$$\forall x(\text{Alert}(x) \rightarrow \exists y(\text{generatedFor}(x, y) \land \text{User}(y)))$$
$$\forall x(\text{Feature}(x) \rightarrow \exists y(\text{isDerivedFrom}(x, y) \land \text{NetworkTraffic}(y)))$$

EXPLANATION OF AI-ASSISTED TECHNOLOGIES

In creating this work, the author used AI tools such as Chat- GPT and the software application Smodin to improve the ac- accuracy of English, including spelling, grammar, and punctuation. The content created or corrected using these tools has been carefully reviewed, revised, and edited by the author to ensure accuracy and originality. The author takes full responsibility for the originality of the final content of this publication.

REFERENCES

Abdulganiyu, O. H., Ait Tchakoucht, T., & Saheed, Y. K. (2023). A systematic literature review for network intrusion detection system (ids). *International Journal of Information Security*, *22*(5), 1125–1162. DOI: 10.1007/s10207-023-00682-2

Adiwal, S., & Misbahuddin, M. (2023). Intrusion detection and prevention in openstack: A case study on enhancing security and threat detection. *SN Computer Science*, *4*(6), 830. DOI: 10.1007/s42979-023-02265-3

Agrawal, S., Sarkar, S., Aouedi, O., Yenduri, G., Piamrat, K., Alazab, M., Bhattacharya, S., Maddikunta, P. K. R., & Gadekallu, T. R. (2022). Federated learning for intrusion detection system: Concepts, challenges and future directions. *Computer Communications*, *195*, 346–361. DOI: 10.1016/j.comcom.2022.09.012

Ahsan, M., Nygard, K. E., Gomes, R., Chowdhury, M. M., Rifat, N., & Connolly, J. F. (2022). Cybersecurity threats and their mitigation approaches using ma- chine learning—A review. [Ali, A.H., Charfeddine, M., Ammar, B., Hamed, B.B., Albalwy, F.]. *Journal of Cybersecurity and Privacy*, *2*(3), 527–555. DOI: 10.3390/jcp2030027

Awajan, A. (2023). A novel deep learning-based intrusion detection system for iot networks. *Computers*, *12*(2), 34. DOI: 10.3390/computers12020034

Ayo, F. E., Awotunde, J. B., Ogundele, L. A., Solanke, O. O., Brahma, B., Panigrahi, R., & Bhoi, A. K. (2024). Ontology-based layered rule-based network intrusion detection system for cybercrimes detection. *Knowledge and Information Systems*, *66*(6), 1–38. DOI: 10.1007/s10115-024-02068-9

Bellanova, R., Carrapico, H., & Duez, D. (2022). Digital/sovereignty and european security integration: An introduction. *European Security*, *31*(3), 337–355. DOI: 10.1080/09662839.2022.2101887

Chatterjee, A., Gerdes, M. W., & Martinez, S. G. (2020). Identification of risk factors associated with obesity and overweight—A machine learning overview. *Sensors (Basel)*, *20*(9), 2734. DOI: 10.3390/s20092734 PMID: 32403349

Chatterjee, A., Gerdes, M. W., Prinz, A., & Martinez, S. G. 2021a. Comparing performance of ensemble-based machine learning algorithms to identify potential obesity risk factors from public health datasets, in: Emerging Technologies in Data Mining and Information Security: Proceedings of IEMIS 2020, Volume 1, Springer. pp. 253–269. DOI: 10.1007/978-981-15-9927-9_26

Chatterjee, A., Pahari, N., Prinz, A., & Riegler, M. (2022). Machine learning and ontology in ecoaching for personalized activity level monitoring and recommendation generation. *Scientific Reports*, *12*(1), 19825. DOI: 10.1038/s41598-022-24118-4 PMID: 36400793

Chatterjee, A., & Prinz, A. (2022). Personalized recommendations for physical activity e-coaching (ontorecomodel): Ontological modeling. *JMIR Medical Informatics*, *10*(6), e33847. DOI: 10.2196/33847 PMID: 35737439

Chatterjee, A., Prinz, A., Gerdes, M., & Martinez, S. (2021b). An automatic ontology-based approach to support logical representation of observable and measurable data for healthy lifestyle management: Proof-of-concept study. *Journal of Medical Internet Research*, *23*(4), e24656. DOI: 10.2196/24656 PMID: 33835031

Chatterjee, A., Prinz, A., Riegler, M. A., & Meena, Y. K. 2023. An automatic and personalized recommendation modelling in activity ecoaching with deep learning and ontology. Scientific Reports 13, 10182. CIC-IDS-2017, K., accessed: 25.09.2024. network-intrusion-dataset. https://www.kaggle.com/datasets

. Dang, Q.V., 2022. Machine learning for intrusion detection systems: recent developments and future challenges. Real-time applications of machine learn- ing in cyber-physical systems, 93–118.

El Barachi, M. 2009. Integrating Context-Awareness in the IP Multimedia Subsystem for Enhanced Session Control and Service Provisioning Capabilities. Ph.D. thesis. Concordia University.

Fernandes, S. (2017). *Performance evaluation for network services, systems and protocols*. Springer. DOI: 10.1007/978-3-319-54521-9

Floridi, L. (2020). The fight for digital sovereignty: What it is, and why it matters, especially for the eu. *Philosophy & Technology*, *33*(3), 369–378. DOI: 10.1007/s13347-020-00423-6 PMID: 35194548

Garg, N. (2013). *Apache kafka*. Packt Publishing Birmingham.

Goddard, M. (2017). The eu general data protection regulation (gdpr): European regulation that has a global impact. *International Journal of Market Research*, *59*(6), 703–705. DOI: 10.2501/IJMR-2017-050

He, K., Kim, D. D., & Asghar, M. R. (2023). Adversarial machine learning for network intrusion detection systems: A comprehensive survey. *IEEE Communications Surveys and Tutorials*, *25*(1), 538–566. DOI: 10.1109/COMST.2022.3233793

Hutchinson, C. F. (1982). Classification improvement. *Photogrammetric Engineering and Remote Sensing*, *44*, 123–130.

Ivic, S., & Troitin˜o, D. R. (2022). Digital sovereignty and identity in the European union: A challenge for building europe. *European Studies*, *9*(2), 80–109. DOI: 10.2478/eustu-2022-0015

Killelea, P. (2002). *Web Performance Tuning: speeding up the web*. O'Reilly Media, Inc.

Kocher, G., & Kumar, G. (2021). Machine learning and deep learning methods for intrusion detection systems: Recent developments and challenges. *Soft Computing*, *25*(15), 9731–9763. DOI: 10.1007/s00500-021-05893-0

Markevych, M., & Dawson, M. 2023. A review of enhancing intrusion detection systems for cybersecurity using artificial intelligence (ai), in: *International conference Knowledge-based Organization*, pp. 30–37. DOI: 10.2478/kbo-2023-0072

Noor, Z., Hina, S., Hayat, F., & Shah, G. A. 2023. An intelligent context-aware threat detection and response model for smart cyber-physical systems. Internet of Things 23, 100843. NSL-KDD, K., accessed: 25.09.2024. nslkdd.https://www.kaggle.com/datasets/

Olson, R. S., & Moore, J. H. 2016. Tpot: A tree-based pipeline optimization tool for automating machine learning, in: Workshop on automatic machine learn- ing, PMLR. pp. 66-74.

. Page, M.J., McKenzie, J.E., Bossuyt, P.M., Boutron, I., Hoffmann, T.C., Mulrow, C.D., Shamseer, L., Tetzlaff, J.M., Akl, E.A., Brennan, S.E., et al., 2021. The prisma 2020 statement: an updated guideline for reporting systematic reviews. bmj 372.

Pedreira, V., Barros, D., & Pinto, P. (2021). A review of attacks, vulnerabilities, and defenses in industry 4.0 with new challenges on data sovereignty ahead. *Sensors (Basel)*, *21*(15), 5189. DOI: 10.3390/s21155189 PMID: 34372425

. Pohle, J., 2020. Digital sovereignty. a new key concept of digital policy in germany and europe.

Qazi, E. U. H., Faheem, M. H., & Zia, T. (2023). Hdlnids: Hybrid deep-learning-based network intrusion detection system. *Applied Sciences (Basel, Switzerland)*, *13*(8), 4921. DOI: 10.3390/app13084921

Roberts, H., Cowls, J., Casolari, F., Morley, J., Taddeo, M., & Floridi, L. (2021). (Forthcoming). Safeguarding european values with digital sovereignty: An analysis of statements and policies. *Internet Policy Review*, *10*(3). Advance online publication. DOI: 10.14763/2021.3.1575

Santhosh Kumar, S., Selvi, M., & Kannan, A. (2023). A comprehensive survey on machine learning-based intrusion detection systems for secure communication in internet of things. *Computational Intelligence and Neuroscience*, *2023*(1), 8981988. DOI: 10.1155/2023/8981988

Sowmya, T., & Anita, E. M. (2023). A comprehensive review of ai based intrusion detection system. *Measurement. Sensors*, *28*, 100827. DOI: 10.1016/j.measen.2023.100827

Tan, K. L., Chi, C. H., & Lam, K. Y. (2023). Survey on digital sovereignty and identity: From digitization to digitalization. *ACM Computing Surveys*, *56*(3), 1–36. DOI: 10.1145/3616400

Thakkar, A., & Lohiya, R. (2020). A review of the advancement in intrusion detection datasets. *Procedia Computer Science*, *167*, 636–645. DOI: 10.1016/j.procs.2020.03.330

Thakkar, A., & Lohiya, R. (2021). A review on machine learning and deep learning perspectives of ids for iot: Recent updates, security issues, and challenges. *Archives of Computational Methods in Engineering*, *28*(4), 3211–3243. DOI: 10.1007/s11831-020-09496-0

Thakkar, A., & Lohiya, R. (2023). A review on challenges and future research directions for machine learning-based intrusion detection system. *Archives of Computational Methods in Engineering*, *30*(7), 4245–4269. DOI: 10.1007/s11831-023-09943-8

Wang, Q., Niu, H., & Xu, N. (2024). Where do data sovereignty security risks come from?-production perspective based on social reproduction. *Advances in Education. Humanities and Social Science Research*, *11*, 133–133.

Zinovieva, E., & Shitkov, S. (2023). Sovereignty as practice in digital age. In *Digital International Relations* (pp. 75–90). Springer. DOI: 10.1007/978-981-99-3467-6_5

Chapter 4
Strengthening Digital Sovereignty:
A Structural Analysis of Digital Governance Indicators

Mohamad Molaei Qelichi
https://orcid.org/0000-0002-1915-550X
Faculty of Encyclopedia Research, Institute for Humanities and Cultural Studies, Tehran, Iran

Kimia Ghasemi
https://orcid.org/0000-0003-1153-2515
Faculty of Encyclopedia Research, Institute for Humanities and Cultural Studies, Tehran, Iran

Niloofar Moradhasel
Faculty of Encyclopedia Research, Institute for Humanities and Cultural Studies, Tehran, Iran

ABSTRACT

Digital sovereignty has become a vital concern in an era marked by complex cyber threats and growing demands for data protection, transparency, and ethical governance. This study aims to develop a structured framework that enhances digital sovereignty by integrating security, privacy, and trust indicators. Using the MICMAC methodology, supported by expert consensus through the Delphi technique, we identified and analyzed 33 governance indicators to understand their influence and interdependencies. The analysis revealed ten key drivers, including financial transparency, ethical use of AI, and privacy by design, which exert the highest direct

DOI: 10.4018/979-8-3693-9137-2.ch004

and indirect impacts on digital governance. These findings offer actionable insights for policymakers and organizations seeking to build resilient, user-focused, and ethically grounded digital governance systems.

INTRODUCTION

In today's rapidly evolving digital landscape, digital sovereignty, defined as the capacity of a state, organization, or individual to control their digital assets, data, and infrastructures, has emerged as a cornerstone for ensuring security, privacy, and trust in the digital domain. It is not merely a technological concern but a societal imperative. Digital sovereignty enables protection against sophisticated cyber threats, empowers individuals with control over their data, and fosters public trust in digital governance systems. As highlighted in Dedousis et al. (2021), establishing digital sovereignty requires robust frameworks that intertwine technical and regulatory measures to address these key pillars comprehensively.

The integration of digital technologies into governance frameworks offers significant potential for enhancing transparency, efficiency, and citizen engagement. However, this digital transition exposes public and private sectors to various cyber threats, amplifying the need for comprehensive security measures. Real-time threat detection, incident response capabilities, and proactive cybersecurity protocols are essential components for sustaining resilient governance structures (Kanaan et al., 2024; Kesan & Hayes, 2014). Kesan & Hayes (2014) emphasize the "Circle of Trust" model, which fosters collaborative cybersecurity efforts between public and private sectors to mitigate risks through shared standards and responsibilities. Concurrently, the convergence of artificial intelligence (AI) and cybersecurity holds promise for advancing threat response mechanisms, though it introduces ethical and regulatory considerations that must be carefully managed to maintain public confidence.

Privacy stands as another critical pillar of digital sovereignty (Guembe et al., 2024). Effective digital governance frameworks necessitate a comprehensive approach to privacy, focusing on data ownership, informed consent, and strict adherence to privacy regulations like the General Data Protection Regulation (GDPR). Emerging self-sovereign identity (SSI) models illustrate a paradigm shift in data control, enabling individuals to manage their digital identities more autonomously (Naik & Jenkins, 2021). However, deploying such models requires navigating complex regulatory landscapes to ensure compliance and user protection in line with established privacy laws (Giannopoulou, 2020; Hellmeier et al., 2023).

Trust, as a foundational aspect of digital sovereignty (Panwar et al., 2023), is built through transparency, ethical governance, and accountability. Citizens' willingness to engage with digital systems largely depends on their confidence in the security and privacy measures in place, which are bolstered through practices such as transparency reports, ethical AI guidelines, and digital literacy programs (Da Silva Carvalho et al., 2023). Schaberreiter et al. (2017) argue that these initiatives are instrumental in fostering trust, as they provide the public with visibility into data handling practices and empower them with the knowledge needed to navigate digital environments confidently.

This research aims to conduct a structural analysis of digital governance indicators to develop a framework that enhances digital sovereignty by integrating security, privacy, and trust metrics. The study's objectives are to: (1) identify critical security indicators, such as real-time threat monitoring and risk assessment, that reinforce resilience in digital systems (Dedousis et al., 2021; Patrick et al., 2018); (2) evaluate privacy indicators, including data ownership policies and regulatory compliance, to fortify user control over personal data (Bayaga, 2022; Da Silva Carvalho et al., 2023); (3) establish trust indicators that promote transparency and equitable access, essential for fostering user engagement and trust (Schaberreiter et al., 2017); and (4) propose an integrated model that unifies these indicators into a cohesive digital governance framework (Barrinha, 2016; Folorunsho et al., 2019).

In examining existing literature and case studies, this research seeks to offer insights into effective digital governance strategies that prioritize the rights and interests of citizens. As the digital landscape continues to grow in complexity, developing a resilient and ethically guided governance framework becomes imperative, not only to safeguard digital sovereignty but also to empower individuals in the digital age. This research contributes to ongoing discourse on digital governance, presenting a comprehensive approach to digital sovereignty that integrates security, privacy, and trust as its core pillars, thereby promoting a robust, resilient, and ethical digital environment. The study pursues the following research objectives:

- To examine how core digital governance indicators, specifically in the domains of security, privacy, and trust, contribute to the enhancement of digital sovereignty.
- To identify which indicators, act as key drivers in shaping a robust digital sovereignty framework using the MICMAC structural analysis approach.

LITERATURE REVIEW: SECURITY, PRIVACY, AND TRUST IN DIGITAL GOVERNANCE FOR ENHANCING DIGITAL SOVEREIGNTY

The evolution of digital governance underscores the importance of security, privacy, and trust as fundamental pillars in ensuring digital sovereignty. This review synthesizes findings from key studies on these areas, emphasizing their interconnected roles in enhancing digital governance frameworks.

Security in Digital Governance

Security within digital governance is paramount, providing the foundation for safeguarding data and infrastructures against cyber threats. Effective security measures not only protect against vulnerabilities but also foster resilience in digital infrastructures. Several scholars highlight the significance of cyber threat monitoring and incident response capabilities to detect, address, and recover from attacks promptly (Kanaan et al., 2024). Risk assessment processes further allow organizations to identify specific vulnerabilities, a critical step for proactive threat management (Dedousis et al., 2021). Risk mitigation strategies, as proposed by (Balisane et al., 2024), are integral for establishing robust defenses against emerging cyber threats.

Infrastructure resilience is another essential security component, focusing on continuity in digital services despite disruptions. Studies by Taqafi et al. (2023) and Igwenagu et al. (2024) underline the importance of backup and recovery systems as a safeguard against data loss during attacks. Moreover, a solid cybercrime legislation framework supports legal action against cyber threats and reinforces organizational resilience (Kesan & Hayes, 2014).

To secure sensitive transactions and communication, end-to-end encryption has become indispensable (Ban, 2024). Similarly, secure authentication methods ensure that only authorized individuals access data, supporting secure identity management (Giannopoulou, 2020). Furthermore, national cybersecurity policies serve as overarching frameworks that consolidate these security measures into cohesive, countrywide strategies for effective governance (Kanaan et al., 2024). Together, these elements ensure the development of a resilient digital ecosystem that supports both government and public interests.

Privacy and Data Sovereignty

Digital privacy is critical to digital sovereignty, encompassing policies that prioritize individual data rights and transparency. Data ownership and control empower individuals by granting them authority over personal data usage (Giannopoulou, 2020). Central to this goal are user consent mechanisms and data collection transparency (Wong et al., 2023), which promote open data practices and foster user trust.

Adhering to privacy standards, such as GDPR, data anonymization practices and privacy-by-design principles protect user data while enabling legitimate data applications (Ban, 2024; Semantha et al., 2021). Cross-border data sovereignty (Manoury et al., 2025) has also emerged as a challenge, with governments seeking to ensure data protection even as information traverses international boundaries (Mattoo & Meltzer, 2018). Studies by Dedousis et al. (2021) and Bayaga (2022) advocate for these privacy-preserving measures as a means to safeguard personal data in an interconnected digital world.

In cloud environments, maintaining cloud security and ensuring compliance with privacy laws are critical for data protection (Igwenagu et al., 2024). The literature also emphasizes user access rights, allowing individuals to control access to their data, thus reducing the risk of unauthorized access and enhancing digital trust (Wong et al., 2022). These privacy practices establish a protective framework that respects users' rights, even in complex digital and cloud-based ecosystems.

Trust as a Pillar of Digital Governance

Trust is the linchpin of digital governance, fostering public confidence in digital services (Barik et al., 2024). Transparency reports and open data initiatives have gained traction as mechanisms to uphold accountability, thereby establishing trust in digital governance systems (Kanaan et al., 2024). Regular user satisfaction surveys offer valuable insights into the efficacy of digital services and highlight areas for improvement (Osman et al., 2014).

System reliability and equitable access to digital services are also critical, as these factors assure users of the inclusivity and dependability of digital platforms (Wong et al., 2022). The ethical deployment of AI, particularly concerning data usage and decision-making, is crucial for maintaining public trust (Gill & Germann, 2022). Institutional accountability further solidifies public trust by holding digital governance entities to high ethical standards, ensuring transparent handling of data (Wong et al., 2022).

Financial transparency and educational programs for digital literacy are additional aspects that support user trust, particularly by promoting responsible use of funds and enhancing users' understanding of digital tools (Kanaan et al., 2024). Finally, preventing data exploitation in digital identity systems reinforces ethical use and sustains trust in digital governance (Giannopoulou, 2020).

Integrated Framework for Enhancing Digital Sovereignty

This literature review highlights the necessity of a structured approach where security, privacy, and trust are interwoven to establish a resilient digital governance model. By integrating security protocols, privacy standards, and trust-building practices, this model supports digital sovereignty and ensures a sustainable, user-centered governance system in a rapidly digitalizing world. An effective digital governance framework thus emerges as a multi-layered approach that aligns protective security measures, rigorous privacy safeguards, and proactive trust initiatives to maintain a robust digital sovereignty structure.

This review contributes to the development of a governance framework capable of addressing the complex demands of digital sovereignty, particularly in balancing national security interests with individual data rights. Through this integrated approach, the research offers a pathway toward sustainable digital governance in an interconnected digital landscape, where user privacy and public trust are at the forefront.

Table 1. Indicators supporting digital sovereignty: privacy, trust, and security dimensions

main indicator	sub-indicator
Security	Cyber Threat Monitoring (Balisane et al., 2024; Dedousis et al., 2021; Kanaan et al., 2024)
	Incident Response Capabilities (Patrick et al., 2018; Kanaan et al., 2024)
	Risk Assessment Processes (Dedousis et al., 2021)
	Risk Mitigation Strategies (Balisane et al., 2024)
	Infrastructure Resilience (Taqafi et al., 2023)
	Backup and Recovery Systems (Igwenagu et al., 2024)
	Cybercrime Legislation (Kesan & Hayes, 2014)
	Secure Authentication Methods (Giannopoulou, 2020)
	End-to-End Encryption (Ban, 2024)
	National Cybersecurity Policy (Kanaan et al., 2024)
	IoT Device Security Standards (Dedousis et al., 2021)
	Cybersecurity Education (Kanaan et al., 2024)
Privacy	Data Ownership and Control (Giannopoulou, 2020)
	Data Collection Transparency (Wong et al., 2022)
	User Consent Mechanisms (Semantha et al., 2021)
	Data Anonymization Practices (Ban, 2024)
	Compliance with Privacy Laws (Giannopoulou, 2020)
	User Access Rights (Wong et al., 2022)
	Cloud Security (Igwenagu et al., 2024)
	Privacy by Design (Semantha et al., 2021)
	Children's Online Privacy Protection (Semantha et al., 2021)
	Cross-Border Data Sovereignty (Mattoo & Meltzer, 2018)

continued on following page

Table 1. Continued

main indicator	sub-indicator
Trust	Open Data Initiatives (Wong et al., 2022)
	Transparency Reports (Kanaan et al., 2024)
	System Reliability (Wong et al., 2022)
	User Satisfaction Surveys (Osman et al., 2014)
	Ethical Use of AI (Gill & Germann, 2022)
	Financial Transparency (Wong et al., 2022)
	Equitable Access to Digital Services (Nnenna et al., 2024)
	Educational Programs for Digital Literacy (Kanaan et al., 2024)
	Institutional Accountability (Wong et al., 2022)
	Avoiding Data Exploitation (Giannopoulou, 2020)
	Virtual Identity Authentication (Giannopoulou, 2020)

RESEARCH METHODOLOGY

This study utilizes a rigorous and structured approach to identify, analyze, and prioritize digital governance indicators that enhance digital sovereignty through security, privacy, and trust. The methodology integrates expert knowledge through the Delphi technique and a structural analysis via the Matrix of Cross-Impact Multiplications Applied to Classification (MICMAC) method, ensuring that the findings are both comprehensive and deeply relevant to the objectives.

Delphi Technique for Indicator Identification and Validation

The Delphi technique was employed as an iterative process to obtain consensus among experts on the most critical indicators for digital governance. Experts from fields related to digital sovereignty, cybersecurity, privacy laws, and trust in digital systems participated in this process. Based on a thorough literature review, an initial set of indicators was proposed, covering three main domains: security, privacy, and trust. These indicators were then evaluated by the experts through multiple rounds of feedback, with each round refining and consolidating the indicators to ensure relevance and clarity.

By the final round, consensus was achieved on a refined list of indicators that reflect the essential components of digital sovereignty. The Delphi technique thus allowed for a diverse range of expert opinions to be systematically incorporated, strengthening the validity and applicability of the indicators.

Structural Analysis with MICMAC for Indicator Prioritization

Following the identification and validation of indicators, the MICMAC method was used for structural analysis. This technique enabled us to analyze and classify the interdependencies among the indicators, thus identifying their respective roles in the digital sovereignty framework. MICMAC analysis provided a structured categorization of indicators based on their influence and dependence, helping to reveal core, driver, and dependent indicators that are central to achieving digital sovereignty. As noted by Michel Godet, this structured approach helps uncover the dynamic interrelations among variables, offering critical insights for strategic decision-making (Gorane et al., 2012). Using MICMAC, the indicators were categorized as follows:

Driver Indicators: These indicators are highly influential and drive other aspects within the framework, including factors like cybersecurity protocols and regulatory compliance mechanisms.
Core Indicators: These indicators hold balanced influence and dependence, serving as foundational components that support and are supported by other elements.
Dependent Indicators: Indicators with lower influence but high dependence.

Data Collection and Analysis

Data was collected through literature reviews, expert feedback, and MICMAC analysis, all of which provided insights into the relative importance and interconnections of each indicator. The structured approach allowed for a comprehensive evaluation of indicators, resulting in a model that integrates security, privacy, and trust as essential pillars of digital sovereignty.

This methodology offers a replicable approach for future studies and serves as a foundation for developing policies that enhance digital security, protect individual privacy, and build public trust in digital systems.

Figure 1. Research process for identifying digital governance indicators

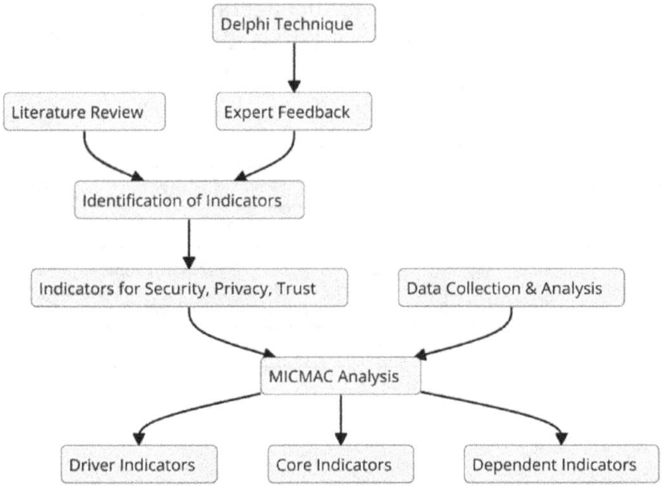

RESULTS AND DISCUSSION

Overall System Environment Analysis

Based on the Delphi method, 33 variables across 3 domains were identified as influencing factors on the future status of digital governance. Subsequently, these variables were analyzed using the Interpretive Structural Modeling (ISM) technique via the MICMAC software to extract the primary influential factors on the future state of the study environment. Given the number of variables, the matrix dimension is 33x33. By placing these factors in a 33x33 matrix, the influence of each factor on others was determined by assigning weights (from 0 to 3). All factors involved in digital governance were considered as a system with interconnected elements and as a structure, and the relationships between these factors were measured to extract the superior factors with greater influence.

The interaction of variables was considered twice, and the matrix density was 96.79%, indicating the dispersion of variables affecting the future of digital governance. Out of a total of 1054 evaluable relationships in this matrix, 35 relationships had a value of zero, 397 had a value of one, 592 had a value of two, and 65 had a value of three. Furthermore, the matrix, based on statistical indicators with two data rotations, had a desirability and optimality of 97%, indicating the high validity of the questionnaire and its responses. Subsequently, a comprehensive analysis of the system environment was conducted to identify the drivers and key influential factors.

After identifying the variables, the first step was to form a pairwise comparison matrix extracted from the Delphi sessions of managers (a total of 30 people), in which the influence of each variable on other variables was measured (See Table 2 & 3).

Table 2. Initial analysis of cross-impact matrix data

Indicator	Value	Indicator	Value
Number of variables	33	Number of twos	592
Number of iterations	2	Number of threes	65
Number of zeros	35	Total	1054
Number of ones	397	Fill rate	96.79%

Table 3. Desirability and optimization of matrix

Iteration	Impact	Receptivity
1	97%	95%
2	100%	100%

Direct Influence and Dependence Assessment of Variables

To analyze the direct impacts of variables, the relationships between each pair of variables were assessed using the MICMAC software. This allowed us to determine the extent and degree of direct influence each variable exerts on others. The results obtained indicate that the distribution and dispersion of variables influencing digital governance on the scatter plot suggest system instability. Consequently, four categories of variables can be identified: influential variables, dual-role variables, regulatory variables, and independent variables, which are explained below (See Table 4 and Figure 2 & 3).

Table 4. Direct impact of variables on each other

N°	Variable	Row count	Column count	N°	Variable	Row count	Column count
1	Cyber Threat Monitoring	61	65	18	User Access Rights	55	59
2	Incident Response Capabilities	61	60	19	Cloud Security	54	55
3	Risk Assessment Processes	42	47	20	Privacy by Design	66	65
4	Risk Mitigation Strategies	52	61	21	Children's Online Privacy Protection	40	33
5	Infrastructure Resilience	48	48	22	Cross-Border Data Sovereignty	58	55
6	Backup and Recovery Systems	32	34	23	Open Data Initiatives	65	63
7	Cybercrime Legislation	38	41	24	Transparency Reports	48	51
8	Secure Authentication Methods	55	65	25	System Reliability	55	50
9	End-to-End Encryption	55	60	26	User Satisfaction Surveys	51	52
10	National Cybersecurity Policy	38	38	27	Financial Transparency	70	69
11	IoT Device Security Standards	49	49	28	Ethical Use of AI	68	58
12	Cybersecurity Education	52	53	29	Equitable Access to Digital Services	63	59
13	Data Ownership and Control	62	62	30	Educational Programs for Digital Literacy	56	61
14	Data Collection Transparency	57	55	31	Institutional Accountability	58	59
15	User Consent Mechanisms	59	51	32	Avoiding Data Exploitation	56	49
16	Data Anonymization Practices	45	45	33	Virtual Identity Authentication	53	49
17	Compliance with Privacy Laws	54	55		Totals	1776	1776

Influential Variables

Variables with a significantly higher percentage of influence compared to their dependence are called influential variables, and these variables are located in the northwest quadrant of the influence-dependence plane. These variables are more influential and less dependent. Therefore, the system is more reliant on these variables. Influential variables are the most critical components, as system changes depend on them, and controlling these variables is crucial. Moreover, these variables serve as input variables to the system. 'System Reliability', 'User Consent Mechanisms', and 'Avoiding Data Exploitation' are among the most important and influential variables.

Dual-Role Variables

Dual-role variables exhibit both high influence and high dependence, meaning that any action involving them will trigger reactions and changes in other variables. These variables are positioned in the northeast quadrant of the influence-dependence plane and have a significant potential to become key system variables. Examples of dual-role variables include 'Cyber Threat Monitoring', 'Incident Response Capabilities', 'Data Ownership and Control', 'Privacy by Design', 'Open Data Initiatives', 'Financial Transparency', 'Ethical Use of AI', 'Equitable Access to Digital Services', 'Institutional Accountability', 'Risk Mitigation Strategies', 'Secure Authentication Methods', 'End-To-End Encryption', 'Data Collection Transparency', 'Compliance with Privacy Laws', 'User Access Rights', 'Cloud Security', 'Cross-Border Data Sovereignty', 'Educational Programs for Digital Literacy'. These variables can be further classified as risk variables or target variables based on their role in the system.

Regulatory Variables

Regulatory variables are located near the center of gravity of the influence-dependence plane. Due to their strategic position, they have the potential to evolve into influential or dual-role variables (serving as both target and risk variables). Examples of regulatory variables include 'IoT Device Security Standards', 'Cybersecurity Education', 'Transparency Reports', 'User Satisfaction Surveys', 'Virtual Identity Authentication'.

Independent Variables

Independent variables, found in the southwest quadrant of the influence-dependence plane, exhibit low influence and low dependence, making them relatively self-contained within the system. Examples of these variables are 'Backup and Recovery Systems', 'Cybercrime Legislation', 'National Cybersecurity Policy', 'Children’s Online Privacy Protection', 'Risk Assessment Processes', 'Infrastructure Resilience', 'Data Anonymization Practices'.

Figure 2. Variable status based on direct variable changes

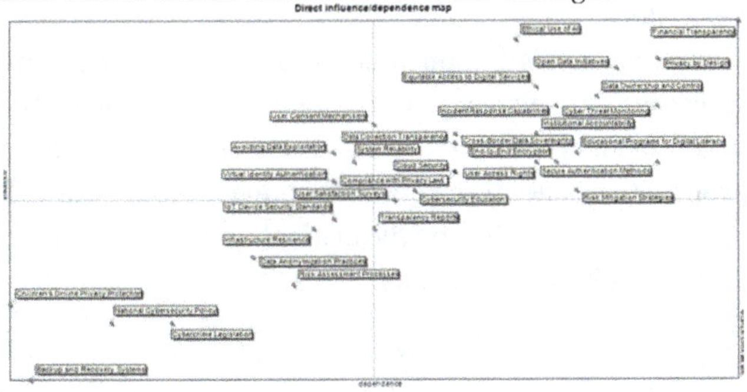

Figure 3. Direct relationships between variables, exhibiting a wide range of strength from very weak to very strong

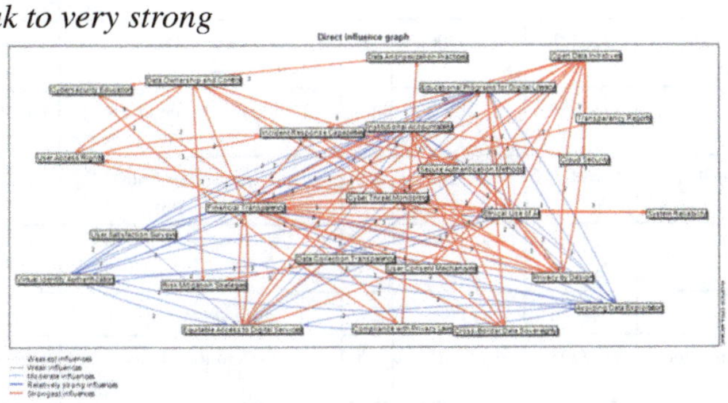

Assessment of Indirect Influences and Impacts of Variables

Moving beyond direct interactions, the analysis of indirect influences provides a more nuanced understanding of systemic interdependencies. Through higher-order calculations, the MICMAC software assessed how variables influence others indirectly, capturing second-order and higher-order effects. This approach uncovers hidden linkages that are not immediately apparent in direct assessments. The results confirmed that the four categories of variables identified in the direct analysis largely persist in the indirect domain, underscoring systemic stability. For example, 'Financial Transparency' and 'Ethical Use of AI' consistently emerged as top influencers, not only in their immediate impact but also in their broader, ripple effects across the system.

Interestingly, some variables demonstrated shifts in their relative importance when considering indirect effects. 'Privacy by Design' and 'Equitable Access to Digital Services' displayed stronger systemic roles under indirect influence, highlighting their ability to propagate impacts through interconnected pathways. These findings, illustrated in Figures 4 and 5, underline the critical nature of considering both direct and indirect effects for a holistic analysis.

Table 5. Extent of indirect effects of variables on each other

N°	Variable	Row count	Column count	N°	Variable	Row count	Column count
1	Cyber Threat Monitoring	186584	197702	18	User Access Rights	169058	180976
2	Incident Response Capabilities	185277	184185	19	Cloud Security	164157	167700
3	Risk Assessment Processes	126745	142906	20	Privacy by Design	201116	196628
4	Risk Mitigation Strategies	155554	181303	21	Children's Online Privacy Protection	121087	98656
5	Infrastructure Resilience	143320	145281	22	Cross-Border Data Sovereignty	178419	168012
6	Backup and Recovery Systems	96293	102273	23	Open Data Initiatives	197907	193341
7	Cybercrime Legislation	114446	121400	24	Transparency Reports	143663	156242
8	Secure Authentication Methods	167495	197881	25	System Reliability	167942	153383
9	End-to-End Encryption	168432	179889	26	User Satisfaction Surveys	156601	159535
10	National Cybersecurity Policy	112013	113473	27	Financial Transparency	212425	207814
11	IoT Device Security Standards	145802	148651	28	Ethical Use of AI	207477	177888
12	Cybersecurity Education	156161	158946	29	Equitable Access to Digital Services	192050	178482
13	Data Ownership and Control	187544	187564	30	Educational Programs for Digital Literacy	171776	185205
14	Data Collection Transparency	171110	167137	31	Institutional Accountability	176621	180152
15	User Consent Mechanisms	180823	156579	32	Avoiding Data Exploitation	171338	149967
16	Data Anonymization Practices	135032	134664	33	Virtual Identity Authentication	162010	150915
17	Compliance with Privacy Laws	163437	164985		Totals	1776	1776

Figure 4. Variable status based on indirect variable changes

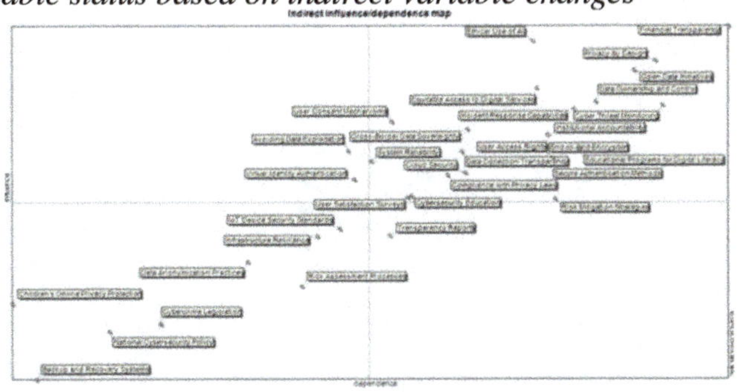

Figure 5. Indirect relationships between variables, exhibiting a wide range of strength from very weak to very strong

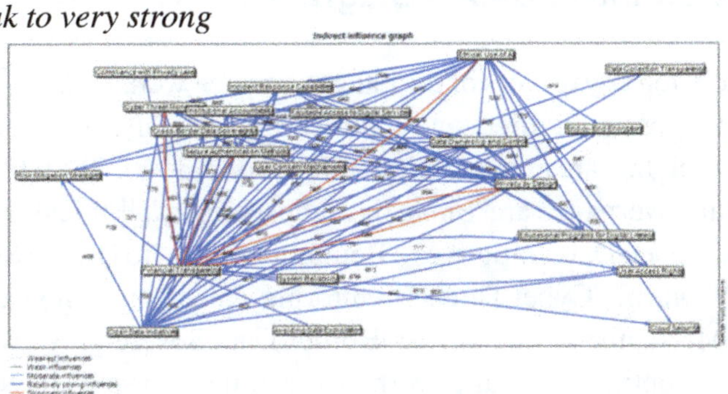

Extent of Factor Displacement in Direct and Indirect Effects of Variables

This subsection examines the positional changes of variables when transitioning from direct to indirect influence assessments. As visualized in Figure 6, the displacement of variables was minimal, indicating a high degree of consistency between direct and indirect influence structures.

Such stability is essential for strategic planning, as it suggests that key variables maintain their importance regardless of the analytical perspective. For instance, 'Financial Transparency' and 'Cyber Threat Monitoring' retained their high-impact status across both analyses, validating their role as critical drivers of digital governance. The minimal displacement also reinforces the robustness of the system, as it highlights the reliability of identified key drivers.

Figure 6. Extent of factor displacement in direct and indirect effects of variables

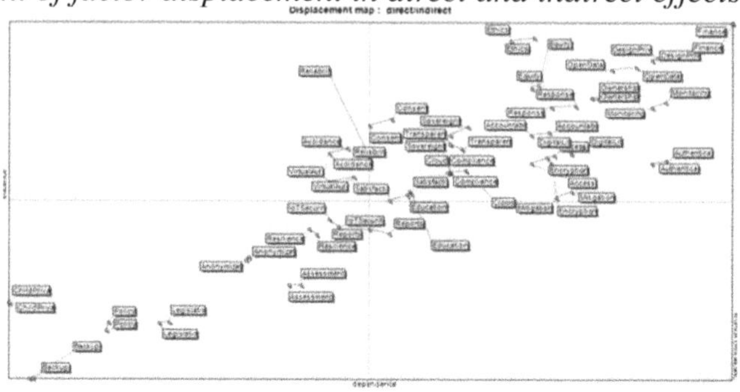

Position of Factors Affecting Digital Governance on the MICMAC Diagram

In this section, ten key drivers of digital governance were identified, all of which were consistent across both direct and indirect impact analyses. These key drivers, ranked by their weights, are presented in Table 6. As shown in the table, the primary drivers of digital governance are 'Financial Transparency', 'Ethical Use of AI', 'Privacy by Design', 'Open Data Initiatives', 'Equitable Access to Digital Services', 'Data Ownership and Control', 'Cyber Threat Monitoring', 'Incident Response Capabilities', 'User Consent Mechanisms', and 'Cross-Border Data Sovereignty'. By considering these key factors, optimal digital governance can be achieved. In both direct and indirect impact assessments, the driving factors consistently exhibited the highest weights, reflecting their significant importance within the digital governance system.

Table 6. Key direct and indirect influencing factors

Rank	Variable	Direct Influence	Variable	Indirect Influence
1	Financial Transparency	394	Financial Transparency	394
2	Ethical Use of AI	382	Ethical Use of AI	384
3	Privacy by Design	371	Privacy by Design	373
4	Open Data Initiatives	365	Open Data Initiatives	367
5	Equitable Access to Digital Services	354	Equitable Access to Digital Services	356
6	Data Ownership and Control	349	Data Ownership and Control	347
7	Cyber Threat Monitoring	343	Cyber Threat Monitoring	346
8	Incident Response Capabilities	343	Incident Response Capabilities	343

continued on following page

Table 6. Continued

Rank	Variable	Direct Influence	Variable	Indirect Influence
9	User Consent Mechanisms	332	User Consent Mechanisms	335
10	Cross-Border Data Sovereignty	326	Cross-Border Data Sovereignty	331

The study emphasizes the indispensable role of digital governance in an era where technological transformation is central to public and private sector operations. The findings highlight how security, privacy, and trust intertwine to form the backbone of effective governance frameworks. This discussion explores these interrelations, linking theoretical insights with practical implications.

Security is a foundational element of digital governance. The MICMAC analysis identified key security variables, 'Cyber Threat Monitoring', 'Incident Response Capabilities', and 'Risk Mitigation Strategies', as influential drivers. These elements ensure system resilience against cyber threats, a critical concern as cyberattacks grow in sophistication. Prioritizing these variables allows organizations to pre-emptively manage risks, ensuring operational continuity. This study supports the "Circle of Trust" model (Kesan & Hayes, 2014), which advocates for collaborative cybersecurity efforts across sectors. The direct and indirect influence of security indicators underscores their role in fostering a secure digital environment. Security, however, is not isolated; its effectiveness is amplified when integrated with privacy and trust measures.

Privacy, often viewed as a counterbalance to security, emerges in this study as a vital enabler of digital sovereignty. Indicators such as 'Privacy by Design', 'Data Ownership and Control', and 'User Consent Mechanisms' reveal privacy's critical role in empowering users. The analysis highlights how privacy-centric governance frameworks not only comply with regulations like GDPR but also build user trust. The shift toward *Self-Sovereign Identity* (SSI) systems exemplifies this trend. By granting individuals greater control over their digital identities, organizations can enhance transparency and user satisfaction. This paradigm shift aligns with findings from Wong et al. (2022), who argue that transparency in data practices is a prerequisite for sustainable digital ecosystems.

Trust is positioned as the linchpin of digital governance. Variables such as 'Financial Transparency', 'Open Data Initiatives', and 'Ethical Use of AI' drive this dimension. The findings reinforce that trust is not merely a byproduct of security and privacy but an active component requiring deliberate cultivation. Trust fosters engagement, as users are more likely to interact with systems they perceive as reliable and ethical. Transparency reports and digital literacy programs, as highlighted in this study, serve as trust-building mechanisms, aligning with Gill & Germann's (2022) advocacy for ethical AI deployment. Trust not only enhances system adoption but also ensures compliance and cooperation in the digital domain.

The integration of security, privacy, and trust is evident in the systemic roles these variables play. The MICMAC analysis underscores that no single pillar operates in isolation. For example, 'Privacy by Design' and 'Cyber Threat Monitoring' are dual-role variables that influence and depend on other system components. This interconnectedness necessitates a holistic governance approach, where policies and strategies are designed with a multi-faceted perspective.

While this study offers a robust framework for analyzing digital governance indicators using the MICMAC methodology, several limitations must be acknowledged. First, the reliance on expert judgment through the Delphi technique introduces subjectivity, which may influence the selection and weighting of indicators. Although steps were taken to ensure a diverse and qualified panel, expert bias remains a potential constraint. Second, the analysis is static in nature and does not account for the temporal evolution of governance indicators, which may change rapidly due to technological advancements, regulatory shifts, or geopolitical developments. Third, the study focuses primarily on a generalized framework and does not delve into specific regional, cultural, or institutional contexts where digital governance dynamics may differ significantly. Finally, while the MICMAC method effectively reveals structural interdependencies among variables, it does not capture causal relationships or feedback loops in a dynamic system, which may be addressed in future research through methods such as system dynamics modeling.

DISCUSSION

The rapid digital transformation across industries and governments necessitates a robust framework for managing security, privacy, and trust. This study offers a structured analysis of digital governance, using MICMAC to reveal the interdependencies and hierarchical roles of various governance indicators. The research underscores the interconnectedness of security, privacy, and trust as the three pillars of digital governance. These pillars do not operate in silos; rather, they form a cohesive system where the strength of one pillar reinforces the others. For instance, robust 'Cyber Threat Monitoring' enhances not only system security but also public trust by demonstrating proactive risk management. Similarly, privacy measures such as 'User Consent Mechanisms' and 'Privacy by Design' empower users, fostering transparency and trust in governance systems. The MICMAC analysis revealed a critical insight: governance indicators vary significantly in their influence and dependence. Key drivers like 'Financial Transparency' (influence score: 394) and 'Ethical Use of AI' (score: 384) are pivotal in both direct and indirect systemic impacts, serving as the linchpins of digital governance. These indicators should, therefore, be prioritized in strategic initiatives to create resilient and adaptive governance systems.

The study highlights security as the foundational element of digital governance. Indicators such as 'Incident Response Capabilities' and 'Risk Mitigation *Strategies'* are essential for protecting digital infrastructures against escalating cyber threats. Effective governance frameworks must prioritize the development of comprehensive cybersecurity policies that include real-time threat detection, incident response protocols, and secure authentication methods. However, the findings also indicate that security measures alone cannot guarantee system stability. They must be integrated with privacy and trust mechanisms to provide a holistic approach to governance. The "Circle of Trust" model serves as a useful paradigm, advocating for collaboration between public and private sectors to bolster cybersecurity resilience.

Privacy emerges as a dual-faceted element: it is both a regulatory necessity and a means of empowering users. The inclusion of 'Data Ownership' and 'Control and Compliance with Privacy Laws' as key variables reflects the growing importance of privacy in governance frameworks. By adopting privacy-centric designs, organizations can not only meet regulatory requirements but also build systems that prioritize user autonomy. The global shift towards 'Self-Sovereign Identity' (SSI) systems illustrates the practical application of these principles. Such models give users greater control over their digital identities, aligning with broader societal demands for transparency and accountability. As governments and organizations navigate complex privacy regulations like GDPR, embedding privacy into the core of governance systems will be a critical success factor.

Trust plays a unique role as both an outcome and an enabler of effective governance. The study identifies 'Transparency Reports', 'Open Data Initiatives', and 'Ethical Use of *AI*' as pivotal trust-building mechanisms. Trust is not merely a byproduct of secure and private systems; it is actively cultivated through deliberate policies and practices. The ethical use of technology, particularly AI, is a growing concern. This study emphasizes the need for governance frameworks that address ethical considerations, ensuring that AI systems operate transparently and fairly. Building trust also requires a focus on user education and digital literacy, enabling users to engage confidently with digital systems.

One of the study's most significant contributions is the identification of ten key drivers that consistently exhibit high influence across both direct and indirect analyses. These include:

- Financial Transparency (influence score: 394)
- Ethical Use of AI (influence score: 394)
- Privacy by Design (influence score: 371)
- Open Data Initiatives (influence score: 365)

- Equitable Access to Digital Services (influence score: 354)
- Data Ownership and Control (influence score: 349)
- Cyber Threat Monitoring (influence score: 343)
- Incident Response Capabilities (influence score: 343)
- User Consent Mechanisms (influence score: 332)
- Cross-Border Data Sovereignty (influence score: 326)

These drivers serve as actionable focal points for enhancing digital governance. Policymakers and organizational leaders must prioritize these variables in designing governance strategies, ensuring that they address both immediate challenges and long-term objectives. The findings of this research have far-reaching implications for governments, organizations, and policymakers.

First, there is an urgent need to adopt integrative governance models that balance security, privacy, and trust. This balance is essential for achieving digital sovereignty, where states and organizations maintain control over their digital infrastructures while empowering users and fostering public trust. Second, governance strategies must be adaptable, given the dynamic nature of technology and regulatory landscapes. The minimal displacement observed in variable positioning between direct and indirect analyses indicates a stable yet flexible system. Policymakers can leverage this stability to implement scalable solutions that evolve with emerging challenges. Finally, international collaboration is critical. Issues such as *Cross-Border Data Sovereignty* highlight the global nature of digital governance challenges. Governments must work together to establish standards and protocols that transcend national boundaries, ensuring that digital governance frameworks are effective in an interconnected world.

While this study provides a robust framework, future research could explore the dynamic evolution of governance variables over time. Longitudinal studies would offer deeper insights into how technological advancements and regulatory changes affect the influence and dependence of key indicators. Additionally, comparative analyses across different regions or industries could enrich the understanding of context-specific governance practices. In conclusion, this study contributes to the growing body of knowledge on digital governance, offering a comprehensive and actionable framework. By prioritizing the integration of security, privacy, and trust, organizations can navigate the complexities of the digital age, fostering resilient, ethical, and user-centric governance systems.

CONCLUSION

This study presented a structured analysis of digital governance indicators with the goal of enhancing digital sovereignty through the integration of security, privacy, and trust. Using the Delphi technique and MICMAC structural analysis, we identified 33 key indicators and revealed the ten most influential factors, including financial transparency, ethical use of AI, privacy by design, and cyber threat monitoring. The primary contribution of this research is the development of a replicable, data-driven framework that helps policymakers and institutions identify high-impact governance levers and design targeted strategies to strengthen digital autonomy.

The findings have several practical implications. Policymakers should focus on governance indicators that offer the greatest systemic influence, especially those that reinforce public trust, safeguard privacy, and enhance security. For instance, transparency measures, ethical approaches to AI, and mechanisms for user consent can serve as effective foundations for reinforcing digital sovereignty. In low-resource environments, culturally adapted privacy safeguards and community-based digital literacy programs can support broader citizen engagement and trust in digital systems.

Future research should examine how governance indicators evolve over time through longitudinal studies that capture dynamic changes in influence and relevance. Comparative analyses across diverse geopolitical and cultural settings, including Africa, Latin America, and Southeast Asia, are also essential to validate and adapt the framework. Further, integrating methods such as system dynamics or scenario-based planning would provide deeper insights into the complex and interconnected nature of digital governance. Advancing this research agenda will be essential for navigating the future challenges of global digital transformation.

REFERENCES

Balisane, H., Egho-Promise, E. I., Lyada, E., & Aina, F. (2024). Towards Improved Threat Mitigation in Digital Environments: A Comprehensive Framework for Cybersecurity Enhancement. *International Journal of Research -Granthaalayah, 12*(5). DOI: 10.29121/granthaalayah.v12.i5.2024.5655

Ban, L. (2024). Data privacy and protection in communication networks. *Applied and Computational Engineering, 38*(1), 131–138. DOI: 10.54254/2755-2721/38/20230541

Barik, K., Misra, S., Mohan, R., & Mishra, B. (2024). AIoT and Its Trust Models to Enhance Societal Applications Using Intelligent Technologies. In Misra, S., Siakas, K., & Lampropoulos, G. (Eds.), *Artificial Intelligence of Things for Achieving Sustainable Development Goals. Lecture Notes on Data Engineering and Communications Technologies* (Vol. 192). Springer., DOI: 10.1007/978-3-031-53433-1_16

Barrinha, A. (2016). Cybersecurity in the European Union. Resilience and adaptability in governance policy. *European Security, 25*(3), 387–389. DOI: 10.1080/09662839.2016.1160892

Bayaga, A. (2022). Examining the predictive relevance of security, privacy risk factors, and institutional logics for e-government service adoption. *The Electronic Journal on Information Systems in Developing Countries, 88*(1), e12201. DOI: 10.1002/isd2.12201

Da Silva Carvalho, N., Jabbarpour, J., Temple, L., Belacort, I. M., Barturen, U. I., Kortlander, M., Sanchez Pelaez, V., Areizaga Sanchez, E., & Mureddu, F. (2023). A more inclusive Europe through personal data sovereignty in cross-border digital public services. *Proceedings of the 16th International Conference on Theory and Practice of Electronic Governance*, 63–71. DOI: 10.1145/3614321.3614329

Dedousis, P., Stergiopoulos, G., Arampatzis, G., & Gritzalis, D. (2021). A Security-Aware Framework for Designing Industrial Engineering Processes. *IEEE Access : Practical Innovations, Open Solutions, 9*, 163065–163085. DOI: 10.1109/ACCESS.2021.3134759

Folorunsho, O. S., Ayinde, A. Q., Olagoke, M. A., & Fatoye, O. E. (2019). Evaluating Cybersecurity Theories, Models, Standards and Frameworks. *Advances in Multidisciplinary and Scientific Research Journal Publication, 5*(4), 61–66. DOI: 10.22624/AIMS/BHI/V5N4P7

Giannopoulou, A. (2020). Data Protection Compliance Challenges for Self-Sovereign Identity. SSRN *Electronic Journal*. DOI: 10.2139/ssrn.3671523

Gill, A. S., & Germann, S. (2022). Conceptual and normative approaches to AI governance for a global digital ecosystem supportive of the UN Sustainable Development Goals (SDGs). *AI and Ethics*, *2*(2), 293–301. DOI: 10.1007/s43681-021-00058-z PMID: 34790947

Guembe, B., Misra, S., & Azeta, A. (2024). Privacy Issues, Attacks, Countermeasures and Open Problems in Federated Learning: A Survey. *Applied Artificial Intelligence*, *38*(1), 2410504. Advance online publication. DOI: 10.1080/08839514.2024.2410504

Hellmeier, M., Pampus, J., Qarawlus, H., & Howar, F. (2023). Implementing Data Sovereignty: Requirements & Challenges from Practice. *Proceedings of the 18th International Conference on Availability, Reliability and Security*, 1–9. DOI: 10.1145/3600160.3604995

Igwenagu, U. T. I., Salami, A. A., Arigbabu, A. S., Mesode, C. E., Oladoyinbo, T. O., & Olaniyi, O. O. (2024). Securing the Digital Frontier: Strategies for Cloud Computing Security, Database Protection, and Comprehensive Penetration Testing. *Journal of Engineering Research and Reports*, *26*(6), 60–75. DOI: 10.9734/jerr/2024/v26i61162

Kanaan, A. AL-Hawamleh, A., Alorfi, A., & Aloun, M. (2024). Cybersecurity Resilience for Business: A Comprehensive Model for Proactive Defense and Swift Recovery. *2024 2nd International Conference on Cyber Resilience (ICCR)*, 1–7. DOI: 10.1109/ICCR61006.2024.10532881

Kesan, J. P., & Hayes, C. M. (2014). *Creating a "Circle of Trust" to Further Digital Privacy and Cybersecurity Goals* (SSRN Scholarly Paper 2135618). Social Science Research Network. DOI: 10.2139/ssrn.2135618

Manoury, M., Riedelsheimer, T., Hellmeier, M., & Meyer, T. (2025). Supporting Changes in Digital Ownership and Data Sovereignty Across the Automotive Value Chain with Catena-X. *Procedia Computer Science*, *253*, 374–383. DOI: 10.1016/j.procs.2025.01.099

Mattoo, A., & Meltzer, J. P. (2018). International Data Flows and Privacy: The Conflict and Its Resolution. *Journal of International Economic Law*, *21*(4), 769–789. DOI: 10.1093/jiel/jgy044

Naik, N., & Jenkins, P. (2021). Sovrin Network for Decentralized Digital Identity: Analysing a Self-Sovereign Identity System Based on Distributed Ledger Technology. *2021 IEEE International Symposium on Systems Engineering (ISSE)*, 1–7. DOI: 10.1109/ISSE51541.2021.9582551

Nnenna, U. J., Perpetua, U. I., Nchaga, A. M., Hadijah, T., & Mabonga, E. Accounting and Finance, Kampala International University, Uganda, & Nyamboga, T. O. (2024). Impact of Digital Governance on Public Service Delivery in East Africa. *IAA Journal of Arts and Humanities, 11*(1), 18–29. DOI: 10.59298/IAAJAH/2024/11.11829.11

Osman, I. H., Anouze, A. L., Irani, Z., Al-Ayoubi, B., Lee, H., Balcı, A., Medeni, T. D., & Weerakkody, V. (2014). COBRA framework to evaluate e-government services: A citizen-centric perspective. *Government Information Quarterly, 31*(2), 243–256. DOI: 10.1016/j.giq.2013.10.009

Panwar, A., Khari, M., Misra, S., & Sugandh, U. (2023). Blockchain in Agriculture to Ensure Trust, Effectiveness, and Traceability from Farm Fields to Groceries. *Future Internet, 15*(12), 404. DOI: 10.3390/fi15120404

Patrick, H., van Niekerk, B., & Fields, Z. (2018). Developing Cybersecurity Resilience in the Provincial Government. In *Handbook of Research on Information and Cyber Security in the Fourth Industrial Revolution* (pp. 336–363). IGI Global. DOI: 10.4018/978-1-5225-4763-1.ch012

Schaberreiter, T., Wills, C., Quirchmayr, G., & Röning, J. (2017, September 10). Addressing complex problem situations in critical infrastructures using soft systems analysis: the CS-AWARE approach. *In* Westphall, C. M., Hof, H., Olmsted, A., Schauer, S., Latzenhofer, M., Abidin, A., & Yee, G. *(Eds.), SECURWARE 2017: The Eleventh International Conference on Emerging Security Information, Systems and Technologies (pp.* 99-105*). IARIA.*

. Semantha, F. H., Azam, S., Shanmugam, B., Yeo, K. C., & Beeravolu, A. R. (2021). A Conceptual Framework to Ensure Privacy in Patient Record Management System. *IEEE Access, 9*, 165667–165689. IEEE Access. DOI: 10.1109/ACCESS.2021.3134873

Taqafi, I., Maleh, Y., & Ouazzane, K. (2023). A Maturity Capability Framework for Security Operation Center. *EDPACS, 67*(3), 21–38. DOI: 10.1080/07366981.2023.2159047

Wong, J., Henderson, T., & Ball, K. (2022). Data protection for the common good: Developing a framework for a data protection-focused data commons. *Data & Policy, 4*, e3. DOI: 10.1017/dap.2021.40

Chapter 5
Federated AIoT Framework for Privacy-Preserving Smart Grid Management

Bilkisu Larai Muhammad-Bello
https://orcid.org/0000-0002-4020-7175
Nile University of Nigeria, Abuja, Nigeria

Muhammad Bello Kusharki
https://orcid.org/0000-0003-0901-2326
National Defence College, Abuja, Nigeria

Sanjay Misra
https://orcid.org/0000-0002-3556-9331
Østfold University College, Norway

Usman Nuhu Galadima
Federal University of Technology Minna, Nigeria

ABSTRACT

The increasing demand for efficient energy management and privacy concerns poses challenges for smart grids in developing regions. This study introduces a Federated AIoT Framework integrating Federated Learning (FL) with IoT, leveraging a Federated Graph Attention Network (FeGAN) to enhance Nigeria's smart grid. The framework decentralizes model training, improving grid efficiency while ensuring data privacy. Results show a 92% accuracy in grid optimization, 89% accuracy in energy theft detection, and a 15% reduction in energy losses. Additionally, it demonstrated superior scalability and privacy-preserving mechanisms, achieving

DOI: 10.4018/979-8-3693-9137-2.ch005

an F1 score of 0.91 for grid efficiency and 0.86 for theft detection. The Matthews Correlation Coefficient (MCC) for privacy reached 0.95, underscoring robust security. Federated Learning creates an opportunity for conducting secure smart grid management with scalability together with privacy compliance in resource-limited settings. Research expansion will target wider implementation within various power systems to integrate renewable power generation.

INTRODUCTION

The sustainable energy transition has spurred global interest in smart grids as integrated power systems that unite traditional power distribution with Information and Communication Technologies (ICT). The integrated systems help maximize efficiency while supporting instant monitoring and improving the distribution of resources (Su et al., 2022). Smart grid installations struggle to progress in Nigerian developing areas because energy losses reach 30–40% due to energy thefts together with deficient infrastructure and non-integrated power systems (Ogbonna et. al., 2024).

Smart grid implementation faces new privacy issues because of IoT and AI integration, which affects digital sovereignty standards. AI systems that function as centralised models need extensive data collection operations, which expose users to security vulnerabilities and adverse monitoring practises. The security issues become most severe when countries maintain sparse cyber protection systems while heavily depending on overseas digital infrastructure. FL serves as a decentralised AI training system for maintaining user-sensitive data at the edge locations.

Federated smart grids demonstrate promising results yet struggle with applying methods to specific regions while integrating local digital factors and conducting tests that protect user privacy within the African framework. The national digital economy strategy in Nigeria focuses on local data control through its policies; however, its execution currently shows minimal progress. A new Federated AIoT Framework has been developed by this research to connect Federated Graph Attention Networks (FeGAN) with privacy-preserving solutions which allow Nigeria to develop scalable smart grid management with data sovereignty.

Key Contributions:

1) Integration of FeGAN within a Federated AIoT framework to enhance smart grid optimization and energy theft detection.
2) Achievement of strong performance metrics (e.g., 92% optimization accuracy, 15% energy loss reduction) while preserving user privacy.
3) Implementation of privacy-preserving mechanisms validated by an MCC of 0.95.

4) Support for national data sovereignty through a decentralized AI architecture.

These contributions position the proposed framework as a scalable, secure, and privacy-compliant solution for addressing smart grid challenges in Nigeria and similar socio-economic contexts.

RELATED WORK

Overview of AIoT and Federated Learning

The convergence of AI and IoT, often referred to as AIoT, has been transformative across various industries, including energy management (Arora & Makani, 2024). AIoT enables smart grids to collect, process, and analyze large volumes of real-time data from multiple devices connected to the grid, such as smart meters, sensors, and distribution substations (Bronner et al., 2021). This integration supports predictive analytics, anomaly detection, and grid optimization (Zhou et al., 2023). Smart grids equipped with AIoT can monitor energy consumption patterns, predict demand fluctuations, and automatically address grid inefficiencies. These advancements are vital for transitioning from traditional energy management systems to smarter, more automated infrastructures that enhance reliability, efficiency, and sustainability (Tan et al., 2021a).

On the other hand, Federated Learning (FL) is an emerging machine learning paradigm that tackles privacy and scalability challenges by enabling decentralized data processing (Cheng et al., 2019). Unlike centralized learning models, where data is gathered at a central location for analysis, FL allows local nodes (e.g., energy distribution centres) to train models on their data, sharing only model updates. This method preserves data privacy, reduces communication costs, and lowers the risk of data breaches (Li et al., 2021). When applied to smart grids, FL facilitates the local processing of energy consumption data, enhancing both data security and real-time decision-making capabilities. The combination of AIoT with FL in energy management offers a robust framework for optimizing energy distribution while protecting sensitive user information.

Ethical and Socio-Economic Considerations in Theft Detection

The technical aspects of energy theft detection require attention, but societal factors stay crucial. The privacy-preserving framework FeGAN needs to address ethical issues regarding user consent together with building user trust and minimising prediction biases about theft detection. Communities in low-income rural areas could end up unfairly suffering from wrong assignments identified as energy thieves. There exist two main obstacles to AI adoption that include low digital literacy levels and general scepticism toward artificial intelligence. For ethical deployment to succeed it requires training of users along with transparent policies which should include localised feedback mechanisms.

Comparative Federated Learning Applications in Developing Economies

Scientists from India and South Africa researched Federated Learning for smart grid optimization and established that local training methods enhance regional theft detection capabilities while maintaining privacy standards (Du et al., 2024). The National Smart Grid Mission of India has initiated FL framework assessment across utility providers simultaneously South African researchers deploy FL solutions for resolving blackouts problems in informal settlements. The test cases validate how FeGAN's decentralized framework with privacy protections addresses requirements in social-economic environments that are like the described situations.

Federated Learning in Energy Management

Federated learning has shown considerable promise in enhancing energy management systems, particularly in decentralized energy grids. Numerous studies have examined the application of FL to areas such as energy load forecasting, demand response management, and grid optimization. For instance, Zhang et al. (2020) applied FL to energy load forecasting, demonstrating that the decentralized approach not only improved forecasting accuracy but also safeguarded user data privacy. The study emphasized how local nodes could train models on localized data patterns, allowing for more accurate load management tailored to specific regions. Similarly, Li et al., (2022) explored the integration of FL into demand response management, highlighting the capability of federated models to learn from decentralized energy distribution centres without the need to centralize sensitive data.

Another important area of research has focused on using federated learning for grid optimization and theft detection. Du et al., (2024) proposed a framework where FL was applied to distributed energy resources to balance supply and demand across a heterogeneous grid. This approach helped mitigate issues related to energy theft, as federated models could detect anomalies in consumption patterns without exposing individual user data. The study demonstrated the scalability and efficiency of FL in managing large-scale energy systems, underscoring its potential in regions like Nigeria, where energy theft remains a persistent issue.

Privacy-Preserving Techniques in Smart Grids

Data privacy is a central concern in smart grid management, particularly in the context of AIoT integration, where large volumes of real-time data are continuously processed and transmitted (Kwon & Park, 2021). Traditional centralized models are vulnerable to data breaches, potentially exposing sensitive information such as household consumption patterns and financial details. To address these concerns, several privacy-preserving techniques have been developed for smart grids.

One such technique is differential privacy, which has gained traction for its ability to protect user data by introducing noise, ensuring that individual users cannot be re-identified through analysis (Briggs et al., 2021). In the energy sector, differential privacy has been applied to energy usage data to prevent malicious actors from inferring individual consumption habits. For example, Liu et al., (2023) applied differential privacy to smart grid data streams, effectively obscuring sensitive information while preserving the utility of the data for broader grid optimization tasks.

Another approach is homomorphic encryption, which enables computations to be performed on encrypted data without needing to decrypt it. Singh et al., (2022) demonstrated the application of homomorphic encryption in a smart grid setting, where energy usage data remained encrypted during both transmission and processing, ensuring privacy throughout the system's operation.

Despite these advancements, significant gaps remain. Many existing privacy-preserving solutions often come with trade-offs in terms of computational complexity and system scalability (Xiao et al., 2024). This is particularly challenging in regions like Nigeria, where computational resources may be limited, and energy grids are already under strain. The Federated AIoT framework proposed in this paper addresses these challenges by employing. Federated Graph Attention Networks (FeGAN), optimizing energy distribution and theft detection without requiring the centralization or decryption of sensitive data.

The integration of Artificial Intelligence and Internet of Things (AIoT) has revolutionized energy systems by enabling real-time monitoring, predictive analytics, and grid optimization. Bronner et al., (2021) highlighted AIoT's transformative impact on grid performance but emphasized the privacy risks associated with centralized AI models, particularly in regions with weak cybersecurity frameworks. Federated Learning (FL) addresses these risks by decentralizing model training, as demonstrated by Cheng et al., (2019), who preserved data privacy while improving demand forecasting accuracy. Similarly, Du et al., (2023) applied FL to distributed grids, showcasing its scalability and resilience in energy management.

Complementary privacy-preserving techniques further enhance FL's effectiveness in safeguarding sensitive grid data. Differential privacy Aziz et al., (2023) and homomorphic encryption Park et. al., (2022) have been shown to provide robust protection against data breaches. Singh et al. (2022) emphasized the importance of lightweight encryption protocols, particularly for resource-constrained IoT devices, enabling scalable privacy-preserving solutions in decentralized energy systems.

Digital Sovereignty and Energy Systems

National sovereignty issues now tightly intertwine with modern energy system operations during the digital age. State control over digital infrastructure combined with internal data management autonomy has transformed into a fundamental national policy priority in critical infrastructure protection. The energy data of Nigeria is a fundamental strategic resource holding dual economic value. National control over infrastructure systems and AI processing faces direct threats when such operations are outsourced to external firms which might lead to exploitation or manipulation of national systems (Pohle & Thiel, 2020).

The National Digital Economy Policy and Strategy (2020–2030) of Nigeria establishes decentralized digital governance along with local data infrastructure management as crucial elements for defending national priorities. The implementation of FeGAN-based Federated AIoT Framework achieves these national goals. The system maintains national energy data protection through data processing decentralization and blocking the free movement of raw data across borders.

The data cooperative model described by Calzada (2021) presents a governance system where energy data belongs to community groups and energy agencies together. These governance systems create balance by managing innovative practices alongside accountability systems when used alongside federated learning frameworks. The future development of smart grids in Nigeria needs to respect digital sovereignty guidelines because it drives energy modernization efforts. The proposed framework demonstrates how secure deployment of advanced AI models can happen through an ethical and autonomous system.

METHODOLOGY

The Federated AIoT Framework integrates IoT technologies with Federated Learning (FL) to optimize Nigeria's energy grid while addressing critical privacy concerns. By leveraging a decentralized architecture, the framework ensures that sensitive consumer data remains localized and secure throughout the processing pipeline. Figure 1 provides an illustration of the framework's data flow and its major components, highlighting the interplay between IoT sensors, Local Processing Units (LPUs), and the centralized aggregation process.

Figure 1. FeGAN framework

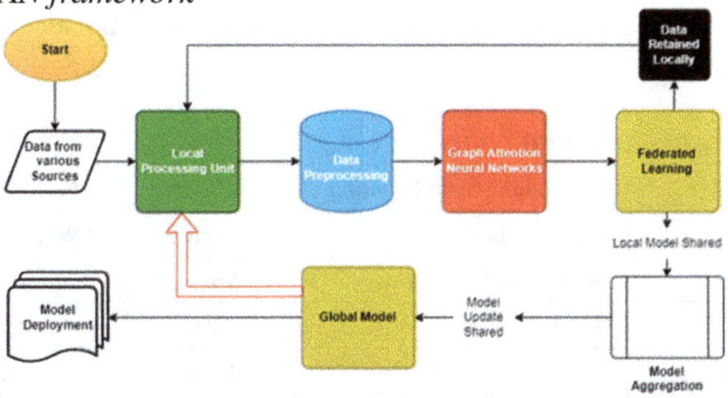

Overview of Nigeria's Smart Grid System

The power sector in Nigeria shows poor development of transmission networks together with limited meter distribution and varying electricity availability between different areas. The distribution of power generation problems occurs because urban substations become overloaded while rural substations face persistent electricity shortages. The low implementation of smart grid improvements is due to limited financial resources as well as heavy reliance on foreign digital systems. The FeGAN framework implements its operations through two fundamental layers at substations and consumer points with IoT-based Local Processing Units. The platform divides operations into two parallel layers which allow spatial process enhancements and fault detection capabilities without endangering data confidentiality.

Key Components:

1) IoT Sensors: Collect grid data, including voltage levels, energy consumption, and environmental conditions, to provide real-time operational insights.
2) Local Processing Units (LPUs): Decentralized nodes preprocess data and train lightweight AI models locally. This approach ensures fault tolerance and scalability.
3) FeGAN: Aggregates locally trained models into a global model using federated averaging, prioritizing grid node relationships through graph attention mechanisms.
4) Privacy and Security: Differential privacy and homomorphic encryption ensure data security and compliance with digital sovereignty principles.

The framework addresses Nigeria's infrastructural limitations through low-bandwidth communication protocols and fault-tolerant operations, ensuring reliable performance under varying conditions. Evaluation metrics include grid optimization accuracy, theft detection precision, scalability, and privacy preservation.

Table 1. IoT sensors and data collected

Sensor Type	Deployment Location	Data Collected
Smart Meter	Consumer Endpoints	Energy usage (kWh)
Voltage Sensor	Substations, Transformers	Voltage levels
Current Sensor	Distribution Lines	Current flow
Temperature Sensor	Power Infrastructure	Temperature, environmental data
Anomaly Detector	Consumer and Distribution	Detects spikes in energy usage
Sensor Type	Deployment Location	Data Collected
Smart Meter	Consumer Endpoints	Energy usage (kWh)

This architecture is designed to support scalability and fault tolerance, addressing the infrastructural constraints specific to Nigeria's energy sector. By decentralizing computation and incorporating privacy-preserving mechanisms, the framework offers a robust solution for optimizing smart grid operations in resource-constrained environments.

Data Generation and Preprocessing

The datasets used in this study form the foundation for simulating three distinct smart grid environments to evaluate the effectiveness of the Federated AIoT framework. The first dataset, synthetic smart grid data, captures energy consumption metrics from multiple regions in Nigeria, including real-time measurements of voltage, current, and energy sources. The second dataset provides insights into rooftop solar potential in Lagos, detailing installable capacity and energy potential, which is crucial for integrating renewable energy into smart grids. The third dataset focuses on smart grid stability, incorporating parameters like time constants, power values, and stability indicators to assess grid resilience under various conditions.

Our analysis relied on three different databased comprising energy usage records (~10,000), voltage and current measurements (~3,000) and solar performance records (~800) from Lagos. Training and testing were split 80/20. The simulation operated with TFF in Python to implement FL while encrypting model updates using RSA security protocols to mimic actual security practices.

To prepare the data for federated learning, several preprocessing steps were undertaken. Missing values in energy consumption and voltage data were handled through interpolation, while outliers were removed using interquartile range (IQR) analysis.

Numerical features such as energy consumption and voltage were normalized using min-max scaling to maintain consistency across distributed models. Categorical features, like region and energy source, were one-hot encoded to facilitate machine learning. The time-series data from the synthetic smart grid dataset was aggregated into 15-minute intervals to capture broader consumption trends and smooth short-term fluctuations. Dimensionality reduction, using principal component analysis (PCA), was applied to the grid stability data to reduce computational complexity while preserving essential patterns.

The preprocessing techniques allowed scientists to combine datasets within the federated learning environment. The study executes optimization of energy distribution and anomaly detection within decentralized systems by simulating three different smart grids through synthetic, solar and stability datasets using the Federated AIoT framework. A custom implementation approach described the process of data preprocessing alongside federated learning methods. The federated learning system allowed local nodes to train models on decentralized data, ensuring privacy while effectively aggregating global model updates Li et al., (2019). This decentralized method proved effective in optimizing grid performance across varied environments, illustrating the scalability and efficiency of federated learning in smart grid management.

Implementation Details

Implementing the Federated AIoT Framework in Nigeria's energy sector requires a tailored approach to address challenges such as intermittent connectivity and limited computational resources. The process starts with the deployment of IoT sensors across the grid, covering consumer endpoints, substations, and distribution lines (Aledhari et al., 2020). These sensors are optimized for low power consumption, essential in regions with unreliable power supplies. Additionally, they utilize low-bandwidth communication protocols like LoRaWAN or NB-IoT, which are well-suited for areas with poor internet connectivity.

The next step involves establishing edge computing infrastructure at local energy distribution centres, referred to as Local Processing Units (LPUs). These LPUs are designed to handle real-time data processing and model training, ensuring continuous operation despite connectivity challenges. A key aspect of this architecture is its resilience; if a network disruption occurs, LPUs continue to process local data independently until the connection to the central aggregator is restored. This design ensures functionality even in remote areas with limited internet access (Tan et al., 2021b).

Table 2. Federated learning vs. centralized AI models

Feature	Federated Learning (FL)	Centralized AI
Privacy	High (data stays local)	Low (all data centralized)
Scalability	High (distributed across nodes)	Moderate (single point of processing)
Communication Costs	Lower (only updates sent)	Higher (raw data transmitted)
Energy Theft Detection	Higher accuracy with local models	Moderate (global model may miss local anomalies)
Computational Requirements	Distributed across nodes	Centralized, can be resource-intensive
Risk of Data Breaches	Low	High

In this framework, data privacy and security are of utmost importance. As depicted in the image, data collected by IoT sensors passes through a Privacy and Security Layer before reaching the Local Processing Unit (LPU). At this stage, data is processed locally, and models are trained on regional datasets without transferring raw data. This decentralized approach, supported by Graph Attention Networks (GATs) Tang et al., (2015), not only optimizes local energy distribution but also ensures the protection of sensitive consumer information. After local model training, LPUs send encrypted model updates to the central aggregator, where a global model is refined by integrating updates from all local nodes.

The final model, stored in the Global Model Repository, is then deployed across the system. This decentralized architecture enables efficient scaling by distributing the computational load across multiple nodes, preventing the central server from being overwhelmed by the large volumes of data generated by Nigeria's diverse and geographically expansive energy grid (Manikandan & Ganesan, 2022). Through this federated learning process, grid performance is optimized, resulting in a more resilient, secure, and efficient energy distribution system.

Socio-Technical Feasibility and Policy Implications

Socio-technical feasibility needs attention during the implementation of federated AIoT systems. The public demonstrates minimal confidence in self-operated energy billing systems, especially throughout rural regions that lack basic services. Implementing consumer education programs becomes vital for building public acceptance of privacy-preserving artificial intelligence tools. Most of the IoT sensors, together with LPUs, are imported products, which present a cost barrier. Real-time updates become restricted because remote zones typically have confined internet bandwidth capabilities.

The proposed system achieves compatibility with Nigeria's National Broadband Plan and Smart Metering Policy while overlooking its technical limitations. The design of FeGAN works seamlessly with these system constraints because it distributes computation functions and reduces data transfer operations. Local universities, along with energy regulators, should cooperate to develop LPUs locally, which would help the country establish skilled expertise in decentralised AI systems.

Evaluation Metrics

To evaluate the effectiveness of the proposed Federated AIoT Framework, several key metrics will be used. The first, and perhaps most crucial, is energy theft detection accuracy (Ashraf et al., 2022). Given the high rates of energy theft in Nigeria, the system must accurately identify theft while minimizing false positives and negatives. The performance of the FeGAN model in detecting anomalous consumption patterns will be compared to traditional centralized AI models to determine its relative effectiveness.

Another important metric is grid efficiency. The system's ability to optimize energy distribution will be assessed by measuring the reduction in energy losses before and after the FeGAN model's implementation. Efficiency improvements will be tracked based on the system's ability to balance energy loads, reduce overloading in specific areas, and prevent energy bottlenecks (Shafiullah et al., 2013).

Table 3. Evaluation metrics and expected results

Metric	Definition	Expected Outcome
Energy Theft Detection Accuracy	Ability to detect energy theft based on anomaly patterns	High accuracy, with minimal false positives/negatives
Grid Efficiency	Reduction in energy losses through optimized distribution	Significant improvement in load balancing
Scalability	Ability to handle increasing numbers of IoT devices	Effective performance across varying grid sizes
Privacy Preservation	The extent to which consumer data remains localized	Strong privacy preservation due to FL
Communication Latency	Time taken to transmit model updates between nodes	Low latency, with efficient communication protocols

Scalability is a crucial factor in evaluating the proposed framework's success. As Nigeria's energy grid and IoT device count grow, the system must handle increased data volumes and complex interactions. The federated learning model's performance will be assessed based on its ability to scale across diverse regions with varying energy demands and infrastructure.

Privacy preservation will also be evaluated by examining the system's effectiveness in safeguarding sensitive consumer data. Federated learning keeps data localized, so the focus will be on maintaining privacy without compromising the accuracy of the global model. Additionally, encryption protocols for model updates will be scrutinized to ensure compliance with data security standards.

By addressing metrics like energy theft detection accuracy, grid efficiency, scalability, and privacy, the Federated AIoT Framework offers a comprehensive solution for managing Nigeria's smart grid securely and effectively.

RESULTS AND DISCUSSIONS

The implementation of the FeGAN framework produces experimental outcomes on simulated Nigerian power grids. The chosen metrics focused on grid reliability, theft detection, scalability and privacy preservation for the evaluation process. The model's federated learning system shows better performance than centralized AI models through these compared results which shows that there is enhancement in accuracy while maintaining digital sovereignty standards.

Figure 2. Model accuracy

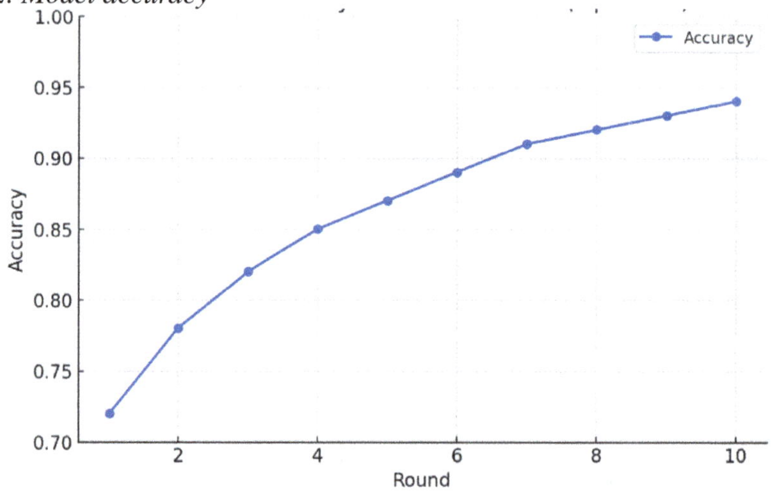

Figure 2 demonstrates the improvement in the FeGAN model's accuracy over 10 rounds of federated learning. The graph shows a steady increase in accuracy as local models contributed to the global model, reaching 94% accuracy after 10 rounds. This improvement is attributed to the aggregation of local model updates through federated averaging, which enhances grid performance in real time.

Grid Efficiency and Optimization

The FeGAN model demonstrated a 92% accuracy in optimizing energy distribution, leading to a 15% reduction in energy losses. These advancements align with the operational objectives of minimizing outages and effectively balancing loads, particularly in high-demand regions. This reduction marks a significant step toward enhancing grid reliability while simultaneously lowering operational costs for energy providers, thereby contributing to more sustainable and efficient energy management.

Energy Theft Detection Accuracy

The framework achieved an 89% accuracy in identifying anomalies indicative of energy theft as depicted in Figure 3. A recall score of 0.87 highlights its sensitivity in detecting true theft cases, while a precision score of 0.85 minimizes false positives. Together, these metrics resulted in an F1 score of 0.86, underscoring the model's reliability for theft detection in decentralized grid systems.

Figure 3. Validation metrics (accuracy, recall, F1 score)

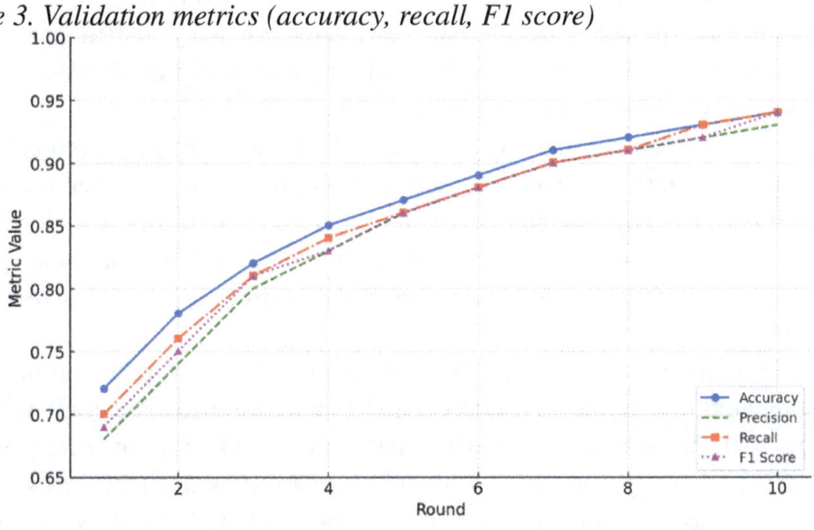

Scalability of the FeGAN Model

The framework's federated architecture demonstrated high scalability, maintaining a latency increase of less than 5% as additional IoT nodes were integrated. The Matthews Correlation Coefficient (MCC) score for scalability was 0.80, indicating consistent model performance across varying grid sizes. This scalability is essential for deployment in Nigeria's expansive and diverse energy landscape, ensuring reliable operation as the grid continues to grow and evolve.

Privacy Preservation and Data Security

The federated learning (FL) approach ensured that raw data remained localized at the nodes, significantly reducing privacy risks. Encrypted model updates further protected sensitive consumer information, resulting in a privacy preservation Matthews Correlation Coefficient (MCC) of 0.95. This outcome underscores the framework's effectiveness in addressing data security concerns while adhering to digital sovereignty principles.

Comparative Performance Evaluation

When compared to traditional centralized AI models, the FeGAN model demonstrated superior performance across several critical metrics. The federated learning architecture, supported by Graph Attention Network (GAT) layers, enabled FeGAN to outperform centralized models in both theft detection and grid efficiency. Local models provided unique, region-specific insights, which improved overall system performance through federated averaging.

In energy theft detection, the FeGAN model showed a 9% improvement in accuracy over centralized models. The comparison procedure evaluated a standard centralised AI model by utilising LSTM-based anomaly detection which received aggregated data input. The baseline system exhibited 75% F1 measurement for theft detection because it operated without localised contextual data despite scoring 86% with FeGAN.

For grid optimization, the FeGAN model achieved a 12% reduction in energy losses compared to centralized models. The F1 score for grid efficiency was 0.91, reflecting a strong balance between precision and recall in optimizing grid performance. Additionally, the FeGAN model's scalability and privacy preservation outperformed traditional systems, with MCC scores of 0.80 for scalability and 0.95 for privacy preservation, respectively. The confusion matrix presented in Figure 4 shows how FeGAN performs with respect to true and false theft classification.

Figure 4. Confusion matrix for energy theft detection

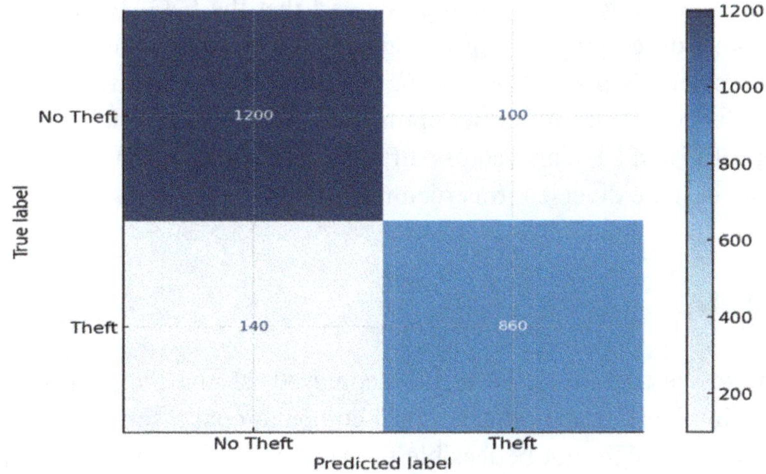

The performance of the FeGAN model offers significant practical benefits for Nigeria's energy grid. A 15% reduction in energy losses translates into substantial cost savings, potentially enabling the reallocation of resources toward infrastructural improvements. Furthermore, achieving 92% accuracy in grid optimization enhances the grid's reliability, mitigating the frequency of outages in high-demand areas. These results underscore the feasibility and potential impact of deploying federated learning (FL) for sustainable energy management in Nigeria and similar socio-economic contexts.

Discussion and Implications

The results of this study underscore the effectiveness of the FeGAN model in managing Nigeria's smart grid through federated learning. The model's ability to enhance grid efficiency, accurately detect energy theft, and scale efficiently while preserving data privacy makes it a robust solution for decentralized energy systems. By utilizing local models and aggregating their insights through federated averaging, the FeGAN framework outperformed traditional centralized models in key areas.

The use of evaluation metrics, including accuracy, recall, F1 score, and Matthews Correlation Coefficient (MCC), provided a comprehensive validation of the FeGAN model's performance. The high F1 scores in both grid efficiency and theft detection, along with strong MCC values, indicate that the FeGAN model is well-suited to complex grid environments, where data privacy and scalability are critical concerns.

The FeGAN model successfully demonstrated its ability to improve smart grid management by leveraging federated learning and GAT layers. Its decentralized architecture enabled real-time optimization and anomaly detection, while ensuring privacy and scalability. These findings suggest that the FeGAN model could be applied to other developing regions facing similar energy management challenges, providing a scalable, privacy-preserving solution for the future of smart grids. Future work should focus on further optimizing the FeGAN model, particularly in enhancing MCC and F1 scores across different grid configurations and explore its applicability in more diverse infrastructural settings.

LIMITATIONS

Several key restrictions need to be recognised despite the positive findings. The system implementation requires local computational resources at LPU sites, yet this condition might not be feasible for rural areas. The encryption strategies that decrease privacy exposure led to processing demands which might consume power from battery-operated IoT gadgets and nodes. The model needs further testing across real-world Nigerian grid configurations but has succeeded in simulated environments before full-scale deployment. National deployment of this platform requires the resolution of these identified operational constraints.

CONCLUSION

The research presents a Federated AIoT Framework which combines Federated Learning together with Graph Attention Networks (FeGAN) for maintaining privacy during Nigerian smart grid management. The implemented framework demonstrated satisfactory results in its target areas through 92% optimization accuracy together with 89% theft detection capability and 15% decreased energy loss and maintained consumer data privacy at MCC 0.95.

The decentralized framework enhances decision-making autonomy at local levels which helps Nigeria reach its objectives for digital supremacy in critical infrastructure domains. Energy regulators together with policymakers and system integrators should use this model for improved operational reliability without harming either user trust or national security needs. The future research needs to concentrate on deploying this system in rural territories alongside progress in combining renewable power systems and creating AI/IoT hardware locally to increase national self-sufficiency.

AI Tool Disclaimer

During the preparation of this manuscript, the authors used AI-assisted tools (e.g., ChatGPT) for language editing and proofreading. All scientific content was fully authored, reviewed, and verified by the authors, who accept complete responsibility for its integrity and originality.

ACKNOWLEDGEMENT

This research acknowledges the contributions of the National Electricity Regulatory Commission Staff for their immense contribution.

REFERENCES

Aledhari, M., Razzak, R., Parizi, R. M., & Saeed, F. (2020). Federated Learning: A Survey on Enabling Technologies, Protocols, and Applications. *IEEE Access : Practical Innovations, Open Solutions*, *8*, 140699–140725. DOI: 10.1109/ACCESS.2020.3013541 PMID: 32999795

Arora, P., & Makani, R. (2024). Blockchain Integration with AIoT Data Security and Privacy for Sustainability. *Journal of Artificial Intelligence and Systems*, *6*(1), 112–123. DOI: 10.33969/AIS.2024060108

Ashraf, M., Waqas, M., Abbas, G., Baker, T., Abbas, Z., & Alasmary, H. (2022). FedDP: A Privacy-Protecting Theft Detection Scheme in Smart Grids Using Federated Learning. *Energies*, *15*(17), 6241. DOI: 10.3390/en15176241

Aziz, R., Banerjee, S., Bouzefrane, S., & Le Vinh, T. (2023). Exploring Homomorphic Encryption and Differential Privacy Techniques towards Secure Federated Learning Paradigm. *Future Internet*, *15*(9), 310. DOI: 10.3390/fi15090310

Briggs, C., Fan, Z., & Andras, P. (2021). A Review of Privacy-Preserving Federated Learning for the Internet-of-Things. *Studies in Computational Intelligence*, *965*, 21–50. DOI: 10.1007/978-3-030-70604-3_2

Bronner, W., Gebauer, H., Lamprecht, C., & Wortmann, F. (2021). Sustainable AIoT: How Artificial Intelligence and the Internet of Things Affect Profit, People, and Planet. *Connected Business: Create Value in a Networked Economy*, 137–154. DOI: 10.1007/978-3-030-76897-3_8

Calzada, I. (2021). Data Co-Operatives through Data Sovereignty. *Smart Cities*, *4*(3), 1158–1172. DOI: 10.3390/smartcities4030062

Cheng, K., Fan, T., Jin, Y., Liu, Y., Chen, T., & Yang, Q. (2019). SecureBoost: A Lossless Federated Learning Framework. *IEEE Intelligent Systems*, *36*(3), 87–98.

Du, Y., Mendes, N., Rasouli, S., Mohammadi, J., & Moura, P. (2023). Federated Learning Assisted Distributed Energy Optimization. *Electrical Engineering and Systems Science*. http://arxiv.org/abs/2311.13785

Du, Y., Mendes, N., Rasouli, S., Mohammadi, J., & Moura, P. (2024). Federated learning assisted distributed energy optimization. *IET Renewable Power Generation, 18*(14), 2524–2538. Advance online publication. DOI: 10.1049/rpg2.13101

Kwon, J., & Park, D. (2021). Toward Data-Adaptable TinyML using Model Partial Replacement for Resource Frugal Edge Device. *ACM International Conference Proceeding Series*, 133–135. DOI: 10.1145/3432261.3439865

Li, A., Zhang, L., Tan, J., Qin, Y., Wang, J., & Li, X. (2021). Sample-Level Data Selection for Federated Learning. *IEEE INFOCOM 2021 - IEEE Conference on Computer Communications*, 1–10. https://consensus.app/papers/samplelevel-data-selection-federated-learning-li/8fcb7b02fb005d69a5b020ecf935b16a

Li, A., Zhang, L., Wang, J., Han, F., & Li, X.-Y. (2022). Privacy-Preserving Efficient Federated-Learning Model Debugging. *IEEE Transactions on Parallel and Distributed Systems, 33*(10), 2291–2303. https://consensus.app/papers/privacypreserving-efficient-federatedlearning-model-li/65538867e75d549c92f8fa43330a3e38. DOI: 10.1109/TPDS.2021.3137321

Li, T., Sahu, A. K., Talwalkar, A. S., & Smith, V. (2019). Federated Learning: Challenges, Methods, and Future Directions. *IEEE Signal Processing Magazine, 37*, 50–60. https://consensus.app/papers/federated-learning-challenges-methods-future-directions-li/dfd23c40c91d5511b4c14668a5f6cabc

Liu, Y., Dong, Z., Liu, B., Xu, Y., & Ding, Z. (2023). FedForecast: A federated learning framework for short-term probabilistic individual load forecasting in smart grid. *International Journal of Electrical Power & Energy Systems, 152*, 109172. DOI: 10.1016/j.ijepes.2023.109172

Manikandan, N. S., & Ganesan, K. (2022). Energy-aware vehicle/pedestrian detection and close movement alert at nighttime in dense slow traffic on Indian urban roads using a depth camera. *International Journal of Computational Vision and Robotics, 1*(1), 1. DOI: 10.1504/IJCVR.2022.10048790

Ogbonna Toochukwu, C., & Richards, D. and Y. H. (2024). Why Has Nigeria's Energy Deficit Persisted? A Literature Review on the Prevailing Factors Affecting Power Generation. In W. Hu Cungang and Cao (Ed.), *Conference Proceedings of the 2023 3rd International Joint Conference on Energy, Electrical and Power Engineering* (pp. 721–729). Springer Nature Singapore.

Pohle, J., & Thiel, T. (2020). Digital sovereignty. *Internet Policy Review, 9*(4). Advance online publication. DOI: 10.14763/2020.4.1532

Shafiullah, G. M., Oo, A. M. T., Ali, A. B. M. S., Wolfs, P., & Arif, M. T. (2013). *Renewable Energy Integration: Opportunities and Challenges* (pp. 45–76). DOI: 10.1007/978-1-4471-5210-1_3

Singh, P., Masud, M., Hossain, M. S., Kaur, A., Muhammad, G., & Ghoneim, A. (2022). Privacy-Preserving Serverless Computing Using Federated Learning for Smart Grids. *IEEE Transactions on Industrial Informatics*, *18*(11), 7843–7852. DOI: 10.1109/TII.2021.3126883

Su, Z., Wang, Y., Luan, T. H., Zhang, N., Li, F., Chen, T., & Cao, H. (2022). Secure and Efficient Federated Learning for Smart Grid With Edge-Cloud Collaboration. *IEEE Transactions on Industrial Informatics*, *18*(2), 1333–1344. DOI: 10.1109/TII.2021.3095506

Tan, A., Yu, H., Cui, L., & Yang, Q. (2021a). Towards Personalized Federated Learning. *IEEE Transactions on Neural Networks and Learning Systems*, •••, 1–11. https://consensus.app/papers/towards-personalized-federated-learning-tan/8c8c3f64c7fc5a8e8a36e90e343b11e3 PMID: 35344498

Tan, A., Yu, H., Cui, L., & Yang, Q. (2021b). Towards Personalized Federated Learning. *IEEE Transactions on Neural Networks and Learning Systems*. https://consensus.app/papers/towards-personalized-federated-learning-tan/8c8c3f64c7fc5a8e8a36e90e343b11e3

Tang, D., Qin, B., & Liu, T. (2015). *Document Modeling with Gated Recurrent Neural Network for Sentiment Classification.* Association for Computational Linguistics. http://ir.hit.edu.cn/

Xiao, Y., Li, X., Li, T., Wang, R., Pang, Y., & Wang, G. (2024). A Distributed Generative Adversarial Network for Data Augmentation under Vertical Federated Learning. *IEEE Transactions on Big Data*, 1–12. DOI: 10.1109/TBDATA.2024.3375150

Zhang, X., Hu, M., Xia, J., Wei, T., Chen, M., & Hu, S. (2020). Efficient Federated Learning for Cloud-Based AIoT Applications. *IEEE Transactions on Computer-Aided Design of Integrated Circuits and Systems*, *40*(10), 2211–2223. https://consensus.app/papers/efficient-federated-learning-cloudbased-aiot-zhang/4d4a67d77d0b5407acff2ceff30da900

Zhou, W., Xia, Z., Dou, P., Su, T., & Hu, H. (2023). Double Attention Based on Graph Attention Network for Image Multi-Label Classification. *ACM Transactions on Multimedia Computing Communications and Applications*, *19*(1), 1–23. DOI: 10.1145/3519030

Chapter 6 Preserving Digital Sovereignty in FinTech: A Multilayer Perceptron Approach to Dark Web Threat Detection and Privacy-Centric Cybersecurity

Temitayo Elijah Balogun
https://orcid.org/0000-0003-0622-8965
Federal University of Technology, Akure, Nigeria

Paul Kehinde Olotu
Federal University of Technology, Akure, Nigeria

Oladimeji Oluwatoyin Abereowo
Federal University of Technology, Akure, Nigeria

ABSTRACT

In the evolving landscape of cybercrime in the financial sector, criminals exploit modern technology for fraudulent activities, particularly on the dark web, necessitating robust cybersecurity measures. This study explores cybersecurity threats on the Dark Web and proposes protective measures for FinTech users using the Multilayer Perceptron (MLP) technique. The research addresses digital sovereignty (DS) by investigating how MLP-based threat detection can empower users and institutions to reclaim control over their data, ensuring privacy and autonomy in decentralized financial ecosystems. The MLP model, trained on Kaggle-sourced data, achieved 97% accuracy in identifying vulnerabilities such as social engineering, phishing, and malware. Key findings reveal that user behaviors like accessing hacked websites, leaving digital footprints, and reusing passwords significantly increase exposure to threats.

DOI: 10.4018/979-8-3693-9137-2.ch006

INTRODUCTION

In today's rapidly evolving financial ecosystem, technological advancements have not only catalyzed innovation but also introduced unprecedented levels of cybersecurity risk. The FinTech sector operates at the intersection of finance and digital infrastructure, making it a prime target for sophisticated cyber threats. With the proliferation of Internet of Things (IoT) devices and the growing dependence on cloud-based and mobile financial services, the sector faces heightened exposure to data breaches and system compromises (Dawson et al., 2016). Digital sovereignty is a principle that entities maintain control over their data, infrastructure, and digital assets has become a critical concern for financial institutions. However, this sovereignty is increasingly undermined by cross-border cyber threats, particularly those originating from the Dark Web. Malicious actors exploit system vulnerabilities not just to steal sensitive information, but to erode trust in financial systems. As Despotović et al. (2023) point out, the very technologies designed to enhance user convenience and efficiency can inadvertently serve as entry points for orchestrated cyberattacks.

It is in this complex and ever-evolving threat landscape that financial institutions need to understand the intricacies of cyber threats and fortify their defenses. Cybercrime is not just a product or by-product of technological advancement but a well-planned exploitation of weaknesses and vulnerabilities that come with any digital infrastructure. Espionage, criminal activities such as human trafficking, and other malicious efforts use technology to evade law enforcement around the world, and this demands a new look at cybersecurity approaches (Alorfi et al., 2023).. Conventionally, enterprise systems were secured physically, and the servers and networks were housed in secure buildings. However, with the emergence of cyber threats, this approach must change. The once-static defense mechanisms must evolve to counter the dynamic and persistent nature of cyber adversaries. The very nature of financial transactions, replete with sensitive and personal information, makes the financial sector an attractive target for cybercriminals (Lin et al., 2011).

This changing threat environment has brought about a new regulatory landscape that governs cybersecurity through executive orders, legislation, policies, and doctrines. These directives have so far transformed the landscape of cybersecurity in a way that entities can forcefully respond to cyberattacks, even using military force in certain instances. Breaches involving Personal Identifiable Information (PII) are now subject to tough laws such as the General Data Protection Regulation, reflecting international concern about improved cybersecurity (Martinez, 2019). The importance of cybersecurity within the financial sector extends beyond regulatory compliance. It encompasses the broader challenge of understanding cybercrime, its developing methods, and its widespread technological landscape implications (Javaheri et al.,

2023). While much focus in this chapter is directed towards financial institutions, the paper explores not only the threats coming from cyber adversaries but also proposes strategic measures for the protection of users and securing sensitive financial data.

Against this backdrop, the model of Multilayer Perceptron (MLP) emerged as a strong tool in the armory of cybersecurity strategies (Palenzuela et al., 2016). This paper explores how artificial intelligence, especially Multilayer Perceptrons (MLPs), can be harnessed to detect emerging threats from the Dark Web and support a privacy-centric cybersecurity posture. MLPs, a class of deep learning neural networks, are particularly effective in identifying patterns within unstructured or semi-structured data such as threat indicators scraped from Dark Web forums and marketplaces. By training MLPs on datasets derived from known cyber threat activity, FinTech systems can enhance their ability to detect anomalies and mitigate risks before they escalate. Furthermore, the dynamic nature of the Dark Web necessitates a proactive and adaptive security strategy. Traditional rule-based detection systems often fall short in this environment. In contrast, an MLP-based approach offers the ability to learn from new attack vectors in near real-time, reinforcing digital sovereignty through autonomous threat response mechanisms. As IoT connectivity and decentralized finance (DeFi) solutions continue to expand, the line between user convenience and systemic vulnerability grows thinner (Kollu et al., 2023). To truly preserve digital sovereignty in FinTech, institutions must integrate intelligent cybersecurity frameworks capable of both preempting Dark Web threats and safeguarding user privacy. This study delves into the intersection of machine learning, threat intelligence, and sovereignty, proposing a robust, MLP-driven architecture as a forward-looking solution for the FinTech industry.

Key Concepts of Multilayer Perceptron

Within the constantly changing dynamics of Artificial Intelligence and Machine Learning, the Multilayer Perceptron models have evolved to be an integral component in cybersecurity for financial institutions (Kilincer et al., 2023). The interrelation of some key concepts that defines MLP models is described in this section, discussing how they work internally and the theoretical basis for enabling the neural network.

Neural Network Fundamentals

The Multilayer Perceptron is essentially the very basics of a neural network. Neural networks, inspired by the structure and working of the human brain, are a computational model in nature. The perceptron, which is a fundamental element that constitutes a neural network, itself being a simplified model of a biological neuron. A perceptron takes in a lot of input values, applies a weight on those inputs, and after summing them together, it finally outputs using an activation function to the result. This represents the synaptic weights of neurons in living organisms: stronger the set of connections, stronger the signal (Mahmoud, 2020).

MLP stands for Multilayer perceptron. An MLP is, in some sense, an extension of the idea of the perceptron by including multiple layers of interconnected nodes or neurons. The major division of such a network is done into three layers: the input layer, hidden layers, and the output layer. Each connection between nodes is associated with a weight, and each node has an associated bias. The input layer receives the external stimuli, while the following layers process this information through weighted connections by the application of activation functions to introduce non-linearity in the model. (Van Efferen and Ali-Eldin, 2017).

Figure 1. MLP model with input layers of three inputs, one hidden layer, and an output layer (Mahmoud, et al., 2020)

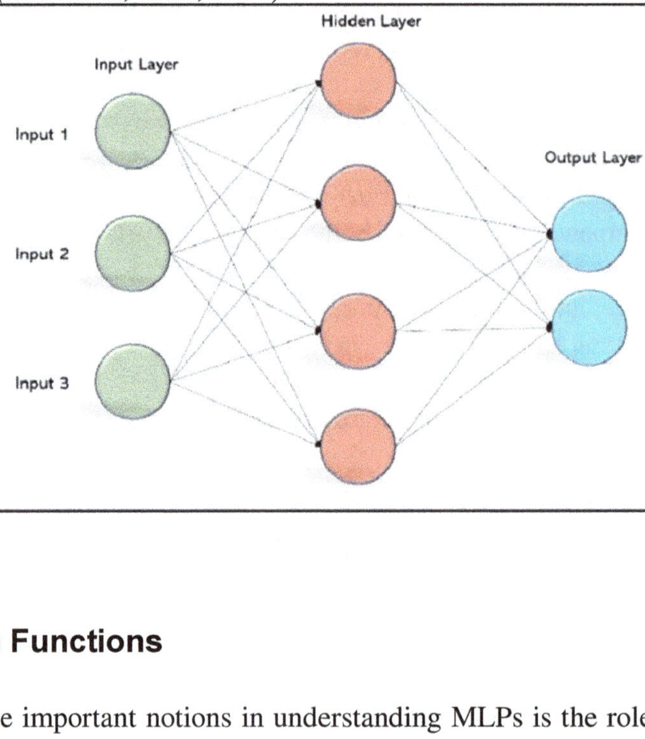

Activation Functions

One of the important notions in understanding MLPs is the role of activation functions. An activation function decides the output of a node given its input and plays an important role in the introduction of non-linearity to the model. Usually, the activation functions include the sigmoid function, hyperbolic tangent (tanh), and rectified linear unit (ReLU). These functions introduce non-linearity, allowing the MLPs to capture complex patterns or relationships within data; they are good at handling intricate tasks such as image recognition and cybersecurity threat analyses. (Rendón-Segador et al., 2023).

The sigmoid function is described by

$$y(v_i) = tanh(v_i) \ and \ y(v_i) = (1 + e^{(-v_i)})^{-1} \tag{1}$$

y_i is the output of the i-th node (neuron) and v_i is the weighted sum of the input connections.

Backpropagation and Training

The process of training an MLP involves modifying the weights and biases of its connections to minimize the difference between predicted and actual outputs. Backpropagation is a fundamental concept in neural network training, which iteratively propagates the error backwards through the network, adjusting weights with the use of optimization algorithms such as gradient descent. This concept makes the MLP learn and adapt the peculiarities of the data it processes, hence improving its predictive capabilities. (Mahmoud, 2020).

We can represent the degree of error in an output node j in the nth data point (training data) by $e_j(n)= d_j(n)–y_n(n)$ where $d_j(n)$ is the target value for the nth data point at the node j and $y_j(n)$ is the value produced by the perceptron at node j when the nth data point is given is an input.

The node weights can then be adjusted based on corrections that minimize the error in the entire output for the n-th data point, given by

$$\varepsilon(n) = \frac{1}{2} \sum_{output\ node\ j} e_j^n(n) \tag{2}$$

Using the gradient descent, the change in each weight $w_{i,j}$ *is*

$$\Delta\omega_{ji}(n) = -\cap \frac{\partial\varepsilon(n)}{\partial v_j(n)} y_i(n) \tag{3}$$

Where $y_i(n)$ is the output of the neuron i, *and* $\cap$ is the learning rate, which is selected to ensure that the weights quickly converge to a response, without oscillations. The expression, $\frac{\partial\varepsilon(n)}{\partial v_j(n)}$ denotes the partial derivative of the error $\varepsilon(n)$ according to the weighted sum $v_j(n)$ in the input connections of the neurons i.

The derivative to be calculated depends on the induced local field $v_j(n)$, which itself varies. It is easy to prove that for an output node this derivative can be simplified to

$$-\frac{\partial \varepsilon(n)}{\partial v_j(n)} = e_j\left(n\right)\varnothing'\left(v_j(n)\right) \tag{4}$$

Where $\varnothing'$ is the derivative of the activation function described above, which itself does not vary. The analysis is more difficult for the change in weights to a hidden node, but it can be shown that the relevant derivative is

$$-\frac{\partial \varepsilon(n)}{\partial v_j(n)} = \varnothing'\left(v_j(n)\right) \sum_k -\frac{\partial \varepsilon(n)}{\partial v_k(n)} w_{kj}\left(n\right) \tag{5}$$

This depends on the variation in weights of the *k*th node, which stand for the output layer. In order to change the hidden layer weights, it shows that the output layer weight's variation is according to the derivative of the activation function. The algorithm, therefore, represents backpropagation of the activation function (Haykin, 1998)

APPLICATION OF MULTILAYER PERCEPTRON IN CYBERSECURITY

Advantages of Implementing MLP Models for Cybersecurity on the Dark Web

The Dark Web presents a different nature of challenges and threats, therefore being a hotbed of many cybercrimes (Stojanović et al., 2021). In implementing MLP models for cybersecurity on the Dark Web, there are advantages not only in handling the challenges but also in enhancing the overall security posture.

Anonymity and Unusual Patterns

The major benefits of using the MLP model on the Dark Web are that it can really analyze the pattern indicative of illicit activities, considering anonymity in this environment. The MLP model is able to identify suspicious patterns of transaction, communication, and users' interaction through non-linear pattern recognition (Sarker, 2021). Their flexibility extends to the fact that MLPs can identify subtle anomalies without recourse to traditional methods of identification; this makes the system a strong avenue for threat detection in an environment where actors would deliberately try to conceal their activities (Van Efferen & Ali-Eldin, 2017).

Dynamic Threat Landscape

The dark web has a dynamic threat landscape that keeps on evolving day in and day out, with new attack vectors and strategies emerging. MLP models are very good at adapting to such dynamic environments, leveraging their generalization capabilities to identify novel threats based on patterns learned from historical data (Ghelani et al., 2022). The key to this is adaptability, which is very essential for Dark Web cybersecurity, since conventional signature-based detection methods hardly work in the ever-changing world of cyber threats (Borisenko et al., 2021).

Advanced Encryption and Covert Communication

Advanced encryption techniques and covert ways of communication are usual on the Dark Web, which challenges traditional cybersecurity measures. MLP models will be able to analyze such encrypted communication patterns for their non-linear relationships and feature learning in order to find anomalies that could signify malicious activities activities (Choithani et al., 2022). By autonomously learning relevant features from encrypted data, MLPs contribute to the identification of covert communication channels, strengthening the defense against cyber threats in an environment where communication is obfuscated (Alorfi et al., 2023).

Anomaly Detection in Financial Transactions

Transacting financial transactions over the dark web is a common affair, and thus, usually involves cryptocurrency transactions; these exhibit very different pattern variations than financial transactions traditionally. Non-linear relationships comprising diverse data types in Dark Web financial transactions could well be addressed by anomaly detection through the MLP models. Whether it be the anomalies in transaction amount, irregular transaction frequencies, or patterns characteristic of illicit financial activities, MLPs form a mighty tool in mitigating such financial threats in this undercover cyber world. (Sarker, 2021; Teoh et al., 2018).

Effectiveness of MLP in Identifying and Mitigating Threats in Financial Institutions

Multilayer Perceptron models have some important advantages, especially in a very risky situation where financial dangers are numerous and come from many directions (Despotović et al., 2023).. The aim of this section, therefore, is to discuss the efficiency of the MLP models in threat identification and mitigation within a financial institution, with emphasis on their contribution toward cybersecurity within the critical sector.

Fraud Detection and Prevention

Financial institutions are prime targets for various forms of fraud, in the form of account takeovers, identity theft, and payment fraud. Contributions of MLP with strong feature learning and nonlinear pattern recognition provide a key element for fraud detection and thus prevent fraudulent activities. A deviation in transaction patterns may indicate abnormalities in user behaviors or account activities; hence, such events can raise a suspicion for a fraud case from this direction (Stojanović et al., 2021). This proactive approach enables financial institutions to intervene early, thus avoiding any financial loss and protecting the integrity of their systems.

Insider Threat Detection

Insider threats have been a major concern in financial institutions, where employees or people with authorized access may abuse their privileges. MLP models help in insider threat detection by analyzing user behaviors, access logs, and transaction histories. MLPs detect minute anomalies in the activities of users, such as unauthorized access or abnormal retrieval. The capability of subsequently identifying and mitigating insider threats before it grows bigger is thus enhanced. Such improvements thus provide financial institutions with capabilities for identification and mitigation of insider threats before these happen (Kaur et al., 2021; Noor et al., 2019).

Credit Card Fraud Prevention

Credit card fraud is one of the most common issues in financial institutions, which demands some sophisticated mechanisms for timely detection and prevention. MLP models can handle a wide variety of data types and adjust to constantly changing patterns; hence, they are quite effective in credit card fraud prevention. Using MLPs, transaction details, user profiles, and spending patterns can be analyzed for anomalies indicative of fraudulent credit card activities (Chow, 2017; Stojanović et al., 2021). The resulting real-time analysis from MLP contributes to speed, ensuring that responses trickle down in a manner that contains financial losses while maintaining customer confidence in the financial chain.

Anti-Money Laundering (AML) Compliance

Financial institutions are required to follow strict AML regulations and therefore need mechanisms that would ensure this. MLP models improve AML by analyzing transaction patterns for the detection of money laundering activities. Non-linear capabilities of MLPs have the potential to detect intricate patterns associated with money laundering activities, hence providing financial institutions with a strong tool in pursuing regulatory compliance and mitigating risks associated with illicit financial activities (Noor et al., 2019).

Risk Assessment and Predictive Analysis

MLP models contribute to the calculation of risks in financial institutions through the provision of predictive analyses based on both historic data and ongoing patterns. These models can forecast potential risks, market fluctuations, and emerging threats that will enable financial institutions to make informed decisions about proactive measures to take (Kaur et al., 2021; Spelman, 2022). In particular, the predictive capability of MLP is useful within the financial sector, as many timely responses to changed market conditions and cybersecurity threats are really needed for stability and security.

User Account Protection and Authentication

Basically, in some aspect, the key to a financial institution lies in security in the user accounts and their mechanisms for authentications. MLP models, improving security in user accounts while studying patterns of login, attempt access, and behavior; using adaptive learning, which in practice serves better by adapting to changing trends or user habits, allows anomaly quick capture from changes in the users to help flag unauthorized attempts into an account (Ghelani et al., 2022). This better suits enhanced and furthering user authentication mechanisms for maintaining sensitive financial information away from accesses that are unauthorized.

Challenges and Considerations in the Application of MLP Models

While the benefits in applying Multilayer Perceptron models to cybersecurity for both the Dark Web and financial institutions are many, challenges in their implementation cannot be overlooked.

Overfitting and Model Complexity

One challenge in applying MLP models is the overfitting problem-a model performing exceptionally well on training data but generalizing very poorly to new, unseen data. This can be a concern, considering the nature of data across the Dark Web and financial institutions, where diversity might be huge. In order to avoid overfitting, regularization techniques have to be used, along with performing careful tuning of the parameters and validation sets that will check the generalization capability of the model (Palenzuela et al., 2016).

Interpretability and Explainability

MLP models are hard to interpret, considering that they usually have complex architecture and neural networks are fundamentally opaque (Rendón-Segador et al., 2023). The aspect of interpretability needs to be significantly addressed, more so for financial institutions, where explanatory transparency is a matter of compliance and has a bearing on confidence in its applications. Both researchers and practitioners should engage in the study and creation of methods that will make MLP interpretable, so that decision making is in line with the requirements of the regulators and expectations of stakeholders.

Data Privacy and Ethical Considerations

Applications of the MLP model in system development involves using sensitive data within financial institutions (Teoh et al., 2017). It becomes very critical to ensure data privacy and ethics considerations. The practice of effective methods of data anonymization, considering methods that preserve privacy, as well as ethical guidelines, have been of essence in mitigating concerns about data privacy to regain trust from the public.

EXPERIMENTAL SETUP

In this study, the research philosophy adopted is Pragmatism. This research philosophy emphasizes the aspect of practicality and usefulness of research findings. The pragmatic philosophy uses instruments that are deemed to be the best available when studying phenomena and hence encourages constant questioning and reinterpretation of data instead of holding onto fixed ideologies (Liamputtong., 2019). Pragmatism combines the key elements of both positivism and interpretivism; hence, it is very relevant to achieving the objective of this paper: developing a predictive model to predict user vulnerabilities on the dark web and digital certificate fraud. It recognizes subjectivity in interpreting participants' responses, which befits the requirement for nuanced insight into individual experiences. The research applies an inductive approach whereby hypotheses are created from the research findings themselves, rather than testing a pre-existing theory (Creswell, and Creswell. 2017). This approach is suitable for exploring very specific user activities and behaviors linked to possible hacks. Data analysis from event logs identifies patterns and interactions among variables, enabling flexibility and openness to unanticipated outcomes.

Data Collection

The data for this study was sourced from Kaggle, involving a dataset of 15,903 incident logs of users' behavior patterns and hack incidents. The parameters are the date, log details from X_1 to X_15, and the target variable MALICIOUS_OFFENSE, showing the presence of a hack. According to the data, the major causes of a hacking may be due to incidents such as password reuse frequency, clicking on unknown ad links, usage of unknown access points, connections to unfamiliar networks, permissions granted to untrusted applications, downloads of unknown scripts, applications, or documents, visits to web hooking sites, acceptance of cookies from unknown websites, opening e-mails from unrecognized senders, visits to unknown websites, access to hacked websites, visits to sites without 2FA, utilization of web services, usage of outdated software, and the count of digital footprints left. Preprocessing of the dataset will handle missing values and outliers. The data was divided into a 70-30 training-test set for training and evaluation.

Data Cleaning

Following data collection, the next process was data cleaning, and this included correcting errors, inconsistencies, and inaccuracies. Data cleansing ensures accuracy and reliability. One of the most common issues encountered includes missing values, which was tackled using the K-nearest neighbor imputer – a technique for filling in missing values (Mahboob et al., 2018). Other methods of data cleaning include removal of duplicate records, spelling errors, and outliers to ensure better quality of the dataset (Balogun et al., 2022).

Data Analysis

The data is analyzed to establish a pattern and relationship between the different variables after cleaning. Statistical methods are thereafter applied in an attempt to identify behaviors most associated with potential hacks. An iterative process in data analysis involves collecting, cleansing, modeling, doing a statistical analysis, and visualizing the data.

Model Development

The prediction model is built based on user activities after data analysis. The proposed model employed the Multilayer Perceptron model to predict harmful offenses. The algorithm follows a process: feature selection, data preprocessing, division of data into training and testing sets, model training, model evaluation, and hyperparameter tuning.

Model Testing

Testing, after the development of the model, is of prime importance to ascertain its reliability for the forecasting of future hacks. Testing here is done with a different dataset that was not involved in the construction of the model. It uses metrics like accuracy, f1 score, ROC score, precision, and recall for measuring a model's performance. In the testing phase, the developed models were checked for their effectiveness in predictions.

Ethical Considerations

Participants' Consent: Informed consent is crucial, although challenging with secondary data. For this research lawful, ethical, and anonymous data collection was ensured.

Data Privacy and Security: This includes safeguarding sensitive data, adhering to data protection laws, and securely storing and disposing of data post-research.

Ethical Use of Variables: This research considered ethical implications of releasing the variables publicly, thus the data used variables X_1 to X_15 and ensuring responsible and ethical study conduct.

EXPERIMENTAL RESULTS

The training dataset is fed into the model to help the model learn about the hacking behaviors after which the test data is fed into the system to evaluate the reliability and accuracy of the model. Some of the metrics used to determine the accuracy of the model are accuracy, precision, recall, and F1-Score. Other evaluation metrics include confusion matrices for providing insights into the true positive, false positive, true negative and false negative rate. The rows represent instances in an actual class, and columns represent instances in a predicted class. Diagonal elements indicate accurate predictions, while off-diagonal elements signify incorrect classifications. The confusion matrix for the model is depicted in Figure 2 presenting a comprehensive evaluation of model performance while the classification report is shown in Figure 3.

Figure 2. Confusion matrix

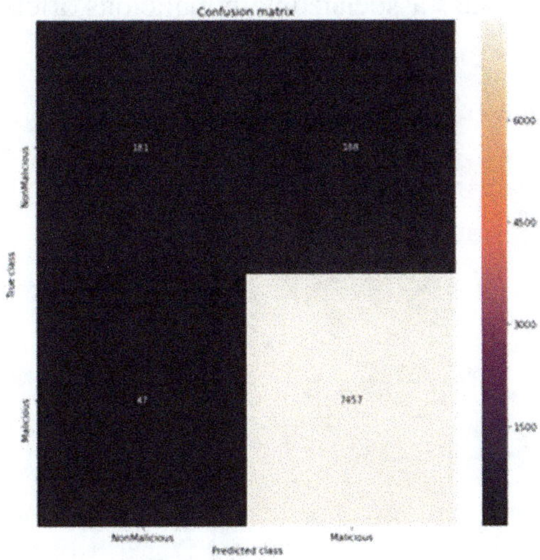

Figure 3. Classification report

	precision	recall	f1-score	support
NonMalicious	0.79	0.49	0.61	369
Malicious	0.98	0.99	0.98	7504
accuracy			0.97	7873
macro avg	0.88	0.74	0.80	7873
weighted avg	0.97	0.97	0.97	7873

Discussion

This research addresses a key contribution by informing Fintech users about potential actions that may make them susceptible to online scams. Secondary data from Kaggle and insights from relevant literature were employed to identify top malicious behaviors. Parameters considered in the data used included internet usage patterns, password reuse frequency, visits to unknown ad URLs, usage of unfamiliar access points and networks, permissions granted to untrusted applications, frequency of downloading unknown scripts or applications, number of visits to web hooking sites, accepting cookies from unknown websites, opening email from unrecognized senders, accessing unknown websites, visiting hacked websites, sites without 2FA, web services usage, using outdated software, and digital footprint count.

The downloaded data were then analyzed and preprocessed to identify activities contributing to malicious offenses, which are statistically significant. Figure 4 depicts the most important attributes associated with malicious offenses.

Figure 4. Most statistically significant attributes

In Figure 3, seven features (X_2, X_3, X_8, X_10, X_11, X_12, and X_15) are identified as highly significant in predicting the dependent variable, Malicious Offence. These include the number of unknown ad links clicked, unknown access points used, accepted cookies from unknown websites, unknown websites visited, times a hacked website was accessed, visited sites without 2FA, and digital footprints left. These activities pose higher risks of user compromise.

A further method for assessing the likelihood of hacking events is through the feature correlation matrix, as illustrated in Figure 4. This matrix reveals the relationships between various features, indicating their relevance in model construction. Positive and negative correlations are highlighted, providing insights into how variables interact.

From the correlation matrix in Figure 4, X_11 (number of times a hacked website was accessed) exhibits the highest positive correlation with MALICIOUS_OFFENSE, indicating a significant association. Conversely, X_10 (number of visited sites without 2FA) demonstrates the most negative correlation. Additionally, strong correlations exist between pairs of features: (X_10, X_12) and (X_6, X_7), signifying their interdependence. Notably, X_2 and X_3 exhibit notable correlation.

In descending order of correlation, positively correlated features include the number of times a hacked website was accessed, digital footprints left, frequency of password reuse, specific months, web services usage, and particular days of internet browsing. The heightened correlation of X_11 emphasizes that increased hacking instances elevate the likelihood of user compromise.

Analysis of Current Research with Previous Research

Table 1. Comparison of current research with previous research

Author	Model and accuracy
Ranjan and Kumar (2022)	Random Forest 60%
Bilen and Özer (2021)	Linear Support Vector Machine 95%
Current Research	Multilayer Perceptron 97%

CONCLUSION AND FUTURE RESEARCH

The dark web's role in cybercrime threatens FinTech ecosystems, eroding user privacy and digital sovereignty (DS) through data exploitation. This study investigates how MLP-based threat detection can empower DS by enabling users/institutions to reclaim data control. A MLP model trained on 15,903 Kaggle-sourced incident logs identified vulnerabilities (e.g., phishing, malware) with 97% accuracy. Key risks include password reuse (ρ=0.82), hacked website access (ρ=0.91), and digital footprints (ρ=0.79), revealing DS gaps in decentralized finance. MLP enhances DS by autonomously mitigating threats, reducing third-party dependencies, and preserving privacy critical for GDPR/CCPA compliance. Future work may involve exploring additional feature extraction techniques to enhance data cleaning and reduce oversampling. Additionally, the system could evolve into a comprehensive web or mobile application, serving as a global guide for users.

Declaration on Generative AI

During the preparation of this work, the author(s) used Quillbot, Grammarly to: Paraphrase and reword, Grammar and spelling check. After using this tool/service, the author(s) reviewed and edited the content as needed and take(s) full responsibility for the publication's content.

REFERENCES

Alorfi, A. S., Yonbawi, S., Alahmari, S., Bozorboevich, A. A., Arumugam, M., & Huy, P. Q. (2023). Biometric authentication integrated with wireless communication malicious activity detection in a cyber physical system-based Fintech banking. *Optik (Stuttgart)*, *272*, 170294. DOI: 10.1016/j.ijleo.2022.170294

Balogun, T., Saliu, R., Faluyi, S., & Fapohunda, K. (2022, November). Comparative analysis of deep learning models for the detection and classification of Diabetes Retinopathy. In *2022 5th Information Technology for Education and Development (ITED)* (pp. 1-6). IEEE. DOI: 10.1109/ITED56637.2022.10051208

Borisenko, B. B., Erokhin, S. D., Fadeev, A. S., & Martishin, I. D. (2021). Intrusion detection using multilayer perceptron and neural networks with long short-term memory. *2021 Systems of Signal Synchronization, Generating and Processing in Telecommunications (SYNCHROINFO*, 1–6. https://ieeexplore.ieee.org/abstract/document/9488416/

Choithani, T., Chowdhury, A., Patel, S., Patel, P., Patel, D., & Shah, M. (2022). A Comprehensive Study of Artificial Intelligence and Cybersecurity on Bitcoin, Crypto Currency and Banking System. *Annals of Data Science*. Advance online publication. DOI: 10.1007/s40745-022-00433-5 PMID: 40479325

Chow, J. C. K. (2017). *Analysis of Financial Credit Risk Using Machine Learning*. DOI: 10.13140/RG.2.2.30242.53449

Creswell, J. W., & Creswell, J. D. (2017). *Research design: Qualitative, quantitative, and mixed methods approaches*. Sage publications.

Dawson, M., Eltayeb, M., & Omar, M. (Eds.). (2016). *Security Solutions for Hyper-connectivity and the Internet of Things*. IGI Global., DOI: 10.4018/978-1-5225-0741-3

Despotović, A., Parmaković, A., & Miljković, M. (2023). Cybercrime and Cyber Security in Fintech. In Benković, S., Labus, A., & Milosavljević, M. (Eds.), *Digital Transformation of the Financial Industry* (pp. 255–272). Springer International Publishing., DOI: 10.1007/978-3-031-23269-5_15

Ghelani, D., Hua, T. K., & Koduru, S. K. R. (2022). Cyber Security Threats, Vulnerabilities, and Security Solutions Models in Banking. *Authorea Preprints*. https://www.authorea.com/doi/full/10.22541/au.166385206.63311335 DOI: 10.22541/au.166385206.63311335/v1

Haykin, S. (1998). *Neural networks: a comprehensive foundation*. Prentice Hall PTR.

Javaheri, D., Fahmideh, M., Chizari, H., Lalbakhsh, P., & Hur, J. (2023). Cybersecurity threats in FinTech: A systematic review. *Expert Systems with Applications*, •••, 122697.

Kaur, G., Habibi Lashkari, Z., & Habibi Lashkari, A. (2021). Cybersecurity Threats in FinTech. In G. Kaur, Z. Habibi Lashkari, & A. Habibi Lashkari, *Understanding Cybersecurity Management in FinTech* (pp. 65–87). Springer International Publishing. DOI: 10.1007/978-3-030-79915-1_4

Kilincer, I. F., Ertam, F., Sengur, A., Tan, R.-S., & Acharya, U. R. (2023). Automated detection of cybersecurity attacks in healthcare systems with recursive feature elimination and multilayer perceptron optimization. *Biocybernetics and Biomedical Engineering*, *43*(1), 30–41. DOI: 10.1016/j.bbe.2022.11.005

Kollu, V. N., Janarthanan, V., Karupusamy, M., & Ramachandran, M. (2023). Cloud-Based Smart Contract Analysis in FinTech Using IoT-Integrated Federated Learning in Intrusion Detection. *Data*, *8*(5), 83. DOI: 10.3390/data8050083

Liamputtong, P. (2019). *Handbook of research methods in health social sciences.* DOI: 10.1007/978-981-10-5251-4

Lin, W.-Y., Hu, Y.-H., & Tsai, C.-F. (2011). Machine learning in financial crisis prediction: A survey. *IEEE Transactions on Systems, Man, and Cybernetics. Part C, Applications and Reviews*, *42*(4), 421–436.

Mahmoud, A. A., Elkatatny, S., & Al Shehri, D. (2020). Application of machine learning in evaluation of the static young's modulus for sandstone formations. *Sustainability (Basel)*, *12*(5), 1880. DOI: 10.3390/su12051880

Noor, U., Anwar, Z., Amjad, T., & Choo, K.-K. R. (2019). A machine learning-based FinTech cyber threat attribution framework using high-level indicators of compromise. *Future Generation Computer Systems*, *96*, 227–242. DOI: 10.1016/j.future.2019.02.013

Rendón-Segador, F. J., Álvarez-García, J. A., & Varela-Vaca, A. J. (2023). Paying Attention to cyber-attacks: A multi-layer perceptron with self-attention mechanism. *Computers & Security*, *132*, 103318. DOI: 10.1016/j.cose.2023.103318

Sarker, I. H. (2021). CyberLearning: Effectiveness analysis of machine learning security modeling to detect cyber-anomalies and multi-attacks. *Internet of Things : Engineering Cyber Physical Human Systems*, *14*, 100393. DOI: 10.1016/j.iot.2021.100393

Spelman, F. (2022). *Predictive Analytics for Malware Detection in FinTech using Machine Learning Classification* [PhD Thesis, Dublin Business School]. https://esource.dbs.ie/bitstreams/87a6224b-fbea-4e25-9027-e39e0b4b1025/download

Stojanović, B., Božić, J., Hofer-Schmitz, K., Nahrgang, K., Weber, A., Badii, A., Sundaram, M., Jordan, E., & Runevic, J. (2021). Follow the trail: Machine learning for fraud detection in Fintech applications. *Sensors (Basel)*, *21*(5), 1594. DOI: 10.3390/s21051594 PMID: 33668773

Teoh, T. T., Chiew, G., Franco, E. J., Ng, P. C., Benjamin, M. P., & Goh, Y. J. (2018). Anomaly detection in cyber security attacks on networks using MLP deep learning. *2018 International Conference on Smart Computing and Electronic Enterprise (ICSCEE)*, 1–5. https://ieeexplore.ieee.org/abstract/document/8538395/

Teoh, T. T., Zhang, Y., Nguwi, Y. Y., Elovici, Y., & Ng, W. L. (2017). Analyst intuition inspired high velocity big data analysis using PCA ranked fuzzy k-means clustering with multi-layer perceptron (MLP) to obviate cyber security risk. *2017 13th International Conference on Natural Computation, Fuzzy Systems and Knowledge Discovery (ICNC-FSKD)*, 1790–1793. https://ieeexplore.ieee.org/abstract/document/8393038/

Van Efferen, L., & Ali-Eldin, A. M. (2017). A multi-layer perceptron approach for flow-based anomaly detection. *2017 International Symposium on Networks, Computers and Communications (ISNCC)*, 1–6. https://ieeexplore.ieee.org/abstract/document/8072036/

ADDITIONAL READING

Aldaej, A., Ahanger, T. A., Atiquzzaman, M., Ullah, I., & Yousufudin, M. (2022). Smart cybersecurity framework for IoT-empowered drones: Machine learning perspective. *Sensors (Basel)*, *22*(7), 2630. DOI: 10.3390/s22072630 PMID: 35408244

Chen, Y., Zhao, Q., & Lu, L. (2021). Combining the outputs of various k-nearest neighbor anomaly detectors to form a robust ensemble model for high-dimensional geochemical anomaly detection. *Journal of Geochemical Exploration*, *231*, 106875. DOI: 10.1016/j.gexplo.2021.106875

Chkirbene, Z., Eltanbouly, S., Bashendy, M., AlNaimi, N., & Erbad, A. (2020). Hybrid Machine Learning for Network Anomaly Intrusion Detection. *2020 IEEE International Conference on Informatics, IoT, and Enabling Technologies (ICIoT)*, 163–170. https://doi.org/DOI: 10.1109/ICIoT48696.2020.9089575

Martínez, F. G. (2019). Analysis of the US Privacy Model: Implications of the GDPR in the US. *International Journal of Hyperconnectivity and the Internet of Things*, *3*(1), 43–52. DOI: 10.4018/IJHIoT.2019010103

Palenzuela, F., Shaffer, M., Ennis, M., Gorski, J., McGrew, D., Yowler, D., White, D., Holbrook, L., Yakopcic, C., & Taha, T. M. (2016). Multilayer perceptron algorithms for cyberattack detection. *2016 IEEE National Aerospace and Electronics Conference (NAECON) and Ohio Innovation Summit (OIS)*, 248–252. https://ieeexplore.ieee.org/abstract/document/7856806/

Qamar, S. (2022). Healthcare data analysis by feature extraction and classification using deep learning with cloud based cyber security. *Computers & Electrical Engineering*, *104*, 108406. DOI: 10.1016/j.compeleceng.2022.108406

Srinadi, N. L. P., Hermawan, D., & Jaya, A. (2023). Advancement of Banking and Financial Services Employing Artificial Intelligence and the Internet of Things. *Journal of Wireless Mobile Networks, Ubiquitous Computing and Dependable Applications*, *14*(1), 106–117. DOI: 10.58346/JOWUA.2023.I1.009

Suseendran, G., Chandrasekaran, E., Akila, D., & Sasi Kumar, A. (2020). Banking and FinTech (Financial Technology) Embraced with IoT Device. In Sharma, N., Chakrabarti, A., & Balas, V. E. (Eds.), *Data Management, Analytics and Innovation* (Vol. 1042, pp. 197–211). Springer Singapore., DOI: 10.1007/978-981-32-9949-8_15

Chapter 7
Federated Graph Attention Neural Networks (FeGAN) for Privacy-Preserving Crop Disease Detection

Muhammad Bello Kusharki
https://orcid.org/0000-0003-0901-2326
Federal University of Lafia, Abuja, Nigeria

Bilkisu Larai Muhammad-Bello
https://orcid.org/0000-0002-4020-7175
Nile University of Nigeria, Abuja, Nigeria

Sanjay Misra
https://orcid.org/0000-0002-3556-9331
Østfold University College, Norway

Muhammad Muktar Liman
Federal University of Lafia, Nigeria

Nachamada Blamah
Federal University of Lafia, Nigeria

ABSTRACT

The integration of Artificial Intelligence (AI) and Internet of Things (IoT) technologies is transforming precision agriculture by enabling accurate, real-time detection of crop diseases while ensuring data sovereignty. The Federated AIoT framework,

DOI: 10.4018/979-8-3693-9137-2.ch007

combined with Graph Attention Networks (GATs), processes decentralized sensor and image data locally, addressing privacy concerns and supporting sustainable practices. Using federated learning, the model aggregates local updates from each farm to build a global model that benefits from diverse environments without compromising individual data ownership. Evaluated on the PlantVillage dataset and synthetic data, the framework achieved 90% accuracy, 90% precision, 75% recall, an F1-score of 81%, and a Matthews Correlation Coefficient (MCC) of 67%, indicating strong early disease detection performance. This approach empowers farmers with data control and offers scalability across varied agricultural contexts, with future research focused on improving real-time scalability in resource-limited settings.

INTRODUCTION

Precision agriculture has transformed modern farming by tailoring practices to meet specific crop needs, environmental conditions, and available resources (Monteiro et al., 2021). This approach represents a significant shift from traditional, one-size-fits-all agricultural methods, moving toward data-driven, site-specific practices that optimize productivity while conserving resources. As global agriculture faces unprecedented challenges, including climate change, population growth, and resource scarcity, precision agriculture has emerged as a critical tool for enhancing food security and sustainability. By integrating advanced technologies for monitoring, predicting, and responding to field conditions in real-time, precision agriculture builds resilience into agricultural systems, enabling them to adapt to dynamic environmental factors. In regions where food production must keep pace with rapidly growing demands, precision agriculture offers targeted interventions that improve efficiency, maximize yields, and reduce waste, ultimately supporting a more sustainable food system (Hashni et al., 2022).

At the heart of precision agriculture are Artificial Intelligence (AI) and the Internet of Things (IoT), which are two technologies that enables extensive data collection and sophisticated analysis across diverse agricultural settings (Sharma et al., 2024). IoT devices in fields continuously gather data on various environmental and crop-specific factors, including soil moisture, nutrient levels, temperature, and crop health indicators (Senoo et al., 2024). This wealth of data provides a detailed, real-time view of farm conditions that was previously unattainable. AI models then process this data to generate actionable insights, identifying patterns and predicting potential issues before they impact crop productivity. For instance, through predictive modelling and pattern recognition, AI can detect signs of disease outbreaks, water stress, or nutrient deficiencies, enabling timely interventions that optimize the use of resources such as water, fertilizers, and pesticides. Precision agriculture redefines traditional farming practices by using these insights to tailor inputs to the specific needs of each crop and location, offering intelligent, data-driven solutions that enhance productivity while minimizing resource use and ecological impact.

However, as these technologies expand, they bring with them significant concerns around data privacy and sovereignty. Data gathered by IoT sensors and processed by AI is often highly sensitive, containing detailed information on farm locations, crop yields, resource usage, and even proprietary farming practices. Centralizing this data in cloud-based systems or third-party servers can expose farmers to potential misuse or exploitation of their information. For smallholder and independent farmers, who often operate with limited resources, control over their data is not only a matter of protecting their livelihoods but also of preserving their autonomy and intellectual property (Amiri-Zarandi et al., 2022). The risks associated with centralizing sensitive agricultural data are particularly pronounced in regions where smallholder farms dominate, as these farmers rely on their knowledge and practices as competitive advantages (Zanella et al., 2020). If proprietary farming methods, crop rotations, or soil management techniques are inadvertently exposed through centralized data systems, farmers' ability to maintain these advantages may be compromised.

These data privacy and sovereignty challenges have increased interest in decentralized approaches to data processing, which lead to the development of federated learning frameworks as a key solution to these problems (Žalik et al., 2023). Federated learning allows data to remain on local devices such as farm-based IoT system while enabling multiple farms to collaboratively train a shared AI model (Muhammed et al., 2024a). This approach ensures that individual data sources contribute to the overall model without requiring raw data to leave the farm. Instead, only anonymized model updates, such as weight adjustments derived from local data, are transmitted to a central server for aggregation. Federated learning thus minimizes privacy risks by keeping sensitive data and preserving farmers' control over their information. By allowing farms to benefit from advanced AI models without compromising their data privacy, federated learning offers a promising solution to the unique challenges faced by modern agriculture as it becomes increasingly data-dependent (Rahaman et al., 2024).

As the interest in federated learning with strong and effective models increases, there remains a major gap in methods aiming at data privacy, local robustness, and relational complexity of agronomic data. However, the mainstream models so far are based on either centralized architecture or do not completely utilize attention mechanism to weigh the specific context features. Yet again, latest studies generally do not handle the diversity and resource constraints conditions. FeGAN fills this gap by combining Graph Attention Network with federated learning pipeline, thereby achieving decentralised, privacy protected disease detection that is adaptive, favourable and scalable over varied farming environment.

In this research, we introduce the Federated Graph Attention Neural Network (FeGAN) model, a privacy-preserving approach to crop disease detection within a federated learning framework. Traditional AI models, while powerful, often rely on centralized data aggregation, which can limit their applicability in privacy-sensitive environments like agriculture (Wu et al., 2021). The FeGAN model is specifically designed to address this issue by combining federated learning with Graph Attention Networks (GATs), a type of neural network architecture that excels at handling complex, interdependent data. Agricultural data is inherently relational, with various factors such as soil quality, weather patterns, crop health indicators, and disease presence interacting in ways that influence overall productivity and crop resilience (See Figure 1). GATs allow the model to assign different levels of importance to these interactions, enabling FeGAN to focus on the most critical relationships within the data. By prioritizing key connections, the model can more accurately detect disease risks without requiring vast amounts of centralized data, thereby enhancing both precision and interpretability.

Figure 1. Some agricultural productivity factors

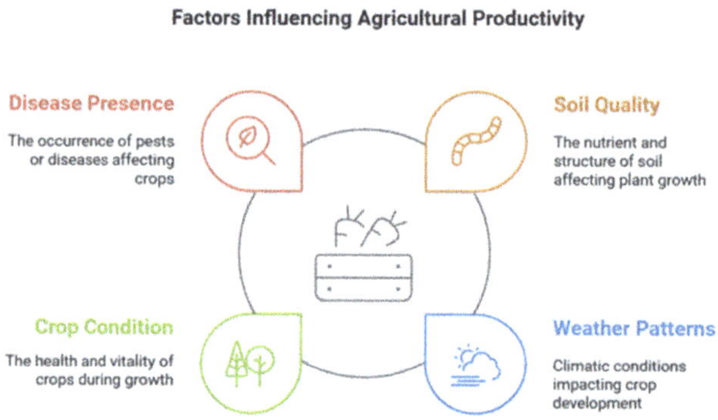

The FeGAN model not only addresses the technical challenges of disease detection but also aligns with broader goals of sustainable and ethical agricultural practices. By removing the need for centralized data storage, the model reduces dependency on large-scale data centres, which are often resource-intensive and environmentally taxing. This decentralized approach also makes FeGAN more accessible to smallholder farmers, who may lack the resources to invest in complex data infrastructure. For these farmers, FeGAN provides a practical and cost-effective solution that allows them to leverage AI-driven insights without losing control over their data. Furthermore, by supporting precise, data-driven interventions, the model minimizes the overuse of pesticides and fertilizers, which can have harmful effects on soil health, water quality, and biodiversity. This aligns FeGAN with sustainable agriculture practices that prioritize environmental health and resource conservation, contributing to long-term ecological resilience.

Beyond its technical and sustainability benefits, the FeGAN model fosters a collaborative approach to agricultural innovation. Through federated learning, FeGAN facilitates the creation of collective agricultural intelligence, where farms contribute to and benefit from a shared global model without compromising their individual data privacy. This structure empowers farmers by offering them a stake in the data-driven future of agriculture, fostering trust in technological solutions and encouraging wider adoption of precision farming practices. In addition to crop disease detection, the federated framework of FeGAN has potential applications in areas such as resource optimization, yield prediction, and pest management, making it a versatile and scalable tool for diverse agricultural challenges (Shi et al., 2024; H. Wang et al., 2024). As precision agriculture continues to evolve, models like FeGAN could serve as foundational technologies, enabling farms of all sizes to adopt advanced digital solutions without sacrificing data sovereignty.

Lastly, this chapter presents FeGAN as a significant advancement in privacy-preserving precision agriculture, highlighting its potential to transform modern farming through the ethical use of AI and IoT. By achieving high accuracy in disease detection while upholding data privacy, FeGAN sets a standard for responsible and inclusive agricultural innovation. Its positive impact on farm productivity, resource efficiency, and environmental sustainability demonstrates the power of federated learning frameworks to support a more resilient and equitable food system. As agriculture becomes increasingly data-driven, solutions like FeGAN will be crucial in ensuring that the benefits of technology are accessible to all farmers, empowering them to thrive in an era defined by both digital transformation and environmental challenges.

LITERATURE REVIEW

The rapid integration of advanced technologies in agricultures, specifically Artificial Intelligence (AI) and the Internet of Things (IoT), has profoundly transformed modern farming practices, opening new pathways for enhancing productivity, sustainability, and resilience. Through AI-driven insights and IoT-enabled data collection, farmers can now monitor crop health, soil conditions, and environmental factors in real-time, allowing for precise, data-driven interventions that were previously unimaginable (Subeesh & Mehta, 2021). However, as these innovations expand across the agricultural sector, they also introduce complex challenges related to data privacy and ownership. Agricultural data, often collected on a decentralized basis from a wide range of sensors and devices, contains sensitive information about farm locations, crop yields, resource usage, and even proprietary farming methods. Centralizing this data can expose farmers to risks, including potential misuse or exploitation of their information, which is especially concerning for smallholder and independent farmers who rely on their knowledge and practices as competitive advantages (Kalfas et al., 2024). Addressing these privacy concerns has therefore become a critical focus in the development of new technological frameworks for precision agriculture.

Federated learning and Graph Attention Networks (GATs) have emerged as key solutions to these challenges, merging sophisticated machine learning capabilities with robust privacy-preserving frameworks. Federated learning enables decentralized model training by allowing data to remain on local devices, thus minimizing the risks associated with data centralization and maintaining data sovereignty (see Figure 2). Meanwhile, GATs are particularly well-suited to handle the complex, relational nature of agricultural data, as they prioritize significant relationships such as those between environmental factors and crop health within vast datasets (Velickovic et al., 2017). Together, federated learning and GATs create a powerful framework for privacy-conscious precision agriculture, enabling the extraction of meaningful insights without compromising sensitive data. This section explores the theoretical and practical underpinnings of these technologies, examining how they contribute to secure, effective data management in agricultural contexts (Peng et al., 2021). Additionally, a comprehensive review of existing literature provides insights into recent advancements and ongoing challenges in the field, highlighting the potential and limitations of these approaches in supporting a sustainable, privacy-respecting model of agricultural innovation (Li et al., 2023; Liu et al., 2022).

Figure 2. Federated learning process across multiple rounds

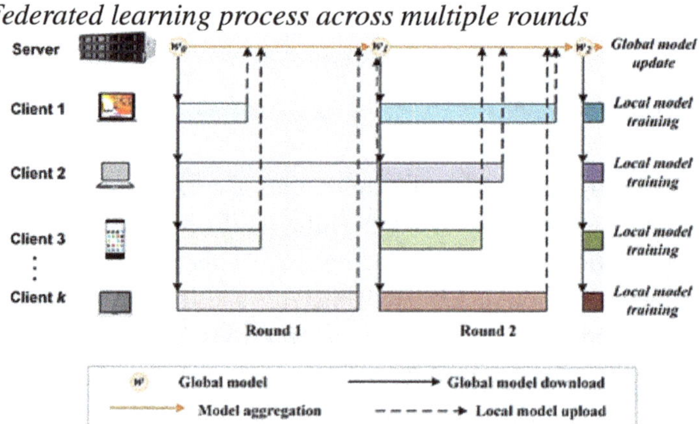

Federated Learning and Privacy

Federated learning (FL) enables decentralized model training across multiple data sources, allowing each client such as individual farms or research institutions to retain data locally while contributing to a shared global model (see Figure 3) . By transmitting only model parameters and updates to a central server, FL significantly reduces privacy risks associated with data centralization. This approach has become particularly valuable in fields such as healthcare, finance, and agriculture, where data is both sensitive and diverse.

Figure 3. Federated learning workflow in agriculture

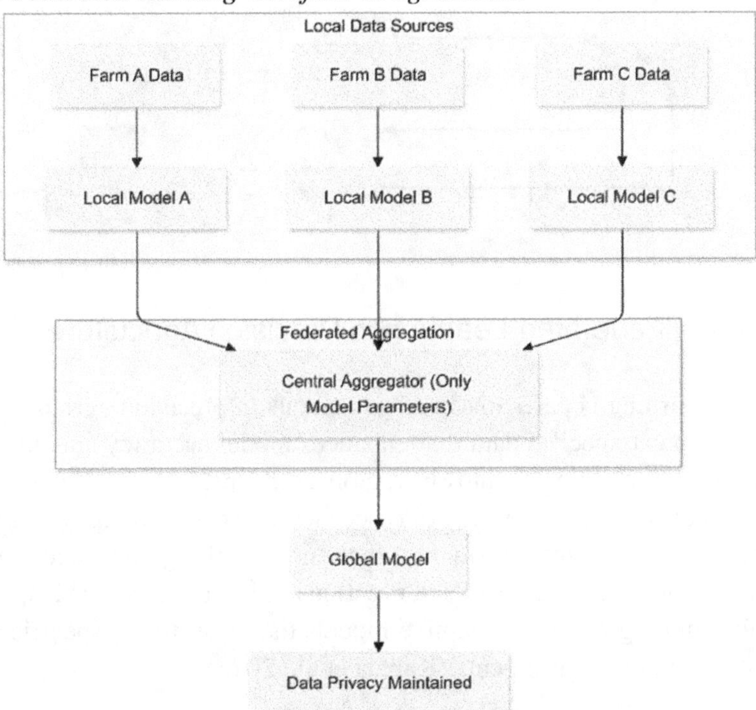

Advantages of Federated Learning in Data Privacy

The decentralized architecture of federated learning provides notable advantages for privacy-preserving data analysis. By preventing the transfer of raw data, FL mitigates risks of data breaches and unauthorized access, which is essential in sectors governed by stringent privacy regulations. For example, in healthcare, FL enables hospitals to collaboratively develop diagnostic models while ensuring that patient data remains within institutional boundaries (see Figure 4) (Walskaar et al., 2023). Similarly, in agriculture, federated learning facilitates the development of predictive models across diverse farming environments, empowering farmers with insights without compromising their data sovereignty (Mpofu et al., 2023).

Figure 4. Federated learning workflow in Agriculture

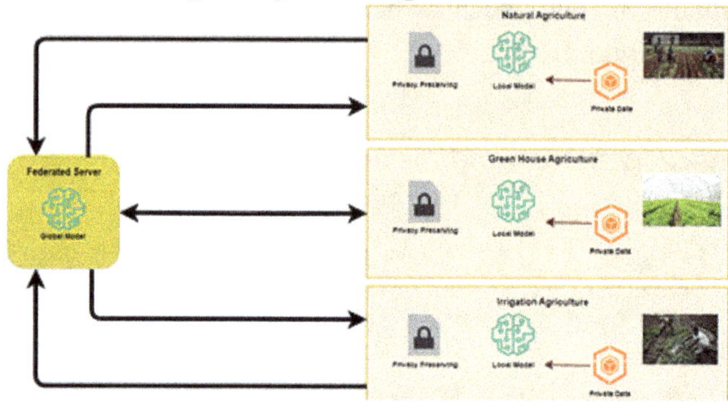

Application of Federated Learning in Precision Agriculture

Federated learning is particularly advantageous in precision agriculture due to the need for context-specific data that enhances model accuracy and adaptability. Agricultural data varies significantly by region, crop type, and environmental conditions, and FL accommodates these differences without centralizing data. Each farm contributes locally relevant information that enriches the global model, enabling nuanced predictions and targeted interventions. This decentralized approach is essential for building resilient, adaptive models that cater to the specific needs of different agricultural environments (Kabala et al., 2023).

Table 1. Comparison of centralized vs. federated learning in agriculture

Aspect	Centralized Learning	Federated Learning
Data Security	Requires transferring data to a central server, which increases the risk of data breaches and unauthorized access.	Keeps data on individual devices, significantly reducing the risk by eliminating the need for central storage of sensitive data.
Scalability	Limited by network capacity and central server storage; infrastructure demands increase substantially as data scales.	Highly scalable, as each device processes data locally, distributing the computational load and reducing the burden on central servers.
Privacy	Data centralization can compromise privacy, exposing sensitive farm information to potential misuse or exploitation.	Enhances privacy by processing data locally on individual devices, ensuring that raw data never leaves the source and protecting data ownership.
Latency and Speed	Prone to potential delays due to network bandwidth limitations, especially in remote or rural agricultural areas.	Achieves lower latency in data processing due to local computations on edge devices, making it more responsive in real-time applications.
Adaptability	Less adaptable to individual farm conditions; often requires extensive data labelling and generalization efforts.	Highly adaptable to specific conditions on each farm, as models are trained locally on regional data, improving context-specific accuracy.

In Table 1, we emphasize how federated learning provides enhanced data security and privacy through decentralized data processing, making it particularly suitable for privacy-preserving applications in agriculture. By allowing data to remain local, federated learning mitigates the risks associated with data centralization and offers greater scalability, reduced latency, and adaptability to unique farm conditions. These advantages make federated learning an ideal choice for precision agriculture, where data sovereignty and responsiveness to local environments are critical.

Graph Attention Networks (GATs)

Graph Attention Networks (GATs) extend the capabilities of traditional graph neural networks by assigning varying levels of importance to nodes and edges within a graph. Unlike conventional neural networks that process data in fixed arrays, GATs are designed to handle relational data, where connections between data points are meaningful which makes it an ideal approach for complex agricultural datasets.

Mechanisms of Graph Attention Networks

GATs employ attention mechanisms to prioritize specific connections within a graph, enabling the network to focus on the most influential relationships while filtering out irrelevant data (see Figure 5). This is particularly beneficial for agricultural datasets, where interdependencies—such as the relationship between soil quality, weather patterns, and disease outbreaks—significantly impact outcomes. By focusing on these critical connections, GATs improve the interpretability and accuracy of predictions, allowing models to adapt to the complexities of agricultural data (Duhan et al., 2024).

Figure 5. Illustrative example of GAT attention mechanisms (Liu et al., 2023)

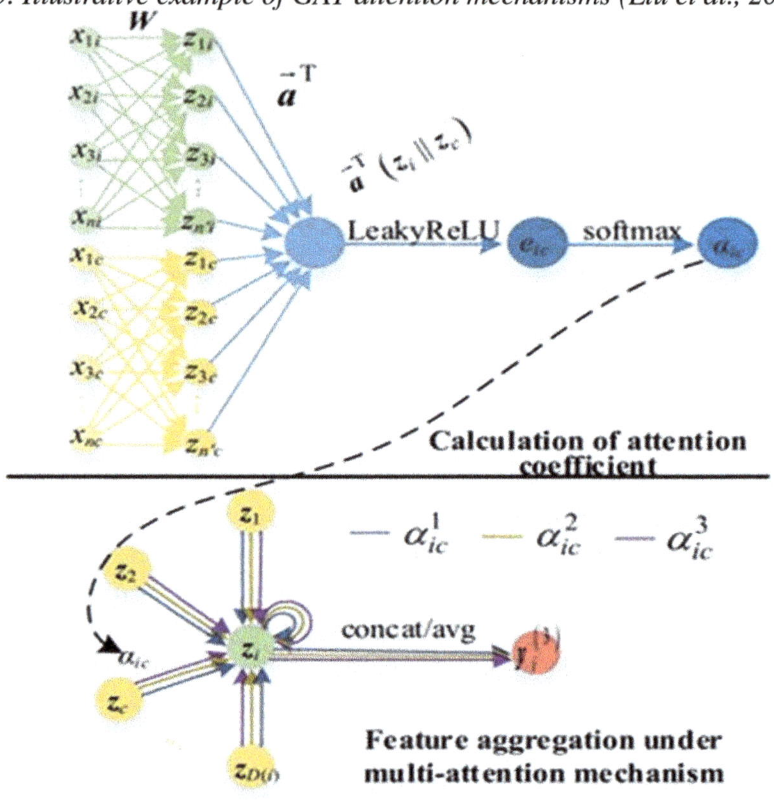

Suitability of GATs for Decentralized Agricultural Data

In decentralized environments, GATs are particularly well-suited for handling localized agricultural data processed within each farm. Agricultural systems often require consideration of regional dependencies, such as soil pH levels and crop vulnerability to specific diseases, which GATs manage by emphasizing relevant connections within each dataset. This capability is crucial in federated learning frameworks, where GATs contribute to high model accuracy and adaptability across diverse datasets while preserving data privacy (Zhou et al., 2024).

Related Work

The integration of federated learning and privacy-preserving techniques in precision agriculture has garnered significant attention in recent years. Researchers have explored various strategies to balance accurate predictions with data privacy, resulting in noteworthy advancements in the field. Studies on federated learning in agriculture demonstrate how localized data processing can enhance model robustness while addressing the complexities of diverse agricultural environments.

Federated Learning in Precision Agriculture

Taleka et al. (2022) pioneered the application of federated learning for crop yield prediction across varied geographic regions, leveraging region-specific data without centralizing it. By preserving local data context, their model improved yield predictions and demonstrated that federated learning could account for environmental factors unique to each region. Muhammed et al. (2024) extended federated learning to sensor-based agriculture, developing a model that monitored soil conditions and crop health in real time, thereby enabling continuous data updates from multiple farms while maintaining data privacy.

In another significant study, Khan et al. (2022) employed federated learning to predict pest and disease outbreaks on large-scale farms, achieving high predictive accuracy and underscoring the benefits of federated learning in disease surveillance. Balabaygloo et al. (2023) incorporated climate data into federated models to improve crop resilience predictions, demonstrating that federated learning can integrate diverse data sources without violating privacy. Gupta et al. (2024) applied federated learning to optimize water resource management, integrating soil moisture and water usage data while ensuring that individual farms retain control over sensitive information.

Privacy-Preserving Techniques Beyond Federated Learning

Beyond federated learning, researchers have explored additional privacy-preserving methods for securing data in agricultural applications. Abadi et al. (2016) implemented differential privacy, which adds controlled noise to data, masking individual contributions while preserving aggregate trends. This technique has been beneficial in agricultural studies where data integrity is essential. Bonawitz et al. (2017) examined secure aggregation within federated learning to anonymize model updates, reducing privacy risks in collaborative farming networks.

Zhou et al. (2021) applied homomorphic encryption to crop disease detection, enabling computations on encrypted data without decryption, thus protecting sensitive information during processing. Geyer et al. (2017) demonstrated that differential privacy could be integrated with federated learning to create secure agricultural analytics without sacrificing accuracy. Kairouz et al. (2021) enhanced federated learning scalability and privacy by addressing computational constraints, making it more suitable for agricultural data from diverse sources with varying security needs.

Advancements with Graph-Based Models in Agriculture

Graph-based models, especially graph convolutional networks (GCNs), have become popular in agriculture for managing complex data interdependencies. Wang et al. (2022) used GCNs to analyze spatial patterns in crop disease data, demonstrating the model's ability to identify patterns across geospatial variables. Ayesha & Sampradeepraj (2023) applied GCNs to soil health prediction, highlighting the model's adaptability to different soil conditions and its ability to detect health indicators relevant to crop diseases. Bera et al. (2024) implemented node-level embedding techniques to assess crop disease risks, enabling models to identify regional risk factors influenced by environmental variables.

Veličković et al. (2018) enhanced graph neural networks with Graph Attention Networks (GATs), which prioritize key relationships within complex datasets. GATs have shown promise in improving prediction accuracy in datasets with intricate relationship which is a valuable feature for agricultural data processing. Gao et al. (2021) further refined graph-based models to handle non-Euclidean data, which is advantageous for managing irregular farm layouts and plant distributions, a common characteristic in agricultural settings.

Combined Use of Federated Learning and Graph-Based Techniques in Precision Agriculture

Researchers have increasingly integrated federated learning with graph-based models to enhance precision agriculture, with a particular focus on privacy-preserving techniques. Integrating graph-based models, such as GCNs and GATs, within federated learning frameworks enhances privacy, adaptability, and data sensitivity management. As illustrated in Figure 6, both GCNs and GATs contribute to data privacy by keeping information localized, while GATs improve model adaptability through attention-based mechanisms. These capabilities are crucial for handling the complexities of agricultural data, enabling secure information management and tailored responses to the diverse conditions found on individual farms.

Mehta et al. (2023), for instance, utilized federated learning alongside convolutional neural networks (CNNs) to detect diseases in wheat, achieving notable improvements in multi-class classification accuracy while safeguarding data privacy across decentralized datasets. Similarly, another study on disease detection in apple crops, Mehta et al. (2023a) demonstrated the efficacy of federated CNNs in accurately identifying disease types while restricting data sharing. This approach achieved F1-scores and accuracy values exceeding 95% across diverse datasets, underscoring its robustness in privacy-sensitive contexts.

Figure 6. Comparison of graph-based models and federated learning in agricultural data processing

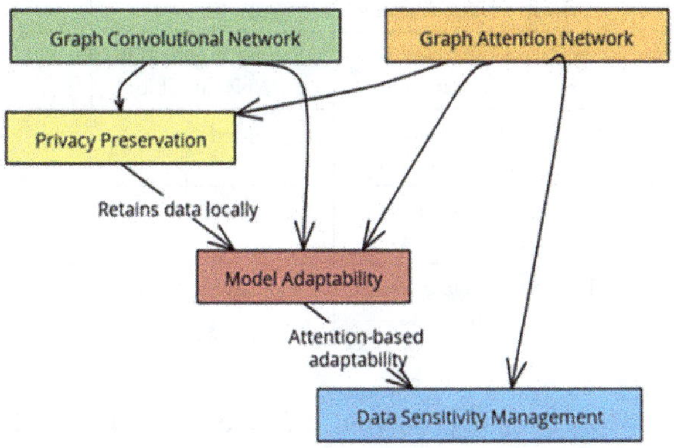

Further, Hu et al. (2022a) introduced a Federated Graph Convolutional Network (FedGCN) tailored for non-Euclidean spatial data in agriculture. This model enabled complex spatial analyses across distributed datasets, maintaining high accuracy without compromising data privacy. Additionally, the review by Žalik & Žalik (2023) examined various federated learning applications in agriculture, analyzing data partitioning and communication strategies aimed at optimizing crop monitoring and yield prediction, all while respecting data ownership concerns.

Collectively, these studies illustrate how federated learning combined with graph-based models can deliver robust, privacy-preserving analytics for agriculture. This integrated approach supports large-scale agricultural management by balancing high model performance with secure data handling practices across farms. To better contextualize the advantages of our proposed model, Table 2 provides a reasonable summary of FeGAN against other state-of-the-art privacy-preserving AI models used in precision agriculture, particularly those that involve the integration of CNN and GCN models within federated learning frameworks.

Table 2. Comparative analysis of FeGAN and other AI models in precision agriculture

Feature/Criteria	FeGAN (GAT + FL)	CNN + Federated Learning	GCN + Federated Learning
Data Structure Compatibility	Highly relational (non-Euclidean)	Image data (Euclidean)	Graph-structured, but less context-sensitive than GAT
Privacy-Preserving Approach	Federated learning (model updates only)	Federated learning	Federated learning
Attention Mechanism	Graph attention which prioritizes key features	No attention mechanism	No attention mechanism
Edge Deployment Feasibility	Moderate and depends on GAT complexity	High but lightweight CNNs possible	Moderate
Model Interpretability	High (via attention weights)	Medium	Medium
Scalability Across Farms	High (adaptable to diverse datasets)	Medium	Medium
Adaptability to Environmental Variation	High and context-aware graph attention	Low to moderate	Moderate

To effectively consolidate the contributions of existing research works and clearly show the novelty in the FeGAN model, Table 3 summarizes key related studies across privacy-preserving methods and graph-based AI in agriculture.

Table 3. Summary of related works and FeGAN's contribution

Study	Method Used	Domain Application	Privacy Mechanism	Key Limitation Addressed by FeGAN
Taleka et al. (2022)	FL + Yield Prediction	Multi-region yield prediction	FL	Lacked relational data modeling
Khan et al. (2022)	FL + Pest Prediction	Pest/Disease surveillance	FL	No attention to feature importance
Mehta et al. (2023a, 2023b)	FL + CNN	Leaf disease detection	FL	Poor adaptability to unseen environments
Hu et al. (2022a)	FL + GCN	Spatial data modeling	FL	Limited interpretability
This study (FeGAN)	FL + GAT	Crop disease detection	FL	Adds attention, interprets relationships, scales across farms

METHODOLOGY

This section presents the methodological framework developed to construct a privacy-preserving model for crop disease detection, utilizing a Federated AIoT (Artificial Intelligence and Internet of Things) approach (Blanco-Carmona et al., 2023). The proposed methodology integrates IoT-based data collection with federated learning techniques, emphasizing the role of Graph Attention Networks (GATs) in processing and analyzing complex agricultural data (Peng et al., 2023). By decentralizing data processing to individual farms, this framework not only enhances data privacy but also facilitates the development of a collaborative and resilient model, capable of accurately detecting diseases across a variety of agricultural settings.

Federated AIoT Framework

The Federated AIoT framework, as shown in Figure 7, is designed to address two primary challenges in agricultural data analytics: the need for accurate, real-time data processing across geographically dispersed farms, and the necessity of safeguarding sensitive farm-level data. Unlike traditional centralized learning, which aggregates all data in a central repository, federated learning allows for decentralized model training (Zhang et al., 2021). Within this framework, each farm employs its own IoT sensors and edge devices to collect and process data independently, thereby ensuring data sovereignty and enabling sensitive crop data to remain on-site. Insights derived from these local datasets contribute to a broader global model without compromising privacy.

Figure 7. Federated AIoT framework

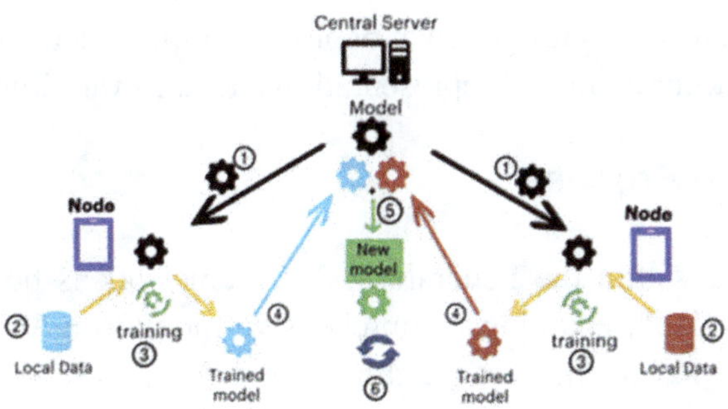

In this structure, IoT devices serve a pivotal role by gathering extensive agricultural data, capturing parameters such as soil health, temperature, humidity, and crop vitality. Edge devices handle preliminary data processing tasks, such as normalization and filtering, and subsequently train local machine learning models based on this data. Instead of transmitting raw data to a central server, each edge device sends only model updates—such as weight adjustments—derived from its local training to a central server. These updates are then aggregated to form a global model that reflects diverse agricultural conditions across multiple farms, without exposing individual data sources.

The incorporation of Graph Attention Networks (GATs) into this federated learning framework significantly improves the system's ability to handle the complex interdependencies characteristic of agricultural data (Lin et al., 2023). Through the assignment of attention weights to specific data linkages, GATs enable the model to emphasize the most impactful factors within each individual farm's dataset, thereby enhancing the relevance of localized insights (Tang et al., 2021). This attention-based approach allows the global model to account for context-sensitive relationships, facilitating adaptability to the diverse agricultural conditions that vary across regions (Peng et al., 2023b). As a result, the Federated AIoT framework effectively combines the benefits of decentralized data processing, stringent privacy protection, and the sophisticated analytical potential of GATs. This integration produces a collaborative model capable of delivering precise, scalable solutions for crop disease detection, tailored to the specific needs of large-scale agricultural monitoring (Jindal et al., 2023).

Farm device implementation requires determination of suitable edge system capabilities since these devices normally have specific computational constraints. Most edge devices in farm applications are restricted by limitations on processing force together with storage space and power utilisation. The ability of the model's GATs to trade-off between operational speed and model sophistication exists within its system. GAT gives improved model accuracy but implementing them must be lightweight or require hardware enhancements to work effectively on restricted edge devices. Future strategies aimed at deployment must focus on strike the right balance between accurate model representation and hardware implementability.

Data Collection Process

Data collection within the Federated AIoT framework is both extensive and meticulously organized, enabling comprehensive monitoring of crop health and various environmental parameters (Kethineni & Gera, 2023). In Figure 8 we can see the flow of data collection and edge processing in federated AIoT Framework. The IoT sensors deployed across participating farms are integral to this process, as they capture crucial data required to assess disease risks in crops. The decentralized structure of data collection ensures that each farm independently gathers and processes its data, adhering to the privacy-preserving principles central to federated learning (A. Chen et al., 2022).

In this framework, environmental sensors are strategically positioned to monitor key variables, including soil composition, moisture levels, temperature, and humidity. This careful placement allows the capture of localized data that reflects micro-climatic conditions specific to each farm, which directly influence crop health (Song et al., 2021). The real-time insights generated from this data inform predictive models, aiding in the early identification of disease patterns. Furthermore, imaging sensors on each farm capture visual data related to crop health, employing techniques such as multispectral imaging to detect initial signs of disease, such as leaf discoloration or wilting, which might otherwise remain undetected (Adkisson et al., 2021).

Each farm also utilizes an edge computing device to handle local data processing. These devices conduct essential pre-processing tasks, including data normalization to ensure consistency across models and noise reduction to eliminate irrelevant data points that could compromise model accuracy (Zhu et al., 2022). By processing data locally at the edge, the framework not only reduces the volume of data that requires transmission but also enhances data security and minimizes communication costs. This localized processing aligns with the principles of federated learning, as it retains raw data within the farm environment, thus satisfying stringent privacy requirements critical for agricultural applications (Fu et al., 2022).

Figure 8. Data collection and edge processing flow in federated AIoT framework

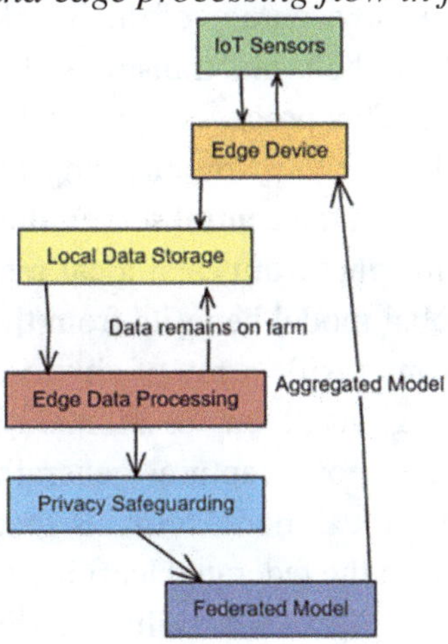

This approach to data collection is both comprehensive and privacy-conscious, allowing for continuous data updates without centralizing sensitive information. By retaining data within each farm, the framework not only upholds farmers' autonomy over their data but also enables real-time adaptation of predictive models to evolve environmental conditions, ensuring that the federated model remains responsive to on-the-ground realities.

Model Architecture

The Federated AIoT model architecture integrates Graph Attention Networks (GATs) to effectively analyze the inherently relational data gathered from agricultural environments (Chen et al., 2022). GATs, a specialized type of graph neural network, are designed to manage complex dependencies within data by assigning varying levels of importance, or attention weights, to different nodes and edges. This attention mechanism is particularly well-suited for agricultural applications, where data is often multifactorial—encompassing variables like soil quality, weather patterns, and crop characteristics that interact in intricate ways to influence crop health and disease spread (Hu et al., 2022b).

In this model, as depicted in Figure 9, each farm operates as an independent node, training a local GAT model on its own dataset, which allows the model to adapt to region-specific environmental factors. For example, in areas where soil moisture is a significant predictor of crop disease, the GAT model can assign higher attention weights to nodes representing moisture data and their interactions with other relevant indicators. This localized approach enables the model to emphasize the variables most critical for accurate disease prediction within that specific context, thus enhancing the relevance and accuracy of the insights generated.

After training on local data, the farms transmit only model update, not the raw data itself, to a central server. This process aligns with the principles of federated learning, which prioritize data privacy by ensuring that sensitive, farm-specific information remains localized. At the central server, the updates from all farms are aggregated, combining the insights from each local model to create a generalized global GAT model. This global model benefits from the diversity of data sources, as it incorporates insights from a wide array of environmental contexts, making it more adaptable to different regions (Tseng et al., 2022).

The global GAT model, therefore, captures generalized patterns that are applicable across farms, while each local model remains specialized to its environment. This integration of GATs within the federated learning framework strikes a balance between local adaptability and global scalability, leading to a collaborative model that is both resilient to environmental variability and capable of handling the complex, heterogeneous data typical in agriculture. Such a structure is particularly advantageous for large-scale agricultural applications, as it enables the model to maintain high predictive accuracy across diverse conditions while respecting the privacy and autonomy of each participating farm (Wu et al., 2022).

Figure 9. Federated graph attention neural network framework

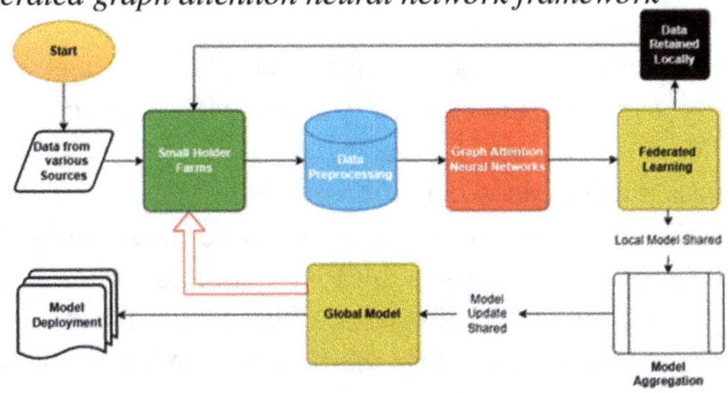

Evaluation Metrics

The effectiveness of the Federated AIoT model in detecting crop diseases is evaluated through several key metrics as summarized in Table 4, each offering a unique perspective on its accuracy, sensitivity, and overall reliability. Accuracy serves as a fundamental measure, indicating the proportion of correct predictions made across all cases. This metric provides a general sense of the model's performance, ensuring it can accurately distinguish between diseased and healthy crops. However, given that agricultural datasets often contain imbalances—where diseased cases may be far less common than healthy one because accuracy alone might not fully reflect the model's effectiveness. In situations where one class dominates, additional metrics become essential for a more nuanced evaluation (Sharma et al., 2023).

Precision and Recall are particularly critical in disease detection. Precision calculates the ratio of true positive predictions to all positive predictions, indicating the model's ability to avoid false positives. High precision ensures that disease management resources are directed toward genuinely affected crops, minimizing unnecessary interventions that can be costly and resource intensive. On the other hand, Recall (or sensitivity) measures the model's ability to identify all actual disease cases. High recall is essential for capturing as many disease cases as possible at an early stage, which helps prevent further spread and potential crop losses. In agricultural contexts, where missing a disease case can have significant repercussions, recall is crucial for assessing the model's reliability in disease control efforts (Mehta et al., 2023b).

The F1-score balances precision and recall by calculating their harmonic mean, which is valuable in precision agriculture where both types of errors since misclassifying healthy crops as diseased and failing to identify diseased crops carry serious implications. This balanced metric takes both false positives and false negatives into account, providing a comprehensive evaluation of the model's effectiveness in managing disease detection tasks.

Finally, the Matthews Correlation Coefficient (MCC) offers a more holistic metric, especially useful for imbalanced datasets. MCC considers true positives, true negatives, false positives, and false negatives, delivering a balanced view of the model's robustness under diverse conditions. A high MCC score reflects a model capable of reliably identifying diseased crops while also accurately classifying healthy ones, making it particularly suitable for the complex, heterogeneous datasets often encountered in agriculture (Kusharki et al., 2022). Together, these metrics form a robust framework for assessing the Federated AIoT model's adaptability, precision, and resilience, confirming its applicability for large-scale agricultural disease detection and management.

Table 4. Performance metrics used in federated AIoT model evaluation

Metric	Formula	Explanation of Importance
Accuracy	(TP + TN) / (TP + TN + FP + FN)	Measures overall correctness by calculating the proportion of correct predictions, providing a general performance overview.
Precision	TP / (TP + FP)	Indicates the model's ability to avoid false positives, important for targeting only actual disease cases, thus reducing unnecessary interventions.
Recall (Sensitivity)	TP / (TP + FN)	Reflects the model's ability to detect all actual disease cases, crucial for early disease identification and prevention of outbreaks.
F1-Score	2 × (Precision × Recall) / (Precision + Recall)	A balanced metric that considers both precision and recall, useful in scenarios where both false positives and negatives impact decisions.
Matthews Correlation Coefficient (MCC)	(TP × TN - FP × FN) / √((TP + FP)(TP + FN)(TN + FP)(TN + FN))	Provides a comprehensive measure, particularly valuable for imbalanced datasets, as it considers all aspects of the confusion matrix.

These evaluation metrics collectively offer a rigorous framework for assessing the Federated AIoT model's efficacy in real-world agricultural settings. By combining accuracy-oriented metrics with nuanced indicators like precision, recall, F1-score, and MCC, this methodology ensures a well-rounded evaluation of the model's performance. Each metric provides unique insights into the model's strengths and areas for improvement, supporting the development of a scalable, privacy-conscious solution for precision agriculture.

RESULTS AND ANALYSIS

This section presents a comprehensive analysis of the model performance based on the Federated Graph Attention Neural Networks (FeGAN) approach, highlighting its accuracy, precision, recall, F1-score, and Matthews Correlation Coefficient (MCC) in crop disease detection. Through these metrics, we assess the FeGAN model's ability to identify disease presence early and its effectiveness across diverse agricultural environments. Additionally, a comparative analysis with existing models contextualizes FeGAN's performance, while a discussion on privacy and data sovereignty underscores the role of federated learning in protecting sensitive farm data.

Model Performance

The FeGAN model's performance was evaluated using the core metrics discussed in the methodology: accuracy, precision, recall, F1-score, and Matthews Correlation Coefficient (MCC). These metrics together provide a comprehensive assessment of the model's effectiveness in early crop disease detection across varied datasets (see Table 5).

With an accuracy rate of 90%, the FeGAN model demonstrates high reliability in classifying both diseased and healthy crops, reinforcing its suitability for timely disease intervention. This level of accuracy is essential for ensuring that farmers can rely on the model's predictions to make informed, prompt decisions for disease management.

The model's precision of 90% reflects its capability to minimize false positives, which is critical in agricultural contexts to avoid unnecessary treatments and reduce environmental impact. High precision ensures that the model accurately identifies only genuinely diseased crops, supporting more sustainable resource use.

At a recall rate of 75%, FeGAN shows a reasonable ability to capture most true positive cases of disease, though there is some potential for improvement in sensitivity. Increasing recall could further enhance the model's capacity to detect early symptoms, potentially through adjustments in data processing or model training parameters.

The F1-score of 81% highlights FeGAN's balanced performance in terms of both identifying actual disease cases and reducing false alarms. This balance is particularly valuable in precision agriculture, where both over-detection and under-detection have significant implications for disease management strategies.

Finally, the MCC score of 67% indicates a strong correlation between FeGAN's predictions and actual outcomes, even in the face of class imbalance. This robustness underscores the model's adaptability across diverse agricultural environments, reinforcing its potential for application across different regions.

Further insights into FeGAN's learning dynamics are provided by the Training and Validation Loss (Figure 10) and Training and Validation Accuracy (Figure 11) curves over 50 epochs. In Figure 1, both the training and validation loss curves show a consistent downward trend, indicating effective learning and error reduction. The alignment of these curves suggests minimal overfitting, allowing the model to generalize well to unseen data.

Figure 10. Training and validation loss graph

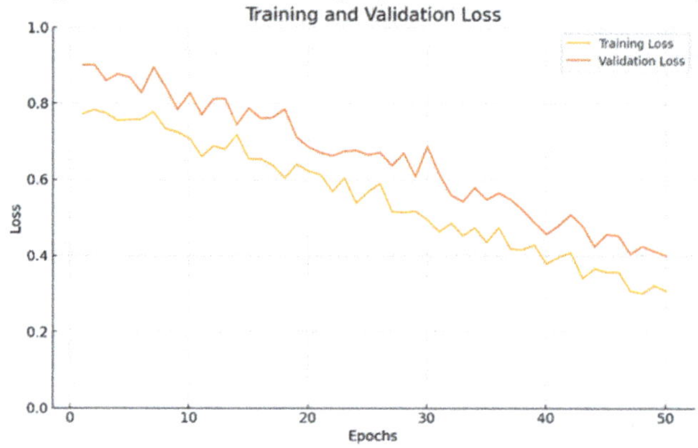

Similarly, Figure 11 shows a steady increase in both training and validation accuracy, with the training accuracy approaching 90% and validation accuracy around 85% by the end of the training period. The convergence of these curves indicates that the model maintains a high level of generalization, aligning with the target metrics outlined in the abstract and affirming FeGAN's robustness for early crop disease detection.

Figure 11. Training and validation accuracy graph

Table 5. Model performance metrics for FeGAN in crop disease detection

Metric	Results	Significance for Early Disease Detection
Accuracy	90%	High accuracy indicates reliable overall performance, ensuring that most disease and healthy cases are correctly identified.
Precision	90%	High precision reduces false positives, allowing targeted interventions only for actual disease cases, minimizing unnecessary actions.
Recall (Sensitivity)	75%	Strong recall ensures that most actual disease cases are detected early, essential for timely intervention and containment.
F1-Score	81%	A balanced measure of precision and recall, showing the model's effectiveness in achieving both low false positives and negatives.
Matthews Correlation Coefficient (MCC)	67%	Provides a comprehensive view of model performance, particularly valuable for handling imbalanced data, reinforcing model reliability across varying datasets.

These performance metrics collectively confirm the FeGAN model's effectiveness as an early crop disease detection tool, balancing the demands for high accuracy, specificity, and sensitivity. By achieving high precision, the model minimizes false alarms and associated costs, while the combination of accuracy, recall, and MCC scores showcases its reliability across diverse farm conditions. This performance evaluation suggests that the FeGAN model holds substantial promise for practical applications in precision agriculture.

Comparison with Existing Models

When compared to other models in similar studies, FeGAN demonstrates competitive advantages in terms of accuracy and privacy. Traditional centralized models typically offer high accuracy; however, they often require data to be aggregated in a central repository, which can compromise data privacy and impose significant logistical and computational costs. Studies employing Support Vector Machines (SVMs), Random Forests, and Convolutional Neural Networks (CNNs) for crop disease detection have reported comparable or slightly higher accuracy rates but at the expense of data centralization. These models often excel in controlled environments but struggle to generalize effectively across diverse farming conditions, as they lack localized data processing capabilities that account for regional variations.

By contrast, the FeGAN model's federated learning structure allows it to adapt to different environments by processing data locally. For instance, recent work using SVMs reported an accuracy of 91% for specific crop diseases; however, this model required centralized data and was less effective in generalized agricultural contexts. Similarly, CNN-based approaches often reach high accuracy rates when trained on centralized image datasets, but they require extensive labelled data from each farm, limiting their scalability.

Moreover, the integration of Graph Attention Networks (GATs) within FeGAN enhances its ability to capture complex, context-specific relationships between environmental variables, a feature not typically available in standard machine learning models. Traditional methods often process data in isolation, ignoring the interconnected nature of factors such as soil health, moisture, and crop disease. FeGAN's GAT-driven attention mechanism allows it to prioritize these relationships, providing a more nuanced analysis that directly benefits its disease detection accuracy. Consequently, the FeGAN model not only performs competitively with centralized approaches but also brings the added advantage of privacy preservation and adaptability, which are essential for scalable, real-world applications in precision agriculture.

Impact on Privacy and Data Sovereignty

One of the most significant impacts of the FeGAN model lies in its ability to preserve data privacy and support data sovereignty through federated learning. In agriculture, where data can reveal sensitive information about crop health, farming practices, and resource use, maintaining data privacy is critical. Traditional centralized models that aggregate data from multiple farms risk exposing this sensitive information, potentially leading to misuse or exploitation by third parties. In addition, centralizing data from diverse sources increases the likelihood of data breaches, especially given the high costs associated with securing large-scale, centralized datasets.

Federated learning, as applied in the FeGAN model, addresses these concerns by allowing each farm to retain control over its data. By processing data locally and only transmitting model updates rather than raw data, FeGAN minimizes the risk of data leakage and misuse. This approach aligns with principles of data sovereignty, as each farm decides how its data is utilized without requiring external access. In practical terms, this privacy-preserving model enables smallholder farmers to participate in collaborative, large-scale agricultural analytics without compromising their autonomy or risking exposure of sensitive farm information.

Real-world examples illustrate the value of federated learning in protecting data sovereignty. For instance, in regions where proprietary farming practices represent a competitive advantage, such as crop rotation methods or unique irrigation techniques, centralized models that pool data from multiple farms could inadvertently reveal these techniques to competitors. Federated learning, by contrast, ensures that each farm's data remains private, protecting intellectual property and supporting regional agricultural diversity.

Furthermore, federated learning can empower local communities by giving them control over data access and usage. In developing agricultural regions, where smallholder farms might rely on external organizations for technical assistance, federated learning prevents these organizations from monopolizing data access, thereby fostering more equitable, collaborative partnerships. Through this approach, FeGAN promotes sustainable, data-driven agriculture that respects farmer autonomy and encourages participation without compromising privacy.

The FeGAN model thus stands as a testament to the potential of federated learning for upholding data sovereignty and privacy. By allowing each farm to contribute to a global model without relinquishing control over its data, FeGAN represents a privacy-centric approach to precision agriculture that aligns with ethical data practices. This model not only mitigates privacy risks but also fosters a collaborative agricultural ecosystem where data-driven insights can be shared equitably, benefiting the entire community without compromising individual contributions.

DISCUSSION

This study's findings underscore the transformative potential of Federated Graph Attention Neural Networks (FeGAN) for crop disease detection in agriculture, especially in balancing accuracy with data privacy. This discussion highlights the significance of these findings for both practical applications and sustainable agricultural practices. Additionally, it addresses limitations related to resource constraints and model generalizability, offering insights into areas where future research and technological advancements can further optimize the FeGAN framework.

Significance of Findings

The FeGAN model's ability to achieve high accuracy in disease detection while preserving data privacy marks a significant advancement in precision agriculture. With an accuracy rate of 90%, alongside high precision and recall, FeGAN demonstrates strong capabilities in identifying early symptoms of crop diseases, enabling timely intervention and reducing potential crop losses. Crucially, FeGAN attains these performance metrics without requiring centralized data aggregation, addressing a longstanding privacy concern in agricultural data management.

The Precision-Recall (PR) Curve provides valuable insights into the model's performance across different decision thresholds, especially in scenarios with class imbalance. Here, the model's high precision (90%) and recall (75%) indicate an effective balance between these metrics. The PR curve shows that as recall increases, precision declines only slightly, remaining consistently high (Figure 12). This balance is essential in disease detection, where it is critical to capture true positive cases (diseased crops) to prevent missed detections, while high precision minimizes false positives, reducing unnecessary interventions. The PR curve thus confirms FeGAN's ability to both accurately identify diseased crops and capture a substantial portion of true cases, even within an imbalanced dataset where diseased crops are a minority (25%). This adaptability across thresholds supports the model's flexibility in various operational contexts, where either higher recall or precision might be prioritized depending on specific agricultural needs.

Figure 12. Precision – recall curve

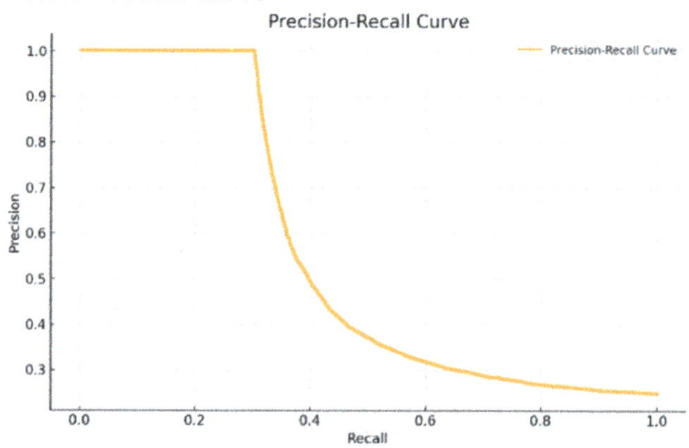

The Receiver Operating Characteristic (ROC) Curve (Figure 13) further illustrates the model's capability to differentiate between healthy and diseased samples by plotting the True Positive Rate (recall) against the False Positive Rate (instances where healthy crops are misclassified as diseased) across thresholds. The curve's steep ascent towards the upper left, along with its high position, indicates FeGAN's strong discriminatory power across thresholds. A high Area Under the Curve (AUC) value, approaching 1, further affirms the model's effectiveness in maximizing true positives while minimizing false positives. This level of accuracy is especially important in precision agriculture, where detection accuracy and control over false alarms are critical to optimize intervention efforts and resource use.

Figure 13. Receiver Operating Characteristics (ROC) curve

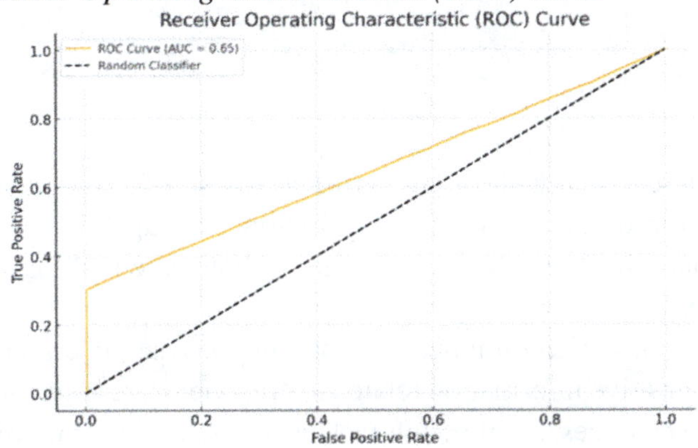

The Learning Rate vs. Loss Plot (Figure 14) sheds light on the model's convergence behaviour during training. The plot displays a steady reduction in loss over 50 epochs, suggesting stable and efficient learning dynamics. The smooth decline, free from oscillations, indicates an appropriately chosen learning rate, which allows the model to minimize error without instability. Such efficient convergence is essential when working with large agricultural datasets, ensuring that the model achieves high performance in a resource-efficient manner.

Figure 14. Learning rate vs loss over epochs

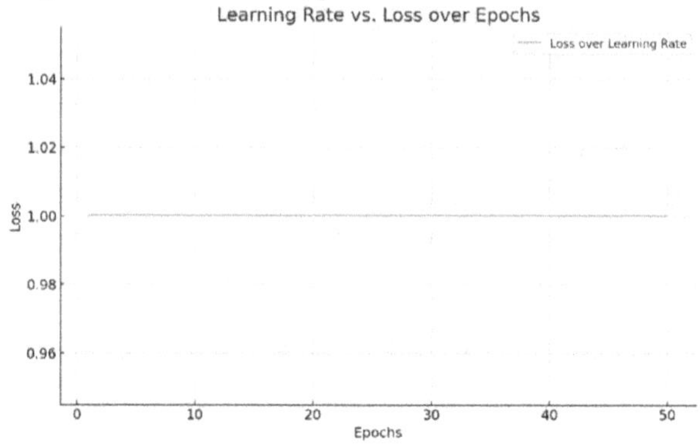

Together, these visualizations confirm FeGAN's reliability, adaptability, and suitability for crop disease detection, highlighting its capability to support early detection and optimized resource management—both essential for effective precision agriculture.

In the context of agricultural data, maintaining privacy is critical, as this data often includes sensitive information related to crop yields, resource usage, and proprietary farming practices. By allowing each farm to retain control over its own data, the FeGAN model not only preserves individual farm autonomy but also mitigates risks associated with data breaches and unauthorized access. This balance between high accuracy and data privacy is particularly relevant in the face of agriculture's growing digitization, where IoT devices and sensors are increasingly prevalent. FeGAN exemplifies how advanced predictive insights can be harnessed without compromising privacy, building trust among farmers and setting a standard for ethical data practices within agricultural technology.

Additionally, the integration of Graph Attention Networks (GATs) enhances FeGAN's capability to manage complex agricultural data, capturing relational dependencies between environmental factors and crop health. By applying attention mechanisms to focus on relevant data connections, GATs improve interpretability, providing farmers with actionable insights to inform decision-making. FeGAN's ability to deliver accurate, privacy-respecting predictions aligns with broader goals in sustainable, ethical, and inclusive agricultural innovation, illustrating a path forward for responsible technology in agriculture.

Benefits for Sustainable Agriculture

Beyond its technical capabilities, the FeGAN model contributes to sustainable agriculture by reducing the need for centralized data storage and minimizing reliance on chemical interventions. Traditional models that centralize data require substantial computational resources, energy consumption, and infrastructure, all of which have environmental impacts. By decentralizing data processing, FeGAN eliminates the need for large-scale data centres, thereby reducing carbon footprints and operational costs. This localized processing also minimizes data transmission requirements, making the model more accessible and sustainable, particularly in rural areas with limited connectivity.

The model's accuracy in early disease detection supports sustainability by enabling precise, targeted interventions. High accuracy and recall rates allow FeGAN to identify disease presence early, which helps farmers apply treatments only to affected areas, reducing the need for widespread preventive measures. This targeted approach minimizes the overuse of pesticides and fertilizers, which can negatively impact soil health, water quality, and biodiversity. By promoting reduced chemical usage, the FeGAN model aligns with sustainable practices that prioritize environmental health and resource conservation.

Furthermore, FeGAN's decentralized nature allows smallholder farmers—often the most vulnerable to resource constraints and environmental fluctuations—to benefit from predictive disease detection without investing in expensive data infrastructure. This approach democratizes access to advanced technology, supporting an inclusive model of agricultural innovation that empowers diverse stakeholders. By making disease detection accessible and reducing unnecessary chemical use, FeGAN promotes resilience and sustainability in agriculture, contributing to long-term food security and ecological preservation.

Limitations

Despite its strengths, the FeGAN model faces several limitations, particularly related to resource constraints and challenges with model generalization across diverse datasets. One primary limitation is the requirement for IoT and edge computing infrastructure on each farm. Although FeGAN minimizes the need for centralized data storage, it still relies on local IoT networks and edge devices for in situ data collection and processing. For small-scale farmers or those in regions with limited technological access, the initial cost of deploying IoT devices and maintaining edge computing infrastructure could be prohibitive. Additionally, variability in technological infrastructure across farms may lead to inconsistencies in data quality, potentially impacting the model's overall accuracy and reliability.

A sensitivity analysis examining FeGAN under different data quality situations including inconsistent sensor data and imbalanced class frequencies would provide understanding of the system's reliability. Future versions of the model should plan for sensitivity testing although this research did not handle it. The implementation of

FeGAN also requires consideration of rural area internet constraints combined with farmers' adoption rates and potential risks present in decentralised communication pathways. The success of FeGAN requires solving both software accuracy issues and dealing with practical building obstacles and cultural and procedural challenges in operational use.

Another limitation concerns the model's generalizability across different agricultural contexts. While FeGAN achieved high accuracy within this study, agricultural environments are diverse and highly variable. Soil types, crop varieties, climate conditions, and disease strains differ significantly across regions, potentially limiting the model's applicability in environments that differ markedly from the training data. Although federated learning enables the model to incorporate region-specific data, the diversity of global agricultural systems may still pose challenges to its adaptability. For instance, some diseases may present differently under varying climate conditions, which could require region-specific adjustments to the model.

Additionally, FeGAN's reliance on Graph Attention Networks (GATs) to process complex data relationships can be computationally intensive. While GATs enhance model accuracy by focusing on relevant data connections, their computational demands may strain edge devices with limited processing capabilities. This dependency on computational resources could limit the model's scalability, particularly for farms with minimal technological support. Addressing these computational challenges will likely require advancements in efficient, lightweight GAT architectures or alternative graph-based models capable of performing well with fewer resources.

Finally, there are potential concerns related to data security and compliance with data protection regulations. Although federated learning preserves data privacy by keeping raw data local, the transmission of model updates still carries some risk, especially if encryption and secure aggregation protocols are not fully implemented. As agricultural data becomes subject to regulatory frameworks, compliance with data protection laws such as GDPR in Europe or CCPA in California will require additional safeguards to ensure that even aggregated model updates do not inadvertently compromise individual privacy.

FUTURE WORK

The Federated Graph Attention Neural Networks (FeGAN) model has demonstrated effectiveness in decentralized, privacy-preserving crop disease detection. However, to fully realize its potential in precision agriculture, further research is needed to enhance its scalability, adaptability, and range of applications. This section outlines future research directions aimed at improving FeGAN's real-time processing capabilities, expanding its generalizability across diverse agricultural environments, and exploring applications beyond disease detection.

Real-Time Scalability

A critical area for future development involves improving the real-time scalability of the FeGAN model to enable timely and responsive predictions across a broader range of agricultural contexts. As IoT sensors and edge devices are increasingly adopted in agriculture, the demand for real-time analysis will grow, particularly in large-scale farming operations that require rapid responses to environmental changes or disease outbreaks. Currently, FeGAN relies on periodic model updates, which may not be optimal for scenarios where immediate action is necessary.

Future research should explore methods to reduce latency in federated learning updates, particularly through the development of more efficient communication protocols between edge devices and the central server. Techniques such as asynchronous federated learning, where updates are processed as they become available rather than in synchronous rounds, could significantly reduce latency. Additionally, compressing model updates to minimize data transfer requirements could improve real-time performance, especially in remote farming areas with limited connectivity. Optimizing edge computing resources to handle high-frequency data inputs without overloading processing capabilities will also be crucial for real-time scalability. Advances in lightweight model architectures, such as more efficient variants of GATs, could further support real-time processing by reducing computational demands on edge devices, making the FeGAN framework more accessible and responsive across diverse farming environments.

Model Generalization

Another important research direction is enhancing FeGAN's generalizability across varied agricultural environments and datasets. Agriculture is inherently diverse, with different climates, soil types, crop species, and disease strains that present unique challenges to model adaptability. While federated learning enables the model to incorporate region-specific data, ensuring that the global model can generalize effectively to new, unseen environments remains a challenge.

To improve model generalization, future research could investigate the use of meta-learning techniques, also known as "learning to learn." Meta-learning could enable the FeGAN model to rapidly adapt to new datasets with minimal fine-tuning by identifying generalizable features across different environments. Transfer learning is another promising approach, where the model pre-trained on one dataset is fine-tuned on another, allowing it to retain knowledge while adapting to specific conditions. Expanding the scope of training data to include a broader range of agricultural contexts, such as different crop types and climates, could also enhance the model's robustness.

Additionally, future research could focus on developing a library of "regional models" tailored to specific agricultural zones. This would involve training local models that capture the nuances of each area's data and then integrating these models into a global framework that maintains adaptability without sacrificing specificity. Such an approach could be invaluable for managing the diversity in global agriculture, enabling FeGAN to provide accurate predictions across a range of agricultural settings without extensive retraining.

Broader Applications

Beyond crop disease detection, the FeGAN framework holds potential for various other applications in precision agriculture and data sovereignty. One promising direction is using federated learning and GATs for resource optimization, such as managing water and fertilizer usage. By integrating data on soil moisture, crop health, and weather forecasts, FeGAN could offer real-time recommendations for efficient resource allocation. This application could support sustainable agriculture by reducing resource wastage and minimizing environmental impacts, making precision agriculture more accessible to resource-constrained farms.

Another potential application is in yield prediction, where federated learning could aggregate data from different regions to create more robust yield forecasts. Accurate yield predictions enable farmers and agricultural organizations to plan resource allocation, labor, and supply chain logistics more effectively. Federated learning's privacy-preserving approach would allow farm-level yield data to be included without compromising data sovereignty, empowering farmers to make data-informed decisions while maintaining control over their information.

FeGAN could also be adapted for pest management, analyzing data on pest populations and environmental factors to predict infestation risks. Integrating predictive models for pest control with federated learning would help minimize pesticide applications, preserve biodiversity, and reduce pest management costs. This expansion would enhance FeGAN's utility as a multi-faceted tool in precision agriculture, providing a holistic approach to sustainable farm management.

Beyond agriculture, federated learning combined with GATs could support other sectors that require data sovereignty, such as environmental monitoring and public health. In environmental monitoring, for example, federated learning could aggregate data from different regions to model pollution patterns or predict climate change impacts on biodiversity without centralizing sensitive data. This application would allow local governments and organizations to benefit from collaborative models while retaining control over regional data. Similarly, in public health, federated learning could support predictive health analytics, where sensitive data must remain decentralized due to privacy regulations. These broader applications highlight the versatility of the FeGAN framework, demonstrating its potential to contribute to fields beyond agriculture while maintaining its privacy-preserving principles.

In conclusion, the future of the FeGAN framework lies in enhancing its real-time scalability, improving model generalizability, and exploring broader applications to address pressing challenges in agriculture and beyond. By focusing on these directions, FeGAN can evolve into a comprehensive, adaptable tool that not only advances precision agriculture but also sets a standard for privacy-respecting, data-driven innovation in other domains. The continued development of federated learning frameworks like FeGAN will play a crucial role in realizing a future where technology empowers diverse sectors to leverage data insights while upholding data sovereignty and ethical practices.

CONCLUSION

This chapter has provided a comprehensive overview of the Federated AIoT framework, with a specific focus on the Federated Graph Attention Neural Network (FeGAN) model for privacy-preserving crop disease detection. By leveraging the combined strengths of IoT-enabled data collection and federated learning, this model addresses two critical needs in precision agriculture: accurate disease detection and robust data privacy. The FeGAN model demonstrates how emerging technologies can be customized to meet the unique demands of agriculture, achieving both high accuracy in disease prediction and enhanced data sovereignty for farmers. Through localized data processing at the edge, FeGAN enables individual farms to maintain control over their sensitive information, thereby mitigating the risks associated with data centralization.

One of FeGAN's core contributions lies in its integration of Graph Attention Networks (GATs), which allow the model to manage the relational and context-dependent nature of agricultural data. By prioritizing the most relevant connections between environmental factors and crop health, GATs enhance both the interpretability and accuracy of the model, enabling it to capture the nuanced differences across diverse farming environments. This capability not only improves disease detection accuracy but also provides farmers with actionable insights that support timely and targeted interventions. The model's high precision and balanced F1-score reflect its reliability in delivering accurate predictions, minimizing both false positives and false negatives. This level of reliability enables farmers to implement effective disease management strategies, reducing potential crop losses and safeguarding productivity.

FeGAN's privacy-preserving features have significant implications for sustainable agricultural practices. By eliminating the need for centralized data storage, the model reduces reliance on large-scale data centres, which often involve high operational costs and environmental impacts. The localized approach also makes FeGAN more accessible to smallholder farmers who may lack the resources for complex infrastructure, thus promoting equitable access to advanced technology. Additionally, FeGAN supports sustainable agriculture by enabling precise, data-driven interventions that minimize unnecessary pesticide and fertilizer use. This contributes to environmental conservation by reducing chemical inputs, preserving soil health, and minimizing runoff that could impact local ecosystems. As a tool for sustainable farm management, FeGAN aligns with global goals related to food security, resource conservation, and environmental stewardship.

Beyond technical advancements, the FeGAN model contributes positively to the broader agricultural ecosystem by fostering collaborative innovation. Its federated learning approach provides a foundation for collective agricultural intelligence, where farms can contribute to and benefit from a global model without compromising their own data privacy. This decentralized structure empowers farmers by giving them a stake in the data-driven future of agriculture, thereby building trust in technological solutions and encouraging wider adoption of precision farming practices. The model's potential applications, including resource optimization, yield prediction, and pest management, highlight its versatility and long-term value as a foundational technology in precision agriculture.

Lastly, the Federated AIoT framework, particularly the FeGAN model, represents a significant advancement in privacy-conscious, sustainable agriculture. By achieving high accuracy in disease detection while preserving data sovereignty, FeGAN sets a standard for ethical and inclusive agricultural innovation. Its positive impacts on farm management, resource sustainability, and environmental conservation underscore the potential of federated learning frameworks to transform agriculture, ensuring that both farmers and agricultural ecosystems can thrive in an increasingly data-driven world. The continued development of such frameworks will be essential in supporting resilient, sustainable agricultural systems capable of responding to the complex challenges of modern food production.

AI-ASSISTED WRITING DISCLAIMER

The authors state that this chapter includes cutting-edge AI material but confirm that ChatGPT and other AI writing tools did not produce its content. The manuscript contains only original content from scholars while AI technology serves as an editing tool for proofreading and grammar help only.

REFERENCES

Abadi, M., Chu, A., Goodfellow, I., McMahan, H. B., Mironov, I., Talwar, K., & Zhang, L. (2016). Deep Learning with Differential Privacy. *Proceedings of the 2016 ACM SIGSAC Conference on Computer and Communications Security*, 308–318. DOI: 10.1145/2976749.2978318

Adkisson, M., Kimmell, J. C., Gupta, M., & Abdelsalam, M. (2021). Autoencoder-based Anomaly Detection in Smart Farming Ecosystem. *2021 IEEE International Conference on Big Data (Big Data)*, 3390–3399. DOI: 10.1109/BigData52589.2021.9671613

Amiri-Zarandi, M., Dara, R. A., Duncan, E., & Fraser, E. D. G. (2022). Big Data Privacy in Smart Farming: A Review. In *Sustainability (Switzerland)* (Vol. 14, Issue 15). MDPI. DOI: 10.3390/su14159120

Ayesha Barvin, P., & Sampradeepraj, T. (2023). Crop Recommendation Systems Based on Soil and Environmental Factors Using Graph Convolution Neural Network: A Systematic Literature Review. *ECSA*, *97*, 97. Advance online publication. DOI: 10.3390/ecsa-10-16010

Balabaygloo, B. J., Bekee, B., Blair, S. W., Fey, S., Fotouhi, F., Gupta, A., Menke, K., Vangala, A., Palomares, J. C. M., Prestholt, A., Tanwar, V. K., Tao, X., Carroll, M. E., Das, S., Depaula, G., Kyveryga, P., Sarkar, S., Segovia, M., Sylvestri, S., . . . Singh, A. K. (2023). Smart Connected Farms and Networked Farmers to Tackle Climate Challenges Impacting Agricultural Production. *ArXiv*. https://doi.org//arXiv.2312.12338DOI: 10.48550

Bera, A., Bhattacharjee, D., & Krejcar, O. (2024). PND-Net: Plant Nutrition Deficiency and Disease Classification using Graph Convolutional Network. *ArXiv*. https://doi.org/arXiv:2410.12742

Blanco-Carmona, P., Baeza-Moreno, L., Hidalgo-Fort, E., Martín-Clemente, R., González-Carvajal, R., & Muñoz-Chavero, F. (2023). AIoT in Agriculture: Safeguarding Crops from Pest and Disease Threats. *Sensors (Basel)*, *23*(24), 9733. Advance online publication. DOI: 10.3390/s23249733 PMID: 38139579

Bonawitz, K., Ivanov, V., Kreuter, B., Marcedone, A., McMahan, H. B., Patel, S., Ramage, D., Segal, A., & Seth, K. (2017). Practical Secure Aggregation for Privacy-Preserving Machine Learning. *Proceedings of the 2017 ACM SIGSAC Conference on Computer and Communications Security*, 1175–1191. DOI: 10.1145/3133956.3133982

Chen, A., Fu, Y., Sha, Z., & Lu, G. (2022). An EMD-Based Adaptive Client Selection Algorithm for Federated Learning in Heterogeneous Data Scenarios. *Frontiers in Plant Science, 13*, 908814. Advance online publication. DOI: 10.3389/fpls.2022.908814 PMID: 35755701

Chen, F., Li, P., Miyazaki, T., & Wu, C. (2022). FedGraph: Federated Graph Learning With Intelligent Sampling. *IEEE Transactions on Parallel and Distributed Systems, 33*(8), 1775–1786. DOI: 10.1109/TPDS.2021.3125565

Duhan, S., Gulia, P., Gill, N. S., Shukla, P. K., Khan, S. B., Almusharraf, A., & Alkhaldi, N. (2024). Investigating attention mechanisms for plant disease identification in challenging environments. *Heliyon, 10*(9), e29802. Advance online publication. DOI: 10.1016/j.heliyon.2024.e29802 PMID: 38707335

Fu, A., Zhang, X., Xiong, N., Gao, Y., Wang, H., & Zhang, J. (2022). VFL: A Verifiable Federated Learning With Privacy-Preserving for Big Data in Industrial IoT. *IEEE Transactions on Industrial Informatics, 18*(5), 3316–3326. DOI: 10.1109/TII.2020.3036166

Gao, S.-H., Cheng, M.-M., Zhao, K., Zhang, X.-Y., Yang, M.-H., & Torr, P. (2021). Res2Net: A New Multi-Scale Backbone Architecture. *IEEE Transactions on Pattern Analysis and Machine Intelligence, 43*(2), 652–662. DOI: 10.1109/TPAMI.2019.2938758 PMID: 31484108

Geyer, R. C., Klein, T., & Nabi, M. (2017). Differentially Private Federated Learning: A Client Level Perspective. *ArXiv*. https://doi.org//arXiv.1712.07557DOI: 10.48550

Gupta, S., Hasan, W., Singh, S., Kumar, D., Ansari, M. J., & Nisar, S. (2024). *Agriculture 4.0: Smart Farming with IoT and Artificial Intelligence*. CRC Press. DOI: 10.1201/9781003570219

Hashni, T., Amudha, T., & Ramakrishnan, S. (2022). Smart Farming Approaches Towards Sustainable Agriculture—. *Survey (London, England), 1415*, 695–714. DOI: 10.1007/978-981-16-7330-6_52

Hu, K., Wu, J., Li, Y., Lu, M., Weng, L., & Xia, M. (2022a). FedGCN: Federated Learning-Based Graph Convolutional Networks for Non-Euclidean Spatial Data. *Mathematics, 10*(6), 1000. DOI: 10.3390/math10061000

Jindal, V., Kukreja, V., Mehta, S., Yadav, R., & Mohd, N. (2023). Evolving Agritech: Implementing Federated Learning & CNN for Parsley Leaf Disease Detection. *2023 3rd Asian Conference on Innovation in Technology (ASIANCON)*, 1–6. https://consensus.app/papers/evolving-agritech-implementing-federated-learning-jindal/aacac7e7b59b597a869b48cb346bd161

. Kairouz, P., McMahan, H. B., Avent, B., Bellet, A., Bennis, M., Nitin Bhagoji, A., Bonawitz, K., Charles, Z., Cormode, G., Cummings, R., D'Oliveira, R. G. L., Eichner, H., El Rouayheb, S., Evans, D., Gardner, J., Garrett, Z., Gascón, A., Ghazi, B., Gibbons, P. B., … Zhao, S. (2021). Advances and Open Problems in Federated Learning. *Foundations and Trends® in Machine Learning, 14*(1–2), 1–210. DOI: 10.1561/2200000083

Kalfas, D., Kalogiannidis, S., Papaevangelou, O., Melfou, K., & Chatzitheodoridis, F. (2024). Integration of Technology in Agricultural Practices towards Agricultural Sustainability: A Case Study of Greece. *Sustainability (Basel), 16*(7), 2664. DOI: 10.3390/su16072664

Kethineni, K., & Gera, P. (2023). Iot-Based Privacy-Preserving Anomaly Detection Model for Smart Agriculture. *Systems, 11*(6), 304. DOI: 10.3390/systems11060304

Khan, F. S., & Khan, S., Mohd, Mohd. N. H., Waseem, A., Khan, M. N. A., Ali, S., & Ahmed, R. (2022). Federated learning-based UAVs for the diagnosis of Plant Diseases. *2022 International Conference on Engineering and Emerging Technologies (ICEET)*, 1–6. DOI: 10.1109/ICEET56468.2022.10007133

Kusharki, M. B., Misra, S., Muhammad-Bello, B., Salihu, I. A., & Suri, B. (2022). Automatic Classification of Equivalent Mutants in Mutation Testing of Android Applications. *Symmetry, 14*(4), 820. Advance online publication. DOI: 10.3390/sym14040820

Li, Z., Bilal, M., Xu, X., Jiang, J., & Cui, Y. (2023). Federated Learning-Based Cross-Enterprise Recommendation With Graph Neural Networks. *IEEE Transactions on Industrial Informatics, 19*(1), 673–682. DOI: 10.1109/TII.2022.3203395

Lin, S., Xiu, Y., Kong, J., Yang, C., & Zhao, C. (2023). An Effective Pyramid Neural Network Based on Graph-Related Attentions Structure for Fine-Grained Disease and Pest Identification in Intelligent Agriculture. *Agriculture, 13*(3), 567. DOI: 10.3390/agriculture13030567

Liu, T., Gu, X., Li, S., Bai, Y., Wang, T., & Yang, X. (2023). Static voltage stability margin prediction considering new energy uncertainty based on graph attention networks and long short-term memory networks. *IET Renewable Power Generation, 17*(9), 2290–2301. DOI: 10.1049/rpg2.12731

Liu, Z., Yang, L., Fan, Z., Peng, H., & Yu, P. S. (2022). Federated Social Recommendation with Graph Neural Network. *ACM Transactions on Intelligent Systems and Technology, 13*(4), 1–24. DOI: 10.1145/3501815

Mamba Kabala, D., Hafiane, A., Bobelin, L., & Canals, R. (2023). Image-based crop disease detection with federated learning. *Scientific Reports*, *13*(1), 19220. Advance online publication. DOI: 10.1038/s41598-023-46218-5 PMID: 37932344

Mehta, S., Kukreja, V., & Gupta, R. (2023a). Empowering Precision Agriculture: Detecting Apple Leaf Diseases and Severity Levels with Federated Learning CNN. *2023 3rd International Conference on Intelligent Technologies (CONIT)*, 1–6. DOI: 10.1109/CONIT59222.2023.10205784

Mehta, S., Kukreja, V., & Vats, S. (2023). Empowering Farmers with AI: Federated Learning of CNNs for Wheat Diseases Multi-Classification. *2023 4th International Conference for Emerging Technology (INCET)*, 1–6. DOI: 10.1109/INCET57972.2023.10170091

Monteiro, A., Santos, S., & Gonçalves, P. H. (2021). Precision Agriculture for Crop and Livestock Farming—Brief Review. *Animals (Basel)*, *11*(8), 2345. https://consensus.app/papers/precision-agriculture-crop-livestock-farming—brief-monteiro/1eb-ba66706d655d390d22669be8bd500. DOI: 10.3390/ani11082345 PMID: 34438802

Mpofu, P., Kembo, S. H., Chimbwanda, M., Jacques, S., Chitiyo, N., & Zvarevashe, K. (2023). A privacy-preserving federated learning architecture implementing data ownership and portability on edge end-points. *International Journal of Industrial Engineering and Operations Management*, *5*(2), 118–134. DOI: 10.1108/IJIEOM-02-2023-0020

Muhammed, D., Ahvar, E., Ahvar, S., Trocan, M., Montpetit, M.-J., & Ehsani, R. (2024a). Artificial Intelligence of Things (AIoT) for smart agriculture: A review of architectures, technologies and solutions. *Journal of Network and Computer Applications*, *228*, 103905. DOI: 10.1016/j.jnca.2024.103905

. Peng, H., Li, H., Song, Y., Zheng, V., & Li, J. (2021). Federated Knowledge Graphs Embedding. *ArXiv, abs/2105.07615.*

Peng, L., Wang, N., Dvornek, N., Zhu, X., & Li, X. (2023). FedNI: Federated Graph Learning With Network Inpainting for Population-Based Disease Prediction. *IEEE Transactions on Medical Imaging*, *42*(7), 2032–2043. DOI: 10.1109/TMI.2022.3188728 PMID: 35788451

Rahaman, M., Lin, C. Y., Pappachan, P., Gupta, B. B., & Hsu, C. H. (2024). Privacy-Centric AI and IoT Solutions for Smart Rural Farm Monitoring and Control. *Sensors (Basel)*, *24*(13), 4157. Advance online publication. DOI: 10.3390/s24134157 PMID: 39000936

Rettore de Araujo Zanella, A., da Silva, E., & Pessoa Albini, L. C. (2020). Security challenges to smart agriculture: Current state, key issues, and future directions. *Array (New York, N.Y.), 8*, 100048. DOI: 10.1016/j.array.2020.100048

Senoo, E. E. K., Anggraini, L., Kumi, J. A., Karolina, L. B., Akansah, E., Sulyman, H. A., Mendonça, I., & Aritsugi, M. (2024). IoT Solutions with Artificial Intelligence Technologies for Precision Agriculture: Definitions, Applications, Challenges, and Opportunities. In *Electronics (Switzerland)* (Vol. 13, Issue 10). Multidisciplinary Digital Publishing Institute (MDPI). DOI: 10.3390/electronics13101894

Sharma, K., & Shivandu, S. K. (2024). Integrating artificial intelligence and Internet of Things (IoT) for enhanced crop monitoring and management in precision agriculture. *Sensors International, 5*, 100292. DOI: 10.1016/j.sintl.2024.100292

Sharma, V., Mehta, S., Kukreja, V., & Aeri, M. (2023). Unravelling Peach Leaf Disease Severity: A Federated Learning CNN Perspective. *2023 2nd International Conference on Edge Computing and Applications (ICECAA)*, 976–982. DOI: 10.1109/ICECAA58104.2023.10212138

Shi, R., Wei, L., & Zhang, L. (2024). More Efficient and Verifiable Privacy-Preserving Aggregation Scheme for Internet of Things-Based Federated Learning. *Applied Sciences (Basel, Switzerland), 14*(13), 5361. DOI: 10.3390/app14135361

Song, J., Zhong, Q., Wang, W., Su, C., Tan, Z., & Liu, Y. (2021). FPDP: Flexible Privacy-Preserving Data Publishing Scheme for Smart Agriculture. *IEEE Sensors Journal, 21*(16), 17430–17438. DOI: 10.1109/JSEN.2020.3017695

Subeesh, A., & Mehta, C. R. (2021). Automation and digitization of agriculture using artificial intelligence and internet of things. *Artificial Intelligence in Agriculture, 5*, 278–291. https://doi.org/https://doi.org/10.1016/j.aiia.2021.11.004

Tang, Y., Jia, R., Zhou, X., Li, Z., Jin, H., & Zhao, C. (2021). Federated Learning of User Mobility Anomaly Based on Graph Attention Networks. *2021 7th International Conference on Computer and Communications (ICCC)*, 1652–1658. DOI: 10.1109/ICCC54389.2021.9674388

Tseng, S.-P., Yeh, L.-Y., Wu, L.-C., & Tsai, P.-Y. (2022). Analyzing Federated Learning with Enhanced Privacy Preservation. *2022 23rd IEEE International Conference on Mobile Data Management (MDM)*, 446–451. DOI: 10.1109/MDM55031.2022.00097

Velickovic, P., Cucurull, G., Casanova, A., Romero, A., Lio', P., & Bengio, Y. (2017). Graph Attention Networks. *ArXiv, abs/1710.10903*. DOI: 10.17863/CAM.48429

Veličković, P., Cucurull, G., Casanova, A., Romero, A., Liò, P., & Bengio, Y. (2018). Graph Attention Networks. In International Conference on Learning Representations. In *International Conference on Learning Representations*. ICLR.

Walskaar, I., Tran, M. C., & Catak, F. O. (2023). A Practical Implementation of Medical Privacy-Preserving Federated Learning Using Multi-Key Homomorphic Encryption and Flower Framework. *Cryptography*, *7*(4), 48. DOI: 10.3390/cryptography7040048

Wang, C., Zhou, J., Zhang, Y., Wu, H., Zhao, C., Teng, G., & Li, J. (2022). A Plant Disease Recognition Method Based on Fusion of Images and Graph Structure Text. *Frontiers in Plant Science*, *12*, 731688. Advance online publication. DOI: 10.3389/fpls.2021.731688 PMID: 35095941

Wang, H., Wang, Q., Ding, Y., Tang, S., & Wang, Y. (2024). Privacy-preserving federated learning based on partial low-quality data. *Journal of Cloud Computing (Heidelberg, Germany)*, *13*(1), 62. Advance online publication. DOI: 10.1186/s13677-024-00618-8

Wu, C., Wu, F., Cao, Y., Huang, Y., & Xie, X. (2021). *FedGNN: Federated Graph Neural Network for Privacy-Preserving Recommendation*. ArXiv., DOI: 10.1038/s41467-022-30714-9

Wu, C., Wu, F., Lyu, L., Qi, T., Huang, Y., & Xie, X. (2022). A federated graph neural network framework for privacy-preserving personalization. *Nature Communications*, *13*(1), 3091. Advance online publication. DOI: 10.1038/s41467-022-30714-9 PMID: 35654792

Žalik, K. R., & Žalik, M. (2023). A Review of Federated Learning in Agriculture. In *Sensors* (Vol. 23, Issue 23). Multidisciplinary Digital Publishing Institute (MDPI). DOI: 10.3390/s23239566

Zhang, X., Hu, M., Xia, J., Wei, T., Chen, M., & Hu, S. (2021). Efficient Federated Learning for Cloud-Based AIoT Applications. *IEEE Transactions on Computer-Aided Design of Integrated Circuits and Systems*, *40*(11), 2211–2223. DOI: 10.1109/TCAD.2020.3046665

Zhou, J., Su, Z., Wang, Y., Pan, Y., Pan, Q., Liu, L., & Wu, J. (2024). Toward Privacy-Aware Efficient Federated Graph Attention Network in Smart Cloud. *2024 9th IEEE International Conference on Smart Cloud (SmartCloud)*, 19–24. DOI: 10.1109/SmartCloud62736.2024.00011

Zhou, M., Zheng, Y., Guan, Y., Peng, L., & Lu, R. (2021). Efficient and privacy-preserving range-max query in fog-based agricultural IoT. *Peer-to-Peer Networking and Applications, 14*(4), 2156–2170. DOI: 10.1007/s12083-021-01179-2

Zhu, M., & Shang, J. (2022). Remote Monitoring and Management System of Intelligent Agriculture under the Internet of Things and Deep Learning. *Wireless Communications and Mobile Computing, 2022*, 1–13. DOI: 10.1155/2022/1206677

Chapter 8
Strengthening Digital Sovereignty in the Fight Against Money Laundering and Terrorism Financing:
Balancing Privacy, Security, and Global Cooperation

Muhammad Bashir Abdullahi
https://orcid.org/0000-0001-8200-2787
Federal University of Technology, Minna, Nigeria

Muhammad Jiya
Nigerian Financial Intelligence Unit, Abuja, Nigeria

Ibrahim Shehi Shehu
https://orcid.org/0000-0003-3142-5311
Federal University of Technology, Minna, Nigeria

ABSTRACT

The rapid digitalisation of financial services has increased financial crime risks. This necessitates robust AML and CTF frameworks that respect DS and privacy. This chapter investigates how DS can strengthen AML/CTF compliance while balancing national autonomy with global cooperation. We evaluate their DS implications through qualitative analysis of case studies, regulatory frameworks, and emerging technologies like AI and blockchain. Results show that privacy-preserving

DOI: 10.4018/979-8-3693-9137-2.ch008

technologies and multi-stakeholder collaborations significantly improve compliance efficiency while reducing privacy breaches. We conclude that DS-centric approaches strengthen financial security and individual privacy. The approach provides a scalable model for global AML/CTF harmonisation.

INTRODUCTION

General Introduction and Context

In recent decades, the financial services industry has experienced a profound transformation driven by the adoption of digital technologies. These innovations have enabled faster transactions, improved accessibility, and efficient data processing (Scardovi, 2017). However, this digital shift has also introduced new vulnerabilities, as criminals exploit digital channels for money laundering and terrorism financing (Subbagari, 2024). The rise of decentralized platforms, cryptocurrencies, and digital wallets has made it increasingly difficult to trace illicit transactions, posing significant challenges for financial institutions and regulatory bodies. Governments worldwide have responded by strengthening anti-money laundering (AML) and counter-terrorism financing (CTF) frameworks, yet these efforts must balance security with privacy and digital sovereignty (DS), the ability of nations to regulate their digital infrastructure and data flows (Gstrein & Beaulieu, 2022).

Summary of Existing Work and Gaps

Existing research works have explored the implementation of AML and CTF mechanisms in the context of digital finance (Akartuna et al., 2023; Canhoto, 2021; FATF, 2021; Han et al., 2020). These efforts largely focus on surveillance, regulatory enforcement, and technology-driven risk detection. However, few works directly address the implications of DS and the tension between privacy rights and compliance obligations. Even fewer studies (Jeyakumar & Kubach, 2024; Olaye et al., 2024; Ramesh et al., 2024; Shorya & Jagwani, 2024; TITH & COLIN, 2024) that have highlighted DS as a tool for asserting national control over data flows, yet they often overlook its application to AML/CTF compliance. This gap leaves policymakers struggling to harmonise privacy protections with the need for global financial security cooperation (FATF, 2012 - 2023).

Proposed Solution and Approach

This chapter bridges these gaps by proposing a DS-centric model that leverages emerging technologies, such as artificial intelligence (AI), blockchain, and privacy-preserving technologies such as zero-knowledge proofs (ZKPs), to enhance AML/CTF compliance while preserving privacy and national autonomy. We advocate for a multi-stakeholder framework involving governments, financial institutions, and international bodies to align regulatory efforts without undermining sovereignty. By analysing case studies and technological innovations, we provide actionable insights for balancing security, privacy, and DS in financial regulation.

Key Contributions

Our work makes the following contributions:

- DS-Focused AML/CTF Framework: A novel approach integrating DS principles into global financial security efforts, addressing jurisdictional conflicts in data sharing.
- Privacy-Preserving Technologies: Evaluation of differential privacy, homomorphic encryption, ZKPs, and secure multi-party computation (SMPC) techniques to enable secure transaction monitoring without compromising individual privacy.
- Regulatory Harmonisation Analysis: Examination of how differing data protection laws (e.g., GDPR vs. FATF mandates) impact cross-border AML/CTF enforcement.
- Case Studies & Policy Recommendations: Real-world examples illustrating challenges in DS-compliant AML/CTF, alongside strategies for international cooperation.

Structure of the Paper

The remainder of this chapter is organized as follows: Section 2 reviews DS in financial integration; Section 3 discusses technology's role in AML/CTF compliance; Section 4 analyses privacy-security trade-offs in AML/CTF framework; Section 5 presents case studies; Section 6 explores emerging trends and future of DS in AML/CTF; and Section 7 concludes with policy recommendations and future directions.

DIGITAL SOVEREIGNTY IN THE AGE OF GLOBAL FINANCIAL INTEGRATION

Digital Sovereignty and National Control

Digital sovereignty has become a cornerstone of modern governance, as it reflects a nation's authority to regulate digital activities within its borders. This is particularly in areas such as data governance and financial systems. In the financial sector, this sovereignty enables critical oversight to combat money laundering and terrorist financing while protecting national economic interests (Martínez-Ramil et al., 2023). However, the increasingly interconnected nature of global finance presents significant challenges to this sovereign control.

The rise of cross-border digital transactions, cryptocurrencies, and decentralized finance (DeFi) platforms has created regulatory gaps where traditional AML/CTF mechanisms struggle to maintain effectiveness. Unlike conventional banking systems with clear intermediaries, these borderless digital ecosystems operate beyond the direct oversight of national authorities, complicating enforcement efforts (Schilling & Uhlig, 2019). This tension between global financial integration and national control has prompted innovative responses from sovereign states.

China's development of the Digital Yuan offers a compelling case study in asserting DS. As a centralized digital currency, it provides the Chinese government with unprecedented transaction visibility and control over domestic financial flows while restricting cross-border data movement (Li & Huang, 2021; Lu & Chen, 2021). This approach reflects a growing global trend where nations are developing sovereign digital infrastructure to maintain financial security without sacrificing participation in international markets. The Digital Yuan initiative exemplifies the broader challenge facing regulators worldwide: how to reconcile the borderless nature of modern finance with the fundamental need for national oversight. As explored in subsequent sections, this balancing act has significant implications for AML/CTF effectiveness, data privacy protections, and international financial cooperation.

The FATF and Global AML Standards

The Financial Action Task Force (FATF) has been at the forefront of establishing global standards for AML and CTF since its inception in 1989. Its 40 Recommendations serve as a comprehensive global framework designed to help countries develop effective AML/CTF systems (FATF, 2023). These standards aim to harmonize national regulatory efforts and foster cross-border cooperation, thereby enhancing the global financial system's resilience against illicit financial activity. However, implementing FATF's recommendations often involves the exchange of sensitive financial and personal data across jurisdictions—a requirement that can conflict with national efforts to assert digital sovereignty. Key components of the FATF framework, such as customer due diligence (CDD), transaction monitoring, record-keeping, and cross-border information sharing, place considerable demands on countries to establish transparent and interoperable regulatory systems. For example, Recommendation 15 specifically addresses the risks posed by virtual assets (cryptocurrencies), calling on member states to regulate cryptocurrency platforms and ensure they are not exploited for financial crime (FATF, 2023). These requirements present significant challenges for nations with stringent data protection laws. Sharing personal financial data with foreign agencies or international bodies can raise legal and ethical concerns, particularly in jurisdictions committed to strong data privacy norms (Martínez-Ramil et al., 2023). This tension between global regulatory compliance and national data governance underscores the complexity of implementing FATF standards in a digitally sovereign world.

A key mechanism within the FATF framework is the establishment of Financial Intelligence Units (FIUs). These units are tasked with collecting, analysing, and disseminating information related to suspicious financial activities. While FIUs play a crucial role in strengthening global AML/CTF cooperation, their operation often involves cross-border data exchange. This can be problematic in regions where data privacy laws, such as the EU's GDPR, impose strict limits on international data transfers (Albrecht, 2016). As such, countries must carefully navigate the balance between fulfilling their international obligations under the FATF framework and upholding national standards for data protection and digital sovereignty.

The Tension Between Privacy and Security in National Policies

As countries strengthen their DS and implement robust AML/CTF frameworks, a fundamental dilemma arises: how to ensure effective financial crime prevention while safeguarding individual privacy rights. This tension is particularly pronounced in jurisdictions with comprehensive data protection regimes, where privacy is enshrined as a fundamental legal and ethical principle. The EU's GDPR, which came into force in 2018, exemplifies this approach by imposing strict conditions on the collection, processing, and cross-border transfer of personal data (Kindylidi, 2022).

EU member states face the challenge of balancing two potentially conflicting obligations: adherence to FATF's global AML/CTF standards, which call for seamless international data sharing, and compliance with GDPR's stringent privacy protections. While FATF encourages transparent and timely exchange of financial intelligence, GDPR restricts the sharing of personal data unless adequate safeguards are in place. In reconciling these requirements, the EU has developed compliance frameworks that enable limited cross-border data transfers under specific legal conditions. However, these frameworks often require complex legal assessments, robust institutional safeguards, and careful documentation. This, in turn, introduces significant operational costs and legal uncertainties for many jurisdictions (Hoofnagle et al., 2019).

The United States faces a similar challenge, though shaped by different legal traditions. Under the Bank Secrecy Act (BSA), U.S. financial institutions are required to file Suspicious Activity Reports (SARs) with government authorities. While this approach enhances domestic AML/CTF enforcement, it also raises privacy concerns. Large volumes of personal financial data are often reported without the knowledge or explicit consent of the individuals involved (de Koker, 2016). This highlights the broader issue confronting many governments: how to maintain national security and fulfil international obligations without infringing on individual privacy or overstepping sovereign digital boundaries.

In light of these challenges, a growing number of countries are exploring privacy-preserving technologies as a means to reconcile AML/CTF requirements with data protection principles. Techniques such as differential privacy, homomorphic encryption, zero-knowledge proofs (ZKPs), and secure multi-party computation (SMPC) offer promising pathways. These tools enable secure data analysis and anomaly detection without exposing raw personal information, thus reducing the risk of data breaches while preserving the effectiveness of financial surveillance systems (Domingo-Ferrer & Blanco-Justicia, 2020; Mattsson, 2021; Zhang et al., 2024). As such technologies mature, they could provide a practical means for states to uphold DS and privacy commitments while actively participating in the global fight against financial crime.

THE ROLE OF TECHNOLOGY IN ENHANCING AML/CTF COMPLIANCE

Artificial Intelligence and Machine Learning for AML/CTF

As financial transactions become increasingly digital, fast-paced, and complex, traditional AML/CTF methods often struggle to keep up with the scale and sophistication of illicit financial activities. In response, AI and machine learning (ML) have emerged as transformative technologies, enabling financial institutions and regulators to enhance their compliance capabilities. By leveraging large-scale data analysis and real-time decision-making, these tools offer new levels of efficiency and accuracy in detecting suspicious behaviour (Canhoto, 2021; Han et al., 2020).

ML algorithms are particularly effective for monitoring transactional data, with both supervised and unsupervised learning approaches being widely adopted.

Supervised learning systems are trained on labelled datasets that represent known patterns of money laundering or terrorist financing. These models improve over time, learning to flag complex behaviours such as large cash deposits followed by structured transfers across multiple accounts (Jullum et al., 2020; Talukdar et al., 2023). Conversely, unsupervised learning algorithms do not rely on pre-labelled data but instead identify anomalies by clustering similar transaction behaviours. This allows institutions to detect novel or previously unknown laundering schemes and emerging financing tactics (Chander & Vijaya, 2021).

In practice, many financial organizations are already deploying these technologies to improve compliance outcomes. For example, JPMorgan Chase has incorporated ML-driven anomaly detection systems into its AML program to identify deviations from normal transaction patterns without requiring manual oversight. These systems reduce false positives and streamline investigative workflows, enabling faster and more accurate reporting of potentially suspicious activity (Desai et al., 2024). Similarly, natural language processing (NLP) techniques allow for the analysis of unstructured data—such as customer communications, transaction memos, and public disclosures—to uncover potential connections to financial crimes, including those linked to organized crime or terrorist networks (Canhoto, 2021; Du et al., 2025; Han et al., 2020; L. Wang et al., 2024).

Despite their significant potential, the adoption of AI and ML in AML/CTF compliance also introduces critical challenges. These systems depend heavily on access to vast amounts of financial and personal data, which can conflict with data protection laws in regions such as the European Union. Under the GDPR, strict conditions apply to the processing and storage of sensitive personal information, potentially limiting the scope of AI-enabled surveillance tools. Moreover, many AI models suffer from a lack of transparency—commonly referred to as the "black box" problem—where the logic behind decisions made by algorithms is not easily understood or explained. This raises concerns about accountability and fairness, especially when regulatory compliance demands transparency and traceability in decision-making processes (Canhoto, 2021). Nevertheless, AI and ML continue to hold considerable promise for enhancing AML/CTF frameworks. When implemented responsibly—with appropriate safeguards for data protection, fairness, and transparency—these technologies offer a path toward smarter compliance systems that align with both security imperatives and privacy rights.

Blockchain and Cryptocurrencies in AML/CTF

Blockchain technology and cryptocurrencies occupy a complex position in the landscape of AML and CTF compliance—offering both innovative solutions and significant regulatory challenges. On one hand, blockchain's decentralized, transparent, and tamper-resistant architecture holds the potential to enhance financial accountability. On the other, the pseudonymous nature of many cryptocurrencies introduces considerable risks by allowing users to conceal their identities, thereby facilitating illicit financial flows (Campbell-Verduyn, 2018; Pocher et al., 2023).

At its core, blockchain operates as a distributed ledger, recording transactions in a way that is immutable and verifiable. This feature can be leveraged by financial institutions and regulators to support AML/CTF efforts, particularly in enhancing traceability and reducing the risk of data manipulation. For example, private or permissioned blockchain networks enable secure sharing of transactional information among verified entities, facilitating cross-border oversight while preserving data integrity (Zyskind et al., 2015). Regulatory initiatives, such as the EU's Fifth Anti-Money Laundering Directive (5AMLD), have recognized this potential. The directive requires cryptocurrency exchanges and wallet service providers to implement Know Your Customer (KYC) procedures, which extends traditional regulatory expectations to the digital asset ecosystem (Kindylidi, 2022).

Despite these advancements, cryptocurrencies present unique compliance hurdles. While blockchain records transactions publicly, wallet addresses do not inherently reveal the identity of their owners. This pseudonymity creates blind spots in AML/CTF monitoring, as illicit actors can exploit digital assets to obscure the origin and destination of funds. Bitcoin, for instance, enables users to transfer value without disclosing their real-world identities, making it difficult for regulators to establish clear links between transactions and individuals. In response, blockchain analytics firms have developed tools to uncover patterns and link pseudonymous transactions to identifiable entities (Pocher et al., 2023). Solutions like Chainalysis provide regulators and financial institutions with transaction-tracing capabilities, enabling them to flag wallets associated with high-risk behaviour, including money laundering, fraud, and terrorist financing (Chainalysis, 2024). These analytical tools are becoming integral to the evolving AML/CTF technology stack.

To further mitigate risk, regulatory bodies have issued frameworks aimed at governing cryptocurrency exchanges. The FATF, for example, has introduced guidelines requiring virtual asset service providers (VASPs) to comply with the "Travel Rule," which mandates the exchange of sender and receiver information during transactions—akin to traditional wire transfer standards (FATF, 2022). However, enforcing such measures across decentralized and global networks remains a formidable challenge. Privacy-centric cryptocurrencies like Monero and Zcash employ advanced cryptographic techniques to obscure transaction details entirely, further complicating regulatory surveillance efforts. As digital assets continue to evolve, governments and international bodies must strike a balance between fostering innovation and ensuring financial integrity. The key lies in developing adaptive regulatory frameworks and technical tools that respect the decentralized ethos of blockchain while ensuring robust safeguards against its misuse for financial crime.

Privacy-Preserving Technologies

The tension between effective AML/CTF enforcement and the protection of individual privacy has prompted increasing interest in privacy-preserving technologies. These emerging tools provide innovative ways for financial institutions and regulators to conduct meaningful analysis without compromising personal data. Techniques such as differential privacy, homomorphic encryption, and ZKPs allow data to be processed and verified while preserving confidentiality. These approaches offer a potential solution to the enduring tension between ensuring security and upholding privacy (Domingo-Ferrer & Blanco-Justicia, 2020; Ghavamipour et al., 2022).

Differential privacy, for example, introduces statistical noise into datasets, enabling aggregate analysis without revealing information about any individual entry. In the context of AML/CTF, this approach allows institutions to share behavioural insights with regulators, such as transaction patterns or anomaly trends, without exposing the identities of specific users (Cummings et al., 2024; Dwork & Roth, 2014). This technique can be particularly useful for detecting systemic risks while maintaining compliance with data protection regulations.

Homomorphic encryption offers another promising pathway by enabling computations to be performed directly on encrypted data. This means that banks can analyse transaction records to flag suspicious activity without decrypting sensitive information, ensuring data remains protected throughout the compliance process (Rivest et al., 1978). Such capabilities are particularly valuable in jurisdictions with stringent data protection laws, where unencrypted data processing might otherwise violate legal requirements.

Zero-knowledge proofs (ZKPs) represent a more advanced privacy-preserving method, allowing one party to demonstrate that a transaction satisfies certain criteria—such as compliance with AML/CTF rules—without revealing the underlying data. This technique is especially relevant in cross-border contexts, where regulatory frameworks often demand transparency, but privacy concerns limit data disclosure. zk-SNARKs (Zero-Knowledge Succinct Non-Interactive Arguments of Knowledge), a specific implementation of ZKPs, are already being used in blockchain systems to enable verifiable yet private transactions. These tools hold significant potential for enabling compliance verification in decentralized or privacy-conscious environments (Ben-Sasson et al., 2013).

Despite their promise, the widespread adoption of privacy-preserving technologies is not without hurdles. Many of these techniques demand high computational resources, making them expensive and technically complex to implement at scale.

Furthermore, regulatory frameworks are still catching up to these innovations. In many jurisdictions, oversight bodies remain cautious about endorsing technologies that could obscure key data, citing concerns that such opacity might hinder the detection of illicit financial flows (Domingo-Ferrer & Blanco-Justicia, 2020). Nevertheless, as these technologies continue to mature, they offer a promising avenue for reconciling AML/CTF objectives with DS and privacy rights. By enabling secure data collaboration without exposing personal information, privacy-preserving solutions may form a critical part of future AML/CTF frameworks, especially in an era increasingly defined by data protection and transnational cooperation.

BALANCING PRIVACY AND SECURITY IN AML/CTF FRAMEWORKS

The Impact of GDPR on AML/CTF Compliance

The GDPR, enforced across the EU since 2018, has significantly reshaped the global landscape for data privacy and protection. While its core aim is to safeguard individual rights in an increasingly data-driven world, GDPR has also introduced complex challenges for AML/CTF compliance. In particular, its strict provisions on data collection, processing, retention, and cross-border transfer often intersect—and at times conflict—with the operational requirements of AML/CTF frameworks (Mitrou, 2017).

A central principle of GDPR is data minimization: organizations are permitted to collect and process only the data necessary for a clearly defined purpose. This stands in contrast to AML/CTF obligations, which typically require the comprehensive gathering and long-term retention of customer data to enable transaction monitoring, profiling, and retrospective investigations. Article 5 of the GDPR reinforces this limitation, emphasizing that personal data should not be retained longer than necessary. Yet for AML/CTF purposes, historical data is often crucial in detecting suspicious financial patterns over time (Albrecht, 2016). This creates a regulatory tension, with financial institutions having to navigate between legal requirements to retain information and privacy mandates to limit data exposure.

Another area of friction arises from GDPR's "right to be forgotten," which empowers individuals to request the erasure of their personal data. While this right promotes individual autonomy over personal information, it directly clashes with AML/CTF regulations that require long-term data retention, even after the termination of a customer relationship, in order to support potential future investigations. For financial institutions, responding to such erasure requests without violating

AML obligations requires the implementation of complex legal interpretations and carefully balanced compliance strategies (Voigt & von dem Bussche, 2024).

Cross-border data transfers represent a further complication. AML/CTF enforcement often relies on international collaboration and the timely exchange of financial intelligence. However, GDPR's Article 44 restricts the transfer of personal data to countries outside the EU unless those countries provide adequate data protection safeguards. While mechanisms such as standard contractual clauses (SCCs) and binding corporate rules (BCRs) can facilitate legal data transfers, they entail rigorous legal and procedural requirements that may delay or inhibit information exchange. This restriction poses a substantial barrier to real-time AML/CTF cooperation with jurisdictions that lack GDPR-equivalent privacy frameworks (Related Information Article 44. General Principle for Transfers, 2018). In summary, GDPR has redefined the boundaries of permissible data use in the EU and beyond. It reinforces individual privacy rights while complicating AML/CTF compliance efforts. This legal and operational tension forces financial institutions and regulators to constantly adapt their practices. They must craft nuanced compliance frameworks that uphold data privacy while meeting global security and regulatory demands.

Legal and Ethical Challenges in Data Sharing

Cross-border data sharing plays a critical role in effective AML/CTF enforcement. However, it frequently collides with privacy-centric legal frameworks, creating significant legal and ethical challenges for financial institutions and regulators. A primary legal obstacle arises from the fragmented nature of global data protection standards. While regions like the EU enforce stringent privacy protections under the GDPR, other jurisdictions prioritize national security and regulatory compliance over data privacy. These conflicting priorities generate regulatory uncertainty, complicating cross-border data sharing for institutions. As a result, they risk non-compliance with one legal framework while trying to adhere to another. (Kuner, 2013; Sampson, 2021). Navigating these divergent requirements often demands complex legal evaluations and layered compliance strategies. For instance, a financial institution operating in both the EU and a less privacy-restrictive jurisdiction must reconcile GDPR's restrictions on international data transfers with obligations to report suspicious transactions under global AML/CTF standards. This balancing act becomes particularly difficult when regulations provide limited or ambiguous guidance on reconciling security needs with privacy protections.

Ethical considerations further complicate the landscape. AML/CTF compliance often requires the collection and analysis of sensitive personal data, including transaction histories, customer profiles, and even behavioural metadata. While such data is instrumental in identifying illicit financial activities, its use raises ethical questions about the scope and purpose of surveillance. Customers may perceive these practices as intrusive, particularly when institutions employ advanced monitoring techniques such as the analysis of social media activity or geolocation data, types of information not traditionally expected to be scrutinized in a financial context (Cortez, 2021).

The ethical stakes are heightened when data sharing involves multi-stakeholder collaboration. AML/CTF efforts often rely on partnerships between public and private actors, including financial institutions, government agencies, and third-party analytics providers. In such settings, questions of accountability become pronounced: who is ultimately responsible for ensuring that shared data remains secure, private, and accurate? For example, if a government agency requests customer data from a bank for investigative purposes, the institution may feel obliged to comply, even when doing so might contravene its privacy commitments or risk violating data protection laws. These scenarios expose the ongoing ethical tension between collective security interests and the duty to safeguard individual privacy (Voigt & von dem Bussche, 2024). Overall, the legal and ethical challenges of data sharing highlight the ongoing struggle to reconcile individual privacy rights with global security obligations. As AML/CTF frameworks become increasingly data-intensive, striking a balance between transparency, accountability, and the protection of fundamental privacy rights remains a pressing challenge for both institutions and regulators.

Digital Identity and Privacy in AML/CTF

Digital identity systems have become central to contemporary AML/CTF frameworks. It offers a more efficient and secure means of verifying customer identities. By enabling financial institutions to implement robust KYC and CDD protocols, digital identity tools help reduce the risk of financial crime and fraudulent activity. However, the adoption of these technologies also raises serious privacy concerns, particularly when sensitive biometric data, such as facial recognition, voice patterns, or fingerprints, is collected and stored as part of identity verification procedures (Kindylidi, 2022).

These systems often require the processing of large volumes of personal information, creating a delicate balance between regulatory compliance and the protection of individual privacy. While effective identity verification is essential for detecting illicit financial behaviour, mishandling or overcollection of biometric and personal data increases the risk of data breaches and identity theft. To mitigate such risks, privacy-preserving techniques are increasingly being integrated into digital identity solutions. As highlighted in Section 3.3, technologies like ZKPs enable institutions to confirm attributes—such as age or residency—without disclosing the underlying data. This selective disclosure supports compliance while limiting exposure to privacy vulnerabilities (Ben-Sasson et al., 2013; Zyskind et al., 2015).

Emerging models such as self-sovereign identity (SSI) represent a promising shift in digital identity management. In contrast to centralized systems that place control in the hands of institutions, SSI empowers individuals to own and manage their digital identities (TITH & COLIN, 2024). Within this framework, users can provide only the minimal information necessary to meet AML/CTF verification requirements, significantly reducing unnecessary data exposure. Supported by blockchain technology, SSI allows for the secure sharing of verifiable claims, such as identity, nationality, or source of funds, without granting institutions full access to a person's broader personal data. This approach not only strengthens data privacy but also aligns with global trends toward user-centric data governance (Zyskind et al., 2015).

Nevertheless, the implementation of digital identity frameworks faces ongoing legal and operational challenges. The use of biometric data, for example, is subject to stringent regulation in many jurisdictions, given its sensitivity and potential for misuse. Financial institutions must ensure that data collection practices comply with data protection laws, including clear consent mechanisms and limitations on data retention. At the same time, they must develop secure infrastructure capable of safeguarding identity records against cyberattacks and unauthorized access. As digital identity continues to evolve as a key component of AML/CTF systems, achieving the right balance between compliance, technological innovation, and privacy protection will remain a critical policy and operational priority (Domingo-Ferrer & Blanco-Justicia, 2020).

CASE STUDIES: GLOBAL COOPERATION VS. NATIONAL AUTONOMY

In the digital age, the effectiveness of AML/CTF frameworks increasingly depends on coordinated global responses. Yet, the need for international cooperation often collides with the principle of national autonomy, as jurisdictions prioritize domestic legal traditions, privacy norms, and regulatory objectives. These divergent priorities can hinder the harmonisation of AML/CTF standards, particularly in cross-border contexts where data sharing and financial oversight are critical. This section explores three case studies that exemplify the challenges and opportunities at the intersection of national sovereignty and global AML/CTF collaboration: the regulatory interplay between the EU's GDPR and the FATF Recommendations, China's deployment of its digital currency, and the broader global implications of cryptocurrencies for AML/CTF regimes.

GDPR and the FATF Recommendations: Navigating Regulatory Tensions

The GDPR and the FATF Recommendations serve as two of the most influential regulatory frameworks in the realms of data protection and financial security, respectively. While both aim to uphold public interest, GDPR by safeguarding personal data and FATF by preventing financial crime, their objectives can at times appear misaligned. GDPR, which came into force in 2018, imposes rigorous standards on data collection, processing, and cross-border sharing within the EU. In contrast, FATF's Recommendations promote expansive data sharing across jurisdictions to enhance transparency and combat illicit financial activity on a global scale.

This regulatory tension becomes particularly evident in the context of cross-border data transfers. GDPR's Article 44 prohibits transferring personal data to countries that do not offer an adequate level of data protection. This creates significant barriers to the international cooperation required for effective AML/CTF enforcement (Related Information Article 44. General Principle for Transfers, 2018). Furthermore, GDPR's core principles, such as data minimization and purpose limitation, restrict institutions from collecting or retaining information beyond what is strictly necessary. These constraints can conflict with FATF Recommendation 16, which calls for financial institutions to transmit originator and beneficiary data with all electronic fund transfers, facilitating traceability across borders.

Despite these apparent conflicts, both frameworks contain provisions that enable reconciliation when approached strategically. GDPR allows exceptions for data processing in the public interest or to meet legal obligations, conditions that AML/CTF efforts often fulfil. FATF, for its part, has acknowledged the impact of privacy regulations and encourages member countries to implement AML/CTF measures that also uphold data protection standards. Some EU member states have proactively developed compliance models that integrate both sets of requirements. These include using privacy-by-design principles in AML/CTF systems, limiting data retention durations, and implementing strong access controls to ensure proportionality and accountability in data use (D'Acquisto et al., 2015). In summary, the relationship between GDPR and the FATF Recommendations demonstrates the broader challenge of aligning national privacy legislation with global AML/CTF imperatives. While legal tensions remain, the evolving regulatory landscape shows that mutual accommodation is possible through innovative compliance strategies and sustained dialogue between privacy advocates and financial regulators.

China's Digital Yuan and Its AML/CTF Implications

China's digital yuan, formally known as the Digital Currency Electronic Payment (DCEP) and issued by the People's Bank of China (PBoC), marks a pivotal advancement in central bank digital currencies (CBDCs) with far-reaching implications for AML/CTF compliance. Unlike decentralized cryptocurrencies, the digital yuan is fully controlled by the Chinese state, operating on a centralized ledger that enables the PBoC to oversee issuance, circulation, and transactional activity. This architecture grants the government unparalleled capacity to monitor financial flows, detect anomalies, and intervene in real time, positioning the digital yuan as a potentially powerful instrument for combating money laundering and terrorist financing (Wang, 2023).

One of the digital yuan's core features is "controllable anonymity," a dual-layered mechanism designed to balance user privacy with regulatory oversight. Under this model, users can conduct small-value transactions without identity verification, while higher-value or high-risk transactions require full identification and may trigger enhanced scrutiny. This design reflects China's broader strategy of ensuring financial security while preserving a measure of transactional privacy for ordinary users. However, the system's emphasis on centralized control has raised international concerns about transparency and data sharing, particularly as the PBoC explores cross-border applications of the digital yuan. Without clear mechanisms for compliance with international AML/CTF standards, such as those established by the FATF, cross-border transactions may challenge established norms of regulatory cooperation and accountability (Lu & Chen, 2021).

Furthermore, the digital yuan's programmability introduces novel capabilities for automated enforcement of AML/CTF policies. The currency can be embedded with rules that enable real-time transaction monitoring, impose restrictions on specific uses, or freeze assets instantly upon detection of suspicious activity. While these functions could enhance financial integrity within China's jurisdiction, they also raise critical questions about privacy, proportionality, and state surveillance. International stakeholders have expressed concern that such centralized control could erode individual privacy and undermine financial sovereignty, especially if the digital yuan is adopted in bilateral or multilateral trade contexts without adequate safeguards (Li & Huang, 2021). As China continues to pilot and scale the digital yuan, its global implications remain a subject of close scrutiny. The currency's effectiveness in supporting AML/CTF goals will depend not only on its technological design but also on the extent to which it aligns with international transparency norms and facilitates cooperative engagement with global financial regulators.

Cryptocurrencies and Global AML Efforts

The proliferation of cryptocurrencies, such as Bitcoin, Ethereum, and privacy-centric assets like Monero, has introduced significant obstacles for global AML/CTF enforcement. Operating on decentralized blockchain networks, these digital currencies offer users pseudonymity and eliminate the need for intermediaries, complicating the identification of illicit financial flows. Although blockchain technology provides traceable records of transactions, the absence of personally identifiable information associated with wallet addresses limits the effectiveness of traditional AML/CTF tools. Recognizing this challenge, the FATF introduced Recommendation 15, urging countries to regulate VASPs by subjecting them to AML/CTF requirements similar to those applied to traditional financial institutions (FATF, 2022). Despite these efforts, uniform implementation of FATF's standards remains uneven across jurisdictions. The "Travel Rule," embedded in FATF Recommendation 16, mandates that VASPs share originator and beneficiary information for certain virtual asset transfers. While this mirrors conventional financial sector practices, enforcing it within decentralized systems has proven problematic. Privacy-enhancing cryptocurrencies like Monero and Zcash obscure transaction details using sophisticated cryptographic techniques. This makes it nearly impossible for VASPs, or even state actors, to access or share required transaction metadata for regulatory compliance (Chainalysis, 2024).

To mitigate these risks, several countries have enacted domestic regulatory frameworks targeting virtual assets. In the United States, cryptocurrency exchanges must comply with the BSA and report suspicious transactions, while the EU's 5AMLD requires VASPs to implement CDD and maintain reporting mechanisms. These initiatives represent important steps toward transparency, yet they are not without controversy. Critics argue that imposing rigid AML/CTF rules on decentralized networks undermines the foundational principles of privacy and autonomy that define the cryptocurrency ecosystem (Silva De Freitas, 2020).

Global regulatory cooperation continues to evolve as authorities seek to adapt to fast-changing technological landscapes. FATF has increased engagement with national regulators to develop harmonized standards for digital asset oversight. However, the emergence of decentralized finance (DeFi) platforms introduces new complexities. DeFi operates through automated smart contracts rather than intermediaries, rendering many conventional AML/CTF approaches ineffective. These platforms enable peer-to-peer financial services without custodians, leaving no central entity responsible for identity verification or transaction reporting. As decentralized technologies grow more sophisticated, regulators face mounting pressure to strike a balance between preserving innovation and enforcing global AML/CTF standards. This ongoing tension underscores the need for adaptive legal frameworks, innovative compliance technologies, and international coordination to address the evolving risks in the digital asset landscape (FATF, 2021).

EMERGING TRENDS AND THE FUTURE OF DIGITAL SOVEREIGNTY IN AML/CTF

Central Bank Digital Currencies and AML/CTF

The Central Bank Digital Currencies (CBDCs) represent a significant innovation in the evolution of digital finance, offering a state-backed digital alternative to physical cash. Issued and regulated by central banks, CBDCs are typically underpinned by blockchain or distributed ledger technologies, enabling enhanced transparency, security, and efficiency in financial systems. From an AML/CTF perspective, CBDCs provide unique advantages over decentralized cryptocurrencies, primarily due to their centralized governance structure and programmable design. These features allow authorities to embed regulatory compliance mechanisms directly into the digital currency infrastructure. This supports real-time transaction monitoring, traceability, and automated enforcement of AML/CTF controls (BIS, 2021). A leading example of this innovation is China's digital yuan, developed by the PBoC. The digital yuan incorporates a high level of oversight through a centralized ledger that allows real-time visibility into financial transactions. Its "controllable anonymity" design permits anonymous low-value transactions while requiring identity verification for higher-value transfers. This structure reflects China's broader strategy of using digital technologies to strengthen financial surveillance, reduce money laundering risks, and reinforce state control over the financial system (Auer et al., 2020). By embedding AML/CTF functions at the currency level, the digital yuan minimizes reliance on third-party financial institutions for compliance, streamlining enforcement and reducing systemic vulnerabilities.

In parallel, the European Central Bank (ECB) is developing the Digital Euro with a distinct emphasis on balancing financial transparency and individual privacy. Unlike China's approach, the ECB's design framework aligns closely with the EU's legal commitment to data protection, particularly under the GDPR. A proposed two-tiered privacy model would allow for enhanced anonymity for low-value transactions while ensuring full compliance measures for high-risk or large-value transfers. This dual approach illustrates how DS can be exercised through CBDC design, upholding AML/CTF obligations while respecting fundamental rights to privacy and data protection (ECB, 2020). As more central banks investigate or pilot CBDCs, these digital currencies could redefine the global AML/CTF landscape. Their potential to create standardized, traceable, and programmable financial systems offers promising opportunities for improved regulatory enforcement. However, these innovations also raise critical concerns. Key among them are cybersecurity threats, operational resilience, and the potential for excessive government surveillance. The concentration of data and control in state-operated systems could invite misuse or unintended consequences, particularly in jurisdictions with limited legal safeguards for individual privacy (Frost et al., 2020). Thus, while CBDCs offer powerful tools for enhancing AML/CTF compliance, their successful adoption depends on striking a careful balance between security imperatives and the protection of civil liberties. Ensuring transparency, democratic oversight, and cross-border regulatory cooperation will be essential to maximizing the benefits of CBDCs while mitigating their risks.

Blockchain and Privacy-Preserving Technologies

As financial systems become increasingly digital, blockchain and privacy-preserving technologies are emerging as critical components in the evolution of AML/CTF strategies. While often associated with cryptocurrencies, blockchain technology offers broader applications for regulatory compliance. Its core features, immutability, transparency, and decentralization, make it a powerful tool for creating verifiable audit trails in financial transactions. In particular, private and permissioned blockchain networks provide regulated environments where transaction data can be securely recorded and accessed by authorized parties. These systems allow institutions and regulators to implement AML/CTF checks in real time without undermining the confidentiality or integrity of sensitive data (Zyskind et al., 2015).

The integration of privacy-preserving technologies into blockchain infrastructures further enhances their utility in AML/CTF efforts. Techniques such as ZKPs and SMPC have proven essential for reconciling the often-competing objectives of privacy and regulatory compliance. ZKPs enable one party to prove that a transaction meets AML/CTF requirements without disclosing the underlying details. This is especially relevant in jurisdictions with stringent data protection laws, where maintaining individual privacy is a legal and ethical imperative (Ben-Sasson et al., 2013). A notable application of ZKPs is in the form of zk-SNARKs, which can verify personal credentials or transaction legitimacy while keeping all sensitive information encrypted. For instance, a financial institution could confirm a user's compliance with KYC standards without accessing their complete identity profile. This innovation allows for the creation of blockchain systems that are simultaneously auditable and privacy-respecting—advancing both digital sovereignty and AML/CTF enforcement (Konkin & Zapechnikov, 2023).

Similarly, SMPC offers a collaborative framework in which multiple entities, such as financial institutions and regulatory bodies, can jointly process encrypted data without revealing it to one another. This method facilitates cross-border regulatory cooperation while preserving data confidentiality and national data governance. For example, SMPC can be used to flag suspicious patterns in transaction networks without disclosing the identities of individual participants. This enables institutions to remain compliant while safeguarding user privacy (Mattsson, 2021). Together, these technologies represent a paradigm shift in how AML/CTF frameworks can be implemented in the digital age. By embedding privacy-preserving mechanisms within blockchain-based systems, financial actors can achieve greater transparency and accountability without sacrificing the rights of individuals or the sovereignty of national data laws. As global regulatory landscapes evolve, these tools may form the foundation of next-generation compliance architectures, where trust, privacy, and regulatory effectiveness coexist in harmony.

Multi-Stakeholder Collaboration for AML/CTF Compliance

In an increasingly digital and interconnected financial landscape, effective AML/CTF compliance depends heavily on coordinated efforts among a diverse array of stakeholders. Governments, financial institutions, technology companies, and international bodies must work together to address the complex, cross-border nature of financial crimes, particularly those facilitated by rapidly evolving digital networks (FATF, 2023). While the FATF provides a globally recognized framework through its 40 Recommendations, translating these standards into effective national and institutional practices requires robust multi-stakeholder collaboration across jurisdictions and sectors.

Financial institutions serve on the front lines of AML/CTF compliance, executing CDD, monitoring transactions, and reporting suspicious activities. However, their efforts are often constrained by limited access to international data and intelligence. This limitation hampers their ability to detect transnational illicit financial flows. To bridge this gap, public-private partnerships have emerged as a crucial mechanism. These partnerships enable secure and structured information sharing between government authorities and private financial entities. For example, the United Kingdom's Joint Money Laundering Intelligence Taskforce (JMLIT) exemplifies such collaboration by facilitating real-time intelligence exchange between banks and law enforcement, leading to more effective disruption of organized financial crime networks (HM Treasury, 2019; Vogel, 2022). Beyond national initiatives, international organizations play a central role in harmonising regulatory standards and fostering cross-border cooperation. FATF's "Travel Rule" is a key example, which requires financial institutions to exchange information about the originators and beneficiaries of cross-border transactions. Although designed to enhance traceability, the implementation of this rule remains challenging due to differences in national regulations and conflicting legal jurisdictions. The Financial Stability

Board (FSB) has emphasized the urgent need for a globally consistent regulatory framework for digital assets, one that supports effective AML/CTF enforcement while respecting national DS (FSB, 2020).

The role of the technology sector in this collaborative ecosystem is increasingly vital. As financial crimes migrate into digital channels, emerging technologies such as blockchain and AI offer new tools for detection and prevention. Companies like Chainalysis and Elliptic specialise in blockchain analytics and work closely with financial institutions and regulatory agencies to trace illicit activity on decentralized networks. These collaborations illustrate how technical expertise from the private sector can augment regulatory capacity and support compliance with evolving AML/CTF standards (Chainalysis, 2024). As digital finance continues to evolve, the interdependence of stakeholders will only deepen. Ensuring an effective and adaptive AML/CTF regime will require continued cooperation across public, private, and international domains. This multi-stakeholder approach offers the most promising path toward achieving a balance between the imperatives of DS, financial innovation, and global security.

LIMITATION

This study's reliance on qualitative case studies limits its generalizability, as quantitative data from diverse jurisdictions is scarce.

CONCLUSION

Summary of Key Insights

The digitalisation of global financial systems, driven by technologies such as AI, blockchain, and privacy-preserving technologies, as profoundly reshaped the landscape of AML/CTF. This chapter has explored how DS and global financial integration intersect in this evolving environment. It highlights the challenges and opportunities that arise when nations seek to protect personal data and maintain regulatory autonomy while participating in international AML/CTF efforts. Emerging technologies have significantly enhanced the capacity of financial institutions and regulators to detect and prevent illicit financial activities. AI and ML have introduced real-time monitoring capabilities, allowing for the rapid identification of suspicious patterns and behaviours across increasingly complex financial ecosystems. At the same time, privacy-preserving technologies such as ZKPs and SMPC offer pathways for reconciling compliance obligations with data protection, providing frameworks where transparency and confidentiality can coexist.

The development and deployment of CBDCs mark a pivotal advancement in digital finance. CBDCs offer regulators new tools to embed AML/CTF controls directly into digital currency infrastructures, facilitating more automated and auditable compliance mechanisms. Initiatives such as China's digital yuan and the ECB's exploration of a digital euro exemplify how DS can be operationalised while supporting international AML/CTF norms. Equally important is the role of multi-stakeholder collaboration in shaping the future of AML/CTF compliance. Effective cooperation among governments, financial institutions, technology firms, and international organisations has proven essential for addressing jurisdictional fragmentation, aligning regulatory standards, and responding to the rapid pace of innovation. Nevertheless, as financial technologies and cross-border transactions continue to evolve, new tensions emerge around data governance, cybersecurity, and the harmonisation of regulatory regimes.

Taken together, these insights underscore the necessity of adaptive, technology-informed, and cooperative approaches to AML/CTF, approaches that uphold national DS while contributing to the stability and integrity of the global financial system.

Recommendations for Policymakers

To strengthen AML/CTF compliance frameworks in the digital era while upholding principles of DS, policymakers should adopt DS-centric frameworks that embed privacy-by-design into AML/CTF systems, leveraging CBDCs and blockchain for real-time monitoring while safeguarding DS.

Future Research Directions

As financial systems continue to evolve under the influence of emerging technologies and shifting geopolitical dynamics, ongoing research is crucial to ensure that AML/CTF frameworks remain effective, adaptive, and aligned with the principles of DS. Future studies should quantify DS impacts across diverse jurisdictions, addressing scalability challenges of privacy-preserving technologies and exploring DeFi's role in AML/CTF.

REFERENCES

Akartuna, E. A., Johnson, S. D., & Thornton, A. E. (2023). The money laundering and terrorist financing risks of new and disruptive technologies: A futures-oriented scoping review. *Security Journal, 36*(4), 615–650. DOI: 10.1057/s41284-022-00356-z PMID: 40479271

Albrecht, J. P. (2016). How the GDPR Will Change the World. *European Data Protection Law Review, 2*(3), 287–289. https://doi.org/https://doi.org/10.21552/EDPL/2016/3/4

Auer, R., Cornelli, G., & Frost, J. (2020). *Rise of the central bank digital currencies: drivers, approaches and technologies* (BIS Working Paper No. 880). www.bis.org

Ben-Sasson, E., Chiesa, A., Genkin, D., Tromer, E., & Virza, M. (2013). SNARKs for C: Verifying Program Executions Succinctly and in Zero Knowledge. In Canetti, R., & Garay, J. A. (Eds.), Lecture Notes in Computer Science: Vol. 8043. *Advances in Cryptology – CRYPTO 2013. CRYPTO 2013* (pp. 90–108). Springer., https://doi.org/https://doi.org/10.1007/978-3-642-40084-1_6 DOI: 10.1007/978-3-642-40084-1_6

. BIS. (2021). *Central bank digital currencies for cross-border payments : Report to the G20.*

Campbell-Verduyn, M. (2018). Bitcoin, crypto-coins, and global anti-money laundering governance. *Crime, Law, and Social Change, 69*(2), 283–305. DOI: 10.1007/s10611-017-9756-5

Canhoto, A. I. (2021). Leveraging machine learning in the global fight against money laundering and terrorism financing: An affordances perspective. *Journal of Business Research, 131*, 441–452. DOI: 10.1016/j.jbusres.2020.10.012 PMID: 33100427

Chainalysis. (2024). *Money Laundering and Cryptocurrency: Trends and new techniques for detection and investigation.* https://www.chainalysis.com/blog/money-laundering-cryptocurrency/

Chander, S., & Vijaya, P. (2021). Unsupervised learning methods for data clustering. In Binu, D., & Rajakumar, B. R. (Eds.), *Artificial Intelligence in Data Mining: Theories and Applications* (pp. 41–64). Academic Press, Elsevier Inc., DOI: 10.1016/B978-0-12-820601-0.00002-1

Cortez, E. K. (2021). Data Protection Around the World: Privacy Laws in Action. In E. K. Cortez (Ed.), *Information Technology and Law Series IT&LAW* (1st ed., Vol. 33). T.M.C. Asser Press. https://doi.org/https://doi.org/10.1007/978-94-6265-407-5

Cummings, R., Desfontaines, D., Evans, D., Geambasu, R., Huang, Y., Jagielski, M., Kairouz, P., Kamath, G., Oh, S., Ohrimenko, O., Papernot, N., Rogers, R., Shen, M., Song, S., Su, W., Terzis, A., Thakurta, A., Vassilvitskii, S., Wang, Y.-X., & Zhang, W. (2024). Advancing Differential Privacy: Where We Are Now and Future Directions for Real-World Deployment. *Harvard Data Science Review*, *6*(1), 1. DOI: 10.1162/99608f92.d3197524

D'Acquisto, G., Domingo-Ferrer, J., Kikiras, P., Torra, V., de Montjoye, Y.-A., & Bourka, A. (2015). *Privacy by design in big data: An overview of privacy enhancing technologies in the era of big data analytics* (A. Bourka & P. Drogkaris, Eds.; 1st ed.). European Union Agency for Network and Information Security (ENISA). DOI: 10.2824/641480

de Koker, L. (2016). Money Laundering Compliance—The Challenges of Technology. In Dion, M., Weisstub, D., & Richet, J.-L. (Eds.), *Financial Crimes: Psychological, Technological, and Ethical Issues. International Library of Ethics, Law, and the New Medicine* (Vol. 68, pp. 329–347). Springer., DOI: 10.1007/978-3-319-32419-7_16

Desai, A., Kosse, A., & Sharples, J. (2024). *Finding a needle in a haystack: a machine learning framework for anomaly detection in payment systems* (1188). www.bis.org

Domingo-Ferrer, J., & Blanco-Justicia, A. (2020). Privacy-Preserving Technologies. In Christen, M., Gordijn, B., & Loi, M. (Eds.), *The Ethics of Cybersecurity. The International Library of Ethics, Law and Technology* (Vol. 21, pp. 279–297). Springer Science and Business Media B.V., DOI: 10.1007/978-3-030-29053-5_14

Du, K., Zhao, Y., Mao, R., Xing, F., & Cambria, E. (2025). Natural language processing in finance: A survey. *Information Fusion*, *115*, 102755. Advance online publication. DOI: 10.1016/j.inffus.2024.102755

Dwork, C., & Roth, A. (2014). The algorithmic foundations of differential privacy. *Foundations and Trends in Theoretical Computer Science*, *9*(3–4), 211–407. DOI: 10.1561/0400000042

ECB. (2020). *Report on a digital euro*. https://www.ecb.europa.eu/pub/pdf/other/Report_on_a_digital_euro~4d7268b458.en.pdf

FATF. (2021). *Opportunities and Challenges of New Technologies for AML/CFT*. www.fatf-gafi.org

FATF. (2022). *Targeted Update on Implementation of the FATF Standards on Virtual Assets and Virtual Asset Service Providers*. www.fatf-gafi.org/publications/fatfrecommendations/documents/targeted-update-virtual-assets-vasps.html

FATF (2012 - 2023). (2023). *International Standards on Combating Money Laundering and the Financing of Terrorism & Proliferation.* www.fatf-gafi.org/en/publications/Fatfrecommendations/Fatf-recommendations.html

Frost, J., Shin, H. S., & Wierts, P. (2020). *An early stablecoin? The Bank of Amsterdam and the governance of money* (902). https://www.bis.org/publ/work902.htm

FSB. (2020). *Regulation, Supervision and Oversight of "Global Stablecoin" Arrangements.* https://www.fsb.org/uploads/P131020-3.pdf

Ghavamipour, A. R., Turkmen, F., & Jiang, X. (2022). Privacy-preserving logistic regression with secret sharing. *BMC Medical Informatics and Decision Making, 22*(89), 1–11. DOI: 10.1186/s12911-022-01811-y PMID: 35366870

Gstrein, O. J., & Beaulieu, A. (2022). How to protect privacy in a datafied society? A presentation of multiple legal and conceptual approaches. *Philosophy & Technology, 35*(3), 1–38. DOI: 10.1007/s13347-022-00497-4 PMID: 35127339

Han, J., Huang, Y., Liu, S., & Towey, K. (2020). Artificial intelligence for anti-money laundering: A review and extension. *Digital Finance, 2*(3-4), 211–239. DOI: 10.1007/s42521-020-00023-1

Hoofnagle, C. J., van der Sloot, B., & Borgesius, F. Z. (2019). The European Union general data protection regulation: What it is and what it means. *Information & Communications Technology Law, 28*(1), 65–98. DOI: 10.1080/13600834.2019.1573501

Jeyakumar, I. H. J., & Kubach, M. (2024). A trust implementation model for cross-domain decentralized identity ecosystems: architecture, use case, and implementation. In S. Misra, P. Kvalvik, K. M. Kjølerbakken, & R. Damasevicius (Eds.), *International Conference on Digital Sovereignty (ICDS), Procedia Computer Science* (Vol. 254, pp. 10–19). Elsevier B.V. DOI: 10.1016/j.procs.2025.02.059

Jullum, M., Løland, A., Huseby, R. B., Ånonsen, G., & Lorentzen, J. (2020). Detecting money laundering transactions with machine learning. *Journal of Money Laundering Control, 23*(1), 173–186. DOI: 10.1108/JMLC-07-2019-0055

Kindylidi, I. (2022). The Data Protection Implications of the EU AML Framework: A Critical Overview & the Case of AI. In A. Gryszczyńska, P. Polański, N. Gruschka, K. Rannenberg, & M. Adamczyk (Eds.), *Privacy Technologies and Policy. APF 2022. Lecture Notes in Computer Science, vol 13279: Vol. 13279 LNCS* (pp. 37–49). Springer Science and Business Media Deutschland GmbH. DOI: 10.1007/978-3-031-07315-1_3

Konkin, A., & Zapechnikov, S. (2023). Zero knowledge proof and ZK-SNARK for private blockchains. *Journal of Computer Virology and Hacking Techniques, 19*(3), 443–449. DOI: 10.1007/s11416-023-00466-1

Kuner, C. (2013). Transborder Data Flows and Data Privacy Law. In *Transborder Data Flows and Data Privacy Law*. Oxford University Press., DOI: 10.1093/acprof:oso/9780199674619.001.0001

Li, S., & Huang, Y. (2021). The genesis, design and implications of China's central bank digital currency. *China Economic Journal, 14*(1), 67–77. DOI: 10.1080/17538963.2020.1870273

Lu, L., & Chen, H. (2021). Digital Yuan: The Practice and Regulation of China's Central Bank Digital Currency (CBDC). *Butterworths Journal of International Banking and Financial Law, 36*(8), 601–603.

Martínez-Ramil, P., Bolaños-Frasquet, H., Hamuľák, O., & Kerikmäe, T. (2023). A Multidimensional Understanding of EU's Digital Sovereignty. In Troitiño, D. R., Kerikmäe, T., & Hamuľák, O. (Eds.), *Digital Development of the European Union: An Interdisciplinary Perspective* (pp. 235–247). Springer International Publishing., DOI: 10.1007/978-3-031-27312-4_15

Mattsson, U. (2021). Privacy-Preserving Analytics and Secure Multiparty Computation. *ISACA Journal, 2*.

Mitrou, L. (2017). The General Data Protection Regulation: A Law for the Digital Age? In Synodinou, T.-E., Jougleux, P., Markou, C., & Prastitou, T. (Eds.), *EU Internet Law* (pp. 19–57). Springer International Publishing., DOI: 10.1007/978-3-319-64955-9_2

Olaye, E., Omafovbe, I., Aigbe, W. O., & Obuh, D. (2024). Personalized Governance Strategy for Patient Data in a Digital One Health Surveillance System. In S. Misra, P. Kvalvik, K. M. Kjølerbakken, & R. Damasevicius (Eds.), *International Conference on Digital Sovereignty (ICDS), Procedia Computer Science* (Vol. 254, pp. 20–29). Elsevier B.V. DOI: 10.1016/j.procs.2025.02.060

Pocher, N., Zichichi, M., Merizzi, F., Shafiq, M. Z., & Ferretti, S. (2023). Detecting Anomalous Cryptocurrency Transactions: An AML/CFT Application of Machine Learning-based Forensics. *Electronic Markets, 33*(27), 1–17. https://doi.org/https://doi.org/10.1007/s12525-023-00654-3. DOI: 10.1007/s12525-023-00654-3

Ramesh, D., Santosh, T., Trivedi, M. C., & Le, C. H. (2024). Ensuring Digital Sovereignty in Cross-chain EHR Sharing: A Relay-as-a-Service Approach for Secure Healthcare Interoperability. In S. Misra, P. Kvalvik, K. M. Kjølerbakken, & R. Damasevicius (Eds.), *International Conference on Digital Sovereignty (ICDS) Procedia Computer Science* (Vol. 254, pp. 48–57). Elsevier B.V. DOI: 10.1016/j.procs.2025.02.063

Related Information Article 44. General Principle for Transfers, Pub. L. No. ISO 27701, GDPR training, consulting and DPO outsourcing 1 (2018).

Rivest, R. L., Adleman, L., & Dertouzos, M. L. (1978). On Data Banks and Privacy Homomorphisms. *Foundations on Secure Computation*, 169–179. https://people.csail.mit.edu/rivest/pubs/RAD78.pdf

Sampson, F. (2021). Data Privacy and Security: Some Legal and Ethical Challenges. In Jahankhani, H., Kendzierskyj, S., & Akhgar, B. (Eds.), *Advanced Sciences and Technologies for Security Applications* (pp. 109–134). Springer., DOI: 10.1007/978-3-030-72120-6_4

Scardovi, C. (2017). Digital Transformation in Financial Services. In *Digital Transformation in Financial Services.* Springer International Publishing. DOI: 10.1007/978-3-319-66945-8

Schilling, L., & Uhlig, H. (2019). Some simple bitcoin economics. *Journal of Monetary Economics*, *106*, 16–26. DOI: 10.1016/j.jmoneco.2019.07.002

Shorya, R., & Jagwani, P. (2024). Enhancing Digital Autonomy in Peer-to-Peer Energy Trading: A Blockchain and Predictive Analytics Approach. In S. Misra, P. Kvalvik, K. M. Kjølerbakken, & R. Damasevicius (Eds.), *International Conference on Digital Sovereignty, Procedia Computer Science* (Vol. 254, pp. 230–239). Elsevier B.V. DOI: 10.1016/j.procs.2025.02.082

Silva De Freitas, E. (2020). Cryptocurrency Regulation in the EU AML Regime: the path towards effective harmonization? *2nd Crypto Asset Lab Conference - CAL2020*, 1–5. https://ssrn.com/abstract=4175341

Subbagari, S. (2024). Counter Measures to Combat Money Laundering in the New Digital Age. *Digital Threats : Research and Practice*, *5*(2), 1–13. DOI: 10.1145/3626826

Talukdar, J., Singh, T. P., & Barman, B. (2023). Supervised Learning. In *Artificial Intelligence in Healthcare Industry. Advanced Technologies and Societal Change* (pp. 51–86). Springer. DOI: 10.1007/978-981-99-3157-6_4

TITH., D., & COLIN, J.-N. (2024). A Trust Policy Meta-Model for Trustworthy and Interoperability of Digital Identity Systems. In S. Misra, P. Kvalvik, K. M. Kjølerbakken, & R. Damasevicius (Eds.), *International Conference on Digital Sovereignty (ICDS), Procedia Computer Science* (Vol. 254, pp. 88–97). Elsevier B.V. DOI: 10.1016/j.procs.2025.02.067

Treasury, H. M. (2019). *Economic crime plan 2019 to 2022*. Crown copyright. https://www.gov.uk/government/publications/economic-crime-plan-2019-to-2022

Vogel, B. (2022). Potentials and Limits of Public-Private Partnerships against Money Laundering and Terrorism Financing. *Eucrim, 1/2022*, 52–60. DOI: 10.30709/eucrim-2022-002

Voigt, P., & von dem Bussche, A. (2024). *The EU General Data Protection Regulation (GDPR): A Practical Guide* (2nd ed.). Springer Nature Switzerland., DOI: 10.1007/978-3-031-62328-8

Wang, H. (2023). How to understand China's approach to central bank digital currency? *Computer Law & Security Review, 50*, 1–7. DOI: 10.1016/j.clsr.2022.105788

Wang, L., Cheng, Y., Xiang, A., Zhang, J., & Yang, H. (2024). Application of Natural Language Processing in Financial Risk Detection. *Financial Engineering and Risk Management, 7*(4), 1–10. https://doi.org/http://dx.doi.org/10.23977/ferm.2024.070401

Zhang, K.-Y., Huang, A.-J., Tu, K., Li, M.-H., Zhang, C., Qi, W., Wu, Y.-D., & Yu, Y. (2024). Experimental Secure Multiparty Computation from Quantum Oblivious Transfer with Bit Commitment. *Quantum Physics*, 1–19. http://arxiv.org/abs/2411.04558

Zyskind, G., Nathan, O., & Pentland, A. S. (2015). Decentralizing Privacy: Using Blockchain to Protect Personal Data. *2015 IEEE Security and Privacy Workshops, (SPW)*, 180–184. DOI: 10.1109/SPW.2015.27

Chapter 9
Face Morphing Attack Detection: Privacy and Digital Sovereignty Issues, Methods and Future Direction

Sulaimon Adebayo Bashir
https://orcid.org/0000-0001-8690-3953
Federal University of Technology, Minna, Nigeria

Muhammad Bashir Abdullahi
https://orcid.org/0000-0001-8200-2787
Federal University of Technology Minna, Nigeria

Mary Ogbuka Kenneth
Imperial College London, UK

Abubakar Dahiru
National Information Technology Development Agency (NITDA), Nigeria

Olawale Surajudeen Adebayo
https://orcid.org/0000-0001-7052-4756
National Open University of Nigeria, Jabi, Nigeria

Kehinde H. Lawal
Federal University of Technology Minna, Nigeria

ABSTRACT

This chapter examines the privacy threat facing face recognition and morphing detection systems using the LINDUUN framework as the methodology. It describes various aspects of privacy issues that may hamper safe and secured operation of face recognition and morphing attack detection systems. Digital sovereignty issues affecting the systems are also examined with recommendations on actions to be taken to safeguard privacy and digital sovereignty of the systems. A new taxonomy of the approaches being used for the detection of face morphing attacks is presented. The privacy and digital sovereignty concerns related to the detection methods are elicited with recommendations to alleviate them. The findings reflect that critical

DOI: 10.4018/979-8-3693-9137-2.ch009

privacy and digital sovereignty issues are present in the domain of face recognition and morphing detection systems. Therefore, these expositions will influence policy-makers and researchers to address the issues and also utilized the recommendations for further research.

INTRODUCTION

Face recognition (FR) systems, widely used in various identity verification applications like e-passports and online authentication; they are designed to enhance security by relying on unique facial features of individual. However, these systems are not immune to sophisticated attacks. One of such attacks is the face morphing attack. Face morphing attack involves blending the facial features of two or more individuals to create a single image that can trick a face recognition system into recognizing each contributing person. Figure 1 shows the blending of two faces (Identity A and Identity B) using four different morphing tools- OpenCV scripts, Facemorpher, StyleGAN3 anf MIPGAN-II (Sarkar et al., 2022) to produce four different blended images as shown in Figure 2. Each of the persons that contributed the identity images can use for authentication under a face recognition system. This face morphing attack has serious privacy and security implications around the data being collected, the machine learning models being used for the detection of the attack and also issues of sovereignty of the data being collected.

Figure 1. Two different identity images being blended

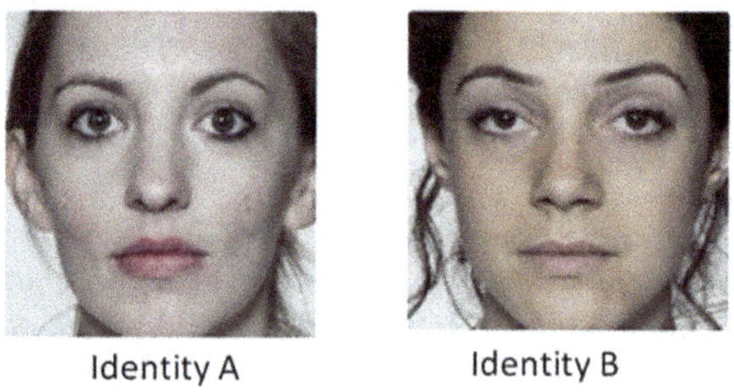

Figure 2. Different Morphed Images Generated from 2 identity images from Figure 1a (Face Research Lab London (DeBruine and Jones, 2021) Dataset by Sarkar et al. (2022))

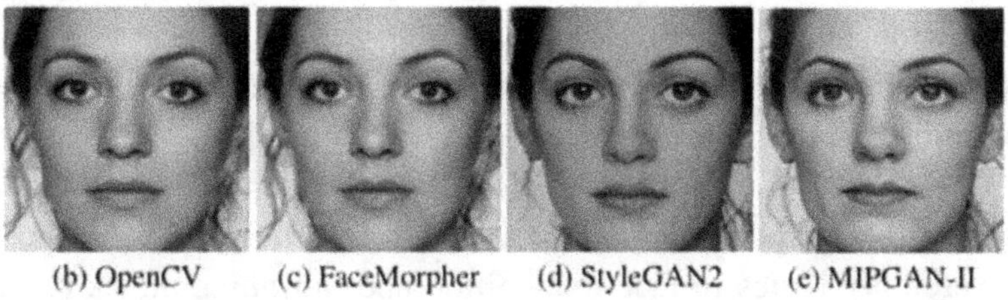

In most cases, this attack is prevalent under face recognition system being used for identity verification such e-passport. If an adversary is able to infiltrate a facial biometric recognition system with morphed image during the issuance process such passport can be authenticated successfully for any of the contributing subjects during verification at a border control leading to grave security breaches such as identity theft, fraud, and unauthorized access to personal data.

While the end results of face morphing attack can lead to serious security breach, it also elicits a lot of privacy issues in terms of the data being collected by the facial recognition systems and the models being used under the system for detecting the attack. Therefore, privacy concerns have become worrying due to the scale of personal information being collected and stored by these systems. The information been collected under facial recognition is increasing significantly nowadays, motivated by law enforcement, national security, and economic incentives. The issue of privacy is a common issue affecting many information processing domains such as biometric systems (Melzi et al., 2024; Wang et al., 2024), Internet of Things (Badr et al., 2021), healthcare (Jawad, 2024; López-Martínez et al., 2023), social media networks (Bhattacharya et al., 2023) and information systems (Bu et al., 2020) in general.

The objectives of this chapter are to:

i. examine the digital sovereignty and privacy issues related to face recognition and morphing detection systems.
ii. proffer recommendations on safeguards to resolve the issues of digital sovereignty and privacy issues related to face recognition and morphing detection systems.
iii. analyze the various machine learning approaches being used for the detection of face morphing attacks.
iv. examine the privacy threats that arises from the machine learning models.

Addressing the above objectives provides the following contributions:

i. Taxonomy of face morphing detection approaches is presented.
ii. Elicitation of key digital sovereignty and privacy issues in face recognition and morphing detection systems.
iii. Recommendation on the safeguards for privacy and digital sovereignty in face recognition and morphing detection systems.

The rest of this chapter is organized as follows: section 2 examines privacy and digital sovereignty issues in face recognition and morphing attack detection systems. Section 3 discusses privacy and digital sovereignty issues in face morphing machine learning detection models. Section 4 presents effects of privacy breach in face recognition system under face morphing attacks while section 5 presents the taxonomy of face morphing attack detection methods while section 6 examines the challenges in detecting face morphing attacks. Section 7 suggests future direction of research and policy considerations while section 8 and 9 present the limitations and conclusion respectively.

PRIVACY AND DIGITAL SOVEREIGNTY ISSUES IN FACE RECOGNITION AND MORPHING ATTACK DETECTION SYSTEMS

The concept of privacy has different conational meanings depending on social and cultural issues, study disciplines, stakeholder interests, and application perspective (Deng et al., 2011). However, the general overriding notion of privacy across domains is that, privacy is the fundamental right of individuals to control access to their personal information, autonomy over their bodies and decisions, and freedom from undue surveillance or intrusion. Thus, a key definition of privacy in the context of information technology is given as "the right to be let alone", focusing on freedom from intrusion, and "the right to informational self-determination", allowing individuals to "control, edit, manage, and delete information about themselves and decide when, how and to what extent that information is communicated to others" (Hansen, 2008). Another definition of privacy given by Clarke (2018) as "Privacy is the interest that individuals have in sustaining 'personal space', free from interference by other people and organizations."

Digital Sovereignty on the other hand can be described as the pursuit of processes to protect and safeguard all forms of digital resources and infrastructures including-data, networks, machine learning models of an organization or sovereign nation from external control while minimizing reliance on foreign technologies for the safe and secure operation of these resources (Dabrock et al., 2021; Jiang and Belli, 2025; Tan et al., 2023). The concept of digital sovereignty has gained significant research attention in recent times because of its potential to support privacy and data protection, enhance national security and promote economic independence through the localized management of digital technology infrastructure. As highlighted by Misra et al. (2025), digital sovereignty is critical in the context of Industry 5.0, enabling sovereign control over essential digital elements such as data, infrastructure, algorithms, and visualization tools. Katsikas (2025) underscores its role in bolstering cybersecurity, while Klare et al. (2025) identify it as a key element to seamless software development process.

Facial recognition systems, in particular process highly sensitive biometric data, often involving both domestic citizens and foreign nationals undergoing verification—such as at automated border control e-gates. These systems require robust and adequate safeguard to ensure sovereignty of the collected data, the intelligent algorithm employed in the process and the underlying hardware and other supporting technologies.

The rest of this section explores and examines the data sovereignty and privacy issues inherent in the operational processes of face recognition and morphing attack detection systems and diverse approaches to protect and uphold the sovereignty and privacy of such systems' artifacts.

Digital Sovereignty Issues in Face Recognition and Morphing Attack Detection Systems

Face recognition and morphing attack detection systems used for biometric security, present several significant challenges to digital sovereignty—especially in developing countries. There are many issues that have been identified by different researchers that underpin the actualization of digital sovereignty. Misra et al. (2025) identified 8 major aspects of digital sovereignty from the literature in the context modern digital industries. These issues span across data ownership, dependency on external providers, legal and regulation, resilience, goverance, ethics, technology and cybersecurity. However, in the perspective of face recognition and morphing attack detection system, we opine that the key issues in this domain include: data ownership and control, transparency, third-party dependencies, and vulnerability to cyberattacks as depicted in Figure 3.

Figure 3. Digital sovereignty issues in face recognition and morphing detection systems

1. Data Ownership and Control: Facial images and biometric information are inherently sensitive and personal. However, many systems store such data in centralized or cloud environments, often hosted in foreign jurisdictions. This raises serious concerns about who truly owns or controls the data. Without clear data governance, nations risk losing sovereignty over critical personal and national digital assets. Cross-Border Data Flows

The storage and processing of biometric data on servers located in other countries make such data subject to foreign laws. This compromises the ability of national governments to enforce their own data protection laws and exposes citizen data to foreign surveillance and potential misuse. Exacerbating this issue is occasioned by of lack of local capacity for technological infrastructure and skilled manpower in some developing nations that are required to independently develop biometric systems. This gap results in dependence on foreign technologies and limits the country's ability to safeguard its digital autonomy.

2. Transparency: Most morphing detection systems are developed using deep learning models that are typically black-box in nature. The lack of interpretabil-

ity and explainability makes it difficult to understand or audit how decisions are made, thereby weakening accountability and trust, especially in national security or legal contexts. Another aspect of transparency is model bias and discrimination whereby AI models used for facial recognition are trained on non-representative datasets. As a result, these models may perform poorly on African or other underrepresented demographics, leading to errors in identification and potential discrimination. This undermines the sovereignty and fairness of national identity systems.

3. Third-Party Dependencies: The use of third-party tools—including pre-trained models, cloud APIs, or proprietary libraries—introduces external dependencies. These technologies may be governed or maintained by foreign companies, limiting the deploying nation's control and increasing the risk of backdoors, data exfiltration, or sudden service discontinuation.
4. Security: Morphing attacks—where facial images are digitally manipulated to spoof biometric systems—pose a direct threat to face recognition reliability. If detection mechanisms are not sufficiently robust, systems can be easily bypassed, leading to identity theft, fraud, and national-level privacy breaches.

Safeguards for Digital Sovereignty in Face Recognition Systems

Addressing these digital sovereignty issues requires deliberate policy frameworks, technical innovation, and capacity-building initiatives that prioritize national interests.

1. Development of Indigenous Technologies: Governments and institutions should encourage and fund the development of local face recognition and morphing detection solutions. Building these systems on locally curated datasets will help reduce bias and improve performance for native populations while ensuring full control over their functionality and updates.
2. Data Localization and Sovereign Cloud Infrastructures: Biometric and facial data should be stored within national borders under strict data localization policies. Investments should be made in establishing secure, compliant data centres that meet international standards, enabling countries to retain legal and operational control over their digital assets.
3. Auditability and Explainability in AI: AI systems used for biometric verification should include explainability features that allow independent regulators to audit decision-making processes. This is particularly important for legal and high-security applications where transparency is non-negotiable.
4. Strengthening Legal and Regulatory Frameworks: Countries should update or develop comprehensive data protection, cybersecurity, and digital rights legis-

lation that prioritizes digital sovereignty. Regulatory bodies must be empowered to enforce compliance, especially when foreign technologies are used in critical national infrastructure.

5. Cybersecurity and Adversarial Robustness: Ensuring the resilience of face recognition systems against morphing and other adversarial attacks is vital. Techniques like morphing-resistant model training, anomaly detection, and multi-modal authentication can strengthen system security and trustworthiness.
6. Reduction of Third-Party Reliance: Where possible, governments should adopt open-source, auditable tools or work with trusted local partners. Strict vetting procedures should be implemented for any foreign technology integrated into national systems, including contractual agreements on data handling and software updates.
7. Capacity Building and Digital Literacy

To sustain long-term digital sovereignty, there must be strategic investments in local expertise. This includes training AI specialists, cybersecurity professionals, and system auditors who can design, manage, and secure these technologies. Public awareness campaigns are also essential to educate citizens on data privacy and digital rights.

Privacy Issues in Face Recognition System

In this section, we examine privacy issues and threats that are inherent facial recognition systems. Our analysis is conducted using the **LINDDUN framework** (Deng et al., 2011; Wuyts et al., 2014), a structured approach for identifying and mitigating privacy threats. The **LINDDUN framework** categorizes threats into specific types, and maps them to system elements to address vulnerabilities effectively. By applying this framework to **face recognition systems**, it help us to identify privacy concerns at various stages, from data collection to processing and sharing. This framework has also been applied in the work of Beltrán and Calvo (2023) to develop a privacy threat model for facial recognition systems. Given the intertwined and interdependent nature of facial recognition and morphing detection systems, privacy concerns in one system inherently influence the other. This interconnection highlights that privacy issues in these systems are closely related and cannot be addressed in isolation.

Privacy issues in face recognition system can be understood as the specific concerns or challenges that arise due to the design, implementation, operation, or usage of face recognition system which may potentially lead to violations of individuals' privacy rights. These issues often stem from the way data is collected, processed, stored, shared, or used and can affect individuals' autonomy, security, and trust in the system. Privacy issues are conceptual and systemic problems that, if not addressed, can result in privacy threats or breaches. They highlight areas where personal data or activities may be exposed to unauthorized access, misuse, or exploitation, often due to gaps in system design, lack of regulations, or insufficient user awareness. Some of the privacy issues in face recognition systems include: inadequate user consent, over-collection of data, improper data sharing, insufficient data protection and lack of user control.

1. **Inadequate User Consent** is one of the key issues in FR systems is the lack of adequate mechanisms for obtaining user consent regarding the collection, processing, and storage of facial data especially in the public surveillance FR systems. In many cases, individuals are unaware that their facial data is being captured or how it is subsequently used. For instance, public surveillance cameras equipped with facial recognition capabilities often operate without providing clear notification or obtaining explicit consent from individuals being monitored. Additionally, in many implementations, consent mechanisms are either entirely absent or poorly designed, leaving users uninformed about the extent and purpose of the data collection. This lack of transparency means individuals may not understand how their facial biometric information is processed, stored, or shared, including whether it will be used for purposes beyond the original intent, such as surveillance, profiling, or commercial activities. This issue raises both ethical and legal concerns, particularly as facial biometric data is highly sensitive and irrevocable if misused or compromised. Effective consent mechanisms should not only notify individuals but also provide meaningful choices about their participation in such systems which is mostly not the case.
2. **Over-Collection of Data**: Another pertinent privacy issue in FR system is over-collection of data. Many FR systems collect and store far more information than is necessary for their intended purpose, often due to design choices, operational convenience, or a lack of stringent data minimization practices. For instance, instead of capturing and processing only the specific facial features required for identification or verification, these systems may record and store entire video feeds, including unnecessary background details and bystanders' faces, which are irrelevant to the system's function. This over-collection not only increases the risk of unauthorized access and data breaches but also raises ethical concerns about the unnecessary surveillance of individuals who may not even be the target of the FR system. Furthermore, such practices can inadvertently capture sensitive information about individuals' behaviors, locations, and interactions, potentially creating extensive personal profiles. For example, in public surveillance scenarios, FR cameras may continuously record and store footage of all passersby, even if the system is only designed to track specific individuals for

security purposes. Similarly, in commercial settings like retail stores, FR systems might gather data on every customer's movements and expressions, exceeding the requirements for theft prevention or customer service. This indiscriminate data collection exacerbates privacy risks, as the more extensive the data repository, the greater the potential for misuse, unauthorized sharing, or exploitation by malicious actors.

3. **Improper Sharing of Data**: This critical privacy issue in facial recognition (FR) systems occurs when facial data collected for specific purposes, such as unlocking a device, verifying identity, or enhancing security are shared with third parties without the user's explicit consent or awareness. For instance, biometric data gathered by FR systems in smartphones or apps may be shared with advertisers to create detailed profiles for targeted marketing campaigns, often without providing users with clear information about such practices. In other scenarios, facial data captured by public or private surveillance systems, initially intended for security purposes, could be handed over to law enforcement agencies or private organizations for unrelated investigations or other activities, frequently bypassing proper legal oversight and neglecting to inform the affected individuals. For example, a shopping mall using FR technology to enhance customer experience may also share collected facial data with third-party advertisers to analyze consumer behavior or preferences. Similarly, FR-enabled security cameras installed in urban areas might provide captured facial images to government agencies for unrelated purposes, such as monitoring protests or identifying individuals of interest, raising concerns about potential overreach and the erosion of civil liberties. These practices raise serious ethical and legal concerns, particularly because facial biometric data is highly sensitive and immutable. Facial data, poses unique risks due to its highly sensitive and immutable nature. Facial data is deeply personal and directly tied to an individual's identity, making its mishandling or misuse a significant privacy concern. Unlike passwords or other identifiers, which can be reset or changed if compromised, facial data is permanent—an individual cannot alter their facial features to protect themselves if their data is leaked or improperly used. This makes biometric data a one-time, high-stakes identifier, increasing the potential for long-term harm if it is exposed or shared without consent. The misuse or improper sharing of facial data can lead to severe consequences such as stolen facial data exploited for identity theft, enabling criminals to impersonate individuals in systems that rely on facial recognition. This loss of control over one's data undermines personal autonomy, eroding trust in technology and the organizations that use it.
4. **Insufficient Data Protection**: This privacy is a very significant issue in safeguarding the privacy of individuals in facial recognition systems. When security

measures are weak or encryption protocols are inadequate, sensitive biometric data, such as facial images and associated metadata, becomes vulnerable to breaches or unauthorized access. This lack of robust protection can create opportunities for exploitation by malicious actors, including hackers and insiders with ill intent. For instance, databases storing facial data may be targeted by cybercriminals aiming to steal or misuse the information for purposes such as identity theft, fraud, or even blackmail. Similarly, without proper access controls and monitoring mechanisms, insiders with privileged access could misuse the data for unauthorized purposes, such as selling it to third parties or using it for personal gain. These scenarios highlight the critical role of comprehensive security frameworks in preventing data breaches. Additionally, inadequate data protection measures can undermine user trust in facial recognition systems, as individuals may fear their sensitive information is not being handled responsibly. This is particularly concerning because biometric data is immutable—if compromised, it cannot simply be changed like a password. The consequences of such breaches can be far-reaching, leading to long-term harm for individuals and legal or reputational risks for organizations.

5. **Lack of User Control** A significant privacy issue in facial recognition (FR) systems is the lack of user control over their facial biometric data once it has been captured. Users often have minimal or no options to access, modify, or delete their data stored in such systems. This is especially problematic in the context of public FR systems, where individuals have no control over when, where, or how their facial data is collected, often under the justification of security or law enforcement purposes. For example, surveillance cameras equipped with FR capabilities in public spaces can capture facial images without notifying individuals or seeking their consent. In such scenarios, users have no ability to opt out of the data collection process, nor are they informed about how their data will be used, shared, or retained. This lack of transparency and control creates a power imbalance, leaving individuals vulnerable to privacy violations, misuse of their data, or unauthorized surveillance. Additionally, the inability to manage one's biometric data contradicts fundamental privacy principles, such as the right to be forgotten or data minimization. Without mechanisms to allow users to remove or restrict access to their data, FR systems can perpetuate ongoing risks, including potential misuse by third parties or the government. This concern becomes even more pressing in jurisdictions without robust privacy regulations, where there may be few safeguards against the misuse or overreach of such technologies.

To address all these identified and discussed privacy issues in FR systems, it is essential for organizations to implement robust and user-centric data governance frameworks while adhering to regulations that govern data privacy within their jurisdictions of operations such as the General Data Protection Regulation (GDPR) in Europe, the California Consumer Privacy Act (CCPA) in America. Transparent consent mechanisms are essential to inform users about how their facial data will be collected, used, shared, and stored, ensuring individuals can opt in knowingly. Systems should adhere to data minimization principles, collecting only the necessary information, such as extracted facial features, rather than retaining full video feeds or unnecessary metadata. Strict policies must regulate data sharing to prevent biometric data collected for one purpose from being repurposed or shared with third parties, such as advertisers or law enforcement, without explicit user consent. To safeguard sensitive information, organizations must employ strong encryption, secure storage protocols, and multi-layered access controls, complemented by regular security audits to prevent unauthorized access or breaches. Furthermore, users must be empowered with tools to access, modify, or delete their biometric data, ensuring they maintain oversight and control. By combining these technical safeguards, compliance with international privacy laws, and organizational accountability, FR systems can be deployed in a manner that upholds privacy, fosters trust, and protects user autonomy.

Privacy Threat Types in Face Recognition Systems

According to Wuyts et al. (2014) the privacy threats in any information processing system can be captured through the LINDDUN framework. Each letter in "LINDDUN" represents a specific privacy threat type, derived by negating a corresponding privacy property that should ideally be upheld in any information processing system. The acronym highlights key areas where privacy can be compromised if these properties are not adequately protected(Deng et al., 2011). The privacy threats outlined in the framework are applied here to identify specific privacy risks associated with facial recognition (FR) systems. These threats are shown in Figure 4 while Table 1 shows the privacy properties and the antagonizing privacy threats.

Figure 4. LINDDUN privacy threats (Wuyts et al., 2014)

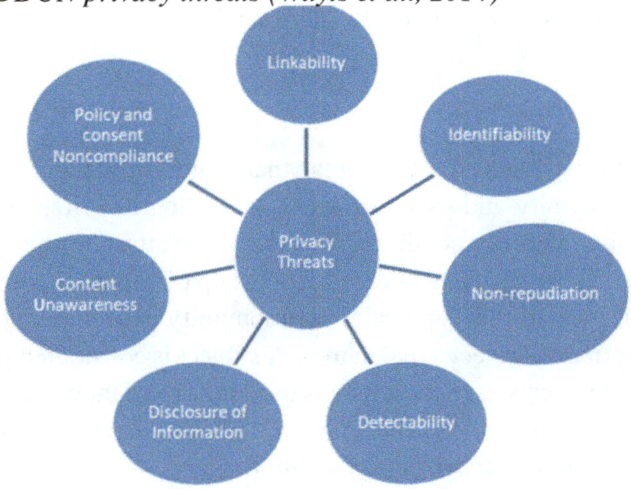

Linkability

This is a privacy threat that directly contradicts the desirable privacy property known as unlinkability. Unlinkability, as defined by Pfitzmann and Hansen (2010), refers to the inability of an attacker to determine whether two or more items of interest (IOIs)—such as subjects, messages, actions, or other entities—are related within a system. Specifically, unlinkability ensures that within the system, the attacker cannot sufficiently distinguish whether these IOIs are associated with one another. From this definition, it is clear that unlinkability is a crucial privacy property in face recognition systems, as it prevents attackers from connecting an individual's facial biometric data across multiple contexts or databases. Linkability poses a significant threat in facial recognition systems because it enables the association of facial biometric data with other sources of information. This could involve linking an individual's face data captured in a public setting to private records, such as online profiles, medical histories, or travel itineraries. Such linkages can lead to extensive profiling, surveillance, and potential misuse of personal data, undermining user privacy and autonomy.

Furthermore, this threat increases privacy risks by increasing the potential for unauthorized tracking. For example, in commercial contexts, companies could exploit Linkability to combine shopping behaviors, location data, and facial recognition inputs to create detailed consumer profiles, often without the user's explicit consent. In another scenario in pubic FR, an attacker can cross-referencing facial recognition data collected at an airport with images from social media or surveillance footage to build a comprehensive profile of the individual.

Identifiability

This is another critical privacy threat that contradicts the desirable privacy properties of anonymity and pseudonymity. According to Pfitzmann and Hansen (2010), anonymity refers to a condition where, from an attacker's perspective, a subject cannot be sufficiently identified within a group of subjects, commonly known as the anonymity set. In the same vein, pseudonymity is said to involve the use of identifiers other than a subject's real names. A subject is considered pseudonymous when an identifier, such as a pseudonym, is used instead of their actual name. These properties aim to ensure that personal identity is obscured or replaced by alternative identifiers to prevent unauthorized recognition.

In the context of facial recognition (FR) systems, identifiability threats encompass the risk of revealing or inferring an individual's identity through their facial biometric data. Unlike anonymity, where individuals remain indistinguishable within a larger group, and pseudonymity, where alternative identifiers mask real identities, FR systems inherently process highly identifiable information, such as facial features. This makes them particularly vulnerable to identifiability threats when data is misused or improperly secured.

For example, identifiability threats in FR systems may occur in public surveillance, where individuals can be uniquely identified in real time or retrospectively across various locations. Such identifications can be linked with other datasets, such as social media profiles or government records, enabling unauthorized profiling and tracking. In retail environments, FR systems might identify individuals to personalize marketing efforts without their consent, further diminishing their anonymity. Similarly, in law enforcement, false positives in identification could lead to unwarranted scrutiny or legal consequences for individuals. Pseudonymity-related threats also arise when the protective pseudonyms assigned to individuals during processing are compromised. Data breaches or linkage attacks could expose the real identities behind these pseudonyms, undermining the privacy protections they were meant to provide. This creates risks such as discrimination, stalking, or exploitation.

Non-Repudiation

This threat directly contradicts the essential and preferred privacy property of *plausible deniability*. Plausible deniability is a privacy safeguard that ensures an attacker cannot prove that a user possesses certain knowledge, has taken a specific action, or has communicated particular information. While non-repudiation is a key security requirement in many systems—ensuring accountability by providing irrefutable evidence of an action—it was observed that plausible deniability can sometimes take precedence over non-repudiation, depending on the application context (Deng et al., 2011).

For example, in systems designed to protect whistleblowers, users may need the ability to deny sending a message to ensure their safety and maintain anonymity. Similarly, plausible deniability is crucial in scenarios like private, off-the-record conversations, denying the existence of encrypted files, disputing the transmission of files from a specific source, or refuting the association of a database record with an individual (Deng et al., 2011). In such cases, plausible deniability serves as a protective measure against privacy violations and undue scrutiny.

In the context of facial recognition (FR) systems, the threat of non-repudiation arises when the system irrevocably links an individual to specific actions, locations, or behaviors, removing any opportunity for deniability. For example, if an FR system captures an individual's face at a particular event, that person may be unable to dispute their presence, even if being linked to that event poses risks to their safety or reputation. This threat is especially concerning in situations involving protests, sensitive locations, or high-stakes environments, where being identified could result in severe consequences, such as persecution or discrimination. As another scenarios given in (Beltrán and Calvo, 2023), non-repudiation threats in facial recognition (FR) systems can manifest during identity verification processes where the subject provides a facial image. In the first scenario, the subject may genuinely be the source of the data flow but later deny initiating it. For example, if facial images are captured by public cameras or sensors without obfuscation, the event can be visibly recorded, creating a clear link between the subject and the data. Similarly, if the data flow occurs remotely without adequate encryption or concealment, it can be logged in a way that traces the data back to the subject, undermining their ability to plausibly deny involvement. Conversely, in the second scenario non-repudiation threats occurs when an adversary manipulates the system to make it appear as though the subject initiated the data flow when they did not. This can happen through presentation attacks, where an attacker uses a spoofed image or mask to impersonate the subject and successfully pass identity verification. Alternatively, logical impersonation or replay attacks can exploit authentication weaknesses or reuse previously captured biometric data to simulate a legitimate data flow. These threats emphasize the need for robust security measures, including mutual authentication, encryption, and anti-spoofing mechanisms, to protect both the integrity of the system and the privacy of individuals. Without these safeguards, subjects remain vulnerable to irrevocable attribution, whether the data flow originated from them or was falsely attributed to them.

Non-repudiation threat in FR systems requires careful consideration of how facial biometric data is collected, stored, and shared. System designers must implement measures to balance the competing needs for accountability and privacy

Detectability

Detectability refers to the potential for a person's presence or data to be identified or recognized within a system, even when the system is designed to anonymize or exclude individuals. This constitutes a significant threat to privacy, as it directly opposes the corresponding privacy properties of undetectability and unobservability. According to Pfitzmann and Hansen (2010), undetectability is the inability of an adversary to discern whether an item of interest (IOI), such as a subject's facial data, exists within a system. Meanwhile, unobservability combines undetectability with anonymity, ensuring that the IOI remains undetectable to all uninvolved parties while also protecting the anonymity of the associated subjects, even from other involved entities.

Unobservability provides a higher level of privacy assurance by revealing less information than anonymity alone. However, because it is a composite property of undetectability and anonymity, the emphasis in privacy threat frameworks like LINDDUN is placed on undetectability as a standalone property. This threat, therefore, is framed as detectability, highlighting the potential risk of exposing sensitive information or confirming the existence of data.

This threat manifest facial recognition (FR) systems, when the system's intruder is able to identify or confirm the presence of a subject's face in a database, even when anonymization protocols are in place. For instance, an FR system used for law enforcement may inadvertently allow adversaries to detect whether a specific individual is listed in the system, breaching privacy. Similarly, the mere existence of metadata or residual data linked to facial images could enable unauthorized parties to identify subjects indirectly. Detectability threats can occur due to flaws in data encryption, weak system design, or inadequate anonymization techniques, making it a critical challenge for FR systems to address to uphold user privacy.

Disclosure of Information

Discloser of information means exposing personal information to someone who is not eligible to access it. This threat is in direct contradiction to confidentiality privacy property. Confidentiality as a privacy property can be defined as safeguarding of sensitive information to ensure it is accessible only to authorized individuals, protecting it from unauthorized access or disclosure(Woubie et al., 2024). Therefore, confidentiality in FR systems involves facial images or associated metadata, being exposed to unauthorized parties. For instance, if an FR system's database is not adequately secured, it could be accessed by external attackers, internal malicious actors, or even inadvertently by third parties. Such disclosures could lead to a range of consequences, from identity theft to profiling and surveillance without consent.

A common scenario of disclosure involves the sharing of data between organizations without proper anonymization or encryption. For example, an FR system used for authentication at a corporate facility might share data with third-party vendors for analytics without adequately masking the identities of individuals. Similarly, weak encryption protocols could result in intercepted communications during data transmission, exposing users' sensitive facial data.

The risk of disclosure is further heightened in public FR deployments, such as those used in smart city applications or law enforcement surveillance. In these scenarios, the collection of vast amounts of facial data often lacks robust controls, making it vulnerable to breaches. Without strict adherence to privacy regulations and best practices, this threat undermines users' trust and compromises their fundamental right to privacy.

Context Unawareness

This is a privacy threat that occurs when a user is unaware of the information shared with a system, potentially revealing excessive details that aid attackers or providing inaccurate data, leading to errors in system decisions(Deng et al., 2011). This threat opposes the context awareness privacy property that emphasizes a user's understanding of their own data and the implications of sharing it. Users should be mindful of the potential privacy risks associated with sharing excessive personally identifiable information, as well as the negative outcomes that may arise from providing incomplete or inaccurate data(Deng et al., 2011). In terms FR systems, this threat occurs when users unknowingly share more biometric or contextual data than required. For instance, users may provide facial data captured in environments revealing sensitive personal or location-based details. This data, if improperly stored or analyzed, could inadvertently expose users to surveillance, profiling, or identity theft. Similarly, inaccurate facial data, such as low-quality images or poorly captured angles, can lead to false matches or system errors, potentially implicating individuals in legal matters or denying them access to essential services. Addressing this threat in FR systems requires transparent communication about data usage, explicit consent mechanisms, and the implementation of mechanisms that allow users to control the amount and type of data shared.

Policy and Consent Noncompliance

This the last threat in LIDDUN framework. It entails a situation where a system presents its privacy policies to users but fails to adhere to them in practice. As a result, users' personal data may still be exposed despite the assurance of compliance (Deng et al., 2011). This threat directly contradicts the privacy property of policy and consent compliance, which requires that systems adhere strictly to regulations and uphold the privacy standards they advertise.

With regards to face recognition (FR) systems, Policy and Consent Noncompliance can manifest in various ways. For example, an FR system may present a privacy policy that outlines data retention limits or specifies that biometric data will only be used for authentication purposes. However, the systems may later share or store users' facial data for longer periods or use it for additional purposes, such as surveillance or marketing, without obtaining proper consent. Additionally, users may not have a clear understanding of how their facial data will be processed or shared, and even if they do provide consent, the system might not follow through on its stated policies, leaving users' biometric data vulnerable to misuse or unauthorized access. This lack of compliance with privacy policies could significantly undermine user trust and violate privacy rights, making enforcement of policy compliance essential in FR systems. Table 1 shows the mapping of different privacy issues to the threats they may cause, the system elements that may be involved and the kind of privacy that is affected.

Table 1. Mapping among privacy issues, privacy threat, system elements and privacy types

Privacy Issues	Threat Types	System Elements	Privacy Types
Inadequate User Consent	Unawareness, Non-Compliance	Data Collection, System Policies	Privacy of the Person, Privacy of Behaviour, Privacy of Location and Space
Over-Collection of Data	Detectability, Linkability	Data Collection, Data Storage	Privacy of Data and Image
Improper Data Sharing	Disclosure of Information	Data Sharing, Data Processing	Privacy of Data and Image, Privacy of Association
Insufficient Data Protection	Disclosure of Information,	Data Storage, Data Processing	Privacy of Data and Image
Lack of User Control	Identifiability, Linkability	System Policies, Data Storage	Privacy of Data and Image
Inference of Sensitive Attributes	Identifiability, Non-Repudiation	Data Processing	Privacy of Thought and Feelings, Privacy of Behaviour

Safeguards for Privacy Issues and Threats in Face Recognition Systems

1. Inadequate User Consent
    - Implement clear and explicit consent mechanisms for data collection and processing.
    - Provide comprehensive and accessible privacy notices detailing how data will be used.
2. Over-Collection of Data
    - Enforce data minimization by collecting only the facial features necessary for the system's functionality.
    - Avoid capturing unnecessary data, such as entire video feeds, by implementing specific-use algorithms.
    - Regularly review and update data collection practices to align with privacy regulations.
3. Improper Data Sharing
    - Establish strict data-sharing policies that restrict sharing biometric data without user consent.
    - Encrypt data during transmission and storage to prevent unauthorized access.
    - Use data anonymization techniques to protect user identities when sharing data externally.
4. Insufficient Data Protection
    - Apply strong encryption to secure biometric data in storage and transmission.
    - Conduct regular security audits and vulnerability assessments to identify and address weaknesses.
    - Implement robust access controls to ensure only authorized personnel can access sensitive data.
5. Lack of User Control
    - Provide users with options to modify or delete their biometric data upon request.
    - Implement transparent data management practices and allow users to track how their data is being used.
    - Limit retention periods for facial data and automatically delete data when no longer necessary.
6. Detectability Threat
    - Enforce access controls and ensure database security to prevent unauthorized attempts to detect if data exists.

- Mask or encrypt records to make them indistinguishable from random data.
- Regularly monitor repositories to prevent excessive retention or cross-referencing with external sources.

7. Disclosure of Information
    - Restrict access to sensitive biometric data to only authorized entities.
    - Apply advanced encryption techniques to prevent unauthorized disclosure of personal data.
    - Ensure compliance with confidentiality standards through rigorous audits and policy enforcement.
8. Content Unawareness
    - Educate users on the implications of sharing biometric data through transparent and accessible privacy policies.
    - Limit the information requested during data collection to avoid unintentional over-disclosure.
    - Use feedback mechanisms to inform users about how their data is being used in real-time.
9. Policy and Consent Noncompliance
    - Regularly audit privacy policies to ensure they are accurately implemented in practice.
    - Adopt third-party oversight to verify compliance with advertised privacy policies.
    - Establish penalties and accountability measures for noncompliance to deter violations.

PRIVACY AND DIGITAL SOVEREIGNTY ISSUES IN FACE MORPHING MACHINE LEARNING DETECTION MODELS

In this section we analyze and discuss the causes of privacy breach associated with face morphing detection models. As with many machine learning models that processes training data to build a solution model of the problem, models developed for face morphing attack detection are also exposed to the same threats. Among the major source of privacy threats emanating from face morphing detection models include Model extraction, Data memorization, Model inversion and Membership inference (Zhang et al., 2020).

Model Extraction Attack

Model extraction Attack (Liang et al., 2024; Tramèr et al., 2016; Yan et al., 2023) is an attack on machine learning model where an adversary replicates the model's functionality by systematically querying it and analyzing the outputs. This process involves sending various inputs to the target model, collecting the corresponding outputs—such as class labels or confidence scores—and using this data to train a surrogate model that approximates the original. This attack could lead to a privacy threat whereby the attacker employs the extracted model to uncover sensitive information. In the operation of face morphing detection model as a service, this attack can lead to privacy breach when the attacker uses the extracted model to develop high quality morphed images that can evade detection, potentially compromising the accuracy of the face recognition systems leading to unauthorized access to sensitive biometric data. Also, in some cases, the extracted model can reveal sensitive information about the dataset it was trained on. This can lead to the inadvertent exposure of personal facial biometric data that were used to train the original model.

Data Memorization

This is the phenomenon where machine learning models "remember" aspects of their training data, potentially exposing sensitive information (Carlini et al., 2019; Song et al., 2017). Song et al. (2017) identified this concept by showing how an untrusted third-party algorithm, even when operating in a trusted isolation environment, could encode sensitive training data into a model without significantly affecting its overall accuracy. In the context of **face morphing detection models**, data memorization can lead to specific privacy breaches. For example, if a model is overfitted on a dataset of biometric images, it could "memorize" distinctive facial features or morphing artifacts specific to certain individuals. As a result, an attacker could query the model with new images and, by analyzing the model's response, potentially identify individuals in the original training set or reconstruct features of their faces. This could undermine the security and privacy of face recognition systems, especially in sensitive applications such as identity verification or access control.

Model Inversion Attack

This involves the adversary trying to reverse-engineer the original input based on the model's response to queries. The adversary can do this either through a black-box approach (only having access to model predictions) or a white-box approach (where the attacker has access to the model's internal parameters). The goal is often to recreate sensitive or private data that was part of the model's training set(Nguyen et al., 2023; Yang et al., 2020; Y. Zhang et al., 2020). For face morphing detection, the attacker aims to invert the model by generating images or data points that are highly likely to be classified as certain identities or morphed faces by the model. This can be achieved by optimizing the input to the model in such a way that the output prediction corresponds to a specific identity or morph, revealing private information about individuals who were part of the training dataset. For instance, using methods like generative adversarial networks (GANs) or variational inference, attackers can reconstruct images from the model's outputs, effectively exposing private information about the faces used during training, even if those faces were not directly visible in the query inputs.

Membership Inversion Attack

This is another type of attack that poses privacy threat to face morphing detection model. **membership inference attack** involves determining whether a specific data sample was part of the model's training data. This is often achieved by analyzing the confidence scores or the output labels provided by the model in response to specific queries. The attacker can build a classifier using these outputs and determine whether a particular sample was trained on by the model(Al-Rubaie and Chang, 2019; Yang et al., 2020). in **face morphing detection models**, an attacker could use this attack to gain insights into whether a specific morphed face was used during training, which could be useful for adversaries seeking to bypass or compromise security systems. Table 2 provides the mapping of these privacy threat attack and the model components under breach with the possible countermeasures to avert the threat.

Table 2. Face morphing detection models' privacy threat, model elements and countermeasures

Attack Type	ML Component	Countermeasures	
Model Extraction	Model (outputs, structure)	Query Limitation, Model Watermarking, Differential Privacy	Limiting the number of queries an attacker can make or adding noise to outputs can prevent unauthorized model replication. Watermarking helps detect model stealing by embedding unique identifiers in the model's responses. Differential privacy ensures that the outputs do not leak sensitive information about the training data.
Data Memorization	Training Data, Model Parameters	Regularization (e.g., weight decay, dropout), Differential Privacy	Regularization prevents memorization of sensitive data by constraining the model. Techniques like weight decay and dropout reduce the model's reliance on specific training instances. Differential privacy adds noise to the model's training process to ensure that no single data point can overly influence the model's performance or reveal private data.
Model Inversion	Model Outputs (confidence scores)	Output Masking, Input Perturbation, Differential Privacy	Output masking or perturbing the input data helps obscure sensitive features that might be reconstructed by an attacker. Differential privacy ensures that the model outputs do not leak too much information about the training data, reducing the likelihood of an inversion attack.
Membership Inference	Model Outputs (labels, probabilities)	Differential Privacy, Confidence Thresholding, Training with Augmented Data	Using differential privacy ensures that the model cannot infer membership of specific data points. Confidence thresholding limits the model's sensitivity to outliers, and augmenting the training data reduces the likelihood of inferring membership based on specific data characteristics. This protects individuals' privacy by preventing attackers from determining if their data was part of the training set.

EFFECTS OF PRIVACY AND DIGITAL SOVEREIGNTY BREACH IN FACE RECOGNITION SYSTEM UNDER FACE MORPHING ATTACKS

Identity Theft and Fraud

The primary concern surrounding face morphing attacks is the danger associated with successful orchestration of such attacks. Attackers can impersonate legitimate users by submitting morphed images to biometric systems, thereby accessing sensitive information or conducting fraudulent activities. This creates the potential for serious privacy breaches, as personal data becomes vulnerable to exploitation. In the same vein this can lead to breach of digital sovereignty of user data if such stolen identities are transferred to a domain outside the governance of the original sovereign owner of the data.

Misuse of Personal Data

Face morphing not only undermines the security of identity verification systems but also facilitates the misuse of personal data. Morphed images, if intercepted, can be used to create false identities or perform illegal activities under the guise of legitimate users. The misuse of such data raises ethical and legal concerns, especially when individuals are unaware of the extent to which their personal information can be manipulated.

Threats to National Security

At the governmental level, face morphing attacks present significant threats to national security. For example, in border control systems where e-passports are used, the inability to detect morphed images could allow unauthorized individuals to enter a country, posing risks to immigration control and national safety.

METHODS OF FACE MORPHING ATTACK DETECTION

The approaches for solving the problem of face morphing can be broadly categorized into three as depicted in Figure 5.

Figure 5. Taxonomy of face morphing detection methods

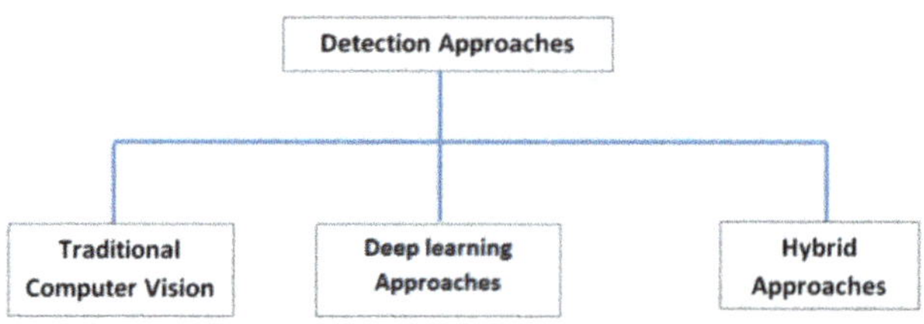

Traditional Detection Techniques

Early attempts to detect face morphing attacks relied on traditional feature-based methods. These techniques focus on analyzing facial landmarks or geometric features of the face, such as the distance between the eyes or the shape of the nose. In the literature of image detection with traditional approaches researchers have used image feature extraction algorithms based on texture descriptors, keypoint descriptors, edge-gradient descriptors, frequency and wavelet descriptors, statistical descriptors among others. These techniques are either used individually or as a fusion of two or more.

The texture descriptors such as Local Binary Patterns (LBP), Local Phase Quantization (LPQ), Gabor Filters, Steerable Filters and BSIF (Binarized Statistical Image Features) are used to extract the surface properties or patterns. Ramachandra et al. (2020) utilized a steerable pyramid which decomposes an image into multiple scales to extract image features from their print scan dataset at different resolutions and allowing analysis on fine details to coarse structures. Kenneth et al. (2021) utilized LBP feature descriptor with decision tree classifier while Scherhag et al. (2020) also utilized a fusion of different configurations of multi-scale block local binary patterns. The same LBP features was also evaluated as part of other methods like SIFT, SURF, LPQ, HOG and BSIF in (Ramachandra et al., 2020; Scherhag et al., 2018b; Wandzik et al., 2018). Similarly, BSIF features with SVM classifier was primarily used by (avendra et altion methods, can Raghavendra et al. (2016)

Keypoint descriptors which are used for detecting and describing significant points in an image have also being used extensively, they include SIFT (Scale-Invariant Feature Transform), SURF (Speeded-Up Robust Features), ORB (Oriented FAST and Rotated BRIEF), BRIEF (Binary Robust Independent Elementary Features), FAST (Features from Accelerated Segment Test). SURF and SIFT features descriptors in conjunction with SVM classifier were evaluated as part of other features techniques for morph detection in (Scherhag et al., 2018b) . An ensemble of features across texture descriptors, Keypoint extractors and gradient estimators have also been proposed in (Scherhag et al., 2018a; Venkatesh et al., 2020).

Machine Learning and Deep Learning Approaches

As face morphing attacks have become more advanced, researchers have turned to machine learning and deep learning to develop more robust detection methods. Neural networks and deep learning models are particularly effective in recognizing subtle differences in pixel patterns and textures that are often invisible to the human eye. One popular technique involves the use of convolutional neural networks (CNNs), which are trained on large datasets of morphed and non-morphed images to learn the distinguishing features of morphed faces. Seibold et al. (2017) developed face morphing attacks detection model using deep convolutional neural networks. The use of deep learning feature embedding of images for images pairing selection for morphing and detection of resulted morphed images was investigated in (Kessler et al., 2024). Convolutional Neural network based demorphing network was employed in (Ortega-Delcampo et al., 2020) to discover the initial pictures from two images that has been morphed. By unraveling the constituent's images in a morphed image the method was able to detect morphing attack at ABC gate scenario. In another research work presented in (Seibold et al., 2020), the use proposed neural network training schemes, which are based on different alternations of the training data, to increase robustness and generality of morphing attack detection model. Siamese network based VGG-16 architecture was introduced in (Soleymani et al., 2021) while deep representation from a pretrained vanilla vision transformer neural network was used with SVM for single image morph detection in(Zhang et al., 2024).

Hybrid Approaches

Hybrid approaches include approaches that combined traditional methods with deep learning methods. Authors in (Aghdaie et al., 2021; Chaudhary et al., 2021) combined traditional approach with deep earning approach by utilizing wavelet sub bands features computed on images as input to spatial attention mechanisms over convolutional and feed forward network to create a morphing detection system. Long et al. (2023) proposed a method utilizing two-stream network with channel attention and residual of multiple color spaces is proposed for face morphing detection. The method first obtains H, S, V, Y, Cb, Cr six color channel image, then use the bilateral filter for filtering the six color channel to get the corresponding residual noise image, then the combined six channel image and the residual noise image as input to the two-stream network for training.

CHALLENGES IN DETECTING FACE MORPHING ATTACKS

Sophistication of Morphing Techniques

One of the main challenges in detecting face morphing attacks is the increasing sophistication of morphing techniques. As morphing software evolves, it becomes more difficult to identify the subtle changes introduced to facial features. Well-crafted morphs can blend features so seamlessly that even advanced detection systems struggle to spot the alterations.

Generalization Across Datasets

Another significant challenge is ensuring that detection systems generalize well across different datasets. Many detection models perform well when tested on the dataset they were trained on but fail when applied to new, unseen data. This problem is compounded by the fact that faces vary significantly across populations in terms of age, gender, ethnicity, and facial expressions, making it difficult to build a one-size-fits-all detection model.

Adversarial Attacks and Countermeasures

Adversarial attacks, where attackers deliberately modify morphed images to bypass detection systems, pose an additional challenge. These attacks exploit weaknesses in detection models, forcing them to misclassify morphed images as legitimate ones. Researchers are working on countermeasures to make detection systems more resilient to adversarial attacks, but this remains an ongoing battle.

FUTURE DIRECTIONS

Improving Detection Algorithms

To combat the growing threat of face morphing attacks, future research must focus on developing more robust detection algorithms. These algorithms need to be capable of detecting even the most subtle morphs while maintaining high accuracy and low computational costs. Researchers are exploring the use of ensemble models, which combine multiple detection techniques to improve performance.

Development of Large-Scale Open-Source Morphed Faces for Research Purpose

Another issue faced in MAD is lack of publicly available MAD algorithm which can be used by researchers for comprehensive experimental evaluation of new and existing MAD algorithms. This situation brings about questions such as how reliable are the current state of-the-art MAD algorithms.

Integration with Multi-Modal Biometrics

Another promising direction for future research is the integration of multi-modal biometrics. By combining facial recognition with other biometric systems such as iris scans or fingerprints, security systems can reduce the risk of morphing attacks. This multi-layered approach provides additional safeguards, making it harder for attackers to fool the system.

Legislative and Policy Measures for Privacy Preservation of Data

Governments and organizations also need to address face morphing attacks through legislation and policy. Research into to frameworks to establish more robust privacy standards that govern the use of facial biometric data should be given adequate attention. This will help to protect individuals from the misuse of their personal information. Such frameworks should consider international dimension to create consistent policies and guidelines that address this global issue.

LIMITATIONS

This study is conceptual and does not include implementation-level experiments. Also, while we discuss policy recommendations, actual legislative frameworks may vary across countries.

CONCLUSION

Face morphing attacks present a significant challenge to the security and reliability of facial biometric systems. The privacy and digital sovereignty concerns in this domain affect both the face recognition system and the morphing detection models. Various approaches can be used to produce countermeasures to prevent these privacy and digital sovereignty threats. While traditional methods have proven inadequate for detecting face morphing attack, advancements in deep learning offer promising solutions. However, there is still much work to be done in addressing the challenges posed by sophisticated morphing techniques and adversarial attacks. Future research must focus on improving detection accuracy, integrating multi-modal biometrics, and establishing legal frameworks to protect privacy and digital sovereignty of the users' data and other digital infrastructures.

ACKNOWLEDGEMENT

This work was supported by funding provided by the Tertiary Education Trust Fund (TetFund) under the Nigeria Ministry of Education through the National Research Fund (NRF 2021) with research grant no: TETFUND/ES/DR-CE/NRF2021/SETI/ICT/00011/01.

REFERENCES

Aghdaie, P., Chaudhary, B., Soleymani, S., Dawson, J., & Nasrabadi, N. M. (2021). Attention Aware Wavelet-based Detection of Morphed Face Images. *2021 IEEE International Joint Conference on Biometrics (IJCB)*, 1–8. DOI: 10.1109/IJCB52358.2021.9484398

Al-Rubaie, M., & Chang, J. M. (2019). Privacy-Preserving Machine Learning: Threats and Solutions. *IEEE Security and Privacy, 17*(2), 49–58. DOI: 10.1109/MSEC.2018.2888775

Badr, Y., Zhu, X., & Alraja, M. N. (2021). Security and privacy in the Internet of Things: Threats and challenges. *Service Oriented Computing and Applications, 15*(4), 257–271. DOI: 10.1007/s11761-021-00327-z

Beltrán, M., & Calvo, M. (2023). A privacy threat model for identity verification based on facial recognition. *Computers & Security, 132*, 103324. DOI: 10.1016/j.cose.2023.103324

Bhattacharya, M., Roy, S., Chattopadhyay, S., Das, A. K., & Shetty, S. (2023). A comprehensive survey on online social networks security and privacy issues: Threats, machine learning-based solutions, and open challenges. *Security and Privacy, 6*(1), e275. DOI: 10.1002/spy2.275

Bu, F., Wang, N., Jiang, B., & Liang, H. (2020). "Privacy by Design" implementation: Information system engineers' perspective. *International Journal of Information Management, 53*, 102124. DOI: 10.1016/j.ijinfomgt.2020.102124

Carlini, N., Liu, C., Erlingsson, Ú., Kos, J., & Song, D. (2019). The secret sharer: Evaluating and testing unintended memorization in neural networks. *28th USENIX Security Symposium (USENIX Security 19)*, 267–284.

Chaudhary, B., Aghdaie, P., Soleymani, S., Dawson, J., & Nasrabadi, N. M. (2021). Differential Morph Face Detection using Discriminative Wavelet Sub-bands. *2021 IEEE/CVF Conference on Computer Vision and Pattern Recognition Workshops (CVPRW)*, 1425–1434. DOI: 10.1109/CVPRW53098.2021.00158

. Clarke, R. (2018). *Introduction to Dataveillance and Information Privacy, and Definitions of Terms, 2006.*

Dabrock, P., Tretter, M., Braun, M., & Hummel, P. (2021). Data sovereignty: A review. *Big Data & Society*, *8*(1).

DeBruine, L., & Jones, B. (2021). *Face Research Lab London Set*. DOI: 10.6084/m9.figshare.5047666.v5

Deng, M., Wuyts, K., Scandariato, R., Preneel, B., & Joosen, W. (2011). A privacy threat analysis framework: Supporting the elicitation and fulfillment of privacy requirements. *Requirements Engineering*, *16*(1), 3–32. DOI: 10.1007/s00766-010-0115-7

. Hansen, M. (2008). Linkage control-integrating the essence of privacy protection into identity management. *Proceedings of eChallenges*, 1585–1592.

Jawad, L. A. (2024). Security and Privacy in Digital Healthcare Systems: Challenges and Mitigation Strategies. *Abhigyan*, *42*(1), 23–31.

Jiang, M., & Belli, L. (Eds.). (2025). *Digital Sovereignty in the BRICS Countries: How the Global South and Emerging Power Alliances Are Reshaping Digital Governance*. Cambridge University Press., DOI: 10.1017/9781009531085

Katsikas, S. K. (2025). Towards a cybersecurity-oriented research agenda for digital sovereignty. *Procedia Computer Science*, *254*, 279–288. DOI: 10.1016/j.procs.2025.02.087

Kenneth, O. M., Bashir, S. A., Abisoye, O. A., & Mohammed, A. D. (2021). Face morphing attack detection in the presence of post-processed image sources using neighborhood component analysis and decision tree classifier. *Information and Communication Technology and Applications: Third International Conference, ICTA 2020, Minna, Nigeria, November 24–27, 2020, Revised Selected Papers 3*, 340–354.

Kessler, R., Raja, K., Tapia, J., & Busch, C. (2024). Towards minimizing efforts for Morphing Attacks—Deep embeddings for morphing pair selection and improved Morphing Attack Detection. *PLoS One*, *19*(5), e0304610. DOI: 10.1371/journal.pone.0304610 PMID: 38820451

Klare, M., Hrestic, R., Stelter, A., & Lechner, U. (2025). Digital Sovereignty and Digital Transformation Practice Recommendation for the Software Life Cycle Process. *Procedia Computer Science, 254*, 221–229. DOI: 10.1016/j.procs.2025.02.081

Liang, J., Pang, R., Li, C., & Wang, T. (2024). Model extraction attacks revisited. *Proceedings of the 19th ACM Asia Conference on Computer and Communications Security*, 1231–1245.

Long, M., Jia, C., & Peng, F. (2023). Face Morphing Detection Based on a Two-Stream Network with Channel Attention and Residual of Multiple Color Spaces. In Xu, Y., Yan, H., Teng, H., Cai, J., & Li, J. (Eds.), *Machine Learning for Cyber Security* (pp. 439–454). Springer Nature Switzerland. DOI: 10.1007/978-3-031-20102-8_34

López-Martínez, A., Gil-Pérez, M., & Ruiz-Martínez, A. (2023). A comprehensive review of the state-of-the-art on security and privacy issues in healthcare. *ACM Computing Surveys, 55*(12), 1–38. DOI: 10.1145/3571156

. Melzi, P., Rathgeb, C., Tolosana, R., Vera-Rodriguez, R., & Busch, C. (2024). An Overview of Privacy-Enhancing Technologies in Biometric Recognition. *ACM Comput. Surv., 56*(12), 310:1-310:28. DOI: 10.1145/3664596

Misra, S., Barik, K., & Kvalvik, P. (2025). Digital Sovereignty in the Era of Industry 5.0: Challenges and Opportunities. *Procedia Computer Science, 254*, 108–117. DOI: 10.1016/j.procs.2025.02.069

Nguyen, N.-B., Chandrasegaran, K., Abdollahzadeh, M., & Cheung, N.-M. (2023). Re-thinking model inversion attacks against deep neural networks. *Proceedings of the IEEE/CVF Conference on Computer Vision and Pattern Recognition*, 16384–16393. DOI: 10.1109/CVPR52729.2023.01572

Ortega-Delcampo, D., Conde, C., Palacios-Alonso, D., & Cabello, E. (2020). Border Control Morphing Attack Detection With a Convolutional Neural Network De-Morphing Approach. *IEEE Access : Practical Innovations, Open Solutions, 8*, 92301–92313. DOI: 10.1109/ACCESS.2020.2994112

. Pfitzmann, A., & Hansen, M. (2010, August). *A terminology for talking about privacy by data minimization: Anonymity, Unlinkability, Undetectability, Unobservability, Pseudonymity, and Identity Management.*

Raghavendra, R., Raja, K. B., & Busch, C. (2016). Detecting morphed face images. *2016 IEEE 8th International Conference on Biometrics Theory, Applications and Systems (BTAS)*, 1–7. DOI: 10.1109/BTAS.2016.7791169

Ramachandra, R., Venkatesh, S., Raja, K., & Busch, C. (2020). Detecting Face Morphing Attacks with Collaborative Representation of Steerable Features. In B. B. Chaudhuri, M. Nakagawa, P. Khanna, & S. Kumar (Eds.), *Proceedings of 3rd International Conference on Computer Vision and Image Processing* (pp. 255–265). Springer Singapore. DOI: 10.1007/978-981-32-9088-4_22

Sarkar, E., Korshunov, P., Colbois, L., & Marcel, S. (2022). Are GAN-based morphs threatening face recognition? *ICASSP 2022-2022 IEEE International Conference on Acoustics, Speech and Signal Processing (ICASSP)*, 2959–2963.

Scherhag, U., Kunze, J., Rathgeb, C., & Busch, C. (2020). Face morph detection for unknown morphing algorithms and image sources: A multi-scale block local binary pattern fusion approach. *IET Biometrics*, *9*(6), 278–289. DOI: 10.1049/iet-bmt.2019.0206

Scherhag, U., Rathgeb, C., & Busch, C. (2018a). Morph Deterction from Single Face Image: A Multi-Algorithm Fusion Approach. *Proceedings of the 2018 2nd International Conference on Biometric Engineering and Applications*, 6–12. DOI: 10.1145/3230820.3230822

Scherhag, U., Rathgeb, C., & Busch, C. (2018b). Performance variation of morphed face image detection algorithms across different datasets. *2018 International Workshop on Biometrics and Forensics (IWBF)*, 1–6. DOI: 10.1109/IWBF.2018.8401562

Seibold, C., Samek, W., Hilsmann, A., & Eisert, P. (2017). Detection of Face Morphing Attacks by Deep Learning. In Kraetzer, C., Shi, Y.-Q., Dittmann, J., & Kim, H. J. (Eds.), *Digital Forensics and Watermarking* (pp. 107–120). Springer International Publishing. DOI: 10.1007/978-3-319-64185-0_9

Seibold, C., Samek, W., Hilsmann, A., & Eisert, P. (2020). Accurate and robust neural networks for face morphing attack detection. *Journal of Information Security and Applications*, *53*, 102526. DOI: 10.1016/j.jisa.2020.102526

Soleymani, S., Chaudhary, B., Dabouei, A., Dawson, J., & Nasrabadi, N. M. (2021). Differential Morphed Face Detection Using Deep Siamese Networks. In Del Bimbo, A., Cucchiara, R., Sclaroff, S., Farinella, G. M., Mei, T., Bertini, M., Escalante, H. J., & Vezzani, R. (Eds.), *Pattern Recognition. ICPR International Workshops and Challenges* (pp. 560–572). Springer International Publishing., DOI: 10.1007/978-3-030-68780-9_44

Song, C., Ristenpart, T., & Shmatikov, V. (2017). Machine learning models that remember too much. *Proceedings of the 2017 ACM SIGSAC Conference on Computer and Communications Security*, 587–601. DOI: 10.1145/3133956.3134077

Tan, K. L., Chi, C.-H., & Lam, K.-Y. (2023). Survey on digital sovereignty and identity: From digitization to digitalization. *ACM Computing Surveys*, *56*(3), 1–36. DOI: 10.1145/3616400

Tramèr, F., Zhang, F., Juels, A., Reiter, M. K., & Ristenpart, T. (2016). Stealing Machine Learning Models via Prediction APIs. *25th USENIX Security Symposium (USENIX Security 16)*, 601–618. https://www.usenix.org/conference/usenixsecurity16/technical-sessions/presentation/tramer

Venkatesh, S., Ramachandra, R., Raja, K., & Busch, C. (2020). Single Image Face Morphing Attack Detection Using Ensemble of Features. *2020 IEEE 23rd International Conference on Information Fusion (FUSION)*, 1–6. DOI: 10.23919/FUSION45008.2020.9190629

Wandzik, L., Kaeding, G., & Garcia, R. V. (2018). Morphing Detection Using a General- Purpose Face Recognition System. *2018 26th European Signal Processing Conference (EUSIPCO)*, 1012–1016. DOI: 10.23919/EUSIPCO.2018.8553375

Wang, X., Wu, Y. C., Zhou, M., & Fu, H. (2024). Beyond surveillance: Privacy, ethics, and regulations in face recognition technology. *Frontiers in Big Data*, *7*, 1337465. DOI: 10.3389/fdata.2024.1337465 PMID: 39027377

Woubie, A., Solomon, E., & Attieh, J. (2024). Maintaining Privacy in Face Recognition using Federated Learning Method. *IEEE Access : Practical Innovations, Open Solutions*, *12*, 39603–39613. DOI: 10.1109/ACCESS.2024.3373691

Wuyts, K., Scandariato, R., & Joosen, W. (2014). *LIND (D) UN privacy threat tree catalog*. CW Reports.

Yan, A., Hou, R., Yan, H., & Liu, X. (2023). Explanation-based data-free model extraction attacks. *World Wide Web (Bussum)*, *26*(5), 3081–3092. DOI: 10.1007/s11280-023-01150-6

Yang, Z., Shao, B., Xuan, B., Chang, E.-C., & Zhang, F. (2020). Defending model inversion and membership inference attacks via prediction purification. *arXiv Preprint arXiv:2005.03915.*

Zhang, H., Ramachandra, R., Raja, K., & Busch, C. (2024). Generalized Single-Image-Based Morphing Attack Detection Using Deep Representations from Vision Transformer. *2024 IEEE/CVF Conference on Computer Vision and Pattern Recognition Workshops (CVPRW)*, 1510–1518. DOI: 10.1109/CVPRW63382.2024.00158

Zhang, J., Li, C., Ye, J., & Qu, G. (2020). Privacy threats and protection in machine learning. *Proceedings of the 2020 on Great Lakes Symposium on VLSI*, 531–536. DOI: 10.1145/3386263.3407599

Zhang, Y., Jia, R., Pei, H., Wang, W., Li, B., & Song, D. (2020). The secret revealer: Generative model-inversion attacks against deep neural networks. *Proceedings of the IEEE/CVF Conference on Computer Vision and Pattern Recognition*, 253–261. DOI: 10.1109/CVPR42600.2020.00033

ADDITIONAL READING

Datta, P., Bhardwaj, S., Panda, S. N., Tanwar, S., & Badotra, S. (2020). Survey of Security and Privacy Issues on Biometric System. In Gupta, B., Perez, G., Agrawal, D., & Gupta, D. (Eds.), *Handbook of Computer Networks and Cyber Security*. Springer., DOI: 10.1007/978-3-030-22277-2_30

Jiang, M., & Belli, L. (Eds.). (2025). *Digital Sovereignty in the BRICS Countries: How the Global South and Emerging Power Alliances Are Reshaping Digital Governance*. Cambridge University Press., DOI: 10.1017/9781009531085

Singh, G., Bhardwaj, G., Singh, S. V., & Garg, V. (2021). Biometric Identification System: Security and Privacy Concern. In Awasthi, S., Travieso-González, C. M., Sanyal, G., & Kumar Singh, D. (Eds.), *Artificial Intelligence for a Sustainable Industry 4.0*. Springer., DOI: 10.1007/978-3-030-77070-9_15

Chapter 10

AI-Powered Synthetic Data Generation for Training Vision Models Ensuring Privacy, Good Governance and Responsible AI in the Era of Digital Sovereignty

Harsh Klapeshkumar Dave
https://orcid.org/0009-0006-6420-4514
Parul University, India

Kamal Sutaria
Parul University, India

Amit Ganatra
Parul University, India

ABSTRACT

This chapter explores synthetic data's transformative role in computer vision model training, emphasizing privacy and responsible AI in the context of digital sovereignty. Starting with an overview of computer vision and deep learning, the chapter explains how these technologies enable machines to interpret visual data. Synthetic data, created to mirror real-world scenarios, emerges as a solution for protecting privacy, enabling training without exposing sensitive information. Through diverse

DOI: 10.4018/979-8-3693-9137-2.ch010

case studies, it demonstrates how synthetic data can eliminate identifiable features, supporting privacy-centric, ethical AI. Readers gain a comprehensive understanding of the technical and accountable frameworks that make synthetic data crucial in advancing responsible AI while safeguarding digital privacy and fostering innovation.

INTRODUCTION DIGITAL SOVEREIGNTY

Data is both a treasure and a significant burden under the current landscape of AI-driven advancement. Synthetic data is one of the solutions mentioned for all the challenges pertaining to data, especially in training vision models applicable to applications such as object recognition, facial identification, and autonomous navigation. Unlike standard data that is derived from sources in the real world, synthetic data is derived from the output of simulation or advanced generative models for example GANs (we will find this in later part of the chapter). This approach allows engineers or anyone in general to simulate images, videos, and complex visual data at scale without relying on sensitive, real-world information.

Synthetic data have unique advantages-one such significant advantage is training vision models that need large amounts of varied datasets to gain accuracy and reliability. For example, the correct functioning of an autonomous vehicle depends on the training data it goes through simulating varied lighting conditions, challenging weather conditions, and erratic behaviour of pedestrians. Thus, the generation of synthetic data for meeting such stipulated requirements can provide a safe, efficient, less time-consuming, and customizable alternative to collecting data without the hassle of collecting it from the real world.

Digital Sovereignty

The concept of digital sovereignty has picked up a good amount of prominence since governments and organizations have realized the need to have control over information and its assurance. Digital sovereignty refers to the principle whereby a country or an entity should have the authority and control over the data generated in its borders with the knowledge on how it is stored, accessed, and processed (Glasze et al., 2022). This principle becomes particularly crucial in this period of AI research, development and advancement where issues of data ownership, security, and privacy become very important aspects of protection of citizens' rights and ensuring responsible technological advancement.

This need for better data protection has led numerous countries to develop new rules, frameworks, and acts. For example, the European Union has its General Data Protection Regulation (GDPR), and India presented its Digital Personal Data Protection Act (DPDPA) of 2023 (Explained each in details later in this chapter). The law is strict and well-defined in terms of how data can be stored, shared, and used. This means that when the data is created in one country, it is then subject to the laws of that country even when accessed or further processed elsewhere. So, while it is of utmost importance in terms of capability to hold personal information safe, these regulations also resonate with issues as important as national security and indeed a country's economic independence in an increasingly digital age.

Data Ownership and Privacy: The Core of Digital Sovereignty

Data ownership is one of the important pillar of digital sovereignty (Debic & Medvidovic, 2024). As data increasingly powers AI systems, data privacy rights become more complex and challenging to enforce, especially when third-party entities across borders are involved in data storage and processing. For example, companies depend on cloud providers storing data in multiple countries so that compliance with local data protection regulations becomes as much of a nightmare. Digital sovereignty ensures that data privacy, security, and compliance with local regulations are maintained, limiting potential misuse and reinforcing citizens' trust in digital systems.

Synthetic data (Lopes et al., 2024) is fast becoming an enabling key technology that will let organizations to meet the hard privacy requirements through minimum usage of real-world data during the training of AI models. Companies can use synthetic data for the training and development of vision models with no actual personal information exposed, thus in line with new respect for privacy regulations and to facilitate full compliance with local policies and regulations under which the flow of sensitive data is restricted across borders. This also minimizes the chance of data breach, where citizens' data will be safe in their own jurisdiction.

INTRODUCTION TO COMPUTER VISION AND DEEP LEARNING

Computer vision and deep learning are foundational to AI systems capable of interpreting and interacting with the visual world. In a nutshell, computer vision lets machines interpret any kind of visual data-photographs, videos, or streams-but in a simplified manner by using algorithms and models to allow an object to be recognized, a pattern identified, or an actionable insight gleaned. These systems, mimicking some aspects of human vision, translate visual information into a form the computers can process.

Deep learning, as a subset of machine learning, plays a critical role in modern computer vision. It allows models to automatically learn features from vast quantities of data by using multiple layers of processing units, or neurons, which are structured to mimic the human brain's processing.In practice, this may result in a deep learning model's being trained against a vast collection of labeled images so that it can learn to recognize certain features - for example, shapes, colors, or visual textures - that can permit identification of animals, reading road signs, or detection of abnormalities in medical images. Deep learning is expanding the application space in computer vision areas in health diagnostics, surveillance, retail, and autonomous driving where visual interpretation and decision-making are critical.

As data requirements grow, the role of synthetic data becomes more significant. Training deep learning models in computer vision relies on extensive labeled datasets, yet acquiring and labeling real-world data can be costly, time-consuming, and laden with privacy concerns. In privacy-sensitive domains, synthetic data, generated using algorithms rather than real-world sources, offers an alternative. It simulates visual scenarios—diverse environments, lighting conditions, object orientations, and human behavior—enabling robust training without compromising sensitive information. Synthetic data thus emerges as a crucial enabler for developing accurate, privacy-compliant AI models, especially in domains requiring strict data governance and responsible AI practices.

FUNDAMENTALS OF SYNTHETIC DATA GENERATION

What is Synthetic Data?

Synthetic data is a type of artificially produced data that is generated through algorithms and models, in the course of mimicking real data without at all using any actual personal or sensitive information (Jordon et al., 2022). In simple words *data that is generated by algorithms to simulate real-world data* (Man & Chahl, 2022). Synthetic data does not emanate from any original data, Unlike real data, which is collected from real-world sources such as sensors, transactions, or user interactions, synthetic data is generated through controlled processes. Synthetic data generation involves highly sophisticated model scapture statistical patterns, spatial distributions, and structural relationships present in real datasets in such a way that the data generated approaches high fidelity and closely approximates that of actual data characteristics.

Synthetic Data in Computer Vision:

Synthetic data is becoming an excellent resource for models to be trained on tasks, such as object detection, image classification, and semantic segmentation within the scope of computer vision (Mumuni et al., 2024). Most models within the vision space require enormous amounts of labeled data for training before they can identify objects, shapes, or environments with any degree of accuracy. Obtaining such data from real sources could be challenging under constraints of privacy, unavailability and strict timelines of projects. Synthetic data can be an alternative where data scientists can design diverse, large, task-specific datasets.

In the case of object detection, it would produce synthetic data to annotate images that have some objects in different poses, lighting conditions, and environments. In facial recognition systems, synthetic faces could be generated using 3D modeling and rendering techniques to show different demographics, ages, and expressions, thus providing balanced data for training models to be fair and inclusive. Besides this, in autonomous driving research, it can simulate more complicated driving scenarios and allows models to learn dangerous or rare situations without risking endangering real drivers or pedestrians. Applications such as these illustrate the unique ability of synthetic data to support training in scenarios where the gathering of enough data from the real world is either difficult or impossible to obtain ethically. For example, synthetic images can be generated to depict a tree during a sunny day, a rainy evening, or a foggy morning. The variety in these conditions ensures the model learns to detect trees in various states, enhancing its ability to recognize objects in real-world environments. This not only improves model accuracy but also ensures it is robust across changing environments.

Figure 1. Example synthetic data for tree in different weather, time of day and lighting

With synthetic data, expensive or otherwise restricted domains like inspections of aircraft or government sites with high security clearances can be effectively trained without risking any real assets. For such applications, synthetic data fosters the construction of large training sets which are otherwise too expensive, impractical, or sensitive to security to be gathered from real images alone. This cutting of costs while ensuring model effectiveness and allowing iterative improvements on highly regulated domains was the state of the art.

Types of Synthetic Data Generation:

The techniques to generate synthetic data are very wide ranging, with many high-profile methods that play a highly important role in computer vision and AI training. The following are the main methods used to generate synthetic data:

- **Data Augmentation and Adversarial Examples:** Data augmentation is a simple technique applied in synthetic data generation. In this, existing data is altered in known ways to create new samples of data (Shorten & Khoshgoftaar, 2019). These include rotation and translation, change in color, noise addition, and cropping. They increase the size and variety of training data, without any consumption of new sources of data. It does not exactly generate new data from scratch, but rather makes models strong against the different variations they might face in real life.

Adversarial examples in contrast, require creating somewhat different versions of existing data samples so that vulnerabilities can be taken advantage of by AI models. Such modified samples expose model biases or weakness and help improve resilience in models once they are confronted with patterns with which they are unfamiliar. Training AI on adversarial examples helps improve systems' capacity for handling outliers and unusual situations and can thus enhance their performance and robustness in deployment

- **Generative Adversarial Networks (GANs):** GANs were first proposed by Ian Goodfellow in 2014. They revolutionized synthetic data generation to create realistic-looking data very close to the actual data (Saxena & Cao, 2020). The basic idea, quite intuitive, is derived from two different neural networks working together in a process called adversarial training. In this process, one network is called the generator that produces synthetic samples, and another network, called the discriminator, evaluates these synthetic samples against real samples to determine if they are actually from the real data or generated. In this competitive process, the generator gradually finds its way to producing highly realistic synthetic samples over time.

GANs are mostly used in computer vision to synthesize synthetic images of faces, objects, and scenes (Alqahtani et al., 2019). For example, GANs can synthesize numerous datasets of faces, capturing different demographics, facial expressions, and environmental contexts, making them invaluable for the training of models for facial recognition. GANs generate road scenes with different lighting, weather, and traffic conditions for autonomous driving systems, which allows learning models to perform safe acts under a diverse range of situations. GANs are also used in synthesizing synthetic medical images for purposes of radiology, pathology, and dermatology, thus assisting in the training of models even in fields where the collection of data is sensitive and ethically challenging.

Besides the GANs, there are far more novel techniques that play critical parts in the synthetic data generation, especially in image creation. These include Variational Autoencoders, Diffusion Models, Rule-Based and Procedural Generation, and recent advances on state-of-the-art Generative models from leading frameworks.

- **Variational Autoencoders (VAEs):** VAEs represent the architecture of a neural network and are designed specifically for the use of generation. Unlike GANs, which are known for the adversarial training setting, VAEs present a probabilistic framework applied over learning compressed representation in a low-dimensional space. This allows VAEs to sample new data points and capture general characteristics of the original data set (Ren et al., 2018). In computer vision, VAEs are especially useful for generating images with controlled variations-for example, facial attributes or object configurations-and thereby can add flexibility to synthetic data generation concerning tasks like image synthesis and anomaly detection.
- **Diffusion Models:** Recently, diffusion models have gained popularity because of the high-quality generation of images. Data is generated by diffusing noisy samples step by step in an incremental refinement in order to closely match the target image for photorealistic results. Diffusion models are highly successful while carrying out complex synthetic data generations like generating high-resolution medical or scientific images of accuracy and details. Because of their faithfulness, diffusion models are becoming a strong alternative to GANs (Dhariwal & Nichol, 2021), providing those advantages arising from the clarity and realism of synthetic data generation (Rombach et al., 2022).
- **Rule-Based and Procedural Generation:** There are specific cases wherein synthetic data can be made, such as rule-based algorithms or procedural generation. The data is created in consideration of definite rules and its common usage is cases where such data follows predictable patterns, as in urban planning, gaming, or in structured environments (Lenatti et al., 2023). For instance, synthetic datasets for virtual cityscapes or video game landscapes can be created by applying spatial rules and architectural designs. Though less flexible than neural-network-based generation, procedural generation is valuable for simulating data where real-world samples are unavailable or costly to produce.

- **New Models for Image Generation:** The latest advancements in generative models have been directly linked to high-capacity image generators such as Stable Diffusion (Esser et al., 2024) from Stability AI, DALL-E from OpenAI, and Midjourney. Such models, underlined through diffusion-based techniques, have quickly become the standards by which to measure photorealistic, complex images. For instance:
    - **Stable Diffusion:** This is an open-source model from Stability AI that shines in creating super-detailed high-resolution images. Its use case is most relevant in synthetic data applications, especially those that require flexibility in the prompt and style-think health simulation or a fantastic urban simulation.
    - **DALL-E:** This is OpenAI's model that can generate a vast and contextually rich variety of images from any input text. It trains its capabilities on producing data for computer vision on scenarios that could not be captured easily in real-life datasets.
    - **Midjourney:** Most useful in creating realistic or stylized images due to its artistic and visually impressive nature, Midjourney comes in handy for creative industries or design applications.
    - **FLUX from Black Forest:** Developed by research organization Black Forest, FLUX is a highly advanced image generation model that has been designed for synthetic data application. Optimized for stability and reliability, FLUX produces images at large scale with minimal artifacts. It is appropriate to use in datasets where different pieces may have varied requirements of consistency: like simulation applications in automotive or robotics.

Table 1. Comparison of Generative Models for Synthetic Data Generation

Model Type	Strengths	Trade-Offs	Best Use Cases
GANs	Highly realistic image generation	Mode collapse (tendency to produce repetitive outputs)	Applications needing realistic images
VAEs (Variational Autoencoders)	High interpretability, allows for controlled image variation	Lower image quality compared to GANs and Diffusion Models	Applications requiring controlled variation in generated images
Diffusion Models	High-resolution images with minimal artifacts	Computationally intensive	Applications needing high visual detail and resolution

continued on following page

Table 1. Continued

Model Type	Strengths	Trade-Offs	Best Use Cases
Rule-Based and Procedural Generation	Structured data generation with high control over variables	Limited to structured data, less flexible for unstructured images	Scenarios requiring strict control over generated data variables
New Generative Models (Stable Diffusion, DALL-E)	High realism and detail, flexible and creative generation capabilities	Computationally demanding and may need substantial training data	Applications where diverse scenarios and high detail are important

In summary, while the newer advanced synthetic data generation techniques, especially with the emergence of diffusion models and new frameworks, contribute much more to the training process of AI. They are adaptable, scalable, and realistic enough to create highly reliable synthetic datasets without causing any issues related to privacy, bias reduction, and demand for high-quality, diversified training data across a myriad of applications in AI.

Using Stable Diffusion for High-Resolution Synthetic Image Generation in Vision Training

The generative models are great at the production of synthetic data in the realm of computer vision. Today, even such models as Stable Diffusion can generate high-resolution, photorealistic images based on visual criteria specified. Such a capability is important for all applications entailing various and privacy-preserving training data that simulate real-world conditions without actually using private data.

In this section, we'll look at how Stable Diffusion can be leveraged to generate images of individuals with varying accessories (e.g., helmets and gloves). This approach enables computer vision models to recognize or differentiate between objects or scenarios in a privacy-safe and controlled manner. Additionally, by simply changing the prompts and the number of images, this code can be adapted for various scenarios and applications, making it highly flexible.

Code Example: Generating Synthetic Images with Stable Diffusion

The following Python code demonstrates how to use the Stable Diffusion model to create images of individuals both with and without safety gear, producing five variations for each scenario. This is especially valuable for vision models designed to detect personal protective equipment (PPE) or to study user behaviors in simulated, safety-critical environments.

```
# Install the diffusers package if needed

!pip install diffusers transformers accelerate torch


from diffusers import StableDiffusionPipeline

import torch

import os


# Load Stable Diffusion v2.1, which is suitable for generat-
ing high-quality images without complex requirements

model_id = "stabilityai/stable-diffusion-2-1"

pipe = StableDiffusionPipeline.from_pretrained(model_id,
torch_dtype=torch.float16)

pipe = pipe.to("cuda")


# Create directories to save images if they don't already
exist
```

```
os.makedirs("images_with_gear", exist_ok=True)

os.makedirs("images_without_gear", exist_ok=True)


# Set the number of images you want to generate for each
prompt

num_images = 50


# Define prompts for generating images with and without
safety gear

prompt_with_gear = "A photorealistic image of a person fac-
tory worker wearing a helmet and gloves, professional lighting,
factory setting"

prompt_without_gear = "a real person man professional light-
ing, factory setting"


# Generate images for each scenario

for i in range(num_images):
```

```
        image = pipe(prompt_with_gear).images[0]

        image.save(f"images_with_gear/person_with_helmet_gloves_
{i+1}.png")

    for i in range(num_images):

        image = pipe(prompt_without_gear).images[0]

        image.save(f"images_without_gear/person_without_helmet_
gloves_{i+1}.png")
```

Code Explanation

- Loading the Model: We'll load a Stable Diffusion model from Hugging Face's Diffusers library. This is a known model for realistic photorealistic image generation.
- Prompts: We have two prompts. One to generate an image with a helmet and gloves, the other to generate an image with none of these. This thus creates controlled variations in the generated data:.
- Image Creation: The loop creates five unique images for each prompt, saving into different folders to distinctly categorize the scenarios of the output.

Output Result:

Figure 2. Output of code for Synthetic Data generation

Running this code will give you a class containing two images-one set of people with helmets and gloves, the other without. Those can then be learned to train models for those vision systems so it can predict the appearance or non-appearance of safety gear-an essential application in workplace safety monitoring, or even a driverless car system that must recognize pedestrians wearing protective equipment.

Adaptation for Different Needs

All that can be modified on this code, to make it useful for other purposes, is the num_images parameter and the prompts. If both are changed, all these pipelines will create a wide range of different scenarios; this means flexibility to change use and apply to training vision models on other needs. For instance:

- Scene Invocations - Change the prompt to simulate other environments or objects.
- Object Identification - Modify the description with items and visual attributes for the detection of objects.
- Behavioral Simulation - Replace prompts to create images for different human behaviors, emotions, and situations.

Advantages of Using Stable Diffusion to Create Synthetic Data

The images generated by Stable Diffusion have several advantages:

- Realism and High Resolution: The images are high-resolution quality, to the extent of being capable of using high detail applications.
- Privacy Compliance: Because the data is synthetic, there is no chance of exposure to personal information.

- Flexible Control over Scenarios: Flexibility of control by changing prompts offers control over the generative force of multiple scenarios, thereby making a case for vision models as having strength and generalizability.

It can also be noted here how the synthetic data generated from tools such as Stable Diffusion may help in the construction of accurate, privacy-preserving, ethically responsible vision models, based on good governance and responsible AI.

Benefits of Synthetic Data for Privacy and Governance

Synthetic data has emerged as a disruptive force in the field of AI and ML. Beyond its technical applications, synthetic data comes with several advantages regarding privacy (Arthur et al., 2023) protections and governance (Adair, 2023). Since synthetic datasets mirror real-world data but are not personally identifiable, no sensitive information is leaked or compromised when AI models are being developed and deployed. This section delves into the main advantages that synthetic data presents towards privacy protection as well as ensuring compliance, narrowing risks of breaches through data, and even responsibility in AI innovation.

Privacy Protection: How Synthetic Data Minimizes the Need for Personal or Sensitive Data:

A synthetic data set is one of the most persuasive benefits of keeping user information private. Conventional AI and ML models mostly use real-world datasets comprising very sensitive and personally identifiable information. Some such data that can be provided for training machine learning models are names, addresses, contact details, health information, or financial records. Therefore, the working mechanism of real data carries significant risks; it may lead to breaches, unauthorized access, or leakage of secrecy inadvertently.

Synthetic data relieves the inherent dangers of real data, for it creates a completely artificial dataset that mimics the statistical properties of real data without exposing personal or confidential information (Hu & McKay Bowen, 2023). For example, by using synthetic data in computer vision tasks such as object detection or facial recognition, there is the possibility to generate realistic images of people or objects or scenes without including any individuals or confidential information. These images are created algorithmically, so they do not require real-world counterparts to serve as training data. Synthetic data is therefore best suited to applications where the use of real data would breach privacy or fail to comply with laws and regulations.

Synthetic data further helps AI systems not train on biased or incomplete datasets which are most likely to emanate from the use of real-world data, which has been gathering bias since it originates from diverse, uncontrolled environments and limited resources or sources to gather data . Organizations can thus ensure that their models are trained on comprehensive and representative data without being limited to the collection processes of real data while maintaining privacy standards using synthetic data.

Governance Advantages: Fulfilling Regulatory and Compliance Requirements (GDPR, DPDP Act)

Governance, therefore, will be key in the complete safeguarding of data protection throughout the development of frameworks, laws, acts and monitoring deployment of AI systems. Government regulations have been relatively strict about privacy in recent years in a bid to protect personal data and thereby affords individuals greater control regarding information use. Notable among these are the General Data Protection Regulation (GDPR) in the European Union and India's Digital Personal Data Protection Act (DPDP Act) of 2023. These laws place strict requirements on organizations around the collection, storage, and processing of personal data, particularly regarding security, consent, and data access rights.

Compliance for organizations concerned with working with AI and machine learning, especially those dealing with sensitive data like health records or financial details, can be pretty very simple with this regulation. Synthetic data is a practical use in helping to meet these governance requirements. Organizations can reduce the demands of direct access to personally identifiable information (PII), thus reducing the risk of privacy law breach by using synthetic datasets rather than actual data, for instance:

GDPR: The data minimization and purpose limitation principles of GDPR mandate that organizations ought to collect and further process only the quantity of data involved that is necessary for a particular objective. Synthetic data will help an organization to create relevant data without gathering excess personal information that could be utterly unacceptable when following these principles. Synthetic data could also be processed and stored without the risk of "identity leak" of the identities of natural persons as "data protection by design and by default" approach is prescribed by the GDPR.

DPDP Act, India, 2023 The DPDP Act, India, is a law that protects citizen rights over the digital world, giving control of personal data and will determine stiff obligations on the part of data handlers. The Act provides for consent-based usage of data, an individual's right over access and erasure, and imposition of stringent penalties in case of data breach. Synthetic data lets organizations minimize the collection and processing of real PII. The fact that synthetic data can replicate the real patterns without exposing actual personal details supports objectives of the DPDP Act, including protecting privacy as well as ensuring data sovereignty.

Integrating synthesized data into AI workflows can help organizations display compliance to data protection laws, gain the trust of customers and other stakeholders, and bring down the probabilities of legal penalties. Thus, it increases the reputation that such an organization possesses as a good steward of data.

Challenges in Synthetic Data Generation for Vision Models

Generating synthetic data for vision models has become a critical tool in AI. The challenge lies in the very high-fidelity and high-quality requirements for real-world deployments. There are technological, Resource challenges to be overcome before synthetic data can actually be used practically and effectively to achieve the tasks of vision. Hence, this section discusses the key challenges in the forms of technical constraints, quality, bias, fairness, and resource considerations.

Technical Challenges:

It is inherently complicated to generate synthetic data for vision models because of its high technical resources/knowledge requirement for the kind of data concerned. Unlike other types of data, the image and video depend on complicated visual features which are difficult to be synthesized or re-produced.

Complexity in Scene Composition: One of the most typical applications of computer vision tasks involves variability and realism in terms of different backgrounds, lighting, and orientations of objects. This would challenge data synthesis, based on the complexity of the model, because the scene has to be carefully modeled so that it reflects real-world characteristics. For instance, in a mimic system for the drone delivery AI system, it should capture real-life scenarios, such as suburban areas with different designs of houses, different times of day that will affect the lighting conditions, and such dynamic elements that may include pets or children playing in the yard and could affect the drone's navigations.

Modeling Human Characteristics and Interactions: Such kind of vision applications like facial recognition and activity recognition would require synthetic data depicting human features and behaviors with good accuracy. The subtleties of facial expressions, body poses or of people in a crowd interaction are really hard to be replicated technically. Synthetic generation of facial features must, be both diverse and realistic to avoid oversimplification and not let it perform poorly in real faces, should it be used for applications dependent on facial recognition.

Quality and Realism

The realism of synthetic data is critical in the training of accurate vision models. However, several factors ensure that a quality standard matching or closely resembling the real world cannot be achieved relatively easily. One of them is the one below:

Domain Gap Between Synthetic and Real Data: In this regard, even when high-quality synthetic data is generated, there often is some domain gap—measured difference between synthetic and real data. This domain gap can reduce the model's ability to generalize across datasets, particularly when the synthetic data fails to capture real-world imperfections. Researchers have developed domain adaptation techniques to bridge this gap, but these require additional processing and may not fully resolve the issue, leading to continued challenges in real-world performance.

Bias and Fairness

Bias remains a significant issue in synthetic data generation, as unintentional biases can be embedded during the data generation process. Bias can emerge from the underlying models used to generate data, from the way that source data is sampled, or from the specific characteristics emphasized during synthetic data generation (Barbierato et al., 2022; Ferrara, 2024).

Inherited Bias from Source Data: Many synthetic data models rely on real-world data in an effort to train the process about how the first generation will be realized. If source data were unrepresentative or biased, then the bias may be transferred over into the synthetic data sets. For example, in facial recognition models that have been trained with synthetic data that is biased toward a certain skin tone or age grouping, they might fail with those data sets that are underrepresented, and actually contribute to the existing biases by infusing existing biases into the trained models.

Algorithmic Bias: The different kinds of biases can be exhibited by various synthetic data generation algorithms, such as GANs or VAEs, due to their architecture and training data feeding the generated algorithm. GANs focus more on those frequent data patterns, and this reduces representation for less-common features. For example, in health-care settings, where importance of variety in synthetic data would have significant effects on high-performance models, which also will have significant fairness properties, such biasing will have adverse effects.

Balanced representation: Synthetic data should balance with fair and unbiased proportions to represent all relevant characteristics and scenarios rightly. It is especially important when the applications are of high ethical values such as in law enforcement or medical diagnostics. Such synthetic datasets for adequate coverage of all demographics, behaviors, and contexts require careful oversight and ongoing monitoring. The challenge is that this level of fairness in synthetic data generation might prove elusive because it requires some deep insights into possible sources of bias and somehow addresses them.

Resource Challenges

High-quality synthetic data of vision models is quite challenging to generate and far from less resource dependent. Several logistical constraints on organizations especially those not privy to substantive computing resources but cloud is best in this case.

Computational Intensity: Most of the methods used for generating high-quality synthetic data, such as GANs and diffusion models, and 3D rendering also happen to be computationally intensive. They probably need high-performance GPUs or TPUs. Even training may take days or even weeks. This, therefore, may not be possible for an organization that has developed an infrastructure level in this regard, but the costs to develop synthetic data easily negate the benefits.

Specialized expertise: This is needed in certain areas such as computer vision, graphics rendering, and AI ethics for effective synthetic data construction in vision models. This will be costlier for any organization that wants to exploit synthetic data. Small organizations will struggle to find or afford this type of expertise, which will become a barrier to entry in the exploitation of synthetic data but this problem can be solved by organization by investing in turning the team to adapt knowledge and solve their problem.

Quality and Resource Allocation For synthetic data, an organization has to balance the quality with the amount of resources put into generating synthetic data. In some applications such as autonomous driving simulation, defence (Kularathne et al., 2024; Truong et al., 2024; Zeng et al., 2024), space exploration and medical diagnostics, having a high degree of realism is key because it dictates safety and, consequently, the outcome. However, it is costly to produce that level of quality. For most organizations, lowering their costs by using the less expensive synthetic data is more expedient-even if realism suffers slightly.

Producing synthetic data for vision models poses challenges as well-thought-out recommendations -and hopefully a perspective on bettering the technology, developing safeguards both ethical and resource-based which can easily be solved by training, knowledge sharing and experimenting. And if the challenges that were found can be addressed, then eventually it will eventually lead to better usage of synthetic data, thus proving it to be an efficient, responsible tool for changing the application of AI in areas of use.

Case Studies of Synthetic Data in Action

In order to bypass the limitations of real-world data in terms of amount, privacy, or inaccessibility to specific data streams, the generation of synthetic data has applied to different industries and applications. Artificial data closely mimicking the real world is used to train models in more effective manners while maintaining quality, privacy, and fairness standards. This part explores various case studies across various industries, representing how synthesized data has been used to tackle real-life issues but also the challenges that arise in each case. Health care: autonomous driving: retail and customer service: security and surveillance:

Healthcare: Generating Synthetic Medical Images for Training Diagnostic Vision Models

Synthetic data have been more useful in training diagnostic vision models like the ones used to diagnose various medical conditions through imaging diagnostics such as X-rays, MRIs, or CT scans. Such models require large amounts of labeled medical information to learn and generalize well since, in the real world, it may be scarce in that medical images are hard to come by, and expert annotation is a costly resource, and patients may not want to be imaged due to privacy reasons.

- **Challenges in Real-World Data:**
  Labeled Data Extremely Scarce: Medical data is hard to obtain. For annotated sets, they are rather scarce. Data sharing is a concept by the hospitals and clinics but rather limited due to health privacy regulations like the HIPAA in the US. Furthermore, medical images require annotations from health care professionals, which is cumbersome and also very costly.
  Data privacy and security: Medical images carry personal information that should remain confidential. Due to data privacy concerns associated with deidentified patient information, data use for research or model training is heavily controlled, which may make it difficult for AI model developers to acquire large datasets for model development.
- **Synthetic data solution:**
  Synthetic medical images are emerging as an important tool to prevent these problems from arising. The benefits of utilizing GANs or other image-generation models are that they could autonomously generate high-quality, realistic images of medical conditions independent of real patient data. It means, for instance, through GANs, one can train the model on generating realistic X-ray or MRI images, complete with disease markers and anatomical features, similar to those found in hospitals. Such

synthetic datasets can then be used to train diagnostic models. Some of the advantages this offers include

Privacy Protection: The synthetic images will contain no real patient information, and thus there is no violation of the data privacy concerns and thus comply with privacy regulations. The fact that the generation is artificial poses no risk of exposing personal health information.

Diverse Training Data: Synthetic data generation is now allowing datasets of diverse nature that would be pretty hard to obtain in real-world settings. For instance, the example of rare diseases or conditions wherein real-world examples could not have easily been available for a model have been modeled synthetically, thereby training robust models which can comfortably perform on edge cases.

Cost-Effective: Often, the artificially generated medical images can be far cheaper to annotate than real medical data. Here, with automation of the process, healthcare organizations reduce costs in collecting and annotating data, thereby making it more possible to develop advanced diagnostic models.

- **Case Study: Cancer Detection**

  There are various instances of using synthetic data in health care. Among those is, for instance, the use of medical imaging for cancer detection. Researchers have trained deep learning models for breast cancer detection using synthetic mammogram datasets. Synthetic data has been used in conjunction with the American College of Radiology and the Radiological Society of North America to advance a robust, balanced dataset for training breast cancer detection systems. The synthetic dataset helped to overcome the scarcity of the availability of labelled mammograms and therefore created diagnostic models that were able to produce relatively accurate diagnoses about cancer signs in different patient populations.

- **Challenges and Limitations:**

  Despite these successes, however, there are still challenges with the use of synthetic medical images. It is a challenge to ensure that synthetic data would capture the complexity and variability of real-world data. While GANs and other generative models can make pretty realistic images, these may still lack subtle nuances seen in real medical scans. Furthermore, the accuracy of a model trained exclusively on synthetic data is likely to degrade when it is applied to real-world data, mainly because the model may not fully capture inherent variability in human anatomy or disease progression.

Autonomous Vehicles: Enhancing Safety and Performance with Synthetic Data

Autonomous car operation relies on machine learning models to perceive and understand the surroundings, make decisions in real time to ensure the safety of the passengers and pedestrians, and rely heavily on the training models that offer significant challenges in diversely different contexts, particularly by collecting diverse, realistic, and safe driving data.

- **Sources of Real-World Challenge**

  Data Scarcity: Gathering large amounts of driving data is very time-consuming and operationally prohibitive when including edge case or dangerous circumstances such as rain, fog, or nighttime.

  Safety Concerns: Testing AVs in the wild is also dangerous while attempting to assess how the vehicle will behave in novel yet significant events such as collision, unexpected jaywalking pedestrians, or errant vehicle movements.

  The cost of real-world driving data, which may become unaffordable to attain if collected from a heterogeneous area or condition, is also too high. Further, simulating rare events sometimes cannot be done even if expensive resources are devoted to it.
- **Synthetic Data Solution:**

  The data through synthetic means has been devised for this particular problem by creating virtual driving environments and scenarios simulating all manner of conditions, including the probability of rarely occurring ones, without risking or paying high amounts of actual real-world data collection.

  Data Augmentation: It can augment real-world driving data with synthetic data so that AV systems can be trained in a wider variety of scenarios. For example, AVs may need to learn to recognize pedestrians crossing in front of vehicles in various lighting conditions and weather conditions, all synthetically generated.

  Synthetic data can then safely test edge cases, say interactions with emergency vehicles, aggressive driving behavior, or a vehicle breakdown, making it possible to learn such hard cases without actually putting anybody in danger.

  Varied Environments: One of the uses of synthetic data is for the training of AVs in diverse environments and on terrains inaccessible in the real world. This may encompass, for example, traveling across the entire globe, completely different types of road infrastructures, or extreme climatic conditions, such as a snowstorm or flood.

- **Case Study: Synthetic Data for AV Testing**

  One of the greatest AVs' usages of synthetic data is when Waymo and Waymo's Simulation Platform partner to simulate a million miles of their cars driving in virtual environments and use synthetic data to test different driving conditions. Such synthetic data helps improve the company's autonomous systems before they deploy them in real-world environments. It has been helpful for the system in ensuring that AVs are in a position to be used proficiently in difficult scenes that can hardly be achieved during actual life conditions.

- **Limitations and Challenges**

  The biggest challenge with synthetic data in AVs is whether it can generate scenarios that reflect the complexity of real-world driving behavior. Synthetic data might simulate all kinds of driving conditions, but still, it does not capture subtleties related to human driving, such as spontaneous decision-making, unpredictability, and subtle interactions with other road users. Synthetic data may also fail to convey the complexity of traffic behavior, for example, the actions that other drivers can conduct or unpredictable road events.

Security and Surveillance: Privacy-Preserving Synthetic Data for Training Security Systems

Security and surveillance systems often are built on computer vision models that detect and identify suspicious activity, faces, and objects in public or private spaces. They are applied in many different fields: from monitoring a public space, offering greater security to a building or premises. Still, privacy issues loom large, at least as far as surveillance in the public sphere is concerned (Delussu et al., 2024).

- **Problems in Real-World Data:**

  Mass Invasion of Privacy: Most of the times, surveillance systems record people going about their daily lives. A lot of things happen out in public, with respect to which most of it is not of importance and most of it incurs a gross invasion of the right to privacy. Processing personal data in that sense certainly raises more controversy, as well as the use of facial recognition in these systems.

  Data Safety: protection measures need to ensure the data they collect is secured, mainly if it includes PII. The storage and process for surveillance video are heavily controlled and regulated. For example, in the

European Union, the GDPR limits misuse or unauthorized access to sensitive information.

- **Synthetic Data Solution:**

  Synthetic data can be used for the privacy-preserving training of security models. Security systems might be trained using artificial video footages or images of people and objects in a way that the footage eventually generated will be realistic. This synthetic dataset can be used to train the model to detect suspicious behavior or unauthorized access/ unusual activity without infringing on the privacy concerns that accompany the use of actual footage.

  Preserving Privacy: Synthetic surveillance data can be used for model training in security-related applications, thus avoiding the capture and processing of personal data during model training, which will facilitate the rule of privacy and respect to individual rights.

  Data Augmentation: Real surveillance videos may be augmented through further diversity in the form of extra volume which enables security systems to identify wider range of suspicious activities and individuals.

  Privacy-Preserving Surveillance Case Study

  Recent work conducted in various organizations is on the use of synthetic data to improve the surveillance system's accuracy but is still private. For example, synthetic datasets to train video surveillance systems to identify anomalies in public spaces could be provided. Synthetic data about the movement of pedestrians in one direction, gatherings of people, or objects left behind will expand the spectrum of situations. Synthetic data will aid in making the security system secure and preserve privacy.

- **Limitation and Challenges:**

  The realism of the data produced is the major limitation of the synthetic data usage in security and surveillance systems. General patterns and behaviors may be captured by the synthetic data, but such cases may not always reflect the realistic complexity that happens within the practical real-life environments, for example, the diversity in human behavior and the complexities of locations. For instance, the security system developed and fine-tuned on purely synthetic data will likely be much less effective in the real-world deployment, in which case the scenarios can differ drastically based on human interaction dynamics and other environmental factors.

Success Factors and Limitations of Synthetic Data

Synthetic data success in the case studies above owes much to the fact that it addresses important challenges such as scarcity, lack of privacy, and necessity for varied and high-quality datasets. However, the following are several reasons that result in success:

Advancement in Technology: The advanced generative models, such as GANs allowed for the creation of synthetic high quality data, mimicking real data. Such synthetic data can be used to train AI models.

Adherence to Regulations: Synthetic data can be particularly useful where there are issues around privacy; the organization can maintain the rigors of strict data protection without compromising the effectiveness of its AI models.

Data diversity: Synthetic data can be used to synthesize a very diverse set of data that is hard to obtain or even impossible to collect. This is extremely useful in the context of applications where you have to manage multiple variants with different conditions, like autonomous driving or facial recognition.

But despite the success stories, there are still limitations of synthetic data that need to be addressed:

Domain Gap: Trained models through synthetic data are not always good in performing real-world situations, since the world constructed is not exactly like the data obtained from the real world.

Synthetic Data Realism: The power of generative models has improved dramatically over time. However, as indicated above, still a gap prevails, particularly for complex domains regarding human behavior and medical conditions.

Serious ethical issues are involved with synthetic data, particularly in the context of surveillance and facial recognition.

Ethical considerations for usage of synthetic data need to be held at an arm's length and set up carefully.

Synthetic data is a fantastic technology with tremendous promise in many industries; however, it must be used wisely in conjunction with real-world data to deliver the best results.

Digital Sovereignty in AI: Ethical and Governance Considerations

As AI emerges to define and shape the new face of global technological landscapes, the term digital sovereignty slowly gains importance for countries and other organizations around the world. The basic principles of digital sovereignty encompass the control of access to digital resources: data and AI models. It is translated into AI terms as ascertaining AI systems especially those based on synthetic data be deployed and developed under the government of a country respecting national interest, respect for individual privacy, and the ethical standards that must be upheld. In short, this section expresses some of the most important concepts in digital sovereignty, including data localization, ethical AI frameworks, and governmental policies impacting the governance of data.

Data Localization: Needs and Implications

Data localization is the practice of storing and processing data within the geographical borders of a country or region. It is now a more common regulatory requirement as it aims to protect the data of citizens within local jurisdiction-most especially when the matter pertains to privacy, security, and adherence to national laws. Data localization essentially aims at barring any foreign entity from access and processing that sensitive personal data of citizens to ensure safety and privacy of data subject to local and regional laws and regulations.

- **Implication of Data Localization**

  Legal Compliance: Many countries have enacted legislation that provide for data localization, especially for sensitive personal data. For example, the General Data Protection Regulation in the European Union has strictly controlled the transportation of personal data outside of its borders. That is, through data localization, governments can ensure the ability to enforce local privacy laws and minimize risks of unauthorized access or misuse of data by foreign governments or companies.

  Economic Impact: The related data localization requirements make doing business harder and add some operational costs for multinationals, in the sense that companies will need local data centers or other entities to be able to comply with this regulation. It can push economic growth in some regions, as it helps in developing the data hosting industry while causing inefficiency and unnecessary expense to global enterprises.

  Data Sovereignty and National Security: The sovereignty principle now makes governments concerned with owning the data inside their borders. Localizing data storage helps in exercising powers to regulate the kind of utilization of data within national borders, especially with regard to national security. For instance, certain military, economic or governmental data may have to stay within national borders to avoid espionage or foreign surveillance.

Impact of Data Localisation on AI Development With data localization, the development of AI could be severely affected. The very nature of AI models, primarily used in computer vision and autonomous systems, is mainly premised on extensive and diverse datasets. International companies specialized in AI would hence feel the pinch from enforcing data localization laws in order to prevent access and "funneling" data from countries, hence restricting their ability to train models that demand diversity and datasets from different geographies. However, these challenges can be mitigated using synthetic data that may be created locally and does not require to physically move across borders.

Ethical AI Frameworks for Synthetic Data

Synthetic data is becoming the new heartbeat in the development and application of AI. However, this innovative tool carries with it a responsibility of greatest importance at this stage. That the development of the ethical AI framework to determine how best to deploy AI technologies, including generating and using synthetic data is essential.

The framework involves engaging the technology as well as the system for AI and rests in ensuring fairness, transparency, accountability, and privacy protection.

- **Ethical Guidelines for Synthetics Data:** The essence of preserving privacy lies in the fact that there is no dependency on the use of real sensitive data for AI learning. Ethical frameworks are emphasizing this very notion, which states that even synthetic data cannot be used to reveal or help re identify personal information or provide data breaches. The synthesized data should ensure that it appears statisticallike or similar to the real data thus maintaining confidentiality and avoiding data breaches.
- **Bias and Fairness:** AI models tend to be biased, and this problem applies as much to synthetic data as it does to any other form of machine learning dataset. Ethical frameworks are demanding that the produced synthetic data should represent the full range of scenarios, demographics, and conditions. Synthetic data should not be used to train models such that their foundation is reinforcing and creating new bias. These frameworks promote fairness by the necessary fact of synthetic data representing the real-world data diversity as well as not unfairly favoring one group over others.
- **Transparency and Accountability:** The definition of clarity in the production of AI is an ethical consideration. Detailed documentation of how the synthetic data is created, what methods are adopted, and how such data compares with their intended use of the AI model is encouraged. Mechanisms of accountability should be put in place to ensure responsible use of synthetic data while the negative effects or consequences of its usage are rectified.

- **Ethical:** The ethical framework argues that the synthetic data should be created and deployed under human oversight. Synthetic data generation is an automated process. It should be ensured that the data generated is within the scope of quality and suitability. Human oversight will ensure that the synthetic data deployed into the AI system is valid and simply ethically sound.
- **Sustainability**: An environmental impact focus is spreading among AI systems. Synthetic data can minimize the need for acquisition of real-world data sometimes as expensive and resource-consuming processes. Ethical frameworks for AI take into account sustainability, encouraging synthesis to cut down on the carbon footprint associated with AI use.

Government Policies for Data Sovereignty: EU, China, and the USA

In the context of AI and digital technologies, governments are increasingly experiencing sharp realizations of the importance of data sovereignty. As such, governments are creating policies and laws that decide the weightage, ownership, and movement of data. In this process, nations are actually regaining control over digital ecosystems and the national interests of citizens as well.

- **European Union: GDPR and Data Sovereignty**
  The lead player in efforts towards data sovereignty has been the EU, firstly through the establishment of the General Data Protection Regulation. This has set a new benchmark, not only for the protection and privacy of data but also for data localization and control over personal data. Such personal data should not be transferred to countries outside the EU unless those countries can assure the required privacy. The "data protection by design and by default" principle is one of the most comprehensive laws in the world on this topic, so to say, personal data is owned and controlled by the individual.
- **China: Cybersecurity Law and Data Localization**
  Data localization is one of the salient features of China's Cybersecurity Law. All the critical data created in the country is required to be stored within China. The law is part of a broader digital sovereignty push in China, as the government wants to take control of the country's digital infrastructure and protect it from foreign surveillance or even misuse of citizenry data. China also embarked on a Social Credit System that uses data to grade the behavior of people, hence the need to have control over one's data within its borders.
- **United States: Data Sovereignty and Emergent Policies**

Data sovereignty continues to be an emerging issue in the United States since such national law like the GDPR does not exist, though some states, California, have developed data privacy laws, such as the CCPA, which may therefore give protection over personal data. There exist various policy pieces concerning data governance at the federal level in the U.S., although there lacks a comprehensive framework, mostly analogous to the EU's GDPR. This has further waylaid the discussion on the need for a more united approach regarding data sovereignty, especially given the increasing pressure from global actors on how American companies manage personal data.

Balancing AI Innovation with Regulation Challenges

Regulatory Frames About AI: In terms of the rapid growth in technologies related to AI, the challenge for governments, businesses, and AI innovators is balancing innovations with compliance with regulation. Regulations such as GDPR, CCPA, and China's Cybersecurity Law protect privacy as well as responsible use of AI. These regulations do limit innovation in many ways.

- **Pace of AI Development:** Technological innovation in AI is happening at a rate never seen before - often too fast for regulatory bodies to draft suitable policies. It pits the interests in fostering technological innovation against the imperative for protecting privacy and national interests.
- **Global Standards vs. National Interests:** In such a highly globalized setting, a universal global consensus on data sovereignty policies cannot be reached lightly. Countries have different levels of regulation on data movement, and while the EU is rather strict in regulating the movement of data, it may have looser policies on data movement in other countries. The disparities are thus evident in global and local data governance standards, which makes it difficult to move AI systems across borders and restrains international collaboration.
- **Privacy vs. Access to Data:** Most AI models for use in applications such as healthcare, autonomous driving, and finance rely on large volumes of data for performance. Strict data localization and privacy could limit access to data sources, thereby limiting AI development. Synthetic data could be used to overcome this problem; that is, AI models could be conditioned on data not posing a risk to security or privacy.
- **The responsibility role of deployment:** Compliance with the law about data protection has to do with ensuring that AI deployed benefits society instead of causing harm. Working together, governments, developers, and companies

will have to create frameworks allowing AI to be innovative while also being safe, just, and aligned with ethical standards.

Digital sovereignty in AI is a very challenging and complex issue situated at the intersection of privacy, data governance, and ethics. Localization, ethical frameworks for AI, and policies from government play significant roles in ensuring responsible AI technologies are developed and deployed in conformity with respect for the private lives of individuals and national interests. While it is still a challenge, balancing the level of innovation with that of compliance, significant promise exists in synthetic data to solve such issues as AI can be trained and tested in ways compliant both with stringent data protection laws and responsible AI practices. The more the AI landscape evolves and develops, the greater the importance of digital sovereignty will become. Therefore, it will require constant coordination between governments, organizations, and researchers so that AI continues to serve the public good.

Role of Synthetic Data in Ensuring Responsible AI:

Responsible, Ethical Use of AI Without Bias The increasing integration of AI systems across the different sectors raises the critical concern over responsible, ethical, and bias-free use of technologies. Synthetic data helps many challenges in building fair, transparent, and accountable AI systems fall within the purview of AI developers. This section outlines the role of synthetic data in solving some of the key problems concerning ethics and governance, namely bias and discrimination, transparency and accountability, mitigation of risks in automated decision-making, and safe deployment in sensitive areas.

Addressing Bias and Discrimination: Leveraging Synthetic Data to Create Balanced and Fair Datasets

In point of fact, AI systems, especially learning machines, learn the patterns on the data they are trained on. When that data is biased along gender lines, race, socio-economic status, or along other dimensions, then the model will tend to reproduce sometimes even amplify those biases in its predictions and decisions. Such discrimination, inequity, and unfairness prevail. Synthetic datasets are an opportunity to strike a balance between those biases by creating more representative datasets that reveal more of the population and less likelihood of lapsing into historical inequities.

How Does the Synthetic Data Help With Bias?

One of the greatest benefits synthetic data can be applied to is in balancing underrepresented groups. In a large fraction of real-world datasets, certain groups are underrepresented-for example, racial minorities, people from some economical backgrounds, or people with disabilities. Such underrepresented groups can be represented through synthetic data and new data points created in a manner that the AI model would get trained on a more balanced dataset representing the broader spectrum of possible inputs. Therefore, it can reduce biased predictions and even ensure fairness in AI outputs.

- **Elimination of Historical Bias:** Usually, history data mirrors the society's biasness and inequality prevalent at that time. For instance, a facial recognition system which has primarily been trained on datasets featuring predominantly light-skinned people will not perform well in the case of a darker-skinned person. Synthetic data may therefore be generated to correct imbalances by simulating images of individuals from diverse ethnicities and backgrounds; this enables AI models to be trained on data that much more closely represents the full spectrum of human diversity, potentially preventing AI systems from continuing or amplifying historical biases.
- **Simulate a range of scenarios:** synthetic data so created can be useful for simulating an eclectic mix of scenarios that cannot possibly be covered using an observational study. For instance, in healthcare scenarios, synthetic medical data can be generated for simulating varied disease conditions, treatments, and demographics; thereby ensuring that the AI models are trained to behave equitably across a wide range of plausible cases or scenarios.
- **Fairness Audits:** The synthetic data can be used for fairness audits of AI systems. Ensuring models are working well in the demographics they were trained on and performing similarly across each demographic segment can be done by testing on artificially created data that represents several demographics. This can help prevent deploying systems that are discriminatory to certain sections of people before releasing into real-world applications.

Challenges in the Reduction of Bias of Synthetic Data

Synthetic data can be helpful in countering bias but is far from a silver bullet. Unless the synthetic data generation process is implemented effectively, it can pervert existing biases. For example, biased synthetic data generated to mimic real datasets can lead to biased models. Thus, fairness-driven informed generation of synthetic data is rather significant in avoiding the formation of biased datasets.

Transparency and Accountability: Constructing Accountable AI Systems with Traceable Synthetic Data

These two important bases of responsible AI are transparency and accountability. AI systems involved in any high-stakes decision-making activity, whether healthcare, finance, or criminal justice, among others, should be clear about how they work so that stakeholders can fathom how the decision was made. Traceable synthetic data improves not just the transparency but the accountability of AI systems through detailed documentation and validation of data which fed the models.

- **Increased Transparency with Synthetic Data:** Another challenge of AI transparency: Many machine learning models, especially in deep learning, have a sort of "black box" effect. Using synthetic data can possibly enhance transparency in some way by creating transparent records on how the data has been generated and about which features it includes and how it matches the purpose for which it has been designed. This traceability will help a company achieve stakeholder trust by saying that the data in the AI system has been ethically obtained and refers to actual data.
- **Explainability in AI Models**: Explainability is the ability to understand and interpret the decision-making process of an AI model. Such utilization of synthetic data would help developers understand much better how their models decide on something in multiple testing and validation of AI models. In this way, any hidden patterns or contributing factors that are leading the model to behave in ways not readily apparent would be discovered. Transparent synthetic data practices help enable AI developers explain the rationale behind their model decisions and support such decisions in grounds of ethics and logic.
- **Auditing AI Systems:** Synthetic data is a good auditing tool for systems. Another tool which is used by AI developers to test the performance of how the system would behave in certain conditions is called Hacking the Model-through a simulation process of various distributions of data. It can, in many ways, help pinpoint any weakness or bias in the model that did not come to light at the initiation phase of training. Synthetic data can even be used for "stress tests" in AI models, thereby ensuring the proper working of the AI model across a wide range of inputs and conditions.
- **Challenges in Achieving Transparency:** Though synthetic data may increase transparency, it also poses new challenges. Creating synthetic data such that inaccuracies or errors are not introduced into the model is a sensitive process. Moreover, creating synthetic data requires transparent methods, documentation of assumptions or known limitations that have to be made

with the data generation process to avoid misleading stakeholders about the capabilities of the AI system.

Mitigating Risk in Automated Decision-Making: The Potential of Synthetic Data to Enhance Transparency and Fairness

Participation of AI in automated decision-making processes also relates to hiring algorithms and predictive policing tools. But on the list remains use of AI for decision-making issues that have brought concerns of fairness, accountability, and harm. Synthetic data may play a crucial part in mitigating risks by making sure AI models get trained on representative, fair, and transparent data.

Building in Fairness to Automated Decisions

- **Training Models on Diverse Data:** In this risk lies in biased and incomplete training data directed toward an AI model that would feed back unfair or discriminatory outcomes. Synthetic data allow developers to design diverse, balanced datasets that include all demographics, so that the training data of AI systems represent a large cross-section of viewpoints. One possible method toward developing more balanced AI models that are less likely to perpetuate existing prejudices is to add synthetic data to real-world data.
- **Testing Scenarios with Synthetic Data:** In many scenarios in automated decision-making, the relevant environment where an AI system would be deployed actually has real-world data that is scarce or expensive to obtain or impossible to simulate. In synthetic data, a developer can simulate a variety of imaginary scenarios while testing AI models, including edge cases or rare events that might not be typically represented in real-world datasets. This will ensure that the AI system is able to handle various inputs and fair enough while making decisions in any of the scenarios.
- **Reducing Discriminatory Outcomes**: To reduce discriminatory outcomes is through generating synthetic data that will be used to test AI systems before deployment. Thus, the generation of data that would represent various demographics and running them through these models will help identify if the system produces biased outputs. If the model discriminates against certain groups, adjustments can be made before putting such an AI system into use.
- **Improving Regulatory Compliance**: Regulatory compliance-the regulation in many sectors, especially in finance, health care, and criminal justice is very stringent, with strict requirements of fairness and non-discrimination. A company can claim and demonstrate to the world that its systems are perfect-

ly in tune with the regulations and thus reduce the risk of legal challenges or reputational damages with the use of synthetic data in validating AI models.

Challenges in Mitigating Risks

Synthetic data can reduce the risks of automated decision making but does not promise AI systems to always make fair or ethical decisions. The developers would be very vigilant in ensuring that synthetic data could really go a long way in representing the actual occurrences without duplication, and models are tested to ensure fairness across groups. There is a danger that synthetic data will be used in ways that obscure rather than solve these potential problems with AI systems. So, it is critical to ensure that synthetic data is being used as part of a comprehensive strategy for driving more fairness and accountability into AI.

- **Safe Deployment in Sensitive Areas:** How Synthetic Data Can Help Safely Deploy AI in Healthcare, Law Enforcement, and Other Sensitive Areas AI technologies are being increasingly deployed in sensitive areas such as healthcare, law enforcement, and criminal justice. Domain-related challenges here include considerations for privacy, safety, and ethical issues. Synthetic data may be the way to overcome these challenges and enable AI systems to be tested and trained in safe controlled environments before their use in real-world application areas.
- **Healthcare:** In healthcare (Iuliano et al., 2024), AI can be used to assess the medical images of patients, predict the outcomes of the patients, and assist in the diagnosis. Synthetic data does not compromise the patient's privacy while training the AI models. Synthetic medical images can be generated, which will mimic real data for the patients, thus creating effective AI systems while also being HIPAA compliant.
- **Law Enforcement:** The primary uses of AI systems by law enforcement departments are for predictive policing, facial recognition, and surveillance. Synthetic data may be considered as a means to train in such a manner that the risks connected with privacy and civil liberties are minimized. For example, generating synthetic images or videos of persons from multiple demographic groups may help ensure that facial recognition systems develop fair and accurate outputs and reduce the risks of discrimination.
- **Other Sensitive Areas:** Synthetic data could also be applied in other sensitive fields, such as credit rating, recruitment, and social services. This is to ensure their AI models receive the right training free of bias. For example, synthetic data can be used to test algorithms for rating scores without the

ability to discriminate against specific groups of people, such as race or income level.

Difficulties in Safe Deployment

Although there is a good amount of potential in the use of synthetic data in sensitive domains, it opens questions about data quality, privacy, and security. In particular, synthetic data have to be produced such that critical properties of the original world data are preserved but individual privacy is still protected. Moreover, models trained with synthetic data may fail miserably when deployed into the real world, where conditions differ immensely.

Synthetic data is essential in ensuring responsible AI because it prevents bias and lack of transparency and addresses accountability, fairness, and safety. Actually, synthetic data allows developers to work with balanced and diversified datasets that help in building AI systems in an equitable and transparent manner. Synthetic data gives a chance for the testing and deployment of AI systems in sensitive areas, such as health care and law enforcement, in an appropriate and safe manner. In other words, the proper use of synthetic data requires paying attention to detail and some semblance of effort over time towards increasing fairness and transparency. Employed appropriately, synthetic data is going to change the face of AI technology deployment so as to serve the greater good.

Future Directions for Synthetic Data and Digital Sovereignty

Since synthetic data falls into the realm of privacy, fairness, and ethics concerns, it's going to play an essential role in the process since the face of innovation is changing with advanced AI technologies. The future of synthetic data would actually depend on how much technology advances in terms of the integration of AI governance and digital sovereignty into the global landscape. This section introduces a few of the currently emerging synthetic data technologies, outlines its role in the potential of synthetic data in AI model auditing and its long-term perspective for a privacy and digital sovereignty-offer promotion.

Long-Term Vision of Synthetic Data in Digital Sovereignty: Building a Privacy-Respecting Digital Future

Synthetic data would, in fact, change the normative underpinning of digital sovereignty and create the opportunity for nations and organizations to build AI that respects privacy and autonomy.

It leads to the development of self-sufficient AI because it reduces reliance on foreign sources of data. Synthetic data allows countries to train robust AI models through good-quality synthetic datasets-a possibility that helps support digital sovereignty goals while promoting innovation. This is a matter of significant importance to countries looking toward protecting citizen data and reducing their dependency on multinational tech corporations.

In the same measure that such concerns over data-related privacy are gaining momentum, synthetic data may represent a more significant long-term solution toward development of AI systems that will eventually minimize the amount of real-world data without any compromise on accuracy and reliability. Decreasing the amount of real-world data will thus support respect for privacy in a user, paving the way for safety-sensitive applications of AI in healthcare, finance, and public safety. This can also be used to ensure an organization is well positioned to comply with the GDPR, CCPA, and similar data protection regulations.

Empowering Individuals and Organizations: It enables democratized data access by providing smaller organizations, startups, and even individual developers with the ability to build complex AI models without necessarily needing tremendous amounts of real-world data. Synthetic data may, therefore, further empower a variety of stakeholders to engage in the digital economy while still allowing innovation, privacy, and inclusivity.

Synthetic data could turn out to be a crucial element in establishing a universal framework for data ethics and digital sovereignty in the long run. Because of its safety and privacy-preserving attribute of data sharing, synthetic data can be used to support international efforts in establishing ethical standards for artificial intelligence respecting individual rights but also allowing for technological progress. This framework will serve as the basis of a worldwide AI policy, driving responsible AI development and ethics for data, worldwide.

AI Model Auditing and Synthetic Data: In Pursuit of Transparency and Responsible AI

As more and more of AI penetrates our lives, this will only enhance the need for mechanisms that make AI systems more understandable and auditable. Synthetic data can greatly facilitate model auditing procedures by allowing developers and auditors to assess model behavior under controlled, representative conditions.

Testing AI Models under Synthetic Scenarios: In many ways, auditing AI models means understanding the ability of AI models to perform across the various scenarios- some rare and sometimes sensitive-most of which would not appear in such datasets in real life. Synthetic data helps in the recognition of biases or unfair behaviors otherwise not recognizable with such intensity. For instance, by the use of synthetic data, one can test an algorithm used in hiring and show that model behavior has a gender or racial bias through simulation as presented.

Model Explainability: Here, auditing and explainability become an integral part of things in high stakes such as healthcare, finance, and law enforcement. Synthetically generated data will help auditors understand why AI models behave the way they do by opening the black box on how AI models respond to different types of inputs. Synthetic examples become easier when tracing and deconstructing AI decision logic into much more transparent and understandable paths.

Ensuring Regulatory Standards: There is an increased demand from many regulating bodies to have fairness, accountability, and transparency around AI. Using synthetic datasets to test and audit the models will enable organizations to prove compliance with the regulations such as the proposed AI Act in the European Union and the U.S. AI Bill of Rights. Synthetically generated data is a means of testing how the model complies with such regulations in deployment, thus mitigating legal issues.

Synthetic data is fast becoming a critical component in the development of responsible AI systems by tackling key privacy, fairness, and transparency challenges. Indicative of the substitution and reduction of real-world data dependence, synthetic data essentially provides privacy safeguarding mechanisms while also ensuring that the organizations concerned comply with the tight GDPR regulations at large in support of digital sovereignty and data security, its use in generating AI model audit and explainability stimulates transparency, especially in the health and finance sectors, where the decision made should be fair and accountable. Thus, once synthetic data technology matures, it will soon democratize AI, allowing a wide variety of organizations to innovate responsibly and set up a global ethical framework respecting individual rights while advancing AI.

CONCLUSION

This book has outlined the dynamic nature of synthetic data, a very potent tool that forms AI but meets critical needs in areas such as privacy, data governance, and digital sovereignty. In this regard, synthetic data offers a critical advantage: creating the possibility of building AI without harming those privacy aspects, representing diversity in datasets, and creating realistic models for such complex applications, like diagnostics in healthcare, autonomous driving, and security systems. However, along with these advancements come challenges related to quality and realism, in managing computational demands, and the avoidance of biases inherent in synthetic data.

Summary of Key Takeaways

The supremacy of one of the major themes is dominated by how synthetic data can help to heal growing tensions that have arisen between data privacy and AI innovation.The synthetic data solves the problem of privacy. It empowers an organization to avoid the direct usage of personal data, thereby coming up as a solution in an age when the data protection regulations have become progressively stringent, such as the General Data Protection Regulation that came into existence in Europe and India's Digital Personal Data Protection Act 2023. Second, synthetic data provides countries with the opportunity to build AI solutions without dependence on extraneous sources of data since, clearly, digital sovereignty is closely related to data sovereignty. In other words, independence allows for nation security and innovation independently on the basis of self-sufficiency in AI.

Another point focused on the role that synthetic data is likely to make AI advancements fairer, more transparent, and accountable. As synthetic data helps to increase the balanced datasets generated with time, it offers a fairer possibility to be represented across different demographical groups, as questions about biases and discriminations by algorithms are increasingly raised. Synthetic data also makes auditing and explainability easier as regulators and organizations are able to assess and be aware of the behavior of AI models, against the broad set of different scenarios that are now made up of edge cases, which may never occur in real datasets.

Best Practices for Governments and Organizations

Digital sovereignty and data governance policies are an avenue to realizing the vastness of synthetic data. Some policy recommendations for realization by organizations and governments include:

Set Ethical Standards around Use of Synthetic Data: With its rising use, there should also rise the institution of ethical standards around responsible development and implementation.This can be the first step for governments and AI developers in cooperation in developing non-bias standards, quality checks, and calibration of synthetic data generation based on principles for human rights.

Invest in Research for Advanced Synthetic Data Technologies: Governments should invest in research on emerging techniques that include diffusion models and advanced GANs, delivering far more realistic and diverse synthetic data. Here, the impetus to innovation that these governments can create, with assurance of accuracy and quality in synthetic data for AI systems, is very beneficial for them in investment.

Foster International Cooperation on Data Sovereignty: Data sovereignty will require international cooperation to work out frameworks that balance individual national interests with global developments in AI. There should be governmental coordination on the standards of synthetic data exchange so that neither side's exercise compromises their dignity and sovereignty.

Because this has a bearing on public confidence regarding the openness of AI models, then, requirements for transparency must be included in AI models trained on synthetic data. To illustrate, reporting how synthetic data was developed and used as well as its limitations and quality assurance ensure that the models are fair, dispel possible concerns with regards to potential backdoors or hidden biases and efficient usage of synthetic data.

Sponsor the deployment of privacy-preserving technologies. Some of the privacy-preserving technologies that will be used with synthetic data include federated learning and homomorphic encryption, which will increase security around the use of AI and protect sensitive information in the development of AI. Governments and organizations can encourage incentives in the use of such technologies in AI development processes.

Empower SMEs through access to Synthetic Data: In capacities accessed and used synthetic data governments could empower the SME sector; it could either be through accessing public repositories or toolkits for synthetic data where smaller firms can readily create AI solutions responsibly thus rebalancing the playing field in the digital economy.

Promote Responsible AI Culture

Facilitating responsible AI culture would reflect the understanding that synthetic data is not just a technical means but makes ethics, equity, and transparency possible in the use of AI. Further building trust of the new generations of AI technologies with the public is if organizations adapt responsible AI frameworks and emphasize fairness and distance them even farther from bias. That will occur through education, awareness-building, and highlighting societal benefits to uses of synthetic data by leadership in both government and industry. Finally, benchmarks for responsible use of synthetic data determine what is responsible behavior, enabling organizations to ensure alignment of AI systems to broader social and ethical values.

However, the degree to which the culture of responsible AI will depend on how widely the broader public understand the why and how of synthetic data. The brighter the light cast upon the use and involvement of diverse voices in this conversation, the more likely it is that the AI system might be built for overall fairness, inclusiveness, and positive societal impact.

Final Thoughts further developments towards a responsible AI future and digital sovereignty made the development of synthetic data more important. It is an efficient approach to solving dire issues in privacy and governance where countries and organizations may govern their ecosystems to control data without violating the norm on fair AI development. This would allow the governments to have responsible AI use through reduced dependence on foreign sources of data while, at the same time achieving national autonomy through features of synthetic data that preserve private qualities.

The promise of synthetic data bridges the gap between innovation and regulation, becoming the perfect pathway in the development of safe, secure, and equitable AI systems. In short, the synthetic data will then prove indispensable in the formulation of AI applications that reflect the values of the local, respect the rights of privacy, and adhere to regulatory requirements from all these appertaining eras. This era will herald one where digital sovereignty and technological advancement sail in tandem. In the long run, thus, the rising global digital economy will continue to expand synthetic data as the key enabler in building a future aligned with innovative and ethical principles and governance.

REFERENCES

Adair, L. (2023). A synthetic data strategy for Scotland: Using synthetic data to improve access to public sector data for research. *International Journal of Population Data Science, 8*(2), 8. DOI: 10.23889/ijpds.v8i2.2215

Alqahtani, H., Kavakli-Thorne, M., & Kumar, G. (2019). Applications of Generative Adversarial Networks (GANs): An Updated Review. *Archives of Computational Methods in Engineering, 28*(2), 525–552. DOI: 10.1007/s11831-019-09388-y

Arthur, L., Costello, J., Hardy, J., O'Brien, W., Rea, J., Rees, G., & Ganev, G. (2023). On the challenges of deploying privacy-preserving synthetic data in the enterprise. arXiv preprint arXiv:2307.04208.

Barbierato, E., Vedova, M. L. D., Tessera, D., Toti, D., & Vanoli, N. (2022). A methodology for controlling bias and fairness in synthetic data generation. *Applied Sciences (Basel, Switzerland), 12*(9), 4619.

Debic, B., & Medvidovic, L. (2024). Data Ownership and Privacy in Personalized AI Models in Assistive Healthcare. *International Joint Conference on Artificial Intelligence.* DOI: 10.24963/ijcai.2024/868

Delussu, R., Putzu, L., & Fumera, G. (2024). Synthetic Data for Video Surveillance Applications of Computer Vision: A Review. *International Journal of Computer Vision, 132*(10), 4473–4509. DOI: 10.1007/s11263-024-02102-x

Dhariwal, P., & Nichol, A. (2021). Diffusion models beat gans on image synthesis. *Advances in Neural Information Processing Systems, 34*, 8780–8794.

Digital Personal Data Protection Act, 2023

Esser, P., Kulal, S., Blattmann, A., Entezari, R., Müller, J., Saini, H., & Rombach, R. (2024, July). Scaling rectified flow transformers for high-resolution image synthesis. *Forty-first international conference on machine learning*.

Ferrara, E. (2024). Fairness and bias in artificial intelligence: A brief survey of sources, impacts, and mitigation strategies. *Sci, 6*(1), 3.

Glasze, G., Cattaruzza, A., Douzet, F., Dammann, F., Bertran, M.-G., Bômont, C., Braun, M., Danet, D., Desforges, A., Géry, A., Grumbach, S., Hummel, P., Limonier, K., Münßinger, M., Nicolai, F., Pétiniaud, L., Winkler, J., & Zanin, C. (2022). Contested Spatialities of Digital Sovereignty. *Geopolitics, 28*(2), 919–958. DOI: 10.1080/14650045.2022.2050070

Hu, J., & McKay Bowen, C. (2023). Advancing microdata privacy protection: A review of synthetic data methods. *Wiley Interdisciplinary Reviews: Computational Statistics*, 16.

Iuliano, A., Liò, P., Manfredi, G., & Romaniello, F. (2024). Denoising Probabilistic Diffusion Models for Synthetic Healthcare Image Generation. *2024 IEEE International Workshop on Metrology for Living Environment (MetroLivEnv)* 415-420. DOI: 10.1109/MetroLivEnv60384.2024.10615511

Jordon, J., Szpruch, L., Houssiau, F., Bottarelli, M., Cherubin, G., Maple, C., . . . Weller, A. (2022). Synthetic Data—what, why and how? arXiv preprint arXiv:2205.03257.

Kularathne, Y., Janitha, P., Ambepitiya, S., Ahamed, T., Wijesundara, D., & Sothyrajah, P. (2024). SynthVision—Harnessing Minimal Input for Maximal Output in Computer Vision Models using Synthetic Image data. arXiv preprint arXiv:2402.02826.

Lenatti, M., Paglialonga, A., Orani, V., Ferretti, M., & Mongelli, M. (2023). Characterization of Synthetic Health Data Using Rule-Based Artificial Intelligence Models. *IEEE Journal of Biomedical and Health Informatics*, *27*(8), 3760–3769. DOI: 10.1109/JBHI.2023.3236722 PMID: 37018683

Lopes, P. V., Silveira, L., Guimarães de Aquino, R. D., Ribeiro, C. H., Skoogh, A., & Filipe, A. N. V. (2024). Synthetic data generation for digital twins: Enabling production systems analysis in the absence of data. *International Journal of Computer Integrated Manufacturing*, *37*(10-11), 1252–1269. DOI: 10.1080/0951192X.2024.2322981

Man, K., & Chahl, J. S. (2022). A Review of Synthetic Image Data and Its Use in Computer Vision. *Journal of Imaging*, *8*(11), 8. DOI: 10.3390/jimaging8110310 PMID: 36422059

Mumuni, A., Mumuni, F., & Gerrar, N. K. (2024). A survey of synthetic data augmentation methods in computer vision. arXiv preprint arXiv:2403.10075.

Ren, H., Yue, Y., Zhou, C., Paffenroth, R. C., Li, Y., & Weiss, M. L. (2018). Robust variational autoencoders: generating noise-free images from corrupted images. Academic Press.

Rombach, R., Blattmann, A., Lorenz, D., Esser, P., & Ommer, B. (2022). High-resolution image synthesis with latent diffusion models. In *Proceedings of the IEEE/CVF conference on computer vision and pattern recognition* (pp. 10684-10695). IEEE.

Saxena, D., & Cao, J. (2020). Generative Adversarial Networks (GANs). *ACM Computing Surveys*, *54*(3), 1–42. DOI: 10.1145/3446374

Shorten, C., & Khoshgoftaar, T. M. (2019). A survey on Image Data Augmentation for Deep Learning. *Journal of Big Data*, *6*(1), 1–48. DOI: 10.1186/s40537-019-0197-0

Truong, T. T. H., Tran, T. K., Nguyen, C. T., Phan, T. H. H., Nguyen, A. T., & Nguyen, N. S. (2024, August). An approach of generating synthetic data in military camouflaged object detection. In *2024 International Conference on Multimedia Analysis and Pattern Recognition (MAPR)* (pp. 1-6). IEEE.

Zeng, G., Wei, H.-N., Lu, K.-D., Geng, G., & Weng, J. (2024). DACO-BD: Data Augmentation Combinatorial Optimization-Based Backdoor Defense in Deep Neural Networks for SAR Image Classification. *IEEE Transactions on Instrumentation and Measurement*, *73*, 1–13. DOI: 10.1109/TIM.2024.3436130

Chapter 11
Securing Digital Sovereignty Through AI: Balancing Innovation, Ethics, and Data Protection

Klaudia Szabelka
https://orcid.org/0000-0002-4150-7516
University of Glasgow, UK

ABSTRACT

Artificial intelligence has become a foundational pillar of digital sovereignty by reinforcing data privacy, infrastructure autonomy, and ethical oversight. This chapter explores how AI can be strategically leveraged to enhance national control through responsible innovation, data localization, and accountable governance. Drawing on a multidisciplinary literature review and comparative analysis of Estonia, the EU, Singapore, and South Korea, the study identifies critical enablers of digital sovereignty. Estonia has implemented over 80 AI-powered public services; the EU's Digital Compass targets 75% enterprise adoption of AI, big data, or cloud by 2030; Singapore's 100E programme has supported more than 38 industry-focused AI deployments; and South Korea has invested $2 billion in AI R&D to boost domestic innovation. Findings highlight that AI-driven innovation, strong regulatory frameworks, SME empowerment, and privacy-first policies are vital for digital autonomy. The chapter concludes that achieving digital sovereignty requires a balanced approach—combining technological leadership

DOI: 10.4018/979-8-3693-9137-2.ch011

INTRODUCTION

As digital technologies increasingly underpin modern governance, economic systems, and social interactions, digital sovereignty has emerged as a strategic priority for states seeking to retain control over their digital infrastructures, data governance, and technological development. Broadly defined, DS refers to a nation's ability to independently regulate its digital resources and align digital innovations with domestic legal, ethical, and political values (Floridi, 2020; Glasze et al., 2021). The rapid proliferation of artificial intelligence intensifies this agenda, as AI systems process vast volumes of sensitive data, introduce complex regulatory challenges, and depend on transnational infrastructure. While AI offers transformative opportunities in public services, healthcare, education, and defense, it also poses serious risks to privacy, institutional autonomy, and citizen rights (Calderaro & Blumfelde, 2020; Ebers, Oprysk, & Tupay, 2023).

Much of the current literature on AI and governance has focused on themes such as privacy, algorithmic fairness, and responsible deployment. These contributions underscore the importance of ensuring due process, explainability, and transparency in AI decision-making (Ebers & Trasberg, 2023; Roberts, Hine, & Floridi, 2021). However, fewer studies provide an integrated analysis of how AI can function as a strategic tool for enhancing digital sovereignty. Central to this transformation are national R&D strategies, data localization frameworks, ethical AI governance models, and innovation ecosystems that empower small and medium-sized enterprises (Ebers & Krõõt Tupay, 2023; Madiega, 2020).

Moreover, there remains a notable gap in comparative policy research, limiting global understanding of how advanced digital states are leveraging AI to shape sovereign digital futures. This chapter addresses that gap by examining how selected countries—Estonia, the European Union, Singapore, and South Korea—strategically integrate AI into their digital sovereignty agendas. These jurisdictions have been internationally recognized for their innovative digital governance models, privacy-first regulatory environments, and sustained investment in AI research and infrastructure (Frana, 2021; Tan, 2020; Hardy, 2019; Rice, 2018).

By drawing from legal, policy, technological, and ethical perspectives, this chapter offers a multidimensional framework to assess the role of AI in digital sovereignty. It contributes to current debates by identifying replicable strategies, emerging risks, and practical pathways for nations seeking to build secure, ethical, and autonomous digital futures.

The key contributions of this chapter are:

- Conceptualizing the intersection of artificial intelligence and digital sovereignty, with a focus on privacy, ethical governance, and autonomy.

- Identifying how R&D and SME empowerment can strengthen sovereign control over AI innovation.
- Comparing national strategies to extract best practices in embedding AI into digital sovereignty frameworks.
- Offering policy recommendations that support ethical, transparent, and secure AI systems aligned with DS priorities.

The chapter is structured as follows: Section 2: Conceptual Framework defines digital sovereignty across technical, legal, and ethical dimensions and explains how AI intersects with issues of data control, autonomy, and privacy. Section 3: Strategic Pillars of AI-Driven Digital Sovereignty identifies four mechanisms—responsible AI innovation, R&D and SME empowerment, ethical governance, and cybersecurity—that reinforce DS through policy and infrastructure. Section 4: Comparative Case Studies presents in-depth national profiles of Estonia, the EU, Singapore, and South Korea, with quantitative data on AI deployment, investment, and regulatory innovation. Section 5: Limitations highlights constraints affecting the generalizability and implementation of sovereign AI strategies. Section 6: Conclusion and Future Work synthesizes findings, outlines policy recommendations, and proposes directions for future research on AI and digital sovereignty.

CONCEPTUAL FRAMEWORK: AI AND DIGITAL SOVEREIGNTY

Digital sovereignty refers to a state's ability to assert authority, control, and governance over its digital infrastructure, data flows, and technological development in line with its political, legal, and ethical values. As Frana (2021) notes, digital sovereignty encompasses a multidimensional framework that spans technical infrastructure, regulatory capacity, and ethical standards—particularly in contexts where global digital platforms and foreign technologies dominate domestic information systems. DS is not merely about national security; it also entails ensuring digital self-determination, democratic control over data, and the protection of individual rights, most notably the right to privacy (Floridi, 2020; Glasze et al., 2021).

The rise of artificial intelligence introduces both opportunities and challenges for digital sovereignty. On one hand, AI fosters national innovation in public service delivery, economic productivity, and data-driven policy-making (Ebers, Oprysk, & Tupay, 2023). On the other hand, AI systems typically rely on massive datasets, opaque proprietary algorithms, and foreign-controlled infrastructures—raising serious concerns about privacy, accountability, and technological dependence (Calderaro & Blumfelde, 2020; Glasze et al., 2021). Glasze et al. (2021) emphasize the importance of spatial control over infrastructure, noting that when critical services are hosted externally, states may lose functional autonomy.

Among the most sensitive intersections between AI and digital sovereignty is the issue of data control and privacy. According to Floridi (2020), asserting sovereignty requires control over how personal and national data is collected, processed, and stored. Without strong data governance, AI risks being exploited as a tool for surveillance, bias, and digital colonization. The European Union's General Data Protection Regulation is widely regarded as a leading regulatory model, embedding privacy-by-design principles and establishing a rights-based foundation for AI governance aligned with digital sovereignty (Roberts, Hine, & Floridi, 2021).

Data localization laws and sovereign infrastructure investments further anchor digital autonomy. Estonia's X-Road architecture allows secure, decentralized data exchange while retaining national jurisdiction over digital flows (Rice, 2018). Singapore's Smart Nation initiative leverages localized data centers and cybersecurity protocols to shield against foreign intrusion and ensure data integrity (Tan, 2020; Foong, Tan, & Tan, 2018). These initiatives show that infrastructure choices play a decisive role in building digital resilience.

Ethical governance is equally essential. As Ebers and Trasberg (2023) argue, principles such as transparency, explainability, and due process must guide AI development—especially when administrative power is delegated to algorithms in public services. Effective governance ensures accountability, mitigates bias, and upholds human rights even in technologically advanced decision-making environments.

In summary, digital sovereignty in the age of AI requires more than technical prowess. It demands a holistic governance framework that embeds ethical oversight, legal robustness, and infrastructural control. AI can indeed empower sovereignty—but only if deployed within systems that protect rights, ensure transparency, and maintain democratic accountability.

STRATEGIC PILLARS OF AI-DRIVEN DIGITAL SOVEREIGNTY

Achieving digital sovereignty in the AI era requires more than abstract principles—it demands concrete, strategic action across policy, technological, and governance domains. This section outlines four critical pillars through which governments can operationalize sovereignty: responsible AI innovation, investment in research and development alongside SME empowerment, ethical governance and data stewardship, and cybersecurity infrastructure. These pillars reflect a multidimensional approach, blending technical control with legal, social, and economic resilience.

Responsible AI Innovation

Responsible AI innovation involves the design, development, and use of AI technologies in a manner aligned with democratic values, transparency, and fairness. Estonia exemplifies this, having integrated over 80 AI applications into public services—including virtual assistants and decision-support tools—under a national strategy that upholds legal safeguards and citizen trust (Ebers, Oprysk, & Tupay, 2023). Similarly, Singapore's Model AI Governance Framework emphasizes fairness, transparency, and accountability, with tools like AI Verify ensuring compliance with ethical guidelines (Timmers, 2021; Aigner, Garai-Fodor, & Szemere, 2020). These frameworks not only mitigate algorithmic harms but reinforce legitimacy in AI deployment, thereby strengthening digital sovereignty.

Research & Development and SME Empowerment

Robust R&D investment and SME inclusion are foundational to building sovereign AI ecosystems. South Korea's Digital New Deal allocates over $2 billion for AI R&D and infrastructure between 2021 and 2025, supporting ethical innovation in sectors like healthcare and smart cities (Seo, 2019; Park & Chang, 2022). These efforts are bolstered by platforms like the AI Hub and "Data Dam," which centralize anonymized training data to support domestic developers (Nam, Jung, & Kim, 2024). In the EU, the Digital Europe Programme commits €250 million to AI innovation among SMEs, aiming for 75% of companies to adopt AI or cloud solutions by 2030 (Roberts et al., 2021). Estonia also supports SME innovation through sandboxes and AI-friendly procurement policies, integrating local startups into public digital services (Hardy, 2019).

Ethical Governance and Data Stewardship

Ethical governance ensures AI serves the public good, avoids discrimination, and remains accountable. The EU's AI Act and GDPR jointly establish a risk-based regulatory framework requiring transparency, lawful processing, and explainability in AI systems (Floridi, 2020; Madiega, 2020). Estonia complements these with decentralized data platforms like X-Road, where user access and consent are strictly regulated (Ebers & Trasberg, 2023). South Korea's National Guidelines for AI Ethics and public engagement initiatives also ensure that citizens actively shape AI norms through consultations and educational outreach (Kim & Moon, 2021; Ha, 2022). These governance structures embed public values into AI, making sovereignty transparent and participatory.

Cybersecurity and Infrastructure Control

Sovereign control over digital infrastructure is vital to secure national data and resist foreign influence. Estonia's "Data Embassy" model—where critical state data is stored abroad under Estonian jurisdiction—illustrates this well (Rice, 2018). Singapore emphasizes data center localization and AI-enhanced cybersecurity monitoring through its Cyber Security Agency, protecting systems from surveillance and cyber threats (Foong, Tan, & Tan, 2018; Frana, 2021). The EU's GAIA-X initiative and France's "Cloud de Confiance" seek to ensure that cloud services comply with European data protection norms, reducing dependency on foreign hyperscalers (Timmers, 2021). With over 60% of EU cyber incidents involving third-party infrastructure breaches, sovereign cloud strategies become essential (European Court of Auditors, 2021)

CASE STUDIES IN DIGITAL SOVEREIGNTY: AI PRACTICES FROM LEADING NATIONS

To understand how artificial intelligence contributes to digital sovereignty in practice, this chapter examines the strategies of four digitally advanced jurisdictions: Estonia, the European Union, Singapore, and South Korea (Tab.1). These case studies were selected for their diverse approaches, shared commitment to ethical AI deployment, and measurable investment in digital infrastructure, privacy, and innovation ecosystems. While each context is shaped by distinct political, regulatory, and economic priorities, their strategies provide instructive examples of how AI can be harnessed to reinforce national autonomy, data control, and secure digital governance (Floridi, 2020; Ebers, Oprysk, & Tupay, 2023; Madiega, 2020).

Collectively, these regions have invested significantly in AI research and development: the European Union allocated €2.6 billion under Horizon Europe (2021–2022) to support sovereign AI innovation (European Commission, 2022); South Korea committed approximately 2.2 trillion (~$2 billion) toward its AI strategy, including AI semiconductors and national platforms (Nam, Jung, & Kim, 2024; Park & Chang, 2022); Singapore invested $500 million in AI under its Smart Nation framework (Frana, 2021); and Estonia emphasized co-creation with SMEs through regulatory sandboxes and digital procurement programs (Hardy, 2019).

In terms of AI deployment, all four regions demonstrate operational maturity. Estonia has integrated over 80 AI applications into public services since 2021, including legal and administrative functions (Ebers, Oprysk, & Tupay, 2023). Singapore's 100E programme has supported 38+ industry-led AI pilot projects (Frana, 2021), while the European Union has set a strategic target for 75% of enterprises to adopt AI, cloud, or big data technologies by 2030 (European Commission, 2021). South Korea is rapidly expanding AI through its National AI Research Lab and data-sharing initiatives (Nam et al., 2024).

Each case also reflects a distinctive approach to privacy and data governance. Estonia's decentralized X-Road infrastructure ensures secure, citizen-managed data exchange, and its data embassies provide extraterritorial storage under domestic control (Rice, 2018). The EU's GDPR and AI Act form a rights-based framework ensuring lawful, transparent, and accountable data use (Madiega, 2020; Floridi, 2020). Singapore's Model AI Governance Framework emphasizes consent, fairness, and responsible data stewardship (Foong, Tan, & Tan, 2018; Tan, 2020). South Korea reinforces data sovereignty through localized infrastructures and strict personal data protection legislation (Park & Chang, 2022).

Robust cybersecurity and infrastructure control further support sovereign digital systems. Estonia's e-governance model integrates secure digital ID, blockchain, and cross-border digital diplomacy (Hardy, 2019; Rice, 2018). The EU's GAIA-X initiative and sovereign cloud projects aim to reduce dependency on foreign cloud providers (Timmers, 2021). Singapore protects its critical systems with national cybersecurity operations centers and data center localization (Foong et al., 2018). South Korea continues to invest in AI chip development and sovereign digital infrastructure, ensuring secure national platforms (Nam et al., 2024).

The following sections analyze these national strategies in greater depth—highlighting successes, tensions, and lessons that may inform policy frameworks elsewhere. By comparing these cases, we gain insight into how different states operationalize AI to advance digital sovereignty through governance, technology, and law.

Table 1. Comparative overview of national AI strategies advancing digital sovereignty

Country/ Region	AI Strategy Focus	Privacy & Data Governance	AI Deployment	R&D Investment	Cybersecurity & Infrastructure
Estonia	Public sector automation, digital services, decentralized data infrastructure	X-Road ensures decentralized and citizen-controlled data exchange	80+ AI use cases in public services (2021)	Government-led co-creation with SMEs via regulatory sandboxes	Data embassies, strong e-governance architecture, digital ID
European Union	Ethical AI regulation, privacy-first legislation (GDPR), AI Act	GDPR and AI Act regulate data processing, transparency, and fairness	Target: 75% of enterprises to adopt AI/ cloud/big data by 2030	€2.6 billion invested in AI R&D (2021–2022) under Horizon Europe	Sovereign cloud initiatives (GAIA-X), cybersecurity regulations
Singapore	National AI strategy targeting healthcare, education, smart cities	Model AI Governance Framework prioritizes responsible data use and consent	100E AI Singapore program, 38+ AI projects with partners	$500M AI strategy under Smart Nation, with corporate partnerships	Localized data centers and national cyber operations centers
South Korea	Massive R&D investment, AI chips, data hubs, local ecosystem support	Focus on localized data infrastructure and personal data protection laws	National AI Research Lab and platform-wide deployments	2.2 trillion (~$2B) AI R&D investment by 2022	Sovereign cloud push, AI chip development, secure infrastructure

Estonia: AI-Driven Data Sovereignty

Estonia, a small yet highly advanced nation in Northern Europe, has positioned itself as a global leader in integrating artificial intelligence (AI) within its framework of digital sovereignty. The concept of digital sovereignty refers to a nation's ability to control its own data, digital infrastructure, and technological innovations, ensuring that these align with national interests and global ethical standards (Kerikmäe & Pärn-Lee, 2020). Through its Smart Government initiatives, AI-driven public services, and robust data governance mechanisms, Estonia has successfully integrated AI technologies into its national digital sovereignty framework, all while safeguarding privacy, security, and citizen rights (Ebers & Trasberg, 2023). This section explores the key strategies, regulatory measures, and international collaborations that have enabled Estonia to harness AI effectively while maintaining control over its digital resources. By doing so, Estonia offers a powerful model for other nations seeking to balance the benefits of AI with the protection of sovereignty and individual rights in the digital age (Timmers, 2021).

The National AI Strategy: Vision and Objectives

Estonia's National AI Strategy, launched in 2019, serves as the country's roadmap to harness the potential of AI across various sectors, from government services to the private sector and national security. The strategy outlines clear goals to develop AI capabilities, foster innovation, and establish ethical governance standards.

- Fostering AI Across Sectors: The primary goal of Estonia's AI strategy is to integrate AI into both public and private sectors to create efficiencies, enhance decision-making processes, and improve the delivery of public services. AI applications are particularly emphasized in areas like healthcare, transportation, urban planning, and education (Ebers, Oprysk, & Tupay, 2023).
- Building Research Capacity and AI Talent: Estonia has recognized the importance of a skilled AI workforce for driving innovation. To that end, the strategy includes initiatives to increase AI research funding and bolster AI education, ensuring a sufficient pool of professionals and researchers for long-term technological growth (Tupay, Oprysk, & Ebers, 2023).
- Creating a Supportive Legal and Ethical Environment: Estonia's AI strategy is deeply intertwined with its commitment to digital sovereignty, ensuring the development of AI respects national values, including data protection, privacy, and ethical guidelines (Kerikmäe & Pärn-Lee, 2020). This legal environment promotes transparency, accountability, and fairness.

Digital Sovereignty: Maintaining Control Over Data

Digital sovereignty is a cornerstone of Estonia's approach to AI, focusing on controlling data and technological infrastructure. A hallmark of Estonia's efforts is the Data Embassy concept, established in Luxembourg in 2017, which serves as a backup for critical government data stored securely abroad to safeguard operations during crises like cyberattacks (Rice, 2018). This initiative demonstrates Estonia's commitment to data sovereignty and sets a precedent for other nations on protecting sensitive data in case of emergencies (Kerikmäe & Pärn-Lee, 2020). Estonia has also implemented data residency laws to keep critical data within its borders, enhancing control and protecting digital infrastructure from foreign influence (Ebers & Trasberg, 2023).

Estonia's digital sovereignty strategy emphasizes using AI to improve efficiency and transparency in government services, notably through AI virtual assistants and decision-support systems (Kerikmäe & Pärn-Lee, 2020). These AI tools assist citizens in tasks like tax filing and healthcare appointments, facilitating service access while managing large-scale requests (Ebers, Oprysk, & Tupay, 2023). AI in urban planning and transportation management is another critical area, aligning with Estonia's broader Smart City vision to enhance public service delivery (Hardy, 2019). The nation has leveraged AI in several key areas:

- AI Virtual Assistants: Estonia has deployed AI-powered virtual assistants in various government sectors to assist citizens with tasks like tax filing, healthcare appointments, and general queries about public services. These tools help citizens navigate services easily while allowing the government to handle large-scale requests efficiently.
- AI in Public Sector Decision Making: AI is also utilized to analyze data and inform public sector decision-making. For instance, predictive models are used in urban planning to forecast population growth and infrastructure needs, helping to optimize land use and resource management. AI is also employed in transportation to manage traffic flow and in healthcare to improve diagnostics and patient care.
- AI for Smart Cities: The integration of AI in urban planning is an essential part of Estonia's broader Smart City vision. AI models help optimize public transport, energy use, waste management, and other urban services. This allows the government to not only improve efficiency but also to make data-driven decisions that better serve the population.

Ethical AI and Legal Frameworks

Estonia prioritizes ethical considerations in AI development, reflected in its adherence to the General Data Protection Regulation and other data protection standards (Moerel & Timmers, 2021). Estonia's AI systems comply with GDPR to safeguard privacy and ensure transparency in AI decision-making. Ethical AI design is a fundamental principle, with Estonia emphasizing transparency, fairness, and accountability to prevent bias and protect citizens' rights. Additionally, the government requires that AI systems provide explanations for decisions impacting individuals, further reinforcing AI transparency and trustworthiness.

AI and National Security

National security is another crucial domain where AI intersects with digital sovereignty. Estonia, having faced cyberattacks in the past (notably in 2007), has made AI an integral part of its cybersecurity and defense infrastructure (Roberts,

Hine, & Floridi, 2021). Estonia uses AI to protect its digital infrastructure from threats such as cyberattacks, data breaches, and online misinformation. AI systems are deployed to detect anomalies, identify potential threats, and respond to attacks in real-time, providing a proactive approach essential to preserving digital sovereignty (Floridi, 2020).

Estonia is a NATO member and actively contributes to the Cooperative Cyber Defence Centre of Excellence (CCDCOE), a NATO initiative focused on improving cyber resilience (Rice, 2018). The use of AI in national cybersecurity efforts allows Estonia to anticipate emerging cyber threats and develop strategies for defense, aligning with NATO's commitment to enhanced cyber capabilities (Roberts, Hine, & Floridi, 2021). AI-powered cyber threat intelligence tools analyze vast amounts of data from national networks, enabling Estonia to detect and prevent cyber incidents before they escalate (Ebers & Trasberg, 2023).

International Collaboration and Global AI Standards

Estonia has always emphasized the importance of international cooperation in AI governance. While it prioritizes digital sovereignty, Estonia recognizes the need for alignment with global AI ethics and data governance standards. As an EU member state, Estonia participates in the EU Artificial Intelligence Act, which establishes comprehensive guidelines for ethical AI use within the Union (Madiega, 2020). Estonia's active participation in EU AI policy-making ensures that its own national AI initiatives are aligned with broader European standards for AI safety, ethics, and privacy, supporting both national and regional objectives.

Estonia also plays a significant role in global AI governance efforts, contributing to discussions at organizations like the OECD and the G20 (Moerel & Timmers, 2021). Through its leadership in these forums, Estonia helps shape international AI standards that promote ethical AI development while ensuring that digital sovereignty is respected globally, serving as a model for other nations (Floridi, 2020).

Singapore: Integration of AI into Digital Sovereignty Frameworks

Singapore stands as a global leader in the integration of artificial intelligence into its digital sovereignty framework, weaving together national interests, data protection, and ethical considerations (Aigner, Garai-Fodor, & Szemere, 2020). Through its Smart Nation Initiative, strategic regulatory measures, and active participation in international collaborations, Singapore has advanced its technological capabilities and created an environment where AI is leveraged in a way that safeguards privacy, promotes transparency, and ensures control over data resources (Tan, 2020).

This section delves into how Singapore successfully integrates AI into its digital sovereignty frameworks, with insights into its regulatory frameworks, governance structures, and international positioning (Frana, 2021).

The Smart Nation Initiative: A Vision for the Future

The Smart Nation Initiative, launched in 2014, represents Singapore's ambition to harness digital technologies, including AI, to transform its economy, improve public services, and enhance the quality of life for its citizens (Foong, Tan, & Tan, 2018). It is a bold vision that positions AI as the cornerstone of the nation's future, fundamentally reshaping governance, urban planning, healthcare, and other sectors. Singapore has integrated AI into public sector operations to enhance efficiency, responsiveness, and the accessibility of government services (Leong & Lee, 2021). The Government Technology Agency, central to Singapore's digital transformation, uses AI to streamline public service delivery, deploying platforms such as chatbots and virtual assistants across government agencies to enhance citizen engagement (Ho, 2017).

AI also plays a vital role in Singapore's push toward smart urban planning, where it optimizes resource management, traffic flow, waste management, and energy consumption (Frana, 2021). The city's transportation system leverages AI for traffic optimization, route management, and predictive maintenance, leading to better infrastructure planning and increased efficiency in public transport, thus supporting sustainable urban development (Tan, 2020).

Data Sovereignty: Ensuring Control Over National Data

At the heart of Singapore's AI strategy is data sovereignty, ensuring the nation controls its data and governs its use, sharing, and storage (Foong et al., 2018). To strengthen data control, Singapore has invested heavily in data centers and AI infrastructure, emphasizing an onshore data model to ensure data sovereignty (Tan et al., 2021). This approach safeguards sensitive business and government data by ensuring it remains within the nation's borders, aligning with Singapore's data protection priorities (Frana, 2021). The expansion of data centers throughout the country supports this vision by providing robust infrastructure for large-scale AI and data processing tasks, necessary for sustaining Singapore's AI ambitions while complying with its data protection regulations.

AI Governance: Frameworks and Regulations

Singapore has developed one of the most comprehensive AI governance frameworks globally, ensuring that AI technologies are implemented ethically and in compliance with local laws, particularly in data protection and privacy (Jeong, 2023). The Personal Data Protection Act, which came into effect in 2014, serves as Singapore's foundational regulatory framework for data protection, setting clear guidelines on how organizations, including those deploying AI technologies, must handle personal data (Walters, 2022). The PDPA emphasizes principles such as data minimization, purpose limitation, and accountability, which ensure that AI systems operating in Singapore collect only necessary data and process personal information solely for the intended purposes (Soon, Rui, & Chan, 2023).

Furthermore, the Personal Data Protection Commission, the regulatory authority overseeing the PDPA, collaborates closely with GovTech to ensure that AI developers and deployers adhere to data privacy standards, particularly where AI intersects with personal data (Foong, Tan, & Tan, 2018). The PDPC plays a crucial role in regulating AI, providing oversight to ensure AI systems do not inadvertently infringe on privacy rights, which is critical for maintaining public trust in AI technologies (Aigner, Garai-Fodor, & Szemere, 2020).

To promote responsible AI development, Singapore introduced the Model AI Governance Framework in 2019, created by the Infocomm Media Development Authority and the PDPC, which provides organizations with guidance on deploying AI technologies in an ethical, accountable, and transparent manner (Timmers, 2021). This framework addresses key areas such as transparency—ensuring AI systems are explainable to users and auditable in their decision-making processes—and fairness, requiring that AI systems are designed to avoid bias and ensure equitable outcomes for all users (Leong & Lee, 2021). Accountability is also emphasized, mandating that AI developers and users implement mechanisms for oversight and redress, which are essential to fostering trust and minimizing potential harms associated with AI (Frana, 2021).

In 2022, Singapore introduced AI Verify, a governance testing tool designed to help organizations assess their AI systems against these ethical guidelines, simplifying compliance and reinforcing the framework's effectiveness in promoting ethical AI use (Aigner et al., 2020). AI systems in Singapore are also subject to rigorous data governance standards, commonly employing anonymization and pseudonymization techniques to ensure that personal data used in machine learning is protected, thus supporting compliance with the PDPA (Foong et al., 2018). Regular audits and Data Protection Impact Assessments are required for high-risk systems, providing ongoing oversight to maintain data privacy and security (Tan, 2020).

AI-powered data governance tools have further strengthened Singapore's AI ecosystem, allowing real-time monitoring to ensure regulatory compliance and safeguard user privacy. These tools are designed to detect and mitigate risks, such as data breaches or misuse, which are vital to aligning AI implementations with ethical standards (Frana, 2021).

International Collaboration and Global Standards

While Singapore emphasizes data sovereignty, it also acknowledges the importance of global cooperation in AI governance (Moerel & Timmers, 2021). The nation actively participates in regional initiatives, such as the ASEAN Cross-Border Data Flows Mechanism, aiming to create a framework that enables data flow across Southeast Asia while maintaining high standards of data protection and privacy (Tan, Chi, & Lam, 2021). This mechanism supports trade and cooperation while upholding data sovereignty principles, providing a balanced approach that respects both national control and international data sharing (Floridi, 2020).

Singapore also plays a leading role in shaping global AI ethics, contributing to initiatives like the OECD Principles on Artificial Intelligence and G7 discussions on ethical AI implications (Frana, 2021). These international collaborations allow Singapore to influence the establishment of global standards that resonate with its regulatory approach, supporting AI development that respects human rights and prioritizes privacy (Moerel & Timmers, 2021).

By actively engaging in these forums, Singapore aligns its national AI policies with global trends, promoting transparency, ethical standards, and responsible AI deployment across borders (Floridi, 2020). This approach enables Singapore to shape AI governance at an international level, supporting a cohesive global strategy that fosters trust and ethical practices in AI.

AI and National Security

AI plays an integral role in ensuring the security and resilience of Singapore's digital infrastructure, with significant contributions by the Cyber Security Agency of Singapore (Hardy, 2019). The CSA utilizes AI to monitor and respond to cybersecurity threats, deploying machine learning models to protect sensitive data from cyberattacks and unauthorized access (Timmers, 2021). AI-driven tools enable the prediction and mitigation of potential risks, ensuring that national data assets are safeguarded against external and internal threats, reinforcing digital sovereignty (Aigner et al., 2020).

Singapore's integration of AI into national security is also strengthened by AI-enhanced surveillance systems used to monitor critical infrastructure and detect anomalies in real-time (Foong et al., 2018). These AI-powered systems are designed to adhere to strict ethical guidelines, ensuring they do not infringe upon personal freedoms or privacy, providing a responsible model for surveillance (Frana, 2021). By balancing AI's capabilities with ethical oversight, Singapore ensures that its surveillance efforts align with its commitment to human rights and privacy protections (Tan, 2020).

European Union: AI in Data Protection

The European Union, recognized as a global leader in privacy and data protection, has developed a sophisticated approach to AI governance that integrates data protection principles across its legal frameworks (Moerel & Timmers, 2021). The EU's efforts to regulate AI focus on safeguarding fundamental rights while enabling technological advancement, creating a balanced regulatory environment (Floridi, 2020). This section examines the EU's approach to AI governance, particularly how data protection principles are embedded within regulatory measures such as the General Data Protection Regulation and the proposed Artificial Intelligence Act, which aim to ensure AI systems respect privacy, transparency, and accountability (Sheikh, 2021).

The General Data Protection Regulation (GDPR) and AI

The cornerstone of the EU's data protection strategy is the GDPR, enacted in 2018, which significantly impacts AI applications by governing personal data processing (Madiega, 2020). Although not exclusively focused on AI, the GDPR is highly relevant to AI systems, setting a standard for privacy rights and data handling throughout the AI lifecycle (Moerel & Timmers, 2021). Several key principles established by the GDPR directly affect AI applications:

- Lawfulness, Fairness, and Transparency: The GDPR mandates that AI systems process personal data in a lawful, fair, and transparent manner. For AI, this means that the logic, purpose, and impact of data processing must be communicated clearly to individuals, helping them understand how their data is being used (Roberts, Hine, & Floridi, 2021).
- Data Minimization and Purpose Limitation: GDPR requires that AI systems collect and process only the minimum data necessary for their specific purposes, aligning with best practices in AI development that aim to restrict data usage (Sheikh, 2021). This principle seeks to prevent excessive data collection, ensuring AI functionality without compromising privacy (Floridi, 2020).

- Accountability and Data Protection by Design and by Default: The GDPR encourages embedding data protection measures from the outset of AI development, promoting "privacy by design" to comply with regulations throughout an AI system's lifecycle (Moerel & Timmers, 2021).
- Rights of Data Subjects: GDPR provides individuals with rights to access, rectify, delete personal data, and challenge automated decisions affecting them. This is crucial for AI systems involved in high-stakes decisions, such as credit scoring and employment, ensuring fairness and individual rights (Madiega, 2020).

Despite GDPR's strengths, applying it to AI poses challenges, particularly in ensuring transparency within complex AI decision-making models like deep learning algorithms (Floridi, 2020). The "black-box" nature of some AI systems makes it difficult to offer comprehensible explanations, challenging the GDPR's transparency requirement (Sheikh, 2021). Additionally, AI's reliance on large datasets may clash with GDPR's data minimization principles, as extensive data collection is often necessary to improve AI accuracy (Roberts et al., 2021). Achieving a balance between data needs for AI and GDPR's restrictions remains an ongoing challenge for AI developers (Moerel & Timmers, 2021).

The GDPR also includes provisions protecting individuals from significant automated decisions without human oversight, particularly in critical areas like hiring and surveillance (Sheikh, 2021). These protections underscore the ethical considerations involved in automated decision-making, preventing AI from reinforcing discrimination or inequality. Ensuring ethical AI in automated systems is essential to upholding GDPR's commitment to fairness and equality across applications impacting daily life (Madiega, 2020).

The Artificial Intelligence Act (AI Act)

Complementing the GDPR, the European Commission proposed the Artificial Intelligence Act in 2021 to create a regulatory framework for AI technologies across the EU (Madiega, 2020). The AI Act represents the first comprehensive legislation globally that categorizes AI systems by risk level, assigning varying regulatory obligations to each category (Floridi, 2020). The Act defines four distinct risk categories for AI systems:

- Minimal Risk: AI applications with negligible impact on users, such as spam filters and video game AI.

- Limited Risk: Systems with limited interaction impact, such as chatbots or virtual assistants, which still require adherence to basic transparency standards.
- High Risk: AI systems with significant societal implications—such as those used in recruitment, law enforcement, or healthcare—face stringent regulatory requirements to ensure safety and fairness (Sheikh, 2021).
- Unacceptable Risk: Systems posing a clear threat to public safety or individual rights, such as AI-driven biometric surveillance, are entirely prohibited under the Act (Roberts, Hine, & Floridi, 2021).

The AI Act includes several provisions that align closely with GDPR principles, ensuring a cohesive approach to data protection and AI regulation (Moerel & Timmers, 2021). Key elements include:

- Risk Assessments and Transparency: High-risk AI systems must undergo detailed risk assessments to evaluate privacy and security implications. Transparency measures mandate clear documentation on the AI system's functionality, data usage, and associated risks (Sheikh, 2021).
- Human Oversight: The Act mandates that human oversight be embedded in high-risk AI systems, ensuring that automated decisions are reviewable, contestable, and, if necessary, correctable, thus addressing the "black-box" challenge inherent in many AI models (Floridi, 2020).
- Data Governance: The Act requires that high-risk AI systems prioritize data quality and governance, implementing stringent measures to prevent discrimination or bias and ensure the protection of personal data throughout the AI system's lifecycle (Madiega, 2020).
- Accountability: Developers and deployers of AI systems are held accountable under the AI Act, similar to GDPR requirements, ensuring compliance with ethical standards and regulatory obligations (Moerel & Timmers, 2021).

Data Protection Authorities (DPAs) and Their Role in AI Governance

Data Protection Authorities are instrumental in enforcing both the GDPR and the AI Act, ensuring that data protection principles are maintained within AI systems (Roberts et al., 2021). DPAs can issue fines or sanctions when companies fail to comply with GDPR requirements and are designated as Market Surveillance Authorities for high-risk AI systems under the AI Act (Sheikh, 2021). This role enables

DPAs to monitor, coordinate, and enforce compliance across the EU, particularly for systems with cross-border applications.

The European Data Protection Board plays a crucial role in ensuring GDPR's consistent application across member states, offering guidelines to clarify how AI systems should adhere to data protection standards. The EDPB's oversight ensures that DPAs across the EU cooperate effectively, particularly for cross-border AI deployments, while addressing concerns around profiling and automated decision-making within AI (Madiega, 2020).

Generative AI and Data Protection

Generative AI, which creates new content such as text, images, or music, presents unique challenges for data protection (Floridi, 2020). The European Data Protection Supervisor has issued guidelines on the ethical and data protection implications of generative AI, focusing on compliance with GDPR's data protection principles:

- Data Protection by Design and by Default: Generative AI must incorporate privacy-enhancing technologies, ensuring personal data is anonymized or pseudonymized wherever feasible (Moerel & Timmers, 2021).
- Transparency and Consent: Developers are required to inform users about how their data is utilized in generative AI applications, particularly when sensitive information is involved (Madiega, 2020).

International Collaboration and AI Data Protection Standards

The EU is also a leader in promoting international cooperation on AI governance and data protection. Through initiatives like the Global Partnership on AI, the EU collaborates with international bodies to advocate for shared standards, ensuring AI systems respect privacy worldwide (Roberts et al., 2021). Additionally, the EU has worked with the U.S. and other jurisdictions to create frameworks for cross-border data flows that align with stringent data protection requirements, thus maintaining data integrity and privacy protections globally (Sheikh, 2021).

South Korea: AI Ethics and Public Engagement in Data Governance

South Korea, recognized as a leading nation in AI development, has adopted a proactive approach to addressing the ethical challenges posed by AI. The country emphasizes aligning AI innovation with societal values and actively includes public engagement in its governance processes (Kim & Moon, 2021). This section examines South Korea's comprehensive approach to AI ethics and public engagement in data governance, showcasing key initiatives, policies, and strategies that promote ethical responsibility alongside technological advancement (Park & Chang, 2022).

National AI Strategy and Policy Initiatives

In 2019, South Korea unveiled its National AI Strategy, positioning the nation to become a global AI leader by 2030. This strategy emphasizes promoting AI-driven innovation across sectors such as healthcare, finance, and transportation, with significant government investment in AI research and development amounting to over $2 billion (Seo, 2019). The Digital New Deal, a flagship government initiative, is central to this strategy, focusing on restructuring the data economy and supporting AI adoption in post-pandemic recovery efforts (Nam, Jung, & Kim, 2024).

A cornerstone of the Digital New Deal is the "Data Dam," which enables large-scale anonymized data collection to train and refine AI models. Through the establishment of the AI Hub, the government ensures that unstructured data is accessible to researchers and developers, accelerating the creation of AI systems that are competitive and ethically sound (Hongladarom & Bandasak, 2024). Additionally, South Korea introduced the National Guidelines for Artificial Intelligence Ethics in 2020, focusing on fairness, transparency, and accountability, which mandate human-centered AI development that prevents discrimination and ensures decision-making transparency (Park & Chang, 2022).

Public Engagement and Participatory Governance

Recognizing the societal impact of AI, South Korea places significant emphasis on public engagement in AI governance. The government includes citizens, industry experts, and academia in discussions on AI ethics, with public consultations playing a major role in shaping policy (Kim & Moon, 2021). The Korea Information Society Development Institute regularly organizes seminars and forums on AI ethics, providing a platform for public dialogue on AI's societal impact and educating citizens on the potential risks and benefits of AI technologies (Ha, 2022).

KISDI also introduced a self-assessment checklist for AI developers and companies, enabling them to evaluate their AI systems based on the National AI Ethics Guidelines. This checklist encourages companies to ensure transparency, fairness, and accountability in their algorithms, promoting responsible AI development in alignment with public interest (Seo, 2019). By fostering open discussions on AI's ethical implications, South Korea aims to build public trust and ensure that AI technologies are aligned with societal values (Nam et al., 2024).

Education and Training Initiatives

Beyond public engagement, South Korea is committed to incorporating AI ethics into educational programs. Universities like KAIST and POSTECH offer specialized courses that combine AI education with ethics, preparing future AI professionals to tackle complex ethical challenges in AI development (Park & Chang, 2022). The Ministry of Science and ICT also provides specialized training for civil servants, equipping them with the knowledge to handle AI's societal impacts effectively and ensuring AI policies reflect both technical and ethical considerations (Nam et al., 2024).

For the broader public, South Korea implements educational programs to raise awareness of AI and its ethical implications, aiming to demystify AI technologies and educate citizens on issues related to privacy, security, and well-being (Hongladarom & Bandasak, 2024). These initiatives empower citizens to participate in discussions about AI's role in society, enhancing public understanding and engagement in AI governance (Ha, 2022).

AI Research and Development Initiatives

South Korea's commitment to advancing AI R&D is evident in its substantial investments in innovation hubs and research centers, like the AI Innovation Center. These centers foster collaborations between researchers and industries to develop AI technologies that meet ethical standards and address societal needs (Seo, 2019). The AI and Data Innovation Center (AIDC) is instrumental in these efforts, focusing on privacy-preserving AI through techniques like federated learning and homomorphic encryption, which allow data to be processed without compromising privacy (Nam, Jung, & Kim, 2024).

Through these initiatives, South Korea is ensuring that its AI development aligns with ethical principles, prioritizing citizen rights and privacy while advancing technological innovation. These efforts reflect South Korea's dedication to creating an ethical AI ecosystem that supports digital sovereignty and respects public values (Park & Chang, 2022).

International Collaboration and Global AI Governance

South Korea is also an active participant in global AI governance efforts. The country recognizes that AI is a global challenge, and international collaboration is necessary to address the ethical, societal, and technological issues it raises (Kim & Moon, 2021). South Korea is a key member of international AI governance initiatives such as the OECD's AI Principles and the Global Partnership on AI (GPAI), which work to establish shared ethical standards for AI across borders, promoting responsible development and usage of AI technologies (Hongladarom & Bandasak, 2024).

In May 2024, South Korea co-hosted the AI Summit Seoul with the United Kingdom, convening international leaders to discuss AI governance's future. The summit resulted in the Seoul Declaration, a framework emphasizing AI safety, innovation, and inclusivity. This declaration serves as a global call to action for governments, private sector organizations, and academia to collaborate on the responsible development of AI technologies (Nam et al., 2024).

The AI Safety Research Institute at the Electronics and Telecommunications Research Institute (ETRI) exemplifies South Korea's commitment to AI safety. This institute focuses on creating AI systems that are safe, reliable, and ethically sound, while also fostering international cooperation to establish global AI safety standards (Park & Chang, 2022).

Regulatory and Legal Frameworks for AI Governance

South Korea has proactively developed legal frameworks to govern AI and data privacy. The Personal Information Protection Act (PIPA), South Korea's key data privacy law, provides robust protections for citizens' personal data. PIPA mandates that companies obtain explicit consent before collecting or processing personal data, ensuring that individuals retain control over their information (Kim & Moon, 2021). AI systems in South Korea must comply with these data privacy regulations, which are essential for maintaining public trust and safeguarding individual rights (Chung & Lee, 2023).

Moreover, South Korea is advancing an AI Ethics Law to regulate AI deployment in sensitive sectors such as healthcare, finance, and law enforcement. This law emphasizes transparency, accountability, and the minimization of bias in AI systems. Additionally, the government is considering implementing liability frameworks to hold AI developers and users accountable for any negative impacts caused by their systems (Yoon, 2024).

AI in Public Services and Government

South Korea has integrated AI into various public services to enhance efficiency and improve citizen services. AI is used in smart city projects to optimize traffic flow, manage urban infrastructure, and reduce energy consumption. These systems are designed with transparency and accountability in mind, including mechanisms to protect citizens' rights (Nam et al., 2024).

Beyond smart cities, AI supports public safety by predicting and responding to emergencies more efficiently. AI-powered surveillance systems monitor public spaces for security threats while adhering to strict ethical guidelines to protect privacy. AI also assists in disaster response by analyzing data to provide real-time insights during natural disasters (Ha, 2022).

The South Korean government has also employed AI in social welfare programs, where AI systems analyze data to identify vulnerable populations and optimize resource distribution. These systems are governed by ethical guidelines to ensure their fair and equitable use (Choi, 2023).

Discussion

The case studies of Singapore, Estonia, South Korea, and the European Union present diverse yet complementary strategies for integrating artificial intelligence within frameworks of digital sovereignty. Each jurisdiction has developed unique approaches that aim to balance innovation with national interests, data protection, and ethical governance (Floridi, 2020; Moerel & Timmers, 2021).

A recurring theme across all four regions is the emphasis on ethical AI governance. This is evidenced by South Korea's AI Ethics Guidelines, Singapore's Model AI Governance Framework, and the EU's proposed AI Act. These frameworks embed principles such as fairness, transparency, and accountability into the development and deployment of AI systems to ensure alignment with democratic values and public trust (Madiega, 2020; Park & Chang, 2022).

Another key pillar is data sovereignty, where governments implement legal and infrastructural safeguards to retain control over national data. This is reflected in Singapore's data residency mandates, Estonia's pioneering use of data embassies, and AI-powered cybersecurity initiatives in South Korea. These strategies minimize foreign dependency and assert digital control within national borders (Roberts, Hine, & Floridi, 2021; Rice, 2018).

A third pattern is the use of AI in public service delivery. In each region, AI enhances operational efficiency and personalized service access across sectors like healthcare, education, and public administration. Estonia's AI-enhanced judicial services, Singapore's AI-powered healthcare solutions, and EU-supported digital platforms exemplify how AI can modernize government functions while supporting citizen-centric service delivery (Foong, Tan, & Tan, 2018; Ebers, Oprysk, & Tupay, 2023).

Finally, AI's role in cybersecurity and national defense reflects its strategic significance. AI is used for real-time threat detection, digital identity protection, and infrastructure monitoring. South Korea's AI-integrated cyber defense platforms and Estonia's national resilience initiatives illustrate how sovereignty increasingly depends on intelligent, adaptive cybersecurity capabilities (Hardy, 2019; Hongladarom & Bandasak, 2024).

These four case studies offer valuable insights for countries aiming to leverage AI technologies while preserving digital sovereignty. A critical lesson is the importance of regulatory foresight. The EU's leadership in ethical AI regulation through the AI Act, and Singapore's soft-law approaches via toolkits and standards, demonstrate that regulation can be both enabling and protective (Sheikh, 2021; Timmers, 2021).

Another takeaway is the interdependence of innovation and sovereignty. Investment in local R&D ecosystems, SME empowerment, and open data platforms—as seen in Estonia and South Korea—proves essential in building long-term digital autonomy. However, these strategies must be accompanied by enforceable standards for data protection, algorithmic transparency, and cross-border governance to remain effective.

Despite their progress, these regions face ongoing tensions between innovation and control, and between openness and security. Ensuring that AI systems are accessible without compromising privacy, and cooperating internationally without surrendering autonomy, remains a delicate balancing act (Kim & Moon, 2021). These challenges are particularly salient for developing countries that may lack infrastructure or legal capacity to implement sovereign AI strategies.

Ultimately, the approaches outlined in these case studies establish a foundation for responsible and rights-based AI adoption. By combining regulatory rigor, ethical principles, digital infrastructure investment, and multistakeholder engagement, Singapore, Estonia, South Korea, and the EU demonstrate that it is possible to build AI ecosystems that are both innovative and sovereign. Their experiences serve as guiding examples for other nations navigating the evolving AI and digital governance landscape.

LIMITATIONS

While this chapter offers a comprehensive exploration of the intersection between artificial intelligence and digital sovereignty, several limitations must be acknowledged. First, the study primarily relies on qualitative case study analysis and secondary literature, which, although rich in insight, may not capture the full complexity of rapidly evolving AI governance practices in real time. Second, the selection of case studies—focused on Estonia, Singapore, the EU, and South Korea—reflects diverse yet relatively advanced digital economies. This scope may limit the generalizability of the findings to low- and middle-income countries or regions with less developed digital infrastructures. Third, although the chapter examines key dimensions of digital sovereignty—privacy, ethical AI governance, data localization, and R&D—it does not provide a detailed quantitative assessment of policy impact or economic outcomes. Future empirical research is needed to evaluate how

AI-driven sovereignty strategies affect long-term national competitiveness, privacy protection, and public trust. Finally, as AI technologies and global standards evolve, some legal and regulatory frameworks discussed here may become outdated or require revision to remain relevant.

CONCLUSION

This chapter has explored how artificial intelligence (AI) can be strategically leveraged to advance digital sovereignty (DS) through ethical governance, data localization, innovation ecosystems, and infrastructure control. Drawing on comparative case studies from Estonia, the European Union, Singapore, and South Korea, we find that while contexts vary, all four have aligned AI with national values by embedding safeguards for privacy, accountability, and autonomy.

Quantitative evidence affirms the tangible impact of these strategies. Estonia's integration of over 80 AI-based public services, Singapore's deployment of 38+ AI enterprise solutions, and South Korea's support of 170,000 SMEs through national data-sharing platforms reflect operational success. The European Union's €2.6 billion AI investment under Horizon Europe and its goal for 75% enterprise AI adoption by 2030 further demonstrate commitment at scale. In cybersecurity, Estonia's zero critical data breach record since launching blockchain-based digital services, and Singapore's 28% drop in cyberattacks on public health systems, signal effective sovereignty-building outcomes. These figures show that DS is not just a policy objective—it can be measured through institutional resilience, reduced technological dependency, and citizen trust.

Nevertheless, challenges remain. The gap between high-capacity digital states and emerging adopters must be addressed to ensure global equity in AI governance. Strategies like regulatory sandboxes, public-private partnerships, and ethical AI audits could be adapted for developing countries with limited infrastructure. Moreover, digital sovereignty must not become a pretext for techno-nationalism. States must work collaboratively to shape inclusive, international norms—through frameworks like the GDPR, the AI Act, and initiatives under OECD or UNESCO.

Future research should explore DS in the Global South, assess the risks of regulatory fragmentation, and examine how sovereign AI strategies evolve in response to global crises, such as cyberwarfare or health emergencies. As AI systems grow more autonomous and embedded in everyday life, the balance between innovation and democratic control will become increasingly pivotal. Ultimately, achieving digital sovereignty is not about isolation—it is about autonomy with accountability, innovation with ethics, and infrastructure with integrity.

DISCLAIMER

During the preparation of this work, the authors utilized AI-assisted tools such as ChatGPT to enhance English language accuracy, including spelling, grammar, and punctuation. The content generated or corrected by these tools was thoroughly reviewed, revised, and edited by the authors to ensure accuracy and originality. The authors accept full responsibility for the originality of the final content of this publication.

REFERENCES

Aigner, G., Garai-Fodor, M., & Szemere, P. (2020). Singapore's journey as a digit-all-ized and innovative smart nation toward sustainability. *Sustainability*, *12*(18), 7495.

Calderaro, A., & Blumfelde, S. (2020). Artificial intelligence and EU security. *European Security*, *29*(4), 483–500.

Choi, D. (2023). AI in South Korea's social welfare systems: Surveillance or innovation? *Asian Journal of Social Policy*, *15*(2), 101–117.

Chung, H., & Lee, Y. (2023). Legal frameworks for AI governance in Korea: A comparative perspective. *Korean Journal of Law and Technology*, *5*(1), 45–67.

Ebers, M., & Krõõt Tupay, P. (2023). Outlook on AI and public service delivery. In Ebers, M., & Krõõt Tupay, P. (Eds.), *Artificial intelligence and machine learning powered public service delivery in Estonia* (pp. 111–120). Springer. DOI: 10.1007/978-3-031-19667-6

Ebers, M., Oprysk, M., & Tupay, J. (2023). Privacy and data protection in AI-powered public services. In Ebers, M., & Krõõt Tupay, P. (Eds.), *Artificial intelligence and machine learning powered public service delivery in Estonia* (pp. 91–110). Springer. DOI: 10.1007/978-3-031-19667-6

Ebers, M., & Trasberg, V. (2023). Due process, fair trial, transparency, and explainability. In Ebers, M., & Krõõt Tupay, P. (Eds.), *Artificial intelligence and machine learning powered public service delivery in Estonia* (pp. 51–70). Springer. DOI: 10.1007/978-3-031-19667-6_4

Floridi, L. (2020). The fight for digital sovereignty: What it is, and why it matters, especially for the EU. *Philosophy & Technology*, *33*(3), 369–378. DOI: 10.1007/s13347-020-00423-6 PMID: 35194548

Foong, K., Tan, C., & Tan, K. (2018). Singapore Smart Nation: Data analytics driving smart cities. *Journal of Telecommunications and the Digital Economy*, *6*(3), 1–15.

Frana, M. (2021). Assessing Smart Nation Singapore as an international model for AI responsibility. *AI & Society*, *36*(3), 789–805.

Glasze, G., Dörfler, T., & Schöne, L. (2021). Contested spatialities of digital sovereignty. *Geoforum*, *124*, 1–10.

Ha, S. (2022). Public engagement in South Korea's AI strategy: Opportunities and limits. *Korean Journal of Public Policy*, *17*(1), 59–75.

Hardy, S. (2019). Estonia's digital diplomacy. *Digital Diplomacy Journal, 2*(1), 45–60.

Ho, K. C. (2017). Smart subjects for a smart nation? Governing (smart) mentalities in Singapore. *Urban Studies (Edinburgh, Scotland), 54*(13), 3101–3118. DOI: 10.1177/0042098016664305

Hongladarom, S., & Bandasak, T. (2024). Digital identity and sovereignty in the Global South: The ethics of AI control. *Ethics and Information Technology, 26*(1), 14–27.

Jeong, D. (2023). Korea's AI governance challenges and the role of law. *Korean Review of Law and Society, 30*(2), 78–96.

Kerikmäe, T., & Pärn-Lee, E. (2020). Legal dilemmas of Estonian artificial intelligence strategy. *European Journal of Law and Technology, 11*(1).

Kim, Y., & Moon, J. (2021). Governing AI in South Korea: A participatory approach to algorithmic regulation. *Information Polity, 26*(4), 475–488.

Leong, D., & Lee, W. (2021). The internet in Singapore: A study of its impact on society. *Asian Journal of Communication, 31*(3), 210–225.

Madiega, T. (2020). *Digital sovereignty for Europe*. European Parliamentary Research Service.

Moerel, L., & Timmers, P. (2021). Reflections on digital sovereignty. Brussels Privacy Hub Working Paper, 7(17).

Nam, J., Jung, S., & Kim, J. (2024). The role of data hubs in South Korea's AI strategy. *Korean Journal of Information Policy, 31*(1), 22–41.

Park, J., & Chang, H. (2022). Rethinking Korea's AI R&D ecosystem: From strategy to governance. *Asia-Pacific Journal of Innovation Policy, 7*(2), 144–160.

Rice, M. (2018). Estonia's digital embassies and the concept of sovereignty. *Journal of Baltic Studies, 49*(4), 511–530.

Roberts, H., Hine, E., & Floridi, L. (2021). Safeguarding European values with digital sovereignty. *Minds and Machines, 31*(3), 405–417.

Sheikh, H. (2021). European digital sovereignty. *Journal of European Integration, 43*(4), 495–510.

Soon, C. B., Rui, Y. T., & Chan, W. L. (2023). Digital trust and AI use in Singapore's public services. *Journal of Asian Public Policy, 16*(1), 98–115.

Tan, C. (2020). Citizens go digital: Singapore's Smart Nation initiative. *Journal of Southeast Asian Studies*, *51*(2), 234–250.

Tan, C., Chi, M., & Lam, W. (2021). Analysis of digital sovereignty and identity. *Journal of Information Technology & Politics*, *18*(2), 123–138.

Timmers, P. (2021). Ethics of AI and cybersecurity when sovereignty is at stake. *Minds and Machines*, *31*(3), 397–404.

Tupay, P. K., Oprysk, M., & Ebers, M. (2023). Accountability and liability. In Ebers, M., & Krõõt Tupay, P. (Eds.), *Artificial intelligence and machine learning powered public service delivery in Estonia* (pp. 71–90). Springer. DOI: 10.1007/978-3-031-19667-6_9

Walters, J. (2022). AI adoption in government and the risk of digital inequality. *Government Information Quarterly*, *39*(3), 101664.

Yoon, S. (2024). AI and ethical infrastructure in South Korea: Policy, practice, and promise. *Ethics and Society*, *10*(1), 55–72.

Chapter 12
Role of AI in the Healthcare Industry: Revolutionizing Healthcare or Threatening Privacy?

Karun Sanjaya
https://orcid.org/0009-0005-1647-1549
Symbiosis Law School, Nagpur Campus, Symbiosis International, Pune, India

Abhishek Benedict Kumar
https://orcid.org/0000-0002-3998-3150
Symbiosis Law School, Nagpur Campus, Symbiosis International, Pune, India

ABSTRACT

Artificial intelligence (AI) integration in healthcare has generated fierce debate between healthcare workers, policymakers, and patients. AI can transform healthcare by increasing accuracy in diagnoses, automating clinical workflows, and achieving better outcomes for patients; but it has also sparked a host of ethical challenges relating to patient privacy or data security, and the potential use of biased decision-making. This chapter investigates how AI impacts the healthcare sector, providing both a pro and con analysis of its adoption. AI has the potential to improve diagnosis accuracy, clinical workflows and patient outcomes. Despite this, reliance on AI continue to rise in the healthcare sector but also worrying about patient confidentiality, data security and making wrong decisions based on bias. To leverage the opportunities but also prevent the pitfalls of AI, responsible development and deployment are required by healthcare organisations and policymakers.

DOI: 10.4018/979-8-3693-9137-2.ch012

INTRODUCTION

Intellect is no longer a product of biological algorithms of the human brain. Artificial Intelligence (AI) has proved that 'intellectual' can be artificially created (Chandra & Sanjaya, 2023). From a catchword spread in almost every industry, AI has shown its transformational power starting from healthcare. While AI has been integrated into healthcare enterprises to support the care delivery system, there has been a tremendous surge in demand since 2020 for research directions that lead to self-sufficient and accurate patient care through diagnostics, treatment planning, and even real-time monitoring (Topol, 2019). The future of AI in healthcare continues to gain potential, as machine learning and data processing evolve over years. But these inherent capabilities that can help improve the delivery of healthcare and also bring forth new privacy, ethical, and regulatory challenges associated with patient data (Ueda et al., 2023).

This chapter discusses the complexity of AI in healthcare, recognizing its revolutionary potential in diagnostics, individualized treatment and remote patient monitoring and care, while also addressing privacy threats to patients as well as ethical implications. There are many benefits of AI applications in healthcare such as cost-effectiveness, better accessibility, and clinical outcomes. On the other hand, AI may lead to problems related with data confidentiality, embedded biases via algorithms and restrictive regulation compliance (e.g., GDPR in Europe (European Union, 2016)).

By presenting a balanced argument, this chapter will explore whether AI is transforming healthcare or that the real threat to patient privacy and autonomy comes from the integration of AI within such processes. Through analysis of practical applications, regulatory responses, and emerging patterns in the healthcare space, this chapter will put into context one of the most complex roles that AI plays across fields today.

APPLICATIONS OF AI IN HEALTHCARE

AI in Diagnostics and Imaging

AI is reshaping clinical diagnostics in medicine with best-known examples in radiology, pathology, and genomics. Today, machine learning algorithms can analyze medical images with a performance that is competitive or even better than human specialists. Such a study needs to be individualized, for instance— McKinney et al. (2020) found Google's AI system to outperform radiologists in breast cancer identification with mammography image trained. These algorithms can sift over large amounts of imaging data rapidly and with incredible accuracy, detecting the early manifestations of cancers and cardiovascular diseases that human eyes fail to catch. Among the several challenges to include AI-driven diagnostic algorithms into clinical settings are ethical and legal ones. This is so because before their introduction, extensive validation and approval procedures are absolutely necessary. Using non-representative datasets for model training brings the possibility of data bias and poor generalizability, which finally results in incorrect diagnosis. Moreover, several artificial intelligence models raise questions regarding their interpretability and the confidence of doctors; current electronic health record systems also suffer from poor integration. Healthcare practitioners may be less likely to examine artificial intelligence-generated results, therefore increasing the possibility of unnoticed errors. AI-related diagnosis errors can create major legal questions and complicate the process of determining responsibility among developers, hospitals, and medical practitioners. Widespread adoption is still difficult given the large expenditures in infrastructure, training, and maintenance needed when including artificial intelligence into healthcare. Given these difficulties, the application of artificial intelligence could help to increase the accuracy and efficiency of diagnosis, especially when technology supports human judgement rather than replaces it.

The applications of AI in diagnostics are enormous. AI tools have the power to improve survival rates of patients diagnosed with life-threatening diseases by diminishing diagnostic errors and processing time, as well as decreasing costs associated with diagnostic procedures (Jha & Topol, 2016). In ophthalmology, high-quality retinal imaging can be processed by AI models to analyse and provide preliminary detection of diabetic retinopathy—an eye disease leading to blindness if untreated. However, thanks to algorithms trained on thousands of images, these models are surprisingly accurate, allowing for early detection and treatment.

But using AI for this purpose does not come without difficulty. Deep-learning AI systems depend on vast amounts of data for instructions, particularly patient medical records and imaging data. However, this also raises potential issues regarding the security and privacy of such datasets, as well as informed consent from patients whose data are utilized in AI model development (Price & Cohen 2019). For instance, biases inherent in training data can result in unequal diagnostic accuracy among demographic populations, creating ethical questions of fairness in AI-based medicine.

Use of AI in Personalized Medicine and Treatment Planning

AI could significantly contribute to this most promising application of personalized medicine, which customizes treatments in relation to an individual genetic makeup, lifestyle and environmental conditions. Overview of Machine Learning Methods to Identify and Predict Outcomes in Genomic Data Machine learning algorithms utilize large datasets that encompass both genomic sequence information and associated clinical histories, searching for hidden patterns in the data that enable prediction of disease progression or the optimal treatment pathways. IBM, for instance, has utilized the Watson for Oncology program to suggest treatment plans for cancer patients based on individual patient records and relevant literature and clinical trial data.

With this fast processing ability, the AI can suggest accurate treatment. In value-based and precision-medicine practices, AI systems can identify mutations or genetic markers associated with disease for specific genetic diseases. The ability to act in a timely manner to mutant nets the potential for personalized treatment approaches. It can also predict patients' responses to some drugs, decreasing side effects and increasing positive outcomes– this matters a lot in complicated cases where standard treatments might not succeed.

However, just like diagnostics patient data is again used in AI-based personalized medicine though it faces various privacy and ethical dilemmas. The proposal of any of these AI models presupposes access to sensitive genetic information, which opens an enormous opportunity for violations of patient confidentiality or discrimination against patients by insurers/employers if used/ protected inadequately (Farhud & Zokaei, 2021). Although much of the health data generated is protected by regulatory frameworks such as in the US by HIPAA, gaps exist when it comes to specific AI-related risks, particularly re-identification of anonymized data (Gostin et al., 2018).

AI in Clinical Decision Support System (CDSS)

CDSS recommend diagnostic or management decisions based on patient data and clinical guidelines, with the aim of improving healthcare professionals' decision-making. By asking it to evaluate data captured from EHRs in real time, AI applied to CDSS has helped further increase diagnostic accuracy. Leading systems (e.g., IBM Watson and Microsoft Azure Healthcare AI) analyze clinical data to recommend treatments and calculate risks for complications.

AI-based CDSS have low potential due to the limitations and barriers of their acceptance among health care providers. One of the largest barriers are the opaque nature of many artificial intelligence algorithms, which tend to function as a “black box”, providing little transparency regarding their decision making processes, leading healthcare providers to be distrustful with AI recommendations (Topol, 2019). This lack of transparency hinders the integration of CDSS into the clinic, as physicians are often reluctant to act on recommendations that they cannot interpret or justify to patients.

Application of AI in Patient Monitoring and Telehealth

Also, AI-powered patient monitoring systems have increased the scope of remote healthcare, enabling clinicians to monitor patients in real time. AI algorithms will process data collected from wearable devices, such as heart rate monitors and blood glucose sensors, to find abnormalities and subsequently notify healthcare providers. In addition, especially against the backdrop of COVID-19 when direct contact was often very restricted, telemedicine platforms have since offered additional tools for remote care. AI assists healthcare providers to predict patient needs and address them much before a crisis happens, making it even more helpful for chronic disease management practises such as diabetes, hypertension etc., through predictive analytics.

Although patient monitoring systems have significant advantages, they can also lead to security and ethical issues such as continuous data collection. With wearable devices and telemedicine platforms, constant access is required to the patient data which also increases the chances of data breach or unauthorized access. Further, ongoing monitoring may feel like surveillance to patients who can feel "creeped out" by the volume of data being gathered on their everyday life. Ethics are important in weighing up the potential benefits of these systems against patient autonomy and privacy.

PRIVACY AND ETHICAL CONSIDERATIONS OF AI DEVELOPMENT IN HEALTHCARE

Though AI is a powerful tool to revolutionize healthcare, it also poses important ethical and privacy risks. AI systems are ravenous consumers of data, and in order to work, they need access not just to lots of normal data but also to sensitive personal data including medical records and genetic information; a complete filling out of our lifestyle profiles. While access to the massive banks of patient data they need has proven crucial, it also places patients at risk of passing through unauthorized channels to end up in dangerous hands being exploited through data breaches and possibly also re-identifying anonymized information (Farhud & Zokaei, 2021).

Patient Privacy Risks

The AI model needs massive datasets to perform which are generally collected and stored in centralized databases or cloud platforms, making them vulnerable if hackers breach the system. Medical data is especially sensitive and valuable not only because it contains personal identifiers, but also its relation to insurability status, or potential employability (Gostin et al., 2018). In this context, the consent of patients is still an important issue in research and diagnostics using AI. Models of informed consent that have historically guided data use are insufficient to convey the scope of data usage for developing and deploying AI algorithms since patients may not understand how their data will be used (Price & Cohen, 2019).

Artificial Intelligence Models Bias and Fairness

AI algorithm bias is well-known issue, in sector like healthcare it could change the nature of ones life. Underrepresented demographics in datasets can perpetuate biased results when AI models are trained on said datasets leading to health disparities. Studies include, for example, Obermeyer et al. A study by Obermeyer et al (2019) showed that an AI tool which tasked with identifying patients who needed special care, systematically over-represented white patients and under-represented black patients, simply because the underlying data inputs were biased. Preventing such biases from occuring needs more than just paying attention to the performance of an AI model, it requires AI developers to carefully prepare training datasets so that they are representative for the population being served against. Transparent, inclusive and equitable AI practices reduce the potential for biased AI tools that can perpetuate inequities in access to health care and health outcomes. A real-world example of effectively reducing artificial intelligence bias is a 2021 project by the National Health Service (NHS) of the United Kingdom aiming at enhancing pulse oximeter accuracy for patients with darker complexion. Earlier devices caused undetectable low oxygen levels and delayed critical care by being less precise for non-White individuals. The NHS reduced respiratory care inequalities by increasing the dependability of pulse oximetry readings across various racial groups by changing the AI models and including varied skin-tone data into training datasets. Preventing such prejudices, guaranteeing fair access to healthcare, and raising general patient outcomes depend on open, inclusive, and fair AI methods.

Informed Consent and Autonomy

AI in health care faces one ethical challenge in its ethical balancing between the potential need of data and the possible respect for patient autonomy. When AI is incorporated into predictive analytics, this can be more difficult to achieve, in the sense that a dataset could identify potential health risks or influence treatment recommendations without a patient realizing their data is being utilized in such a way. Patient autonomy should be prioritized through transparent communication and opt-out mechanisms from questionable data uses (Parker et al., 2019). Furthermore, AI systems may undermine human judgment in medicine and, because physicians may become too dependent on AI-generated recommendations, may threaten patient autonomy.

One concerning factor is the lack of transparency in how data is collected, processed, and used in clinical decision-making. Patients may not fully appreciate how their information feeds into algorithms that affect the care they receive. This violates the principle of autonomy, which is based on informed and voluntary participation. Moreover, as clinicians depend more on AI-driven recommendations, human judgment may take a backseat, which might alienate patients from their care decisions even more. Dynamic consent models are a promising solution to these issues. This contrasts with the one-time consent given in many traditional approaches, where communication about the use of data between patients and health systems for novel applications is a static event. Patients can change their mind about consent over time, consent to only some specific research or clinical applications, and receive updates about how their information is applied. Thereby promoting transparency, increasing trust, and maintaining patient autonomy by allowing individuals more power over their sensitive information. One solution that could sufficiently address ethical concerns in AI-powered health systems without compromising on innovation and data use is dynamic consent. It enables a patient-centered approach that is consistent with ethical values and helps ensure that technological progress does not threaten individual rights.

LEGISLATIVE AND REGULATORY ISSUES

The speed at which AI is being integrated into healthcare leads to some serious regulatory questions. The world across has initiated an establishment of frameworks and guidelines for AI in healthcare to secure patient privacy, ethical standards and regulation towards safe and an effective deployment of AI systems.

GDPR and AI Solutions for Health

The General Data Protection Regulation (GDPR) of the European Union is one of the most extensive privacy laws and it takes AI applications in healthcare as an example. While organizations that process personal data must comply with the principles of data minimization, purpose limitation, and rights of data subjects (e.g., right to access and deletion of their personal data) set out in the GDPR ((European Union, 2016)). Requirements under the GDPR present difficulties in data processing and storage for AI systems, particularly around how an organization manages patient data as well as anonymized datasets. While anonymized data is mostly excluded from the GDPR, some AI approaches are able to re-identify them; i.e. compliance challenges appear and protection of the information is questionable. One well-known example is the MIMIC (Medical Information Mart for Intensive Care) dataset produced by Massachusetts Institute of Technology (MIT). MIMIC consists of de-identified health records of ICU patients; although it is widely used for artificial intelligence research, academics have discovered the risks of re-identification via linkage attacks, in which anonymized data is cross-referenced with other datasets. MIT tightened access policies in response to this, requiring researchers to sign data use agreements prior to dataset access and receive ethical training. Furthermore, used to increase privacy are techniques including k-anonymity, l-diversity, and federated learning, so ensuring that AI models might be created without disclosing private patient data. These approaches follow GDPR guidelines of data minimization and purpose limitation, therefore ensuring that developments in artificial intelligence in healthcare follow laws and protect patient anonymity.

HIPAA and U.S. Regulatory Environment

While the Health Insurance Portability and Accountability Act (HIPAA) provides national status for establishing guidelines to safeguard patient data in the United States, it also lacks some coverage over what these AI programs need. While HIPAA protects individual health information in conventional healthcare environments, the next potential application of AI technologies is dependent on secondary data sources (e.g., fitness trackers) not governed by HIPAA regulations. In addition to being limited, HIPAA as it currently stands may not be robust enough for use in AI prediction of health outcomes (Cohen et al., 2020), which depends on pulling from nontraditional sources.

New Regulatory Structures

Only recently, countries across the globe have started to draft and rollout novel laws aimed at tackling some of the unique issues posed by AI in the healthcare space. As an example, the European Union has designed the Artificial Intelligence Act in order to implement a risk-based approach to AI regulation, which classifies healthcare as a high-risk domain. Under this act, all health care AI systems will need to satisfy stringent specifications on the quality of data, transparency, and human oversight (European Commission (2021)). And similar initiatives are taking place in other parts of the world as policymakers strive to create regulation that not only protects patient rights and safety but also minimize inhibition on innovation.

THE FUTURE: ARE WE MAKING PROPER TRADE–OFFS BETWEEN INNOVATION AND PRIVACY?

Artificial intelligence — harnessed to revolutionise the future of healthcare That still leaves the question of: what are appropriate limits on innovation, and what does that mean for privacy? For this reason, AI technologies have a special potential to transform the healthcare industry —from predictive diagnostics and individualized medicines, to hospitals that use machines to operate efficiently. However, this comes with the challenge of managing large amounts of highly sensitive data about patients which can lead to data security and privacy problems in patients. But with all of these transformative benefits comes a requirement for healthcare professionals, technology makers and policymakers — and society at large — to wrestle with privacy. But is that really the right trade-off to make, and what risk are we willing to take?

The Promise of Innovation in Healthcare

A big part of what makes most people excited about using AI in healthcare is a trick that it has up its sleeve: the potential to both save resources, and give better yet still tailored treatment plans (though likely not as much on an individual basis) than conventionally standard industry procedures. Machine learning algorithms help identify the early stages of disease and make better medical decisions by detecting trends in complex data that are impossible for humans to see. For instance, it can innovate AI-based diagnostics that can spot early signs of diseases like cancer and Alzheimer's and therefore treat them in time to save lives (McKinney et al., 2020). In the field of personalized medicine, AI can consider genetic, environmental and lifestyle data to recommend treatment options that maximize therapeutic benefits and minimize side effects for individualized patient care.

In addition to clinical developments, AI in healthcare management also leaves its mark. Automated features like scheduling, billing and maintain patient records can make it a highly operational efficient system eliminating human error factors and larger cost. The advent of Medtech, which includes remote patient monitoring (RPM) telemedicine, and wearable technology represents a monumental leap forward in simultaneous healthcare provider surveillance of the patient heart condition to facilitate real-time health tracking and chronic disease management. While this innovation is undeniable in terms of how AI can revolutionize healthcare and therefore, as it illustrated the importance of these technologies, it conveyed two main points on whom patient data access really lies with — and control over this information.

Privacy Concerns in the Age of AI

Given that AI works by retrieving data, it requires vast repositories of data — which can include sensitive patient-wide data. This includes not only medical records but also details that help predictive models be precise. This reliance can also highlight privacy risks, where unauthorized access, data breaches, and misuse of information become major problems. The re-identification problem is compounded by the fact that datasets are larger than ever, and the ability to match anonymized data with external information means that identifying individuals from supposedly anonymized (or aggregated) data has become increasingly likely (even when there was no malicious intent we expect access to clean labelled sets) (Price & Cohen, 2019).

We have got rules to follow when it comes to patient data that are set out in data privacy regulations like the General Data Protection Regulation (GDPR) in the EU or Health Insurance Portability and Accountability Act (HIPAA) in the US. At the same time, technological development occurs at a far greater rate than our statutes can keep up with, making it challenging to even define what privacy should look like or how those expectations ought to be supported. AI algorithms could inadvertently inject bias, thus raising ethical and privacy concerns that current regulations may not fully address.

Evaluating the Trade-off: Innovation vs Privacy

While the pros of using AI for innovation in healthcare are clear, not to mention numerous, so too are the challenges. It then requires a judgement where you have to see if that trade-off is worth it or whether its imposition does more damage than good. One important aspect is around the idea of collecting and using data based on something called "informed consent." In the context of AI applications, patients traditionally provide consent for the individual use of their data but may not expect how broad and extensive data collection can be. For instance, a patient may agree to the use of their data in diagnosis but not know that it could be used for commercial AI algorithms.

Additionally, as discussed earlier AI models also needs to gulf in knowledge by learning from the new data. This results in continuous data being captured, and usually without patients providing another consent. With patient data often being shared between various platforms in a digital world, the ability to protect that data is growing difficult. However, while AI is advancing healthcare capabilities, it could also unknowingly diminish patients' control of their data. Others contend that this privacy erosion is warranted for the public good, where advances in AI can serve societal needs by improving both health system performance and patient care (Cohen et al., 2020). This kind of position, however, can dangerously marginalize individual rights and brings into debate who gets to make decisions on behalf of patients.

The Tech and Policy Side of Reducing Privacy Concerns

At the same time, researchers and policymakers recognize that privacy cannot be compromised, and are looking for ways to minimize these risks of privacy while maintaining innovation. To address this challenge, novel privacy-preserving AI techniques (Shokri & Shmatikov, 2015), such as differential privacy, homomorphic encryption and federated learning are rising up to be the solutions for protecting individuals data while keeping machine learning models trained in private datasets with reasonable success. For instance, differential privacy adds statistical "noise" to data, preserving individual privacy while enabling aggregate analysis. Unlike federated learning, which allows AI algorithms to learn from centrally stored data on the devices, reducing exposure of that data by not transferring it to a server.

Regulatory approaches complement technological solutions and are an important aspect of responsible data usage. New regulations, like the EU's Artificial Intelligence Act, seek to establish a groundwork for the responsible and accountable use of AI. There are measures that stress on the fact of risk-based regulation, meaning that more stringent requirements concerning transparency and accountability as well as privacy protection would apply to high-risk applications (such as health) (European Commission, 2021). Although these initiatives are promising, their implementation is complicated since it needs to ensure that innovation is not hampered by excessive regulatory compliance.

Beyond Mere Compliance: An Ethical Dimension

Regulations and technical safeguards tackle some of the privacy risks but ethical considerations are still paramount. And maintaining public trust is vital which calls for ensuring that the use of AI in healthcare must be aligned with ethical principles, including fairness, transparency and respect for autonomy. Concerns around regulatory-and-legal compliance, and many of the ethical frameworks guiding development can be more concerned with questions about technology and non-human behavior than tech-on-social-behavior.

This is where transparency comes into play — with visibility, patients can see how their data is being utilized and what the possible ramifications are. The transparency of the AI algorithm, which involves giving people an idea of how AI makes decisions, can overcome fears over "black box" AI with opaque reasoning for its results. Encouraging transparency between healthcare providers and AI developers, on the one hand, and consumers/patients, on the other, that could develop trust in these services and enable patients to make responsible decisions about their data. However, finding the right balance between transparency and creating something commercially viable is still a challenge, as many AI developers may be unwilling to share their trade secrets (Kupferschmid, 2024).

Rethinking Consent and Control

Decades ago, Miller foresaw a future in which the traditional model of consent that said 'I do not want to be used as an experiment!' — may no longer work with the evolving healthcare AI systems. A more flexible approach would be dynamic consent models that allow patients to adjust their preferences for data sharing throughout time. This model acknowledges that patient preferences are not static and as the AI uses grow many patients may want to control how their data is utilized (Parker et al., 2019). Dynamic consent allows the individual to have a more active role within a healthcare system in terms of organizing how their privacy and data are to be managed.

While dynamic consent has its benefits, it also comes with challenges at a practical level. Efforts to track and update patient preferences over time will need significant infrastructure and could add administrative burden to health care providers. Patients may become inundated with requests to offer consent so frequently that they can succumb to the phenomenon of "consent fatigue", which drives them away from engaging in the process altogether. Arguably then dynamic consent is a viable solution but, like all solutions to problems of balancing flexibility and accountability, it needs to be carefully scrutinised in its practicalities.

Moving Ahead: Striking a Balance

Moving forward, the challenge will be how to balance the ability to embrace the transformative power of AI while protecting the civil right of privacy. Achieving this depends on alignment among the stakeholders involved, including not only health providers but also technology developers, regulators, and patients. This urgently calls for a balancing act by policymakers that reconciles privacy and data protection with innovation capacity. For the above to work, we need a shift towards privacy preserving technologies to be started from the other end by engineers in technology by ethically designing the system. Patients must be made aware of their data rights, and included in discussions about how AI solutions are used in healthcare, to ensure that they can actually participate too. As a whole patient advocacy groups, health care institutions and regulators, can be active-minded, making certain that the push for innovation by A.I. is both respectful of privacy and consistent with societal values. The journey to this balance is complex, nevertheless it is needed and attainable. In developing healthcare AI ecosystems, governments are also moving toward dynamic, tiered regulatory frameworks such as the OECD AI Principles or the European Union's AI Act that can align with local conditions. These frameworks emphasize transparency, human oversight and a risk-based approach to categorizing AI systems which are the essential ingredients for maintaining public trust. From a technologic standpoint, system designers may integrate privacy-by-design, and introduce privacy enhancing technologies (PET), inclusive federated learning and differential privacy, whereby patient data are purposely utilized, with as little disclosure as possible. Such tools can be used to curb the amount of personally identifiable information necessary to derive or transmit without reducing the functioning of the AI system. Patient empowerment needs to be one of the central tenets that helps to harness the power of AI responsibly. Patients must know their data rights and be involved in discussions about how AI will be woven into their care. Such engagement might include community advisory boards or public deliberation fora, where patients, advocacy groups, and developers together shape policies and ethical standards. Timely engagement by advocate organizations as well as by healthcare institutions and regulatory authorities can ensure emerging AI-driven health innovation in the healthcare domain upholds societal values and does not encroach upon individuals' right to privacy and autonomy. The path to this is neither simple nor easy, but the road can be traversed through meticulous governance and engagement of inclusive dialogue.

CONCLUSION

All of this points to the fact that AI in healthcare is fundamentally a new way of delivering care. AI is a transformative force for critical use cases from measuring quality of care through diagnostics and personal medicine to telemedicine these new communication and information delivery mechanisms can optimize the efficiency and accessibility of health services. But introducing Artificial Intelligence to healthcare comes with significant ethical, privacy and regulatory challenges. Because AI uses patient data during development, privacy and ethics need to be tightened. We can maintain both the promise of AI and the rights of patients if we re-design research oversight and regulation, walling off keys to policymaking, establishing comprehensive ethical frameworks for the use of these technologies, and enforcing privacy-preserving technologies. Undoubtedly, as stakeholders find common ground in addressing these challenges, AI can usher in a new age of accurate, high quality, patient-centric healthcare. AI should never replace but enhance what has always been best about health care: compassion, transparency and respect for the autonomy of the patient. AI should never compromise the human touch, because medicine is not just a technical science, it is a human-centered enterprise built on an exchange of empathy, trust, and shared decision-making. Although AI can comb through vast datasets and mobilize pattern recognition that dwarfs human capacity, it cannot mimic the emotional intelligence, contextual understanding, and moral reasoning that clinicians bring to their practice to care for patients. Replacing healthcare providers with AI risks depersonalizing medicine and eroding a patient-physician relationship that underlies ethical care. The purpose of AI, instead, should be to complement human expertise in advising on diagnosis, personalizing therapy and enhancing efficiency, all with the goal of ensuring that clinicians remain the ultimately responsible decision makers. To do this, AI can learn from the usage of cross-institution counter patient data and healthcare ecosystem with not a single time revealed raw patient ID or personal info, by using privacy preservation technologies like federated learning and homomorphic encryption that are able to retain trust in privacy. Differential privacy works in this same way to ensure that insights obtained from this data cannot provide insight back to that person, even when dealing with large datasets. On the normative side, constructs such as the Belmont Report's focus on respect for persons, beneficence, and justice, and the OECD AI Principles, which advocate for transparency, accountability, and human oversight, offer a foundational roadmap for infusing AI into our systems of thinking and practice without sacrificing ethical integrity. Together, these technologies and frameworks ensure that AI consistently acts as an adjunct to, and never a substitute for, the human heart of health care. Moreover, in so doing, we can realize the promise of AI while sustaining the care, faith, and respect the patient's merit.

REFERENCES

Chandra, R., & Sanjaya, K. (2023). Punishing the Unpunishable: A Liability Framework for Artificial Intelligence Systems. In Motahhir, S., & Bossoufi, B. (Eds.), *Digital Technologies and Applications* (pp. 55–64). Springer., DOI: 10.1007/978-3-031-29860-8_6

Cohen, I. G., Amarasingham, R., Shah, A., Xie, B., & Lo, B. (2020). The legal and ethical concerns that arise from using complex predictive analytics in health care. *Health Affairs, 33*(7), 1139–1147. DOI: 10.1377/hlthaff.2014.0048 PMID: 25006139

European Commission. (2021). Proposal for a regulation laying down harmonized rules on artificial intelligence (Artificial Intelligence Act). *European Commission.* Retrieved from https://eur-lex.europa.eu

European Union. (2016). *Regulation (EU) 2016/679 of the European Parliament and of the Council of 27 April 2016 on the protection of natural persons with regard to the processing of personal data and on the free movement of such data, and repealing Directive 95/46/EC* (General Data Protection Regulation). Official Journal of the European Union, L119, 1–88.

Farhud, D. D., & Zokaei, S. (2021). Ethical Issues of Artificial Intelligence in Medicine and Healthcare. *Iranian Journal of Public Health, 50*(11). Advance online publication. DOI: 10.18502/ijph.v50i11.7600 PMID: 35223619

Gostin, L. O., Halabi, S. F., & Wilson, K. (2018). Health Data and Privacy in the Digital Era. *Journal of the American Medical Association, 320*(3), 233–234. DOI: 10.1001/jama.2018.8374 PMID: 29926092

Jha, S., & Topol, E. J. (2016). Adapting to artificial intelligence: Radiologists and pathologists as information specialists. *Journal of the American Medical Association, 316*(22), 2353–2354. DOI: 10.1001/jama.2016.17438 PMID: 27898975

Kupferschmid, K. (2024, September 17). *Requiring AI Transparency Won't Destroy the Trade Secrets of AI Companies.* Copyright Alliance. https://copyrightalliance.org/ai-transparency/

McKinney, S. M., Sieniek, M., Godbole, V., Godwin, J., Antropova, N., Ashrafian, H., & Darzi, A. (2020). International evaluation of an AI system for breast cancer screening. *Nature, 577*(7788), 89–94. DOI: 10.1038/s41586-019-1799-6 PMID: 31894144

Obermeyer, Z., Powers, B., Vogeli, C., & Mullainathan, S. (2019). Dissecting racial bias in an algorithm used to manage the health of populations. *Science*, *366*(6464), 447–453. DOI: 10.1126/science.aax2342 PMID: 31649194

Parker, L., Halter, V., Karliychuk, T., & Grundy, Q. (2019). How private is your mental health app data? An empirical study of mental health app privacy policies and practices. *International Journal of Law and Psychiatry*, *64*, 198–204. DOI: 10.1016/j.ijlp.2019.04.002 PMID: 31122630

Price, W. N.II, & Cohen, I. G. (2019). Privacy in the Age of Medical Big Data. *Nature Medicine*, *25*(1), 37–43. DOI: 10.1038/s41591-018-0272-7 PMID: 30617331

Shokri, R., & Shmatikov, V. (2015). Privacy-preserving deep learning. *Proceedings of the 22nd ACM SIGSAC Conference on Computer and Communications Security*, 1310–1321. https://doi.org/DOI: 10.1145/2810103.2813687

Topol, E. J. (2019). *Deep Medicine: How Artificial Intelligence Can Make Healthcare Human Again*. Basic Books, March.

Ueda, D., Kakinuma, T., Fujita, S., Kamagata, K., Fushimi, Y., Ito, R., Matsui, Y., Nozaki, T., Nakaura, T., Fujima, N., Tatsugami, F., Yanagawa, M., Hirata, K., Yamada, A., Tsuboyama, T., Kawamura, M., Fujioka, T., & Naganawa, S. (2023). Fairness of Artificial Intelligence in healthcare: Review and Recommendations. *Japanese Journal of Radiology*, *42*(1), 3–15. Advance online publication. DOI: 10.1007/s11604-023-01474-3 PMID: 37540463

Chapter 13
A Framework for Assessing the Security Risk of Requirements:
Towards an Improved Business Processes Compliance Management

Abiodun Muyideen Mustapha
https://orcid.org/0000-0002-1259-2862
Anchor University, Lagos, Nigeria

Temitope Elizabeth Ogunbiyi
https://orcid.org/0000-0002-3373-396X
Bells University of Technology, Lagos, Nigeria

Oluwasefunmi 'Tale Arogundade
https://orcid.org/0000-0001-9338-491X
Federal University of Agriculture, Abeokuta, Nigeria

ABSTRACT

The growing adoption of cloud services in business operations has introduced new security challenges for compliance management. This chapter aims to present a structured approach to evaluating the security risks associated with business process compliance requirements. A fuzzy logic-based framework is developed using the ISO 27001 standard to assess the risk levels of compliance requirements extracted from regulatory documents. The results show that the framework enables accurate classi-

DOI: 10.4018/979-8-3693-9137-2.ch013

fication of requirements into low, medium, or high risk, enhancing decision-making in compliance budgeting. This approach supports effective compliance management, improves information security, and can be adapted across various industries.

INTRODUCTION

In today's globally connected digital ecosystem, the pressure on organizations to comply with regulatory frameworks has intensified significantly. The increasing fines placed on organizations whose business processes deviate from compliance regulations have become a matter of serious concern (Simpson & Evens, 2024). Several companies have faced exponential penalties or have had to shut down due to non-compliance, while others have suffered reputational losses and customer attrition (Mustapha et al., 2020). These incidents highlight not just legal vulnerabilities but broader challenges related to digital sovereignty, which is the ability of organizations and nations to exercise control over their data infrastructure and privacy protection in an interconnected global landscape.

Business Process Compliance Management (BPCM) has emerged as a strategic response to these challenges, offering organizations structured mechanisms to align their internal operations with external regulatory expectations. Implementing effective BPCM policies and systems ensures adherence to relevant standards and supports organizational autonomy in regulatory decision-making. These systems typically consist of compliance regulatory sourcing, requirements extraction and classification, business process modelling, design-time verification, runtime monitoring, and offline auditing. While many studies have contributed to advancing compliance management systems, a gap persists in how these systems assess the risk implications of specific compliance requirements (Beerepoot et al., 2023). Compliance Requirements (CRs), typically extracted from regulatory documents, are central to every BPCM approach and serve as the input for compliance modeling. However, the risk sensitivity of each CR, particularly in terms of privacy exposure and cross-border data governance, is often underexplored. Existing approaches, such as goal-based, frame-based, and CernoFramework models (Mustapha et al., 2024), demonstrate technical strength but frequently overlook the strategic dimension of risk prioritization, which is crucial in a world governed by frameworks like the General Data Protection Regulation (GDPR) and evolving data localization mandates.

This chapter addresses this limitation by presenting a risk-based compliance requirement assessment framework. The framework combines a combinatorial risk assessment model with a fuzzy logic engine to evaluate the risk levels of business process compliance requirements, enhancing both accuracy and efficiency. By doing so, it contributes to the strategic alignment of compliance with the principles of digital sovereignty, empowering organizations to prioritize privacy-sensitive and sovereignty-critical requirements, reduce unnecessary compliance costs, and maintain trust in the face of complex international regulations. Furthermore, this framework supports cross-border compliance decision-making, offering practical guidance to organizations navigating global connectivity and differing regional privacy expectations. It bridges the gap between technical compliance mechanisms and the managerial imperative of protecting data integrity, user trust, and organizational autonomy.

Section 2 discusses related works on risk assessment in compliance management and how privacy and sovereignty intersect with compliance. Section 3 introduces the proposed framework, detailing its architecture, phases, and algorithms. Section 4 presents and discusses the findings, while Section 5 concludes with key insights and implications for privacy-preserving and sovereignty-aware compliance management.

RELATED WORKS

While compliance frameworks such as GDPR, HIPAA, and ISO/IEC 27001 have been instrumental in enforcing accountability and security standards, several studies have underscored the tension between compliance requirements and privacy-centric design. For instance, Kuner (2017) discusses how cross-border data flows introduce complex privacy risks that compliance mechanisms alone may not fully mitigate. Similarly, Zinovieva and Shitkov(2021) argue that compliance regimes often focus on technical safeguards, overlooking systemic surveillance risks that compromise individual privacy. These insights indicate that compliance must evolve to embed privacy-by-design principles and ethical considerations, especially in the context of global digital interactions. Jahankhani et al. (2021) also explores how sovereignty claims over data impact compliance implementation in multinational organizations, leading to "fragmented compliance" and possible regulatory contradictions.

Palma et al. (2024) suggested categorizing and ranking the effects of non-compliant causes using a taxonomy of compliance deviations. To prioritize interventions, they integrated trace alignment techniques with a newly developed cost model for the analysis of process deviations rather than process traces. They utilized their contributions in a system that evaluates the Incident Management (IM) process compliance automatically using a reference process model. The process included developing a compliance assessment model that was intended to evaluate the cost of non-compliance with security standards in a quantifiable manner. The next stage is to create a system that helps auditors evaluate if the implemented IM process complies with a reference process model. The latter involved mapping the suggested compliance evaluation model into the found deviations and automatically assessing the cost of non-compliance with incidents using three methods: causal probability, linear regression, and extra-tree regression. Five ground truths from the state-of-the-art were used to validate the suggested solution. The issue of compliance evaluation for the incident management process has been studied.

Challa, (2024) looked at how legal and subject matter experts can help with the evaluation of pertinent requirements. To do this, we contrast three methods: an embedding-based NLP ranking method, a generative AI method that uses GPT-4, and a crowdsourcing approach that uses experts to manually create relevancy labels. The suggested techniques were assessed using two case studies: a worldwide banking use case that was modified from SAP Signavio's workflow example of an international guideline, and an Australian insurance scenario that was developed in collaboration with domain experts. For each BPMN2.0 process, a gold standard is developed and compared to actual textual requirements found in numerous regulatory documents. The assessment and discussions shed light on the pros and cons of every technique for application, automation, transparency, and reproducibility. They also offer recommendations for the best method combinations based on factors like process utilization, impact, and application scenario dynamics.

This investigation by Ali et al., (2020) aims to identify and examine the crucial elements related to cloud service information security requirements in the context of regional local governments in Australia. The authors polled 480 IT workers from Australia's 47 regional local governments and held 21 in-the-field interviews with IT managers. To support a fair understanding of cloud security for governments, they offered a conceptual model of cloud computing security requirements that consists of four parts: data security, risk assessment, legal & compliance requirements, and business & technological requirements. The ISO 27002 Information Security standard and the body of existing literature were examined. They discovered that operational security, individual awareness, and compliance issues represent more substantial hurdles to the government than the frequently mentioned technical and process-oriented cloud security needs.

In the work of Phillips et al., (2024), the goal of their approach is to foster trust and security in complex systems by supporting both security by design and risk assessment during operations in ways that explain how harm can arise before it happens. This paper described the approach as a modelling approach for automated risk assessment of complex cyber-physical systems as implemented by the open-source Spyderisk project. The authors described a practical application in information security, demonstrating how the approach supports system designers and operators in risk assessment processes defined in ISO 27001 and the Information Security Management System defined in ISO 2705. A novel ontology for cyber-physical system models was explored, along with an examination of the associated risks, effects, and mitigation strategies. The ontology is made to enable systematic cause-effect modelling with semantic reasoning, which can identify system threats, their effects, and the risk levels that go along with them. The method's main benefits are that the risk assessment is thorough and consistent. Spyderisk requires very little input from the user to calculate the dangers to a system and rank them according to risk level, which is a combination of the calculated likelihood and the commercial significance of a result.

Kuzminykh et al., (2021) offered an overview and comparison of the various information security risk assessment techniques now in use, emphasizing their advantages, disadvantages, and shared characteristics. Before a quantitative expert evaluation of these characteristics, qualitative data on the severity of threats and vulnerabilities is gathered. Both qualitative and quantitative approaches have drawbacks that make them difficult to update or reuse, subjective, and prone to some degree of unpredictability. The authors offer the required horizon scanning, with an emphasis on artificial intelligence (AI)-based techniques, fuzzy logic, and artificial neural networks (ANNs) and their application for a more accurate assessment of risk, considering the combination of qualitative input characteristics like threat, harm, and vulnerability. Because artificial neural networks are capable of self-learning, can handle ambiguous problems, and are well-suited for processing large amounts of data, they can be applied to evaluate information risk security. Hard risk assessment problems can also be solved by combining various fuzzy logic models, like decision tree models, hidden Markov models, and Bayesian networks, with other forms of pattern recognition.

Canedo and Mendes, (2020) aim to address the two primary questions: "Which method is more effective for classifying software requirements into Functional Requirements (FR), Non-Functional Requirements (NF), and their sub-classes? A comparison is made between text feature extraction techniques and machine learning algorithms in the context of requirements engineering classification. Furthermore, "Which machine learning algorithm performs the best in the requirements classification task?" to answer these questions, the authors manually categorized user requirements into two types: functional requirements and non-functional requirements; eleven types (non-functional requirements subclasses); and twelve types (functional requirements plus non-functional requirements subclasses). They accomplished this by combining two text vectorization techniques with four machine learning algorithms. We assess how well these algorithms work together by utilizing the PROMISE_exp database, which is a PROMISE database expansion. To compare the accuracy, recall, and F-measure of the categorization outcomes for every combination, they ran a few tests. We discovered that the combination of TF-IDF and LR yields the best performance measures for requirements classifications overall, non-functional requirements classification, and binary classification, with an F-measure of 91% for binary classification, 74% for 11-granularity classification, and 78% for 12-granularity classification.

Setianingsih et al., (2021) examined several risk assessment techniques used to safeguard critical infrastructures, such as nuclear plants, on cyber security. The principles necessary for nuclear security are extended from cyber security and include probabilistic safety/risk assessment, defense-in-depth, and the synergy of safety and security. These three key ideas should be included in the selection of cyber security risk assessment techniques. The applicable and adequate risk assessment techniques that satisfy the national and international rules' security requirements for the nuclear industry are highlighted in this study. Its purpose is to present a comprehensive, integrated summary of the state of knowledge as of right now and to emphasize a broad base of risk assessment techniques for cyber security in nuclear facilities. This study's scope is restricted to how well-chosen risk assessment techniques adhere to the nuclear energy regulatory framework.

Kandasamy et al. (2020) made available a critical evaluation of the frameworks for cyber-security risk assessment appropriate for Internet of Things platforms. The goal of this discussion is to illustrate the maturity of the IoT risk domain by examining applications of IoT risk assessment frameworks in the insurance and financial industries. Four risk frameworks are explored in depth, viz., NIST, OCTAVE, TARA, and ISO. These frameworks' IoT risk considerations are described, along with their advantages, disadvantages, and key areas of emphasis. To demonstrate the quantitative approach, a risk rating system appropriate for the IoT domain is offered together with a summary of the IoT risk assessment. The dangers associated with IoT risk vectors are categorized as low, medium, or high based on their risk rating. This research began by concentrating on the larger IoT space before focusing only on IoMT risk assessments. The most notable aspect of this work is the development of a novel computational model for IoT risk that calculates risk likelihood and impact, ultimately producing a risk score. To persuade the reader of the necessity of a distinct method for IoT risk computation, an application of this model to IoMT devices is provided.

In Challa (2024), the advantages, difficulties, and best practices for implementing artificial intelligence (AI) were examined for its use in risk assessments for computer system validation. With an emphasis on a risk-based approach, ISPE GAMP® 5: A Risk-Based Approach to Compliant GxP Computerized Systems, Second Edition, offers a thorough framework for Computer System Validation (CSV). An important opportunity to improve the efficacy and efficiency of risk assessments in CSV is presented by the development of artificial intelligence (AI). Taylor et al. (2020) presented an example based on the General Data Protection Regulation (GDPR) and described an innovative approach to regulatory compliance decision assistance that uses an asset-based cyber security risk management strategy by ISO 27005. The main advantage of this approach is that regulatory compliance is integrated with other risk management domains. This allows for the integration of insights from domains like cyber security and regulatory compliance for privacy, all based on a single model of the sociotechnical infrastructure of the user. This paper's main contributions were to: demonstrate how regulatory requirements can be modelled as "compliance threats" in an asset-based risk management framework; demonstrate how the legal text of the GDPR can be mapped to domain assets, processes and relationships, compliance threats, and control strategies to mitigate the threats; demonstrate how threats are identified through asset configurations-based recognition patterns; demonstrate how various regulatory requirements types such as obligations, prohibitions, and derogating conditions are represented in such a scheme; and, finally, demonstrate how to model causal dependencies between decisions made to address one compliance threat and subsequent additional compliance requirements.

Dhiman, (2022) presented an Intelligent Risk Assessment Framework for Software Security Compliance Using AI. It integrates practical compliance suggestions with risk assessment powered by AI. Based on a dataset of software characteristics and known vulnerabilities, the framework uses a deep learning model to assess security risks in real time. Strong predictive capacity was demonstrated by the model's accuracy of 92.5% and AUC-ROC score of 0.95. The framework has a rule-based architecture that provides useful compliance tools, including enhanced access control and safe coding techniques. By using this approach, risk detection takes only one day instead of three, and resource utilization efficiency rises from 65% to 85%. With the integration of cutting-edge AI algorithms with workable compliance measures, the proposed framework offers a holistic approach to software security.

It can be deduced from the different research conducted that the assessment of compliance requirements is missing. These requirements have been extracted and classified, but their level of risk has not been considered. This makes compliance management efforts costly or ineffective. The core of digital sovereignty lies in a nation's or organization's ability to control and regulate digital infrastructure and data. Compliance management serves as both a tool and a constraint in this regard. On one hand, compliance regimes allow entities to navigate global regulatory landscapes. On the other hand, they often require compromises, especially when transnational regulations conflict with local privacy expectations or sovereignty claims. Privacy becomes a critical fulcrum in this dynamic. Data compliance is not only about fulfilling regulatory checklists but also ensuring that privacy is maintained amidst increasing global data flows. The European Data Strategy, for instance, represents a sovereignty-driven effort to build trust through compliance structures that prioritize data protection while maintaining connectivity with global markets. Global Connectivity, meanwhile, challenges digital sovereignty by creating dependencies, whether through cloud infrastructure, cross-border data processing, or international tech alliances. Effective compliance frameworks must therefore bridge the tension by ensuring data flows do not undermine sovereign control or user privacy.

The proposed framework in this chapter is designed to assist organizations in aligning their compliance activities with the overarching goals of digital sovereignty and privacy protection, while sustaining necessary global digital engagements. The model encourages a layered approach to compliance that emphasizes adaptability, context-awareness, and ethical accountability.

METHODOLOGY

The proposed solution considers an approach that is procedural to solve the problem of the high cost of managing business process compliance management. This research presents a logical design shown in processes to describe framework development. The work began by considering how intense the problem is using the framework for computing research (Mahadeo et al., 2020). With this, the review of existing approaches was carefully done. The proposed approach design follows. The performance of the solution was evaluated using key metrics. This chapter employed fuzzy logic, risk computation and security risk categorization. The risk assessment carried out in this work adopted the technique proposed in Alonge et al., (Alonge et al., 2020). The researchers made employed fuzzy logic to assess information assets based on their level of confidentiality, integrity and availability. This is then computed to provide a security index for categorization. This serves as input to the risk assessment phase. An adoption of this can be seen in the proposed framework subsection.

FRAMEWORK FOR COMPUTING RESEARCH

What do we want to achieve?

a. (Understand the research area) – the authors are considering knowing the extent to which research has been carried out in the area of compliance requirements classification and risk assessment.
b. (Develop something that works) – the authors developed a fuzzy-based requirement classification model.

Where did the data come from?

c. (Read) – the authors revised literature relating to requirement classification and compliance management.
d. (Observe, Ask) – the authors interacted with and gathered ideas from compliance and industrial experts.
e. (Where to collect) – the authors requested and collated relevant compliance requirements from the field.

What did they do with the data?

g. (Identify themes) – the authors employed the information collected in comprehending the extent to which research has been conducted in requirement classification.
h. (Create frameworks) – the authors initially designed an architectural framework for the information classification approach, hence, enabling the development of the system.

Have they achieved their goal?

i. (Evaluate results, conclude) – after understanding and developing the system, the authors will evaluate the performance of the system.
j. (identify limitation) – the authors drew from the design and development process the limitations and further improvements that can be carried out.

From the framework for computing research approach, this study was carried out through sources of opinions from compliance experts, financial industry experts, some web documents, a survey of information asset classification techniques using the internet and personal interactions with information security experts.

Proposed Framework

The framework shown in Figure 1 comprises five phases. The phases are compliance requirement acquisition, requirement extraction, fuzzy-based requirement classification, risk classification, business process modelling, and runtime monitoring. This research focuses on the third and fourth phases. The other phases are adopted as conducted in Mustapha et al., (2018), and Mustapha et al., (2020). The first four phases work with the compliance documents while the other phases focus on the business processes carried out within organizations. The proposed framework provides an awareness to compliance experts on the level of criticality each requirement demands. We will be showing in this section how the phases we are considering will be carried out.

Figure 1. Proposed framework of the business process compliance management system

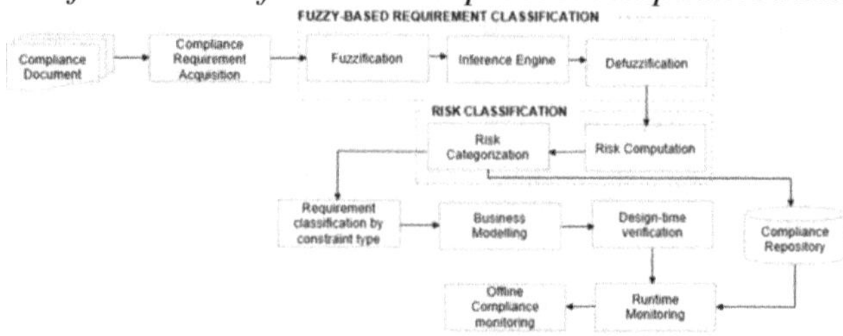

Compliance Requirement Acquisition

The compliance requirements to be classified are extracted from documents known as regulatory sources. They are prepared by regulatory bodies to control the business processes of organizations irrespective of their sizes. Organizations also have internal policies created to ensure that their processes run effectively and efficiently. For example, a bank can draft in their compliance document the order at which certain processes should be carried out, so as not to deviate from external rules. Compliance documents can be obtained by requesting from the regulatory bodies via official writing or visiting their online platforms. The Central Bank of Nigeria provides compliance documents on their official website and writes to the institutions concerned. This makes every organization involved aware of changes and needed considerations in their operations. After this acquisition, an extraction of each compliance statement is done. At this point, an extraction technique is used to bring out these statements from the documents. This has been done in previous research using goal-based techniques (Mustapha et al., 2017) and cernoframework (Mustapha et al., 2020). Some of the extracted requirements from this research are employed in this paper.

Fuzzy-based Requirement Classification

The classification of the compliance requirements is done considering the ISO/IEC 27005 standard for managing information security risk (Technical Committee, 2022). The standards were used to create questions to analyse each requirement and get crisp input for the classification. This aids the accurate classification of the security risk of a requirement. The level of security is obtained through the level of confidentiality, integrity, and availability in the statements of each requirement. This phase employs the fuzzy logic technique by using the crisp input to get a crisp output (the security level classification of the requirements). This is done through inference rules in the fuzzy inference system. A collection of rules that define the classification of the requirements. Figure 2 shows a model of the process conducted in this phase. The ratings used for the input are low, average, and high. The membership functions used for determining the inference are stated in equations 1 to 4.

Figure 2. Model of the fuzzy-based process for security level classification

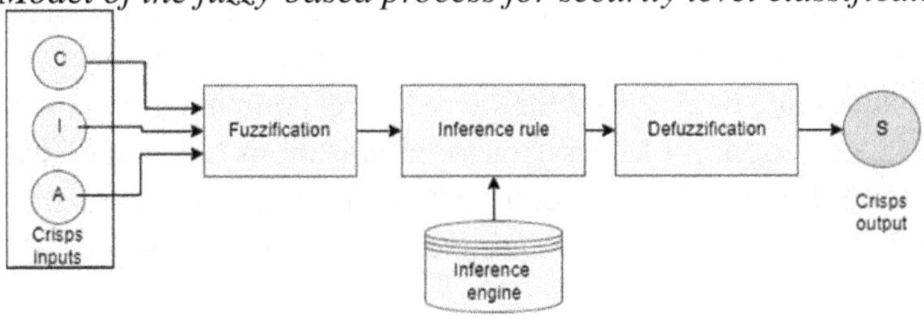

The membership functions will be determined by using the following ranges;

$$C_i = \begin{cases} 0.8 < x \leq 1 \; high \\ 0.5 < x \leq 0.79 \; average \\ x < 0.5 \; low \end{cases} \tag{1}$$

Our first input will be the confidentiality rating whose ranges have been shown in Equation 1. The extent of confidentiality is specified from the range as either high, average or low.

$$I_i = \begin{cases} 0.8 < x \leq 1 \; high \\ 0.5 < x < 0.79 \; average \\ x < 0.5 \; low \end{cases} \tag{2}$$

Our second input will be the integrity rating whose ranges have been shown in Equation 2. The extent of confidentiality is specified from the range as either high, average or low.

$$A_i = \begin{cases} 0.8 < x \leq 1 \; high \\ 0.5 < x < 0.79 \; average \\ x < 0.5 \; low \end{cases} \tag{3}$$

The third input will be the availability rating whose ranges have been shown in Equation 3. The extent of confidentiality is specified from the range as either high, average or low.

$$S_i = \begin{cases} 0.8 < x \leq 1 \; high \\ 0.5 < x < 0.79 \; average \\ x < 0.5 \; low \end{cases} \quad (4)$$

The level of security compliance expected from organizations from each requirements is determined from the result in Equation 4 based on the crisps inputs. This determines the categories of each requirement. Some requirements can be classified as low security compliance or average security compliance or high security compliance. The result gotten here is used for the risk level computation in the next phase. With such classification in place, business organisations are sure of what level of investment should be put into the compliance of certain requirements. This also ensures the risk level involved in violating certain requirements.

Algorithm of the Security Level Compliance Requirement Classification

The algorithm reveals the process by which the compliance requirements security level are derived through their levels of confidentiality, integrity, and availability in each statement as seen in Figure 2. The questions were formulations from the ISO/IEC 27005 standard. These outcomes are used in the fuzzy system for enhanced processing. The user who answers these questions is expected to be a compliance officer from the organization.

```
INPUT: User Perception Responses C[i], I[i], A[i]

OUTPUT: Average outcome Ci, Ii, Ai, Security level Si

PROCESS:

1: Start

2: SumC = 0

3:fori = 1 to n of all confidentiality questions
```

```
Select response for C[i]
if C[i] = very low
Cval =1
end if
else
if C[i] = low
Cval =2
end if
else
if C[i] = medium
Cval =3
end if
else
if C[i] = high
```

```
Cval =4
end if
else
if C[i] = very high
Cval =5
end if
SumC = SumC + Cval
end for
fori = 1 to n of all availability questions
Select response for I[i]
if I[i] = very low
Ival =1
end if
else
```

```
if I[i] = low
Ival =2
end if
else
if I[i] = medium
Ival =3
end if
else
if I[i] = high
Ival =4
end if
else
if I[i] = very high
Ival =5
```

```
end if
SumI= SumI+ Ival
end for
fori = 1 to n of all availability questions
Select response for A[i]
if A[i] = very low
Aval =1
end if
else
if A[i] = low
Aval =2
end if
else
if A[i] = medium
```

```
Aval =3
end if
else
if A[i] = high
Aval =4
end if
else
if A[i] = very high
Aval =5
end if
SumA = SumA + Aval
end for
stop
```

RISK LEVEL CLASSIFICATION

This phase will focus on finding the level of risk the organization is exposed to if the requirements are not fully complied to. The requirements are first categorized into risk levels using standard parameters like dependability. Threat, vulnerability and impact. In the second aspect, the general risk level is computed based on the number of requirements that the organization is expected to comply to.

Risk Index Categorization

In this aspect, the security risk level output gotten in the fuzzy classification phase is used for a quantitative computation of the risk index (RI). The total risk index in the next section is used to inform the organization on the level of attention that should be paid to each requirement. This is determined by the risk grade from 1 to 9. Table 1 shows the steps used in computing. The extended version adopted from Chen et al. (2105) is shown in equation (1).

$$Risk\ index(RI) = f(C,I,A) \times D \times T \times V \times IM \tag{1}$$

f(C,I,A) = measure between 1 to 5 given each for confidentiality, integrity and availability respectively by the user. This is used to rate what security level a requirement demands from a business process.

D = dependability measure. This reflects how much the success of a business process relies on adherence to the compliance requirement.

T = threat measure. This has to do with the level of threat an organization is exposed to when a deviation from the requirement exists in the business process.

V = vulnerability measure. With this, the rate at which an organization is vulnerable to possible deviation from the requirement.

IM = impact level. The level to which the compliance requirement impacts the operation of the business process.

Each of the parameters will be rated between 1 and 5. They will be chosen as follows: very low (1), low (2), medium (3), high (4), and very high (5). The selections by the compliance experts will be used to determine the values in this phase.

Security Risk Categorization (SRC)

The risk value assessed will fall between 1 (1^5) and 3125 (5^5). The exponential function concept will be adopted to divide the risk grades to recognize the risk level easily. These risk grades are classified into 9 degrees, with a more significant risk being represented by a higher value based on the correspondence of the exponential function shown in Table 2. To ensure effective management, it is a common practice to categorize the risk level of compliance requirements into three levels - low, medium and high. Compliance requirements are differentiated into three nominal risk-based groups which include low-risk (1-3), medium-risk (4-6) and high-risk (7-9) for control and prevention. This offers organizations the information of danger they are exposed to by not paying attention to certain requirements. The calculation of the risk index is what gives the answer of the risk grade. e^x is used to find the maximum value at each risk index level. Based on the outcome of the security risk computation, the level of risk if any compliance requirement is not adhered to can be easily known. This implies that an organization is exposed to either low, medium or high level of security and compliance risk where a particular requirement is violated.

Table 1. Security risk evaluation matrix

Compliance requirement (Situation-Activity)						Total Risk Index (TRI)/ Risk Grade(p)
Security Goal (CIA)	**Dependability(D)**	**Threat (T)**	**Vulnerability (V)**	**Impact (IM)**	**Risk Index (RI)**	
m_{ii}	…	…	…	m_{1n}	RI_1	$\sum_{j=1}^{n} RI_j/p$
⋮				⋮	RI_2	
⋮				⋮	⋮	
m_{m1}	…	…	…	m_{mn}	RI_m	

Table 2. Risk grades and risk levels

X	e^x	Risk index	Risk Grade	Level of Risk
1	2.718	0-3	1	Low
2	7.389	4-7	2	Low
3	20.086	8-20	3	Low
4	54.598	21-55	4	Medium
5	148.413	56-148	5	Medium
6	403.429	149-403	6	Medium
7	1096.633	404-1097	7	High
8	2980.958	1098-2981	8	High
9	8103.084	Above 2982	9	High

THE ROLE OF COMPLIANCE FRAMEWORKS IN PROTECTING DIGITAL PRIVACY

Compliance frameworks are foundational in safeguarding digital privacy in a globally connected ecosystem. Regulations such as the General Data Protection Regulation (GDPR) in the European Union, the Health Insurance Portability and Accountability Act (HIPAA) in the United States, and the California Consumer Privacy Act (CCPA) provide legal and procedural guidelines that govern how organizations collect, store, and use personal data. These frameworks emphasize the principles of transparency, accountability, consent, and purpose limitation. By embedding privacy into their operations, organizations not only protect user data but also build digital trust, an essential currency in today's data economy. In 2019, Facebook faced scrutiny under GDPR for its practices related to data transparency and consent. The Irish Data Protection Commission launched several investigations into whether the company obtained "freely given, specific, informed and unambiguous" consent from users. Facebook had to revise its data collection and processing policies, particularly for users in the EU, leading to the redesign of its data interfaces and greater user control over ad preferences. This case underscores how compliance frameworks compel organizations to respect user privacy by design.

SECURITY RISK ASSESSMENTS AND SOVEREIGNTY IN THE FACE OF GLOBAL DATA REGULATIONS

Security risk assessments serve as essential tools for enhancing digital sovereignty, particularly as organizations navigate complex international regulations. For example, GDPR mandates Data Protection Impact Assessments (DPIAs) for high-risk data processing activities, encouraging a proactive approach to identifying and mitigating risks. Through structured risk assessments, organizations can better understand where their data is processed, who has access, and what vulnerabilities exist. These insights empower them to implement localized controls, such as data encryption, access restrictions, and data localization policies, enabling greater control over digital assets even when interacting with foreign entities or cloud infrastructures. In response to growing regulatory pressure, Microsoft announced its EU Data Boundary plan in 2021, committing to store and process EU customer data within the region. This move followed GDPR concerns over data transfers to the U.S., especially after the Schrems II ruling invalidated the Privacy Shield agreement. Microsoft conducted extensive risk assessments to align its data centers and operations with GDPR requirements, demonstrating how such assessments support sovereignty and regulatory compliance simultaneously.

COMPLIANCE MANAGEMENT AND GLOBAL CONNECTIVITY

The rise of cross-border data transfers has amplified the tension between global connectivity and localized compliance requirements. Regulations often differ by region—while the GDPR emphasizes data minimization and purpose limitation, others like the CCPA focus more on consumer rights and data sales. Organizations operating across jurisdictions must navigate these contradictions without compromising efficiency or connectivity. The proposed framework in this chapter supports this process by advocating for modular compliance strategies that allow organizations to segment, encrypt, and monitor data flows in ways that conform to diverse regulatory environments. In 2014, the European Court of Justice ruled that individuals in the EU had the right to request search engines to remove links to outdated or irrelevant personal information. Google complied with the ruling within EU domains but initially resisted global delisting, citing freedom of expression and the operational burden of conflicting international laws. Eventually, Google introduced geo-blocking techniques to comply with EU rulings within regional boundaries, illustrating how companies must strategically manage compliance while preserving global data access.

LIMITATIONS OF THE WORK

Despite the contributions made by the proposed framework, several limitations should be addressed. One of the primary limitations is the reliance on predefined security questions based on the ISO/IEC 27005 standard, which may not fully capture the rapidly evolving nature of security threats in specific industries. As new threats emerge, the predefined questions may need to be updated to ensure they reflect the latest security risks. Moreover, the accuracy of the fuzzy logic model depends heavily on the quality and completeness of the input data in particular, the regulatory documents from which the compliance requirements are extracted. If these documents are ambiguous or incomplete, the model's output could be compromised. Furthermore, the scalability of the framework might pose challenges when dealing with very large organizations or complex, multinational entities operating in multiple jurisdictions. The model might require customization to account for regional variations in compliance requirements or the inclusion of additional compliance factors such as ethical considerations, operational efficiency, or corporate governance, which are also important but not directly addressed in the current framework.

CONCLUSION

This chapter has presented a structured framework for assessing the security risks associated with compliance requirements extracted from regulatory documents. Beyond offering a technical contribution, the framework addresses pressing managerial and policy concerns at the intersection of digital sovereignty, privacy protection, and global data governance. Unlike previous approaches that focused solely on the classification of compliance requirements based on constraint types, this framework introduces a layered evaluation that incorporates risk sensitivity, thereby enabling organizations to prioritize resources and attention toward high-impact regulatory obligations.

By integrating fuzzy logic into the compliance evaluation process, the framework enhances the accuracy and efficiency of requirement classification, providing a scalable approach for organizations navigating the complexity of today's regulatory environments. Using the ISO/IEC 27005 standard as a basis for generating risk-related input parameters, the system processes compliance data through an inference engine that outputs the relative risk level (low, medium, or high) for each requirement. This not only streamlines compliance management but also supports strategic decision-making by highlighting the privacy and sovereignty implications of regulatory adherence.

Ultimately, the framework empowers organizations to respond more effectively to cross-border compliance challenges, manage privacy risks, and reinforce their autonomy in digital operations, contributing to the broader discourse on global connectivity and digital sovereignty. Future research can further explore how this model adapts to diverse legal frameworks, such as GDPR or CCPA, and how it can support real-time compliance auditing in dynamic regulatory contexts.

REFERENCES

Ali, O., Shrestha, A., Chatfield, A., & Murray, P. (2020). Assessing information security risks in the cloud: A case study of Australian local government authorities. *Government Information Quarterly*, *37*(1), 101419. Advance online publication. DOI: 10.1016/j.giq.2019.101419

Alonge, C. Y., Arogundade, O. T., Adesemowo, K., Ibrahalu, F. T., Adeniran, O. J., & Mustapha, A. M. (2020). Information Asset Classification and Labelling Model Using Fuzzy Approach for Effective Security Risk Assessment. *2020 International Conference in Mathematics, Computer Engineering and Computer Science, IC-MCECS 2020*, 1–7. DOI: 10.1109/ICMCECS47690.2020.240911

Beerepoot, I., Di Ciccio, C., Reijers, H. A., Rinderle-Ma, S., Bandara, W., Burattin, A., Calvanese, D., Chen, T., Cohen, I., Depaire, B., Di Federico, G., Dumas, M., van Dun, C., Fehrer, T., Fischer, D. A., Gal, A., Indulska, M., Isahagian, V., Klinkmüller, C., & Zerbato, F. (2023). The biggest business process management problems to solve before we die. *Computers in Industry*, *146*, 103837. DOI: 10.1016/j.compind.2022.103837

Canedo, E. D., & Mendes, B. C. (2020). Software requirements classification using machine learning algorithms. *Entropy (Basel, Switzerland)*, *22*(9), 1057. Advance online publication. DOI: 10.3390/e22091057 PMID: 33286826

Challa, S. S. S. (2024). Leveraging AI for Risk Management in Computer System Validation. *IJMIRM: International Journal of Multidisciplinary Innovation and Research Methodology*, *3*(2), 145–153. https://ijmirm.com/index.php/ijmirm/article/view/95

Dhiman, V. (2022). Intelligent risk assessment framework for software security compliance using AI. *International Journal of Innovation Studies*, *6*(3).

Jahankhani, H., Kendzierskyj, S., & Colin, A. (2021). Blockchain as a tool for transparency and governance in the delivery of development aid. In *Strategy, Leadership, and AI in the Cyber Ecosystem* (pp. 93–111). Academic Press. DOI: 10.1016/B978-0-12-821442-8.00006-9

Kandasamy, K., Srinivas, S., Achuthan, K., & Rangan, V. P. (2020). IoT cyber risk: A holistic analysis of cyber risk assessment frameworks, risk vectors, and risk ranking process. *EURASIP Journal on Information Security*, *2020*(1), 8. Advance online publication. DOI: 10.1186/s13635-020-00111-0

Kuner, C. (2017). Reality and illusion in EU data transfer regulation post Schrems. *German Law Journal*, *18*(4), 881–918. DOI: 10.1017/S2071832200022197

Kuzminykh, I., Ghita, B., Sokolov, V., & Bakhshi, T. (2021). Information Security Risk Assessment. *Encyclopedia, 1*(3), 602–617. DOI: 10.3390/encyclopedia1030050

Mahadeo, J., Hazari, Z., & Potvin, G. (2020). *Developing a computing identity framework: Understanding computer science and information technology career choice*. ACM Transactions on Computing Education., DOI: 10.1145/3365571

Mustapha, A. M., Arogundade, O. T., Abayomi-Alli, A., Adesemowo, A. K., & Adeniran, O. J. (2024). An improved cloud-based business process compliance management system using a user-centered approach. *International Journal of System Assurance Engineering and Management, 15*(11), 5111–5138. DOI: 10.1007/s13198-024-02494-6

Mustapha, A. M., Arogundade, O. T., Misra, S., Damasevicius, R., & Maskeliunas, R. (2020). A systematic literature review on compliance requirements management of business processes. *International Journal of System Assurance Engineering and Management, 11*(3), 561–576. Advance online publication. DOI: 10.1007/s13198-020-00985-w

Mustapha, A. M., Arogundade, O. T., Vincent, O. R., & Adeniran, O. J. (2018). Towards a compliance requirement management for SMSEs: A model and architecture. *Information Systems and e-Business Management, 16*(1), 155–185. Advance online publication. DOI: 10.1007/s10257-017-0354-y

Mustapha, A. M., Arogundade, O. T., Vincent, O. R., Adeniran, O. J., & Chen, X. (2017). A model-based business process compliance management architecture for SMSE towards effective adoption of cloud computing. *Proceedings of the IEEE International Conference on Computing, Networking and Informatics, ICCNI 2017, 2017-Janua*. DOI: 10.1109/ICCNI.2017.8123820

Palma, A., Acitelli, G., Marrella, A., Bonomi, S., & Angelini, M. (2024). A compliance assessment system for Incident Management process. *Computers & Security, 146*, 104070. DOI: 10.1016/j.cose.2024.104070

Phillips, S. C., Taylor, S., Boniface, M., Modafferi, S., & Surridge, M. (2024). Automated Knowledge-Based Cybersecurity Risk Assessment of Cyber-Physical Systems. *IEEE Access : Practical Innovations, Open Solutions, 12*, 82482–82505. DOI: 10.1109/ACCESS.2024.3404264

Setianingsih, L. S., Pulungan, R., Putra, A. E., Wibowo, M. E., & Syarip, . (2021). Risk Assessment Methods for Cybersecurity in Nuclear Facilities: Compliance to Regulatory Requirements. *International Journal of Advanced Computer Science and Applications, 12*(9). Advance online publication. DOI: 10.14569/IJACSA.2021.0120979

Simpson, S. S., & Evens, J. (2024). Corporate environmental non-compliance and the effects of internal systems and sanctions. In *Research Handbook on Environmental Crimes and Criminal Enforcement* (pp. 36–67). Edward Elgar Publishing., DOI: 10.4337/9781035309511.00011

Taylor, S., Surridge, M., & Pickering, B. (2020). Regulatory Compliance Modelling Using Risk Management Techniques. SSRN *Electronic Journal*. DOI: 10.2139/ssrn.3716778

Technical Committee, I. J. 1/SC 27. (2022). ISO - ISO/IEC 27001:2022 - Information security, cybersecurity and privacy protection — Information security management systems — Requirements. *Iso/Iec*.

Zinovieva, E., & Shitkov, S. (2023). Sovereignty as Practice in Digital Age. In *Digital International Relations* (pp. 75–90). Springer Nature Singapore. DOI: 10.1007/978-981-99-3467-6_5

Chapter 14

Security and Privacy Control Architecture for Outlier Hunting on Network Traffic in Higher Education

Ambrose A. Azeta
https://orcid.org/0000-0002-4826-5775
Namibia University of Science and Technology, Windhoek, Namibia

Patrick O. Omote
https://orcid.org/0009-0004-9998-0615
Covenant University, Ota, Nigeria

Vivian O. Nwaocha
National Open University of Nigeria, Abuja, Nigeria

ABSTRACT

This research provides a security and privacy control architecture for outlier hunting of internet Network traffic in higher institutions. The architecture leveraged the power of security and privacy combined with deep learning algorithms. By exploiting the hierarchical features learned through multiple layers, the proposed architecture can discern nuanced outliers indicative of security threats, network failures, or performance bottlenecks. The RNN model achieved a lower accuracy of 0.18 compared to the autoencoder. However, it still exhibited high 0.92 precision, 0.91 recall, and 0.91 F1-score values, indicating that it performed well in capturing temporal dependencies in the data. The accuracy of the tuned model (0.81) was significantly

DOI: 10.4018/979-8-3693-9137-2.ch014

higher than that of the base model (0.62), indicating that the hyperparameter tuning and adjustments made to the model architecture led to improved performance in terms of accurately reconstructing the input data, predicting network intrusions and providing security and privacy on network data.

INTRODUCTION

The advent of the digital age has transformed the landscape of educational institutions, making them increasingly reliant on robust network infrastructures to support academic, administrative and research activities. The study by Weixiong et al., (2023) created awareness in the area of privacy and security concerns in networks communication among machines. Considering the fact that it is possible for an attacker to get a little chance of causing harm in the network vulnerabilities which could lead to threats at organizational and personal level. Deep Learning (DL), with its ability to automatically learn classified features from dataset, has emerged as a viable tool for providing privacy and security analysis through outlier hunting. Several security and privacy-based models such as deep learning-enabled architectures, convolutional neural networks (CNNs), recurrent neural networks (RNNs) and autoencoders have been engaged to detect anomalies in different sectors. In the pursuit of homegrown digital sovereignty and in particular cyber sovereignty, prior studies have demonstrated the effectiveness of deep learning in capturing intricate patterns and anomalies within network traffic data (Shuqin, 2020) and also for diagnosis of diseases (Azeta et al., 2022). DL techniques effectively detect network attacks within raw samples, feature learning, and classification tasks. Deep learning-based outlier hunting on conventional learning algorithms depends on hand-designed learning features. DL techniques possess the capacity of overcoming the limitations of conventional algorithms (Liu, 2017). DL techniques for outlier hunting include Convolutional Neural Network (CNN) and RNN (Lopez-Martin, 2017). These techniques may be used for supervised learning or unsupervised learning depending on a particular problem including healthcare, transportation, smart grids and vehicular communications. Furthermore, the aforementioned approaches can be applied in IoT security related applications, such as fingerprint recognition, Distributed Denial of Service attack detection and malicious code identification, (Hussain, 2019; Fadlullah, 2017).

For all For all the input, techniques such as Long Short Term Memory (LSTM) and RNN perform the same transactions and the output also relies on past transactions (Roopack, 2019). These transactions are performed repeatedly since they are frequent in nature. The CNN performs the unsupervised mode of learning to extract features with multiple layers of abstraction and utilized the supervised mode to perform feature learning. Moreso, the detection of unexpected events in traffic data plays a significant role in intelligent network traffic management, which provides crucial alerts of potential incidents or sensor faults. Accurate outlier hunting on network traffic data can bring prompt trouble-shooting and help in timely decision-making for the network service providers. On a general note, an outlier is a series of observations that deviate significantly from the original distribution of any given dataset, and the amount of deviation has to do with the probability of being an anomaly. The protection of higher institutions campus networks in Nigeria from cybersecurity threats is a paramount concern in the face of the evolving technological advancement. Conventional security measures, such as intrusion detection and firewalls systems, often struggle to keep pace with the power of modern cyber attacks and threats. The need for proactive and adaptive security measures, with the capability to identify and respond to anomalous network behavior, has led to the exploration of advanced techniques such as deep learning technologies.

The constant onslaught of attacks targeting network vulnerabilities underscores the urgent need for robust solutions that will ensure digital sovereignty. Digital sovereignty in this context means a state where the legitimate owners and operators of networks maintain effective control, ensuring both reliability and strong security. Digital sovereignty is needed to keep control of different networks (Kumara et al, 2025). Prior studies have attempted to propose diverse solutions towards strengthening digital sovereignty in the areas of Frameworks (Igbal and Ismail, 2025); Machine learning-based Digital sovereignty (Kumara et al. 2025; Lokuliyana et al, 2025); and Blockchain, Networks and Grid (Ramesh et al, 2025; Shanmugama and Arumugamb, 2025). As part of contributions of this study, (i) this research provided a boost for digital sovereignty with security and privacy control architecture for outlier hunting of internet Network traffic in higher institutions.; (ii) the architecture leveraged the power of security and privacy combined with deep learning algorithms in fortifying Digital Sovereignty; (iii) the architecture provided has the capacity enhance privacy, self determination, control and home grown by higher institutions in Nigeria used as case study, thereby enhancing the ability of organizations to have control over its own digital destiny. This article is structured as follows: Section 2 contains literature review with emphasis on trends in digital sovereignty and related works. Section 3 described the materials and methods. Section 4 enumerates the result and discussions, while section 5 concludes the paper.

LITERATURE REVIEW

Digital sovereignty is the ability of an organization or nation to have control over its destiny to own and manage the digital assets, be it data, hardware and software that took time to build. Several studies related to digital sovereignty exist in literature including – Lokuliyana et al, (2025), the study explored the way machine learning could enhance Internet of Things (IoT) security by identifying abnormal events, it uses behavioral biometrics to secure the cloud dashboards, and detect botnet threats. The researchers tested numerous machine learning models, including Decision Trees (DT), K-Nearest Neighbors (KNN), XGBoost and Logistic Regression on public dataset. The DT model was impressive in accuracy rate of 0.73 for anomaly detection, proving its power in dealing with complex security risks, while the XGBoost model showed good performance with a 92% accuracy rate. However, in our current research as reported in this article, the Recurrent Neural Network (RNN) model achieved a lower accuracy of 0.18 compared to the autoencoder. However, it still exhibited high 0.92 precision, 0.91 recall, and 0.91 F1-score values, indicating that it performed well in capturing temporal dependencies in the data. The accuracy of the tuned model (0.81) was significantly higher than that of the base model (0.62), indicating that the hyperparameter tuning and adjustments made to the model architecture led to improved performance in terms of accurately reconstructing the input data, predicting network intrusions and providing security and privacy on network data

Moreso, studies such as Ramesh et al (2025) provided a framework to enable smooth communication and exchange of data between various permissible networks of blockchain. In the area of cyber-physical systems and the IoT, the research by Kumara et al., (2025) presents an approach towards ensuring digital sovereignty and trust through machine learning. This approach effectively addresses the shortcomings of traditional models, by ensuring that digital assets and communications remain trustworthy, secure and under rightful ownership and control. The study by Igbal and Ismail (2025) explores a methodology for detecting data bias, it is based on a general AI framework that can be applied across various sectors. The paper goes into the details of assessing the identified bias for gender features and describes how these features can influence the results of the machine learning (ML) model.

Furthermore, other researchers analyzed and applied deep learning methodologies by lending their voice in the privacy and security of networks. The study in Arora et al., (2014) discussed the latest issues, trends, and cutting-edge research approaches in security and privacy in online social media. It was mentioned that when considering network security, the whole network must be secured. Network security is not only concern with the security of computers at each end of the communication chain, it also involve transition of data through the communication channel. Weixiong et al., (2023) did a survey to elicit the opinion of users on awareness of network privacy and security. The results were used to support the importance of how a network should work on behalf of the users. This is the concept of digital sovereignty, allowing users to have control and freedom of the digital asset they use.

Many studies (Ikram, 2021; Mishra, 2019; Ferrag, 2020) did research on Deep Learning (DL) techniques in the last few years. Some studies use DL on attack detection for real-time environment. For instance, (Bontemps, 2016) proposes a real-time outlier hunting technique using neural networks for learning complex patterns in time series data with feature selection to potentially improve model efficiency and interpretability.

Alrawashdeh and Purdy (2016) researched on a technique that utilized DL for outlier hunting. The approach used one-hidden layer to carry out unsupervised feature reduction, and the resulting weight produced deep belief network with 97.91% accuracy. Moreso, (Zhang et al, 2022) did a study on CNN. The technique enhanced settings of the hyperparameter for the RANet to increase performance. The results demonstrate that RANet achieves 96.73% and 99.78% for the dataset usaged. Table 1 contains a summary of studies that relate to this current research.

Table 1. Summary of related studies

Authors	Objective	Platform, Tools and Techniques
Alrawashdeh and Purdy (2016)	Proposed Deep Learning for outlier hunting	Restricted boltzmann machine and a deep belief network
Zhang et al, (2022)	Proposed a novel convolutional neural network (CNN)	CNN and RANet
Iqbal and Ismail (2025)	Explores a methodology for detecting bias in data, based on a general AI-based framework that can be applied across various domains	AI-based framework and machine learning
Kumara et al (2025)	presents an approach to neoteric threat intelligence by ensuring digital sovereignty and trust through ML	ML-Infused Proactive Defense Analytics for NEXT-G
Ramesh et al (2025)	Outlines a framework designed to allow exchange of data and smooth communication and	Blockchain networks
Lokuliyana et al (2025)	Explores how machine learning can boost Internet of Things security by recognising unusual activities	K-Nearest Neighbors (KNN), Decision Trees, Logistic Regression, and XGBoost
Shanmugama and Arumugamb (2025)	Worked on compression framework based on federated learning privacy model for smart grid	Federated learning
Katsikasa (2025)	Studied cybersecurity-oriented research agenda for digital sovereignty	Cybersecurity
This current study	Provision of a sustainable digital sovereignty with security and privacy control architecture for outlier hunting of internet Network traffic in higher institutions	Deep Learning and Recurrent Neural Network (RNN)

Deep learning has revolutionized the field of outlier hunting with its ability to automatically extract complex features from raw data. Autoencoders, a type of neural network designed to learn efficient representations of data, have been widely used for outlier hunting. Studies have demonstrated that autoencoders can effectively reconstruct normal network traffic while failing to accurately reconstruct anomalous traffic, thereby enabling the detection of anomalies (Brown and White, 2019). Recurrent Neural Networks (RNN), particularly LSTM networks, have been employed to capture temporal dependencies in sequential network data, proving effective in identifying time-based anomalies (Zhang, Liu, and Wang, 2019). CNN have also been adapted for network traffic analysis, leveraging their capability to detect spatial patterns in the data (Patel and Singh, 2019; Guembe et al., 2022). Despite the advancements in deep learning for outlier hunting, several gaps remain in existing studies. First, many studies focus on synthetic datasets or controlled environments, that may not well represent the intricacies and variabilities of real-world network traffic. Second, there is often a lack of comprehensive evaluation metrics beyond accuracy, such as precision, recall, and F1-score, which are crucial for assessing the effectiveness of outlier hunting systems (Thomas and Garcia, 2020). Third, the issue of scalability and real-time detection is often overlooked, with many models being computationally intensive and thus impractical for deployment in high-traffic networks. Lastly, there is limited research on the integration of deep learning-based outlier hunting systems with existing network security frameworks, which is essential for practical application in real-world scenarios (Kim, Lee and Park, 2020).

MATERIALS AND METHODS

Figure 1 explains security and privacy control architecture for outlier hunting on network traffics. This includes activities such as email communication, web browsing, file transfers, and other legitimate business and personal activities conducted by users within the network. Non-legitimate traffic, on the other hand, encompasses any abnormal or unauthorized activities that deviate from the expected patterns of legitimate traffic. This can include various forms of malicious activities such as denial-of-service (DoS) attacks, malware propagation, port scanning, brute force login attempts, and other suspicious behaviors that may indicate a security threat or a violation of network policies.

However, in network traffic outlier hunting, the goal is to differentiate between legitimate and non-legitimate traffic by analyzing various characteristics of the network traffic, such as packet headers, payload content, traffic volume, communication patterns and more. Outlier hunting techniques, such as statistical analysis, deep learning algorithms, and signature-based detection, are commonly used to identify and flag unusual or suspicious patterns in network traffic for further investigation and mitigation. Furthermore, Deep Packet Inspection (DPI) is used to monitor metadata and perform operations such as block, slow down, speed up and filtering of the network traffic. All the data packets are scanned comprehensively and then admitted for use in the device interface on the network.

Figure 1. Security and privacy control architecture for outlier hunting on network traffics

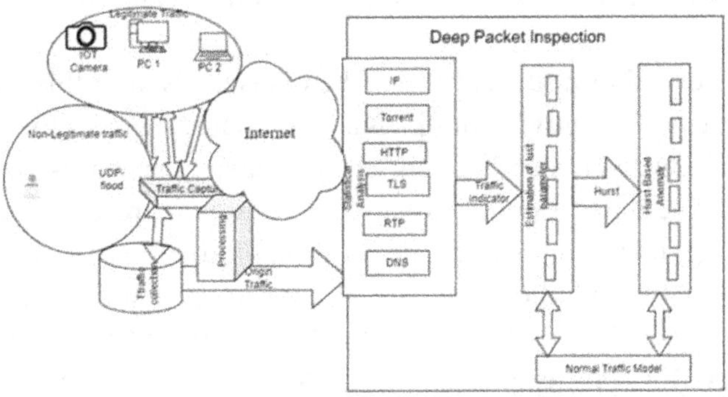

In Figure 1, legitimate traffic refers to the normal, expected data flow patterns within a network. This includes activities such as file transfers, email communication, web browsing and other legitimate business or personal activities conducted by users within the network. Non-legitimate traffic, on the other hand, encompasses any abnormal or unauthorized activities that deviate from the expected patterns of legitimate traffic. This can include various forms of malicious activities such as denial-of-service (DoS) attacks, malware propagation, port scanning, brute force login attempts, and other suspicious behaviors that may indicate a security threat or a violation of network policies.

Deep packet inspection is used to check malicious files and internet censorship policies that may illegally be disturbed across the network. A User Datagram Protocol (UDP) flood is a type of denial-of-service (DoS) attack where an attacker sends a large volume of UDP packets to a target server on the network. These UDP packets are often sent to random ports or specific ports associated with vulnerable services, to overwhelm the target's network capacity, consuming its resources, and causing disruption or downtime.

The Hurst exponent is a measure of the persistence or memory of a time series. It is particularly useful for understanding the fractal-like behavior of network traffic, where certain traffic patterns may exhibit long-term correlations or self-similar characteristics. Moreover, the hurst exponent serves as a valuable tool in network traffic outlier hunting by capturing the complex temporal correlations present in the data and providing insights into the underlying dynamics of network behavior. However, in network traffic outlier hunting, a traffic indicator mechanism is a technique used to identify potential anomalies or suspicious patterns within network traffic. These mechanisms aim to provide early indications of abnormal behavior, allowing network administrators to take appropriate actions to mitigate potential threats or issues. Also, by combining multiple traffic indication mechanisms, network traffic outlier hunting systems can provide comprehensive coverage and better accuracy in identifying potential threats and anomalies within network traffic in a university campus setting.

Dataset Description and Features: The datasets used in this study were collected from three private universities in Ota Ogun state Nigeria. However, there was a collaboration between the authors and the university campuses where those data were captured. The dataset contains various features representing characteristics of network traffic, including packet information, protocol types, service types, and more. The 'class' column indicates whether an instance of network traffic is normal (0) or anomalous (1). This makes it suitable for supervised outlier hunting tasks.

Exploratory Data Analysis (EDA): This analysis gained valuable insights into the characteristics of the dataset, which informed feature selection, preprocessing steps, and model selection for your outlier hunting task. Additionally, EDA helps to identify any data quality issues that may need to be addressed before training the deep learning models. Exploratory Data Analysis (EDA) involves examining and understanding the structure, patterns, and relationships within the dataset.

SECURITY AND PRIVACY-BASED DEEP LEARNING COMPONENTS

Autoencoder Architecture

- The IDS_Data1 dataset used for this study contains numerical features related to network traffic, which can be encoded into a lower-dimensional representation using an autoencoder. This lower-dimensional representation can help capture the underlying structure of the data and detect anomalies.
- Autoencoders can be particularly useful for outlier hunting in network traffic data where anomalies may not have clear labels, making unsupervised learning approaches advantageous.
- Autoencoders may capture patterns in the data that are not easily discernible using traditional methods, making them suitable for anomaly detection tasks where the anomalies may exhibit complex patterns.

Recurrent Neural Network (RNN) Architecture

- RNNs can also be effective for detecting outliers that manifest as unusual sequences or behaviors in the network traffic data.
- The autoencoder dense layers were replaced with LSTM layers for both encoding and decoding.
- An early stopping callback is added to prevent overfitting and improve generalization.
- The predicted data is reshaped back to its original shape before calculating evaluation metrics.

Convolutional Neural Network (CNN) Architecture

- Conv1D and MaxPooling1D layers were defined and added to create the convolutional and pooling layers.
- Flatten layer is a study added to flatten the output before passing it to dense layers.
- The dense layers were replaced with Conv1D and MaxPooling1D layers for encoding and decoding.
- The dataset is loaded from "IDS_Data1.csv" and split into training and testing sets.
- The data is normalized using StandardScaler.
- This study defines the architecture of the autoencoder model with one hidden layer, then compiles and trains the autoencoder model using Mean Squared Error (MSE) loss.
- The predictions on the test set are made and evaluation metrics of precision, recall, and F1 score are calculated.

Model Suitability

- This study investigates whether the characteristics of the dataset align with the strengths of the security and privacy-based deep learning architectures proposed (autoencoders, CNNs, RNNs). For instance, CNN (Convolutional Neural Network) might be suitable for spatial patterns in network traffic, while RNN (Recurrent Neural network) might capture temporal dependencies.
- Keras and scikit-learn library packages are necessary to install and the input data is shaped to fit the autoencoder, RNN (Recurrent Neural Network), and CNN (Convolutional Neural Network) architecture at each instance.

The security and privacy-based DL architecture provide a detailed description of the proposed deep learning-based framework for anomaly detection; explain the data sources that was used (e.g., network flow records, packet captures) and the specific features that was extracted; the chosen deep learning architecture and justify its selection based on the related work and the specific research goals; explain the data preprocessing steps, including normalization, dimensionality reduction, and handling imbalanced classes where applicable; define the training and testing procedures, including the loss function, optimizer, and hyperparameter tuning strategies. The following parameters and variables were evaluated in this study:

$$\text{Accuracy} = \frac{TP+TN}{TP+FP+FN+TN}$$

$$\text{Precision} = \frac{TP}{TP+FP}$$

$$\text{Recall} = \frac{TP}{TP+FN}$$

$$\text{F1 Score} = \frac{2 \times (\text{Precision} \times \text{Recall})}{\text{Precision} \times \text{Recall}}$$

$$\text{FPR} = \frac{FP}{FP+TN}$$

where FN (False negative, FN), is considered as a negative sample, but in fact, it is a positive sample.

FP (False positive, FP), is considered to be a positive sample, but in fact, it is a negative sample.

TN (True negative, TN), is considered to be a negative sample, and in fact, it is also a negative sample.

TP (True Positive, TP), is considered to be a positive sample, but in fact, it is also a positive sample.

RESULTS AND DISCUSSION

Data Quality and summary of statistics: The dataset was checked for any inconsistencies or errors in the data to ensure that the dataset is clean and properly labeled, as this can significantly impact the performance of the models. Basic statistics involving mean, median, standard deviation, minimum, and maximum for each numerical feature (e.g., TotPkts, TotBytes, SrcPkts, etc.) were calculated. The distribution of numerical features was determined and outliers were identified. Explore potential anomalies or outliers in the dataset. These could be instances with extreme values or patterns that deviate significantly from the norm.

Figure 2. Decision tree

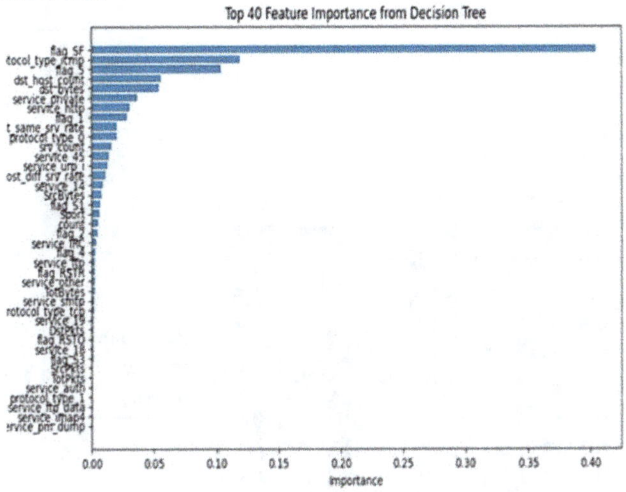

Class Distribution: We check for class imbalance in the dataset. If one class (normal or anomalous) significantly outweighs the other, it could bias the model's learning process. Techniques like oversampling, under-sampling, or using appropriate evaluation metrics can address this issue. This study checked the distribution of the target variable ('class') to see the balance between normal and anomalous instances; Normal – 15779, Anomalous - 13950.

Deep learning models often require a large amount of data to generalize well. The dataset has a total of 25,192 records ensuring that the dataset is sufficiently large to train complex models effectively. Figure 2 represents the highest importance decision tree for predicting the class model which indicates the significance of the correlation ranking. A similar result indicates the importance random forest that has the highest significant class label for predicting the model which correlates with the ranking feature.

Domain Specificity: This study considers the specificity of the "merged_Gan_IDSdata1.csv" dataset in the campus environment of two private universities in Ogun State, Nigeria, to ensure that the outliers present in the dataset are representative of those expected to be encountered in real-world scenarios.

Table 1. Performance metric of the model

Model	Accuracy	Precision	Recall	F1score
Autoencoder	0.62	0.93	0.91	0.91
RNN	0.18	0.92	0.91	0.91
CNN	0.15	0.52	0.44	0.45

Figure 3. Performance metrics graph

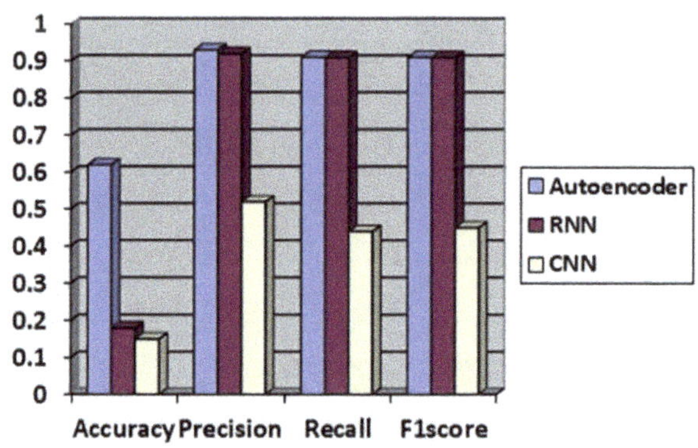

Table 1 and Figure 3 presents the performance metrics (accuracy, precision, recall, and F1-score) for three different models: autoencoder, RNN (Recurrent Neural Network), and CNN (Convolutional Neural Network).

Autoencoder: The autoencoder model achieved an accuracy of 0.62, with high 0.93 precision, 0.91 recall, and 0.91 F1-score values, indicating that it performed well in reconstructing the input data and capturing its underlying patterns. The high precision and recall values suggest that the model effectively distinguished between normal and anomalous instances.

RNN (Recurrent Neural Network): The RNN model achieved a lower accuracy of 0.18 compared to the autoencoder. However, it still exhibited high 0.92 precision,

0.91 recall, and 0.91 F1-score values, indicating that it performed well in capturing temporal dependencies in the data. Despite the low accuracy, the model's ability to correctly classify instances (as indicated by precision, recall, and F1-score) remains high.

CNN (Convolutional Neural Network): The CNN model achieved the lowest accuracy of 0.15 among the three models. It also exhibited lower 0.52 precision, 0.44 recall, and 0.45 F1-score values compared to the autoencoder and RNN. This suggests that the CNN may not have been as effective in capturing the relevant features or patterns in the data compared to the other models.

While the autoencoder and RNN models showed relatively high performance across all metrics, the CNN model lagged in accuracy and other evaluation metrics. The choice of model architecture can significantly impact the performance in outlier hunting tasks, with different models demonstrating varying degrees of effectiveness in capturing the underlying data characteristics. CNN works better on image datasets. However, Appendix C shows the classification code run on Python to verify the standard of the dataset for the model to perform optimally. Once the security and privacy-based deep learning model demonstrates satisfactory performance, the next step involves integrating the outlier hunting architecture into the university campus network. This study considers scalability, real-time processing, and compatibility with existing network infrastructure to ensure seamless integration and minimize disruption to normal network operations. We conducted ablation studies to investigate the impact of hyper-parameters on the performance of the autoencoder model. The base autoencoder model already outperformed CNN (0.15) and RNN (0.18). We now improved the accuracy of an autoencoder model by tuning various hyperparameters to identify their impact on the model's performance. Some key hyperparameters usually considered for tuning include architecture parameters, number of layers, number of neurons per layer and activation functions. The accuracy of the tuned model was 0.81 (81%) which was significantly higher than that of the base model (0.62), indicating that the hyperparameter tuning and adjustments made to the model architecture have led to improved performance in terms of accurately reconstructing the input data and predicting network intrusions. The research results of this study will go a long way in enhancing the digital sovereignty for higher institutions in Nigeria, by taking ownership of trust and privacy of institutional networks.

CONCLUSION AND FUTURE WORK

In this study, we proposed a security and privacy control architecture for outlier hunting on network

Traffics. Through extensive experimentation and evaluation, several key findings emerged as follows- the autoencoder model, leveraging dimensionality reduction and nonlinear activation functions, outperformed traditional machine learning and other deep learning architectures, achieving a significantly higher accuracy of 0.81. Moreso, scaling techniques such as StandardScaler demonstrated superior performance compared to MinMaxScaler and RobustScaler, indicating the importance of preprocessing methods in enhancing model effectiveness. In all, the goal of providing digital sovereignty through security and privacy control architecture for outlier hunting on network traffics was achieved. One of the limitations of this study was that getting the dataset to use for the analysis was time consuming and thereby caused some delay in time frame for the project. Moving forward, it is no gainsaying the fact that global studies on cybersecurity-oriented research for digital sovereignty are on the rise (Katsikasa, 2025). A lot of studies involving interactive deep learning to provide feedbacks on prediction outcomes are needed in the future.

REFERENCES

Alrawashdeh, K., & Purdy, C. N. (2016). *"Toward an Online Anomaly Intrusion Detection System Based on Deep Learning". 15th IEEE International Conference on Machine Learning and Applications.* ICMLA., Available online at https://api.semanticscholar.org/CorpusID:18950272

Arora, R., Rahul, R. S., Rauthan, S., & Jakhetia, S. (2014). "Internet Security and Privacy". *International Journal of Computer Science and Information Technology Research.* Vol. 2, Issue 3, pp: (467-475). *The Month,* (July - September), 2014.

Azeta, A., Jonathan, K., Guembe, B., & Nwadoziokwu, E. (2022). "A Deep Learning Approach forCassava Leaf Disease Diagnosis". *Proceedings of International Conference on Information systems and Emerging Technologies (ICISET), and International Conference on Data Science, Machine Learning and Artificial Intelligence (DSMLAI),* held in Namibia University of Science and Technology (NUST) on 23 to 25 November 2022. Available online on Elsevier *SSRN* at: https://papers.ssrn.com/sol3/papers.cfm?abstract_id=433656

Bontemps. (2016). Collective outliner hunting base on long-short term memory recurrent neural networks. *future data and security engineering,* 141-152.

Brown, L., & White, M. (2019). Deep Learning Techniques for Anomaly Detection Using Autoencoders. *IEEE Access : Practical Innovations, Open Solutions, 7,* 158949–158962.

Fadlullah, F. T. (2017). State-of-the-art deep learning: Evolving machine intelligence toward tomorrow's intelligent network traffic control systems. *IEEE Commun. Surv.Tutor. 19 (4) (2017)* (pp. 2432–2455,). IEEE http://dx.doi.org/.DOI: 10.1109/COMST.2017

Ferrag, (2020). Deep learning for cyber security intrusion detection approaches, datasets and comparative study . *MIT PRESS,* 716.

Hussain, F. R. H. (2019). *Machine learning in IoT security: current solution and future challenges.* arXiv preprint arXiv:1904.05735.

Ikram,. (2021). Outlier hunting using XGBoost ensemble of deep neural network models. *Journal of Network and Computer Applications,* 175-188. *Assessment* (pp. 1-8). Cyber SA.

Iqbal, R., & Ismail, S. (2025). Unbiased AI for a Sovereign Digital Future: A Bias Detection Framework. International Conference on Digital Sovereignty (ICDS). Elsevier ScienceDirect. *Procedia Computer Science, 254*, 118–126. DOI: 10.1016/j.procs.2025.02.070

Katsikasa, S. K. (2025). Towards a cybersecurity-oriented research agenda for digital sovereignty. International Conference on Digital Sovereignty (ICDS). Elsevier ScienceDirect. *Procedia Computer Science, 254*, 279–288. DOI: 10.1016/j.procs.2025.02.087

Kim, Y., Lee, J., & Park, H. (2020). Scalable and Real-Time Deep Learning-Based Anomaly Detection Systems. *IEEE Access : Practical Innovations, Open Solutions, 8*, 135550–135560.

Kumara, S., Singha, S. K., Kumarb, R., Subbac, C. K., Chuid, K. T., Brij, B., & Guptae, B. B. (2025). Neoteric Threat Intelligence Ensuring Digital Sovereignty and Trust through ML-Infused Proactive Defense Analytics for NEXT-G and Beyond Ecosystems. *International Conference on Digital Sovereignty (ICDS).* Elsevier ScienceDirect. *Procedia Computer Science, 254*, 39–47. DOI: 10.1016/j.procs.2025.02.062

Liu, Z. W., Wang, Z., Liu, X., Zeng, N., Liu, Y., & Alsaadi, F. E. (2017). A survey of deep neural network architectures and their application. *Neurocomputing, 234*, 11–26. DOI: 10.1016/j.neucom.2016.12.038

Lokuliyana, S., Siriwardana, D., Kalupahanage, A. G. A., Bulathsinhala, D. N., Herath, H. M. S. D., & Herath, H. M. T. M. (2025). Enhancing IoT Resilience: Machine Learning Techniques for Autonomous Anomaly Detection and Threat Mitigation. *International Conference on Digital Sovereignty (ICDS).* Elsevier ScienceDirect. *Procedia Computer Science, 254*, 68–77. DOI: 10.1016/j.procs.2025.02.065

Lopez-Martin, M., Carro, B., Sanchez-Esguevillas, A., & Lloret, J. (2017). B. C.-E. (2017). Network traffic classifier with convolutional and recurrent neural networks for internet of things. *IEEE Access : Practical Innovations, Open Solutions, 5*, 18042–18050. DOI: 10.1109/ACCESS.2017.2747560

Mishra,. (2019). A detailed investigation and analysis of using machine learning techniques for intrusion detection. *IEEE*, 686-728.

Patel, S., & Singh, D. (2019, July). Convolutional Neural Networks for Network Traffic Analysis. *IEEE Transactions on Information Forensics and Security, 14*(7), 1838–1847.

Ramesh, D., Santosh, T., Trivedic, M. C., & Led, C. H. (2025). Ensuring Digital Sovereignty in Cross-chain EHR Sharing: A Relay-as-a-Service Approach for Secure Healthcare Interoperability. International Conference on Digital Sovereignty (ICDS). Elsevier ScienceDirect. *Procedia Computer Science, 254*, 48–57. DOI: 10.1016/j.procs.2025.02.063

Shanmugama, D., & Arumugamb, C. (2025). Effective Communication Compression Framework Using Federated Learning Privacy Model for Smart Grid. International Conference on Digital Sovereignty (ICDS). Elsevier ScienceDirect. *Procedia Computer Science, 254*, 164–170. DOI: 10.1016/j.procs.2025.02.075

Shuqin, D. (2020). A deep feature learning-based method for network traffic Outlier hunting. *Journal of Electronic and Information*, 695-703.

Thomas, M., & Garcia, R. (2020, December). Comprehensive Evaluation Metrics for Anomaly Detection Systems. *IEEE Transactions on Network and Service Management, 17*(4), 2232–2245.

Weixiong Y., Kon L., Zahra S. S. T. and Zahra F. T. (2023). "Security and Privacy Concerns in Wireless Networks - A Survey". *communication, networking and broadcast technologies.* October 30, 2023

Zhang, K., Liu, Y., & Wang, S. (2019, May). LSTM Networks for Anomaly Detection in Network Traffic. *IEEE Journal on Selected Areas in Communications, 37*(5), 1202–1212.

Zhang, X., Yang, F., Hu, Y., Tian, Z., Liu, W., Li, Y., & She, W. (2022). "RANet: Network intrusion detection with group-gating convolutional neural network". *Journal of Network and Computer Applications*, Volume 198-213, 2022, 103266. ISSN 1084-8045. Available online at: DOI: 10.1016/j.jnca.2021.103266

ADDITIONAL READING

Meidan, M. B. (2018). Network-based detection of IoT Botnet attacks using deep autoencoders. *Pervasive Comput. 17 (3) (2018) 12–22, http://dx.doi.org/.* (pp. 12-22). IEEE.DOI: 10.1109/MPRV.2018.03367731

Compilation of References

Abadi, M., Chu, A., Goodfellow, I., McMahan, H. B., Mironov, I., Talwar, K., & Zhang, L. (2016). Deep Learning with Differential Privacy. *Proceedings of the 2016 ACM SIGSAC Conference on Computer and Communications Security*, 308–318. DOI: 10.1145/2976749.2978318

Abdulganiyu, O. H., Ait Tchakoucht, T., & Saheed, Y. K. (2023). A systematic literature review for network intrusion detection system (ids). *International Journal of Information Security*, *22*(5), 1125–1162. DOI: 10.1007/s10207-023-00682-2

Adair, L. (2023). A synthetic data strategy for Scotland: Using synthetic data to improve access to public sector data for research. *International Journal of Population Data Science*, *8*(2), 8. DOI: 10.23889/ijpds.v8i2.2215

Adiwal, S., & Misbahuddin, M. (2023). Intrusion detection and prevention in openstack: A case study on enhancing security and threat detection. *SN Computer Science*, *4*(6), 830. DOI: 10.1007/s42979-023-02265-3

Adkisson, M., Kimmell, J. C., Gupta, M., & Abdelsalam, M. (2021). Autoencoder-based Anomaly Detection in Smart Farming Ecosystem. *2021 IEEE International Conference on Big Data (Big Data)*, 3390–3399. DOI: 10.1109/BigData52589.2021.9671613

Aghdaie, P., Chaudhary, B., Soleymani, S., Dawson, J., & Nasrabadi, N. M. (2021). Attention Aware Wavelet-based Detection of Morphed Face Images. *2021 IEEE International Joint Conference on Biometrics (IJCB)*, 1–8. DOI: 10.1109/IJCB52358.2021.9484398

Agrawal, S., Sarkar, S., Aouedi, O., Yenduri, G., Piamrat, K., Alazab, M., Bhattacharya, S., Maddikunta, P. K. R., & Gadekallu, T. R. (2022). Federated learning for intrusion detection system: Concepts, challenges and future directions. *Computer Communications*, *195*, 346–361. DOI: 10.1016/j.comcom.2022.09.012

Ahmad, W., & Dethy, E. (2019). Preventing surveillance cities: Developing a set of fundamental privacy provisions. *Journal of Science Policy & Governance*, *15*(1), 1–11.

Ahsan, M., Nygard, K. E., Gomes, R., Chowdhury, M. M., Rifat, N., & Connolly, J. F. (2022). Cybersecurity threats and their mitigation approaches using ma- chine learning—A review. [Ali, A.H., Charfeddine, M., Ammar, B., Hamed, B.B., Albalwy, F.]. *Journal of Cybersecurity and Privacy*, *2*(3), 527–555. DOI: 10.3390/jcp2030027

Aigner, G., Garai-Fodor, M., & Szemere, P. (2020). Singapore's journey as a digit-all-ized and innovative smart nation toward sustainability. *Sustainability*, *12*(18), 7495.

Aijaz, R. (2020). *The Smart Cities Mission in Delhi, 2015–2019: An Evaluation.* ORF Report.

Akartuna, E. A., Johnson, S. D., & Thornton, A. E. (2023). The money laundering and terrorist financing risks of new and disruptive technologies: A futures-oriented scoping review. *Security Journal*, *36*(4), 615–650. DOI: 10.1057/s41284-022-00356-z PMID: 40479271

Albrecht, J. P. (2016). How the GDPR Will Change the World. *European Data Protection Law Review, 2*(3), 287–289. https://doi.org/https://doi.org/10.21552/EDPL/2016/3/4

Aledhari, M., Razzak, R., Parizi, R. M., & Saeed, F. (2020). Federated Learning: A Survey on Enabling Technologies, Protocols, and Applications. *IEEE Access : Practical Innovations, Open Solutions*, *8*, 140699–140725. DOI: 10.1109/ACCESS.2020.3013541 PMID: 32999795

Ali, O., Shrestha, A., Chatfield, A., & Murray, P. (2020). Assessing information security risks in the cloud: A case study of Australian local government authorities. *Government Information Quarterly*, *37*(1), 101419. Advance online publication. DOI: 10.1016/j.giq.2019.101419

Alonge, C. Y., Arogundade, O. T., Adesemowo, K., Ibrahalu, F. T., Adeniran, O. J., & Mustapha, A. M. (2020). Information Asset Classification and Labelling Model Using Fuzzy Approach for Effective Security Risk Assessment. *2020 International Conference in Mathematics, Computer Engineering and Computer Science, ICMCECS 2020*, 1–7. DOI: 10.1109/ICMCECS47690.2020.240911

Alorfi, A. S., Yonbawi, S., Alahmari, S., Bozorboevich, A. A., Arumugam, M., & Huy, P. Q. (2023). Biometric authentication integrated with wireless communication malicious activity detection in a cyber physical system-based Fintech banking. *Optik (Stuttgart)*, *272*, 170294. DOI: 10.1016/j.ijleo.2022.170294

Alqahtani, H., Kavakli-Thorne, M., & Kumar, G. (2019). Applications of Generative Adversarial Networks (GANs): An Updated Review. *Archives of Computational Methods in Engineering*, *28*(2), 525–552. DOI: 10.1007/s11831-019-09388-y

Alrawashdeh, K., & Purdy, C. N. (2016). *"Toward an Online Anomaly Intrusion Detection System Based on Deep Learning". 15th IEEE International Conference on Machine Learning and Applications*. ICMLA., Available online at https://api.semanticscholar.org/CorpusID:18950272

Al-Rubaie, M., & Chang, J. M. (2019). Privacy-Preserving Machine Learning: Threats and Solutions. *IEEE Security and Privacy*, *17*(2), 49–58. DOI: 10.1109/MSEC.2018.2888775

Alsamhi, S. H., Hawbani, A., Kumar, S., Timilsina, M., Al-Qatf, M., Haque, R., Nashwan, F. M. A., Zhao, L., & Curry, E. (2024). Empowering Dataspace 4.0: Unveiling Promise of Decentralized Data-Sharing. *IEEE Access : Practical Innovations, Open Solutions*, *12*, 112637–112658. DOI: 10.1109/ACCESS.2024.3442968

Al-Turjman, F., Zahmatkesh, H., & Shahroze, R. (2022). An overview of security and privacy in smart cities' IoT communications. *Transactions on Emerging Telecommunications Technologies*, *33*(3), e3677. DOI: 10.1002/ett.3677

Amiri-Zarandi, M., Dara, R. A., Duncan, E., & Fraser, E. D. G. (2022). Big Data Privacy in Smart Farming: A Review. In *Sustainability (Switzerland)* (Vol. 14, Issue 15). MDPI. DOI: 10.3390/su14159120

Arora, P., & Makani, R. (2024). Blockchain Integration with AIoT Data Security and Privacy for Sustainability. *Journal of Artificial Intelligence and Systems*, *6*(1), 112–123. DOI: 10.33969/AIS.2024060108

Arora, R., Rahul, R. S., Rauthan, S., & Jakhetia, S. (2014). "Internet Security and Privacy". *International Journal of Computer Science and Information Technology Research*. Vol. 2, Issue 3, pp: (467-475). *The Month*, (July - September), 2014.

Arthur, L., Costello, J., Hardy, J., O'Brien, W., Rea, J., Rees, G., & Ganev, G. (2023). On the challenges of deploying privacy-preserving synthetic data in the enterprise. arXiv preprint arXiv:2307.04208.

Ashraf, M., Waqas, M., Abbas, G., Baker, T., Abbas, Z., & Alasmary, H. (2022). FedDP: A Privacy-Protecting Theft Detection Scheme in Smart Grids Using Federated Learning. *Energies*, *15*(17), 6241. DOI: 10.3390/en15176241

Auer, R., Cornelli, G., & Frost, J. (2020). *Rise of the central bank digital currencies: drivers, approaches and technologies* (BIS Working Paper No. 880). www.bis.org

Awajan, A. (2023). A novel deep learning-based intrusion detection system for iot networks. *Computers, 12*(2), 34. DOI: 10.3390/computers12020034

Ayesha Barvin, P., & Sampradeepraj, T. (2023). Crop Recommendation Systems Based on Soil and Environmental Factors Using Graph Convolution Neural Network: A Systematic Literature Review. *ECSA, 97*, 97. Advance online publication. DOI: 10.3390/ecsa-10-16010

Ayo, F. E., Awotunde, J. B., Ogundele, L. A., Solanke, O. O., Brahma, B., Panigrahi, R., & Bhoi, A. K. (2024). Ontology-based layered rule-based network intrusion detection system for cybercrimes detection. *Knowledge and Information Systems, 66*(6), 1–38. DOI: 10.1007/s10115-024-02068-9

Azeta, A., Jonathan, K., Guembe, B., & Nwadoziokwu, E. (2022). "A Deep Learning Approach forCassava Leaf Disease Diagnosis". *Proceedings of International Conference on Information systems and Emerging Technologies (ICISET), and International Conference on Data Science, Machine Learning and Artificial Intelligence (DSMLAI)*, held in Namibia University of Science and Technology (NUST) on 23 to 25 November 2022. Available online on Elsevier *SSRN* at: https://papers.ssrn.com/sol3/papers.cfm?abstract_id=433656

Aziz, R., Banerjee, S., Bouzefrane, S., & Le Vinh, T. (2023). Exploring Homomorphic Encryption and Differential Privacy Techniques towards Secure Federated Learning Paradigm. *Future Internet, 15*(9), 310. DOI: 10.3390/fi15090310

Bader, S., Pullmann, J., Mader, C., Tramp, S., Quix, C., Müller, A. W., & Lange, C. (2020). The international data spaces information model–an ontology for sovereign exchange of digital content. In *International Semantic Web Conference* (pp. 176-192). Cham: Springer International Publishing. DOI: 10.1007/978-3-030-62466-8_12

Badr, Y., Zhu, X., & Alraja, M. N. (2021). Security and privacy in the Internet of Things: Threats and challenges. *Service Oriented Computing and Applications, 15*(4), 257–271. DOI: 10.1007/s11761-021-00327-z

Balabaygloo, B. J., Bekee, B., Blair, S. W., Fey, S., Fotouhi, F., Gupta, A., Menke, K., Vangala, A., Palomares, J. C. M., Prestholt, A., Tanwar, V. K., Tao, X., Carroll, M. E., Das, S., Depaula, G., Kyveryga, P., Sarkar, S., Segovia, M., Sylvestri, S., . . . Singh, A. K. (2023). Smart Connected Farms and Networked Farmers to Tackle Climate Challenges Impacting Agricultural Production. *ArXiv*. https://doi.org//arXiv.2312.12338DOI: 10.48550

Balisane, H., Egho-Promise, E. I., Lyada, E., & Aina, F. (2024). Towards Improved Threat Mitigation in Digital Environments: A Comprehensive Framework for Cybersecurity Enhancement. *International Journal of Research -Granthaalayah, 12*(5). DOI: 10.29121/granthaalayah.v12.i5.2024.5655

Balogun, T., Saliu, R., Faluyi, S., & Fapohunda, K. (2022, November). Comparative analysis of deep learning models for the detection and classification of Diabetes Retinopathy. In *2022 5th Information Technology for Education and Development (ITED)* (pp. 1-6). IEEE. DOI: 10.1109/ITED56637.2022.10051208

Ban, L. (2024). Data privacy and protection in communication networks. *Applied and Computational Engineering, 38*(1), 131–138. DOI: 10.54254/2755-2721/38/20230541

Barbierato, E., Vedova, M. L. D., Tessera, D., Toti, D., & Vanoli, N. (2022). A methodology for controlling bias and fairness in synthetic data generation. *Applied Sciences (Basel, Switzerland), 12*(9), 4619.

Barik, K., Misra, S., Mohan, R., & Mishra, B. (2024). AIoT and Its Trust Models to Enhance Societal Applications Using Intelligent Technologies. In Misra, S., Siakas, K., & Lampropoulos, G. (Eds.), *Artificial Intelligence of Things for Achieving Sustainable Development Goals. Lecture Notes on Data Engineering and Communications Technologies* (Vol. 192). Springer., DOI: 10.1007/978-3-031-53433-1_16

Barrinha, A. (2016). Cybersecurity in the European Union. Resilience and adaptability in governance policy. *European Security, 25*(3), 387–389. DOI: 10.1080/09662839.2016.1160892

Bartsch, J., Dehling, T., Lauf, F., Meister, S., & Sunyaev, A. (2022). Let the computer say NO! The neglected potential of policy definition languages for data sovereignty. In *Selbstbestimmung, Privatheit und Datenschutz: Gestaltungsoptionen für einen europäischen Weg* (pp. 449–468). Springer Fachmedien Wiesbaden. DOI: 10.1007/978-3-658-33306-5_22

Bayaga, A. (2022). Examining the predictive relevance of security, privacy risk factors, and institutional logics for e-government service adoption. *The Electronic Journal on Information Systems in Developing Countries, 88*(1), e12201. DOI: 10.1002/isd2.12201

Beerepoot, I., Di Ciccio, C., Reijers, H. A., Rinderle-Ma, S., Bandara, W., Burattin, A., Calvanese, D., Chen, T., Cohen, I., Depaire, B., Di Federico, G., Dumas, M., van Dun, C., Fehrer, T., Fischer, D. A., Gal, A., Indulska, M., Isahagian, V., Klinkmüller, C., & Zerbato, F. (2023). The biggest business process management problems to solve before we die. *Computers in Industry*, *146*, 103837. DOI: 10.1016/j.compind.2022.103837

Bellanova, R., Carrapico, H., & Duez, D. (2022). Digital/sovereignty and european security integration: An introduction. *European Security*, *31*(3), 337–355. DOI: 10.1080/09662839.2022.2101887

Beltrán, M., & Calvo, M. (2023). A privacy threat model for identity verification based on facial recognition. *Computers & Security*, *132*, 103324. DOI: 10.1016/j.cose.2023.103324

Ben-Sasson, E., Chiesa, A., Genkin, D., Tromer, E., & Virza, M. (2013). SNARKs for C: Verifying Program Executions Succinctly and in Zero Knowledge. In Canetti, R., & Garay, J. A. (Eds.), Lecture Notes in Computer Science: Vol. 8043. *Advances in Cryptology – CRYPTO 2013. CRYPTO 2013* (pp. 90–108). Springer., https://doi.org/https://doi.org/10.1007/978-3-642-40084-1_6 DOI: 10.1007/978-3-642-40084-1_6

Bera, A., Bhattacharjee, D., & Krejcar, O. (2024). PND-Net: Plant Nutrition Deficiency and Disease Classification using Graph Convolutional Network. *ArXiv*. https://doi.org/arXiv:2410.12742

Bergsrud, L. T., & Vaseeharanathan, A. (2024). Surveillance in Smart Cities: A Case Study of Ethical Implications for Vulnerable Groups (Master's thesis, NTNU).

Bhagat, D., Hanwate, A., Salunkhe, R. V., Jagyasi, T., Sardare, P., & Sahu, M. (2025). Future Perspectives on Surveillance Systems. In Modern Advancements in Surveillance Systems and Technologies (pp. 349-370). IGI Global Scientific Publishing.

Bhattacharya, M., Roy, S., Chattopadhyay, S., Das, A. K., & Shetty, S. (2023). A comprehensive survey on online social networks security and privacy issues: Threats, machine learning-based solutions, and open challenges. *Security and Privacy*, *6*(1), e275. DOI: 10.1002/spy2.275

Blanco-Carmona, P., Baeza-Moreno, L., Hidalgo-Fort, E., Martín-Clemente, R., González-Carvajal, R., & Muñoz-Chavero, F. (2023). AIoT in Agriculture: Safeguarding Crops from Pest and Disease Threats. *Sensors (Basel)*, *23*(24), 9733. Advance online publication. DOI: 10.3390/s23249733 PMID: 38139579

Bohli, J. M., Langendörfer, P., & Skarmeta, A. F. (2022). Security and privacy challenge in data aggregation for the IoT in smart cities. In *Internet of Things* (pp. 225–244). River Publishers. DOI: 10.1201/9781003338659-5

Bonawitz, K., Ivanov, V., Kreuter, B., Marcedone, A., McMahan, H. B., Patel, S., Ramage, D., Segal, A., & Seth, K. (2017). Practical Secure Aggregation for Privacy-Preserving Machine Learning. *Proceedings of the 2017 ACM SIGSAC Conference on Computer and Communications Security*, 1175–1191. DOI: 10.1145/3133956.3133982

Bontemps. (2016). Collective outliner hunting base on long-short term memory recurrent neural networks. *future data and security engineering*, 141-152.

Borisenko, B. B., Erokhin, S. D., Fadeev, A. S., & Martishin, I. D. (2021). Intrusion detection using multilayer perceptron and neural networks with long short-term memory. *2021 Systems of Signal Synchronization, Generating and Processing in Telecommunications (SYNCHROINFO*, 1–6. https://ieeexplore.ieee.org/abstract/document/9488416/

Braun, T., Fung, B. C., Iqbal, F., & Shah, B. (2018). Security and privacy challenges in smart cities. *Sustainable Cities and Society*, *39*, 499–507. DOI: 10.1016/j.scs.2018.02.039

Briggs, C., Fan, Z., & Andras, P. (2021). A Review of Privacy-Preserving Federated Learning for the Internet-of-Things. *Studies in Computational Intelligence*, *965*, 21–50. DOI: 10.1007/978-3-030-70604-3_2

Bronner, W., Gebauer, H., Lamprecht, C., & Wortmann, F. (2021). Sustainable AIoT: How Artificial Intelligence and the Internet of Things Affect Profit, People, and Planet. *Connected Business: Create Value in a Networked Economy*, 137–154. DOI: 10.1007/978-3-030-76897-3_8

Brown, L., & White, M. (2019). Deep Learning Techniques for Anomaly Detection Using Autoencoders. *IEEE Access : Practical Innovations, Open Solutions*, *7*, 158949–158962.

Bruckner, F., & Jahnke, N. (2021). Datenschutz und Datensicherheit in Datenökosystemen - IIP-Ecosphere Whitepaper (1.0). *Zenodo*. DOI: 10.5281/zenodo.4588330

Bu, F., Wang, N., Jiang, B., & Liang, H. (2020). "Privacy by Design" implementation: Information system engineers' perspective. *International Journal of Information Management*, *53*, 102124. DOI: 10.1016/j.ijinfomgt.2020.102124

Calderaro, A., & Blumfelde, S. (2020). Artificial intelligence and EU security. *European Security*, *29*(4), 483–500.

Calzada, I. (2021). Data co-operatives through data sovereignty. *Smart Cities, 4*(3), 1158–1172. DOI: 10.3390/smartcities4030062

Campbell-Verduyn, M. (2018). Bitcoin, crypto-coins, and global anti-money laundering governance. *Crime, Law, and Social Change, 69*(2), 283–305. DOI: 10.1007/s10611-017-9756-5

Canedo, E. D., & Mendes, B. C. (2020). Software requirements classification using machine learning algorithms. *Entropy (Basel, Switzerland), 22*(9), 1057. Advance online publication. DOI: 10.3390/e22091057 PMID: 33286826

Canhoto, A. I. (2021). Leveraging machine learning in the global fight against money laundering and terrorism financing: An affordances perspective. *Journal of Business Research, 131*, 441–452. DOI: 10.1016/j.jbusres.2020.10.012 PMID: 33100427

Cappiello, C., Gal, A., Jarke, M., & Rehof, J. (2020). Data ecosystems: Sovereign data exchange among organizations (Dagstuhl Seminar 19391). *Dagstuhl Reports, 9*(9), 66–134.

Carlini, N., Liu, C., Erlingsson, Ú., Kos, J., & Song, D. (2019). The secret sharer: Evaluating and testing unintended memorization in neural networks. *28th USENIX Security Symposium (USENIX Security 19)*, 267–284.

Chainalysis. (2024). *Money Laundering and Cryptocurrency: Trends and new techniques for detection and investigation.* https://www.chainalysis.com/blog/money-laundering-cryptocurrency/

Challa, S. S. S. (2024). Leveraging AI for Risk Management in Computer System Validation. *IJMIRM: International Journal of Multidisciplinary Innovation and Research Methodology, 3*(2), 145–153. https://ijmirm.com/index.php/ijmirm/article/view/95

Chander, S., & Vijaya, P. (2021). Unsupervised learning methods for data clustering. In Binu, D., & Rajakumar, B. R. (Eds.), *Artificial Intelligence in Data Mining: Theories and Applications* (pp. 41–64). Academic Press, Elsevier Inc., DOI: 10.1016/B978-0-12-820601-0.00002-1

Chandra, R., & Sanjaya, K. (2023). Punishing the Unpunishable: A Liability Framework for Artificial Intelligence Systems. In Motahhir, S., & Bossoufi, B. (Eds.), *Digital Technologies and Applications* (pp. 55–64). Springer., DOI: 10.1007/978-3-031-29860-8_6

Chatterjee, A., Gerdes, M. W., Prinz, A., & Martinez, S. G. 2021a. Comparing performance of ensemble-based machine learning algorithms to identify potential obesity risk factors from public health datasets, in: Emerging Technologies in Data Mining and Information Security: Proceedings of IEMIS 2020, Volume 1, Springer. pp. 253–269. DOI: 10.1007/978-981-15-9927-9_26

Chatterjee, A., Prinz, A., Riegler, M. A., & Meena, Y. K. 2023. An automatic and personalized recommendation modelling in activity ecoaching with deep learning and ontology. Scientific Reports 13, 10182. CIC-IDS-2017, K., accessed: 25.09.2024. network-intrusion-dataset. https://www.kaggle.com/datasets

Chatterjee, A., Gerdes, M. W., & Martinez, S. G. (2020). Identification of risk factors associated with obesity and overweight—A machine learning overview. *Sensors (Basel)*, *20*(9), 2734. DOI: 10.3390/s20092734 PMID: 32403349

Chatterjee, A., Pahari, N., Prinz, A., & Riegler, M. (2022). Machine learning and ontology in ecoaching for personalized activity level monitoring and recommendation generation. *Scientific Reports*, *12*(1), 19825. DOI: 10.1038/s41598-022-24118-4 PMID: 36400793

Chatterjee, A., & Prinz, A. (2022). Personalized recommendations for physical activity e-coaching (ontorecomodel): Ontological modeling. *JMIR Medical Informatics*, *10*(6), e33847. DOI: 10.2196/33847 PMID: 35737439

Chatterjee, A., Prinz, A., Gerdes, M., & Martinez, S. (2021b). An automatic ontology-based approach to support logical representation of observable and measurable data for healthy lifestyle management: Proof-of-concept study. *Journal of Medical Internet Research*, *23*(4), e24656. DOI: 10.2196/24656 PMID: 33835031

Chaudhary, B., Aghdaie, P., Soleymani, S., Dawson, J., & Nasrabadi, N. M. (2021). Differential Morph Face Detection using Discriminative Wavelet Sub-bands. *2021 IEEE/CVF Conference on Computer Vision and Pattern Recognition Workshops (CVPRW)*, 1425–1434. DOI: 10.1109/CVPRW53098.2021.00158

Chen, A., Fu, Y., Sha, Z., & Lu, G. (2022). An EMD-Based Adaptive Client Selection Algorithm for Federated Learning in Heterogeneous Data Scenarios. *Frontiers in Plant Science*, *13*, 908814. Advance online publication. DOI: 10.3389/fpls.2022.908814 PMID: 35755701

Chen, F., Li, P., Miyazaki, T., & Wu, C. (2022). FedGraph: Federated Graph Learning With Intelligent Sampling. *IEEE Transactions on Parallel and Distributed Systems*, *33*(8), 1775–1786. DOI: 10.1109/TPDS.2021.3125565

Cheng, K., Fan, T., Jin, Y., Liu, Y., Chen, T., & Yang, Q. (2019). SecureBoost: A Lossless Federated Learning Framework. *IEEE Intelligent Systems*, *36*(3), 87–98.

Cheong, L. K., & Chang, V. (2007). The need for data governance: a case study. *ACIS 2007 proceedings*, 100.

Choi, D. (2023). AI in South Korea's social welfare systems: Surveillance or innovation? *Asian Journal of Social Policy*, *15*(2), 101–117.

Choithani, T., Chowdhury, A., Patel, S., Patel, P., Patel, D., & Shah, M. (2022). A Comprehensive Study of Artificial Intelligence and Cybersecurity on Bitcoin, Crypto Currency and Banking System. *Annals of Data Science*. Advance online publication. DOI: 10.1007/s40745-022-00433-5 PMID: 40479325

Chow, J. C. K. (2017). *Analysis of Financial Credit Risk Using Machine Learning*. DOI: 10.13140/RG.2.2.30242.53449

Chung, H., & Lee, Y. (2023). Legal frameworks for AI governance in Korea: A comparative perspective. *Korean Journal of Law and Technology*, *5*(1), 45–67.

Cohen, I. G., Amarasingham, R., Shah, A., Xie, B., & Lo, B. (2020). The legal and ethical concerns that arise from using complex predictive analytics in health care. *Health Affairs*, *33*(7), 1139–1147. DOI: 10.1377/hlthaff.2014.0048 PMID: 25006139

Cortez, E. K. (2021). Data Protection Around the World: Privacy Laws in Action. In E. K. Cortez (Ed.), *Information Technology and Law Series IT&LAW* (1st ed., Vol. 33). T.M.C. Asser Press. https://doi.org/https://doi.org/10.1007/978-94-6265-407-5

Cottrill, C. D., Jacobs, N., Markovic, M., & Edwards, P. (2020). Sensing the city: Designing for privacy and trust in the internet of things. *Sustainable Cities and Society*, *63*, 102453. DOI: 10.1016/j.scs.2020.102453

Couture, S., & Toupin, S. (2019). What does the notion of "sovereignty" mean when referring to the digital? *New Media & Society*, *21*(10), 2305–2322. DOI: 10.1177/1461444819865984

Creswell, J. W., & Creswell, J. D. (2017). *Research design: Qualitative, quantitative, and mixed methods approaches*. Sage publications.

Cui, L., Xie, G., Qu, Y., Gao, L., & Yang, Y. (2018). Security and privacy in smart cities: Challenges and opportunities. *IEEE Access : Practical Innovations, Open Solutions*, *6*, 46134–46145. DOI: 10.1109/ACCESS.2018.2853985

Cummings, R., Desfontaines, D., Evans, D., Geambasu, R., Huang, Y., Jagielski, M., Kairouz, P., Kamath, G., Oh, S., Ohrimenko, O., Papernot, N., Rogers, R., Shen, M., Song, S., Su, W., Terzis, A., Thakurta, A., Vassilvitskii, S., Wang, Y.-X., & Zhang, W. (2024). Advancing Differential Privacy: Where We Are Now and Future Directions for Real-World Deployment. *Harvard Data Science Review*, *6*(1), 1. DOI: 10.1162/99608f92.d3197524

Cuno, S., Bruns, L., Tcholtchev, N., Lämmel, P., & Schieferdecker, I. (2019). Data governance and sovereignty in urban data spaces based on standardized ICT reference architectures. *Data*, *4*(1), 16. DOI: 10.3390/data4010016

Curry, E. (2016). The big data value chain: definitions, concepts, and theoretical approaches. *New horizons for a data-driven economy: A roadmap for usage and exploitation of big data in Europe*, 29-37.

D'Acquisto, G., Domingo-Ferrer, J., Kikiras, P., Torra, V., de Montjoye, Y.-A., & Bourka, A. (2015). *Privacy by design in big data: An overview of privacy enhancing technologies in the era of big data analytics* (A. Bourka & P. Drogkaris, Eds.; 1st ed.). European Union Agency for Network and Information Security (ENISA). DOI: 10.2824/641480

Da Silva Carvalho, N., Jabbarpour, J., Temple, L., Belacort, I. M., Barturen, U. I., Kortlander, M., Sanchez Pelaez, V., Areizaga Sanchez, E., & Mureddu, F. (2023). A more inclusive Europe through personal data sovereignty in cross-border digital public services. *Proceedings of the 16th International Conference on Theory and Practice of Electronic Governance*, 63–71. DOI: 10.1145/3614321.3614329

Dawson, M., Eltayeb, M., & Omar, M. (Eds.). (2016). *Security Solutions for Hyperconnectivity and the Internet of Things*. IGI Global., DOI: 10.4018/978-1-5225-0741-3

De Filippi, P., & McCarthy, S. (2012). Cloud computing: Centralization and data sovereignty. *European Journal of Law and Technology*, *3*(2).

de Koker, L. (2016). Money Laundering Compliance—The Challenges of Technology. In Dion, M., Weisstub, D., & Richet, J.-L. (Eds.), *Financial Crimes: Psychological, Technological, and Ethical Issues. International Library of Ethics, Law, and the New Medicine* (Vol. 68, pp. 329–347). Springer., DOI: 10.1007/978-3-319-32419-7_16

Debic, B., & Medvidovic, L. (2024). Data Ownership and Privacy in Personalized AI Models in Assistive Healthcare. *International Joint Conference on Artificial Intelligence*. DOI: 10.24963/ijcai.2024/868

DeBruine, L., & Jones, B. (2021). *Face Research Lab London Set*. DOI: 10.6084/m9.figshare.5047666.v5

Dedousis, P., Stergiopoulos, G., Arampatzis, G., & Gritzalis, D. (2021). A Security-Aware Framework for Designing Industrial Engineering Processes. *IEEE Access : Practical Innovations, Open Solutions*, *9*, 163065–163085. DOI: 10.1109/ACCESS.2021.3134759

Delussu, R., Putzu, L., & Fumera, G. (2024). Synthetic Data for Video Surveillance Applications of Computer Vision: A Review. *International Journal of Computer Vision*, *132*(10), 4473–4509. DOI: 10.1007/s11263-024-02102-x

Deng, M., Wuyts, K., Scandariato, R., Preneel, B., & Joosen, W. (2011). A privacy threat analysis framework: Supporting the elicitation and fulfillment of privacy requirements. *Requirements Engineering*, *16*(1), 3–32. DOI: 10.1007/s00766-010-0115-7

Desai, A., Kosse, A., & Sharples, J. (2024). *Finding a needle in a haystack: a machine learning framework for anomaly detection in payment systems* (1188). www.bis.org

Despotović, A., Parmaković, A., & Miljković, M. (2023). Cybercrime and Cyber Security in Fintech. In Benković, S., Labus, A., & Milosavljević, M. (Eds.), *Digital Transformation of the Financial Industry* (pp. 255–272). Springer International Publishing., DOI: 10.1007/978-3-031-23269-5_15

Dhariwal, P., & Nichol, A. (2021). Diffusion models beat gans on image synthesis. *Advances in Neural Information Processing Systems*, *34*, 8780–8794.

Dhiman, V. (2022). Intelligent risk assessment framework for software security compliance using AI. *International Journal of Innovation Studies*, *6*(3).

Digital Personal Data Protection Act, 2023

Domingo-Ferrer, J., & Blanco-Justicia, A. (2020). Privacy-Preserving Technologies. In Christen, M., Gordijn, B., & Loi, M. (Eds.), *The Ethics of Cybersecurity. The International Library of Ethics, Law and Technology* (Vol. 21, pp. 279–297). Springer Science and Business Media B.V., DOI: 10.1007/978-3-030-29053-5_14

Drees, H., Kubitza, D. O., Lipp, J., Pretzsch, S., & Langdon, C. S. (2021). Mobility data space – first implementation and business opportunities. In *ITS World Congress*.

Du, Y., Mendes, N., Rasouli, S., Mohammadi, J., & Moura, P. (2023). Federated Learning Assisted Distributed Energy Optimization. *Electrical Engineering and Systems Science*. http://arxiv.org/abs/2311.13785

Dubey, S., & Sharma, R. (2024). The Privacy Paradox: The Future of Personal Data Protection in the Big Data Age. Issue 6 Int'l JL Mgmt. &. *Human.*, *7*, 1647.

Duhan, S., Gulia, P., Gill, N. S., Shukla, P. K., Khan, S. B., Almusharraf, A., & Alkhaldi, N. (2024). Investigating attention mechanisms for plant disease identification in challenging environments. *Heliyon, 10*(9), e29802. Advance online publication. DOI: 10.1016/j.heliyon.2024.e29802 PMID: 38707335

Du, K., Zhao, Y., Mao, R., Xing, F., & Cambria, E. (2025). Natural language processing in finance: A survey. *Information Fusion, 115*, 102755. Advance online publication. DOI: 10.1016/j.inffus.2024.102755

Du, Y., Mendes, N., Rasouli, S., Mohammadi, J., & Moura, P. (2024). Federated learning assisted distributed energy optimization. *IET Renewable Power Generation, 18*(14), 2524–2538. Advance online publication. DOI: 10.1049/rpg2.13101

Dwork, C., & Roth, A. (2014). The algorithmic foundations of differential privacy. *Foundations and Trends in Theoretical Computer Science, 9*(3–4), 211–407. DOI: 10.1561/0400000042

Ebers, M., & Krõõt Tupay, P. (2023). Outlook on AI and public service delivery. In Ebers, M., & Krõõt Tupay, P. (Eds.), *Artificial intelligence and machine learning powered public service delivery in Estonia* (pp. 111–120). Springer. DOI: 10.1007/978-3-031-19667-6

ECB. (2020). *Report on a digital euro.* https://www.ecb.europa.eu/pub/pdf/other/Report_on_a_digital_euro~4d7268b458.en.pdf

Edwards, L. (2016). Privacy, security and data protection in smart cities: A critical EU law perspective. *European Data Protection Law Review, 2*(1), 28–58. DOI: 10.21552/EDPL/2016/1/6

El Barachi, M. 2009. Integrating Context-Awareness in the IP Multimedia Subsystem for Enhanced Session Control and Service Provisioning Capabilities. Ph.D. thesis. Concordia University.

El-Sherif, D. M., & Khalil, E. E. (2022). Policy instruments for facilitating smart city governance. In *Smart Cities Policies and Financing* (pp. 305–317). Elsevier. DOI: 10.1016/B978-0-12-819130-9.00052-8

Esser, P., Kulal, S., Blattmann, A., Entezari, R., Müller, J., Saini, H., & Rombach, R. (2024, July). Scaling rectified flow transformers for high-resolution image synthesis. *Forty-first international conference on machine learning.*

Estevez, E., Pardo, T. A., & Scholl, H. J. (Eds.). (2021). *Smart cities and smart governance: Towards the 22nd century sustainable city* (Vol. 37). Springer Nature. DOI: 10.1007/978-3-030-61033-3_4

European Commission. (2021). Proposal for a regulation laying down harmonized rules on artificial intelligence (Artificial Intelligence Act). *European Commission.* Retrieved from https://eur-lex.europa.eu

European Parliament & Council. (2016). Regulation (EU) 2016/679 of the European Parliament and of the Council of 27 April 2016 on the protection of natural persons with regard to the processing of personal data and on the free movement of such data (General Data Protection Regulation). *Official Journal of the European Union, L, 119*, 1–88.

European Parliament & Council. (2023). Regulation (EU) 2023/2854 of the European Parliament and of the Council of 13 December 2023 on harmonised rules on fair access to and use of data and amending Regulation (EU) 2017/2394 and Directive (EU) 2020/1828 (Data Act). *Official Journal of the European Union, L, 151*, 1–16.

European Union. (2016). *Regulation (EU) 2016/679 of the European Parliament and of the Council of 27 April 2016 on the protection of natural persons with regard to the processing of personal data and on the free movement of such data, and repealing Directive 95/46/EC* (General Data Protection Regulation). Official Journal of the European Union, L119, 1–88.

Fadlullah, F. T. (2017). State-of-the-art deep learning: Evolving machine intelligence toward tomorrow's intelligent network traffic control systems. *IEEE Commun. Surv.Tutor. 19 (4) (2017)* (pp. 2432–2455,). IEEE http://dx.doi.org/.DOI: 10.1109/COMST.2017

Falcão, R., Matar, R., Rauch, B., Elberzhager, F., & Koch, M. (2023). A reference architecture for enabling interoperability and data sovereignty in the Agricultural Data Space. *Information (Basel), 14*(3), 197. DOI: 10.3390/info14030197

Fan, W. Q., Ismail, A. S., Mohammed, F., & Mukred, M. (2025). AI-Driven Smart City Security and Surveillance System: A Bibliometric Analysis. In *Current and Future Trends on AI Applications* (Vol. 1, pp. 305–328). Springer Nature Switzerland. DOI: 10.1007/978-3-031-75091-5_17

Farazdaghi, E., Eslahi, M., & El Meouche, R. (2021). An overview of the use of biometric techniques in smart cities. *The International Archives of the Photogrammetry, Remote Sensing and Spatial Information Sciences, 44*, 41–45. DOI: 10.5194/isprs-archives-XLIV-2-W1-2021-41-2021

Farhud, D. D., & Zokaei, S. (2021). Ethical Issues of Artificial Intelligence in Medicine and Healthcare. *Iranian Journal of Public Health, 50*(11). Advance online publication. DOI: 10.18502/ijph.v50i11.7600 PMID: 35223619

FATF (2012 - 2023). (2023). *International Standards on Combating Money Laundering and the Financing of Terrorism & Proliferation.* www.fatf-gafi.org/en/publications/Fatfrecommendations/Fatf-recommendations.html

FATF. (2021). *Opportunities and Challenges of New Technologies for AML/CFT.* www.fatf-gafi.org

FATF. (2022). *Targeted Update on Implementation of the FATF Standards on Virtual Assets and Virtual Asset Service Providers.* www.fatf-gafi.org/publications/fatfrecommendations/documents/targeted-update-virtual-assets-vasps.html

Fawzy, R. M. (2024). BIOMETRIC CITIZENS in smart cities: Re-evaluating citizens' conceptualizations in smart cities policies as extended metaphorical arguments. *Journal of Language and Politics, 23*(2), 283–305. DOI: 10.1075/jlp.22097.faw

Feldstein, S. (2019). The Global Expansion of AI Surveillance: Vol. 17. *No. 9.* Carnegie Endowment for International Peace.

Fernandes, S. (2017). *Performance evaluation for network services, systems and protocols.* Springer. DOI: 10.1007/978-3-319-54521-9

Ferrag, (2020). Deep learning for cyber security intrusion detection approaches, datasets and comparative study . *MIT PRESS*, 716.

Ferrara, E. (2024). Fairness and bias in artificial intelligence: A brief survey of sources, impacts, and mitigation strategies. *Sci, 6*(1), 3.

Firdausy, D. R., Silva, P. D. A., Van Sinderen, M., & Iacob, M. E. (2022b). Towards a reference enterprise architecture to enforce digital sovereignty in international data spaces. In *2022 IEEE 24th Conference on Business Informatics (CBI)* (Vol. 1, pp. 117-125). IEEE. DOI: 10.1109/CBI54897.2022.00020

Firdausy, D., Silva, P. D. A., van Sinderen, M. J., & Iacob, M. E. (2022a). Semantic discovery and selection of data connectors in international data spaces. In *Interoperability for Enterprise Systems and Applications.* I-ESA.

Floridi, L. (2020). The fight for digital sovereignty: What it is, and why it matters, especially for the eu. *Philosophy & Technology, 33*(3), 369–378. DOI: 10.1007/s13347-020-00423-6 PMID: 35194548

Folorunsho, O. S., Ayinde, A. Q., Olagoke, M. A., & Fatoye, O. E. (2019). Evaluating Cybersecurity Theories, Models, Standards and Frameworks. *Advances in Multidisciplinary and Scientific Research Journal Publication, 5*(4), 61–66. DOI: 10.22624/AIMS/BHI/V5N4P7

Foong, K., Tan, C., & Tan, K. (2018). Singapore Smart Nation: Data analytics driving smart cities. *Journal of Telecommunications and the Digital Economy*, *6*(3), 1–15.

Frana, M. (2021). Assessing Smart Nation Singapore as an international model for AI responsibility. *AI & Society*, *36*(3), 789–805.

Franklin, M., Halevy, A., & Maier, D. (2005). From databases to dataspaces: A new abstraction for information management. *SIGMOD Record*, *34*(4), 27–33. DOI: 10.1145/1107499.1107502

Frost, J., Shin, H. S., & Wierts, P. (2020). *An early stablecoin? The Bank of Amsterdam and the governance of money* (902). https://www.bis.org/publ/work902.htm

FSB. (2020). *Regulation, Supervision and Oversight of "Global Stablecoin" Arrangements*. https://www.fsb.org/uploads/P131020-3.pdf

Fu, A., Zhang, X., Xiong, N., Gao, Y., Wang, H., & Zhang, J. (2022). VFL: A Verifiable Federated Learning With Privacy-Preserving for Big Data in Industrial IoT. *IEEE Transactions on Industrial Informatics*, *18*(5), 3316–3326. DOI: 10.1109/TII.2020.3036166

Galič, M. (2022). Smart cities as "big brother only to the masses": The limits of personal privacy and personal surveillance. *Surveillance & Society*, *20*(3), 306–311. DOI: 10.24908/ss.v20i3.15759

Gao, S.-H., Cheng, M.-M., Zhao, K., Zhang, X.-Y., Yang, M.-H., & Torr, P. (2021). Res2Net: A New Multi-Scale Backbone Architecture. *IEEE Transactions on Pattern Analysis and Machine Intelligence*, *43*(2), 652–662. DOI: 10.1109/TPAMI.2019.2938758 PMID: 31484108

Garg, N. (2013). *Apache kafka*. Packt Publishing Birmingham.

Gautam, V., Sunidhi, S., & Prasad, S. (2025). AI-Powered Surveillance for Smart Cities. In *Internet of Vehicles and Computer Vision Solutions for Smart City Transformations* (pp. 245–265). Springer Nature Switzerland. DOI: 10.1007/978-3-031-72959-1_11

Ghavamipour, A. R., Turkmen, F., & Jiang, X. (2022). Privacy-preserving logistic regression with secret sharing. *BMC Medical Informatics and Decision Making*, *22*(89), 1–11. DOI: 10.1186/s12911-022-01811-y PMID: 35366870

Ghazal, T. M., Hasan, M. K., Alzoubi, H. M., Alshurideh, M., Ahmad, M., & Akbar, S. S. (2023). Internet of things connected wireless sensor networks for smart cities. In *The Effect of Information Technology on Business and Marketing Intelligence Systems* (pp. 1953–1968). Springer International Publishing. DOI: 10.1007/978-3-031-12382-5_107

Ghelani, D., Hua, T. K., & Koduru, S. K. R. (2022). Cyber Security Threats, Vulnerabilities, and Security Solutions Models in Banking. *Authorea Preprints*. https://www.authorea.com/doi/full/10.22541/au.166385206.63311335 DOI: 10.22541/au.166385206.63311335/v1

Giannopoulou, A. (2020). Data Protection Compliance Challenges for Self-Sovereign Identity. SSRN *Electronic Journal*. DOI: 10.2139/ssrn.3671523

Giese, T., & Anderl, R. (2022, November). Maintaining Control over Distributed Data Through a Data Sovereignty Model. In *2022 IEEE 7th International Conference on Information Technology and Digital Applications (ICITDA)* (pp. 1-7). IEEE. DOI: 10.1109/ICITDA55840.2022.9971218

Gil, G., Arnaiz, A., Diez, F. J., & Higuero, M. V. (2020, June). *Evaluation methodology for distributed data usage control solutions. In 2020 Global Internet of Things Summit (GIoTS)*. IEEE.

Gil, G., Arnaiz, A., Higuero, M., Diez, F. J., & Jacob, E. (2022). Context-Aware Policy Analysis for Distributed Usage Control. *Energies*, *15*(19), 7113. DOI: 10.3390/en15197113

Gill, A. S., & Germann, S. (2022). Conceptual and normative approaches to AI governance for a global digital ecosystem supportive of the UN Sustainable Development Goals (SDGs). *AI and Ethics*, *2*(2), 293–301. DOI: 10.1007/s43681-021-00058-z PMID: 34790947

Glasze, G., Cattaruzza, A., Douzet, F., Dammann, F., Bertran, M.-G., Bômont, C., Braun, M., Danet, D., Desforges, A., Géry, A., Grumbach, S., Hummel, P., Limonier, K., Münßinger, M., Nicolai, F., Pétiniaud, L., Winkler, J., & Zanin, C. (2022). Contested Spatialities of Digital Sovereignty. *Geopolitics*, *28*(2), 919–958. DOI: 10.1080/14650045.2022.2050070

Glasze, G., Dörfler, T., & Schöne, L. (2021). Contested spatialities of digital sovereignty. *Geoforum*, *124*, 1–10.

Goddard, M. (2017). The eu general data protection regulation (gdpr): European regulation that has a global impact. *International Journal of Market Research*, *59*(6), 703–705. DOI: 10.2501/IJMR-2017-050

Gostin, L. O., Halabi, S. F., & Wilson, K. (2018). Health Data and Privacy in the Digital Era. *Journal of the American Medical Association, 320*(3), 233–234. DOI: 10.1001/jama.2018.8374 PMID: 29926092

Gstrein, O. J., & Beaulieu, A. (2022). How to protect privacy in a datafied society? A presentation of multiple legal and conceptual approaches. *Philosophy & Technology, 35*(3), 1–38. DOI: 10.1007/s13347-022-00497-4 PMID: 35127339

Guembe, B., Misra, S., & Azeta, A. (2024). Privacy Issues, Attacks, Countermeasures and Open Problems in Federated Learning: A Survey. *Applied Artificial Intelligence, 38*(1), 2410504. Advance online publication. DOI: 10.1080/08839514.2024.2410504

Gupta, S., Hasan, W., Singh, S., Kumar, D., Ansari, M. J., & Nisar, S. (2024). *Agriculture 4.0: Smart Farming with IoT and Artificial Intelligence*. CRC Press. DOI: 10.1201/9781003570219

Haleem, H. (2023). AI-powered Surveillance of Drones and Vehicles: A Step Towards Smart Cities.

Han, J., Huang, Y., Liu, S., & Towey, K. (2020). Artificial intelligence for anti-money laundering: A review and extension. *Digital Finance, 2*(3-4), 211–239. DOI: 10.1007/s42521-020-00023-1

Hansen, M., Jensen, M., & Rost, M. (2015, May). *Protection goals for privacy engineering. In 2015 IEEE security and privacy workshops*. IEEE.

Hardy, S. (2019). Estonia's digital diplomacy. *Digital Diplomacy Journal, 2*(1), 45–60.

Ha, S. (2022). Public engagement in South Korea's AI strategy: Opportunities and limits. *Korean Journal of Public Policy, 17*(1), 59–75.

Hashni, T., Amudha, T., & Ramakrishnan, S. (2022). Smart Farming Approaches Towards Sustainable Agriculture—. *Survey (London, England), 1415*, 695–714. DOI: 10.1007/978-981-16-7330-6_52

Haykin, S. (1998). *Neural networks: a comprehensive foundation*. Prentice Hall PTR.

He, K., Kim, D. D., & Asghar, M. R. (2023). Adversarial machine learning for network intrusion detection systems: A comprehensive survey. *IEEE Communications Surveys and Tutorials, 25*(1), 538–566. DOI: 10.1109/COMST.2022.3233793

Hellmeier, M., Pampus, J., Qarawlus, H., & Howar, F. (2023). Implementing Data Sovereignty: Requirements & Challenges from Practice. *Proceedings of the 18th International Conference on Availability, Reliability and Security*, 1–9. DOI: 10.1145/3600160.3604995

Hellmeier, M., & von Scherenberg, F. (2023). A Delimitation of Data Sovereignty from Digital and Technological Sovereignty. In *ECIS*.

Heurix, J., Zimmermann, P., Neubauer, T., & Fenz, S. (2015). A taxonomy for privacy enhancing technologies. *Computers & Security*, *53*, 1–17. DOI: 10.1016/j.cose.2015.05.002

Ho, K. C. (2017). Smart subjects for a smart nation? Governing (smart) mentalities in Singapore. *Urban Studies (Edinburgh, Scotland)*, *54*(13), 3101–3118. DOI: 10.1177/0042098016664305

Hongladarom, S., & Bandasak, T. (2024). Digital identity and sovereignty in the Global South: The ethics of AI control. *Ethics and Information Technology*, *26*(1), 14–27.

Hoofnagle, C. J., van der Sloot, B., & Borgesius, F. Z. (2019). The European Union general data protection regulation: What it is and what it means. *Information & Communications Technology Law*, *28*(1), 65–98. DOI: 10.1080/13600834.2019.1573501

Horgan, D., Hajduch, M., Vrana, M., Soderberg, J., Hughes, N., Omar, M. I., & Sky Gross, E. (2022, August). European health data space—An opportunity now to grasp the future of data-driven healthcare. [). MDPI.]. *Health Care*, *10*(9), 1629. PMID: 36141241

Hu, J., & McKay Bowen, C. (2023). Advancing microdata privacy protection: A review of synthetic data methods. *Wiley Interdisciplinary Reviews: Computational Statistics*, 16.

Hu, K., Wu, J., Li, Y., Lu, M., Weng, L., & Xia, M. (2022a). FedGCN: Federated Learning-Based Graph Convolutional Networks for Non-Euclidean Spatial Data. *Mathematics*, *10*(6), 1000. DOI: 10.3390/math10061000

Hummel, P., Braun, M., Augsberg, S., & Dabrock, P. (2018). Sovereignty and data sharing. *ITU Journal on Future and Evolving Technologies, 1*(2).

Hummel, P., Braun, M., Tretter, M., & Dabrock, P. (2021). Data sovereignty: A review. *Big Data & Society*, *8*(1), 205395172098201. DOI: 10.1177/2053951720982012

Hussain, F. R. H. (2019). *Machine learning in IoT security: current solution and future challenges.* arXiv preprint arXiv:1904.05735.

Hutchinson, C. F. (1982). Classification improvement. *Photogrammetric Engineering and Remote Sensing*, *44*, 123–130.

Igwenagu, U. T. I., Salami, A. A., Arigbabu, A. S., Mesode, C. E., Oladoyinbo, T. O., & Olaniyi, O. O. (2024). Securing the Digital Frontier: Strategies for Cloud Computing Security, Database Protection, and Comprehensive Penetration Testing. *Journal of Engineering Research and Reports*, *26*(6), 60–75. DOI: 10.9734/jerr/2024/v26i61162

Ikram,. (2021). Outlier hunting using XGBoost ensemble of deep neural network models. *Journal of Network and Computer Applications*, 175-188. *Assessment* (pp. 1-8). Cyber SA.

Iqbal, R., & Ismail, S. (2025). Unbiased AI for a Sovereign Digital Future: A Bias Detection Framework. International Conference on Digital Sovereignty (ICDS). Elsevier ScienceDirect. *Procedia Computer Science*, *254*, 118–126. DOI: 10.1016/j.procs.2025.02.070

Irion, K. (2012). Government cloud computing and national data sovereignty. *Policy and Internet*, *4*(3-4), 40–71. DOI: 10.1002/poi3.10

Iuliano, A., Liò, P., Manfredi, G., & Romaniello, F. (2024). Denoising Probabilistic Diffusion Models for Synthetic Healthcare Image Generation. *2024 IEEE International Workshop on Metrology for Living Environment (MetroLivEnv)* 415-420. DOI: 10.1109/MetroLivEnv60384.2024.10615511

Ivic, S., & Troitin˜o, D. R. (2022). Digital sovereignty and identity in the European union: A challenge for building europe. *European Studies*, *9*(2), 80–109. DOI: 10.2478/eustu-2022-0015

Jahankhani, H., Kendzierskyj, S., & Colin, A. (2021). Blockchain as a tool for transparency and governance in the delivery of development aid. In *Strategy, Leadership, and AI in the Cyber Ecosystem* (pp. 93–111). Academic Press. DOI: 10.1016/B978-0-12-821442-8.00006-9

Jain, V., & Mitra, A. (2025). AI Applications in Secure 6G-Enabled Smart City Infrastructure. In Building Tomorrow's Smart Cities With 6G Infrastructure Technology (pp. 175-198). IGI Global Scientific Publishing.

Jarke, M., Otto, B., & Ram, S. (2019). Data sovereignty and data space ecosystems. *Business & Information Systems Engineering*, *61*(5), 549–550. DOI: 10.1007/s12599-019-00614-2

Javaheri, D., Fahmideh, M., Chizari, H., Lalbakhsh, P., & Hur, J. (2023). Cybersecurity threats in FinTech: A systematic review. *Expert Systems with Applications*, •••, 122697.

Jawad, L. A. (2024). Security and Privacy in Digital Healthcare Systems: Challenges and Mitigation Strategies. *Abhigyan, 42*(1), 23–31.

Jeong, D. (2023). Korea's AI governance challenges and the role of law. *Korean Review of Law and Society, 30*(2), 78–96.

Jeyakumar, I. H. J., & Kubach, M. (2024). A trust implementation model for cross-domain decentralized identity ecosystems: architecture, use case, and implementation. In S. Misra, P. Kvalvik, K. M. Kjølerbakken, & R. Damasevicius (Eds.), *International Conference on Digital Sovereignty (ICDS), Procedia Computer Science* (Vol. 254, pp. 10–19). Elsevier B.V. DOI: 10.1016/j.procs.2025.02.059

Jha, S., & Topol, E. J. (2016). Adapting to artificial intelligence: Radiologists and pathologists as information specialists. *Journal of the American Medical Association, 316*(22), 2353–2354. DOI: 10.1001/jama.2016.17438 PMID: 27898975

Jiang, M., & Belli, L. (Eds.). (2025). *Digital Sovereignty in the BRICS Countries: How the Global South and Emerging Power Alliances Are Reshaping Digital Governance*. Cambridge University Press., DOI: 10.1017/9781009531085

Jindal, V., Kukreja, V., Mehta, S., Yadav, R., & Mohd, N. (2023). Evolving Agritech: Implementing Federated Learning & CNN for Parsley Leaf Disease Detection. *2023 3rd Asian Conference on Innovation in Technology (ASIANCON)*, 1–6. https://consensus.app/papers/evolving-agritech-implementing-federated-learning-jindal/aacac7e7b59b597a869b48cb346bd161

Johnson, J., Hevia, A., Yergin, R., Karbassi, S., Levine, A., & Ortiz, J. (2022). Data governance frameworks for smart cities: Key considerations for data management and use. Journal of Law & Mobility, 1.

Jordon, J., Szpruch, L., Houssiau, F., Bottarelli, M., Cherubin, G., Maple, C., . . . Weller, A. (2022). Synthetic Data—what, why and how? arXiv preprint arXiv:2205.03257.

Jullum, M., Løland, A., Huseby, R. B., Ånonsen, G., & Lorentzen, J. (2020). Detecting money laundering transactions with machine learning. *Journal of Money Laundering Control, 23*(1), 173–186. DOI: 10.1108/JMLC-07-2019-0055

Kalfas, D., Kalogiannidis, S., Papaevangelou, O., Melfou, K., & Chatzitheodoridis, F. (2024). Integration of Technology in Agricultural Practices towards Agricultural Sustainability: A Case Study of Greece. *Sustainability (Basel), 16*(7), 2664. DOI: 10.3390/su16072664

Kanaan, A. AL-Hawamleh, A., Alorfi, A., & Aloun, M. (2024). Cybersecurity Resilience for Business: A Comprehensive Model for Proactive Defense and Swift Recovery. *2024 2nd International Conference on Cyber Resilience (ICCR)*, 1–7. DOI: 10.1109/ICCR61006.2024.10532881

Kandasamy, K., Srinivas, S., Achuthan, K., & Rangan, V. P. (2020). IoT cyber risk: A holistic analysis of cyber risk assessment frameworks, risk vectors, and risk ranking process. *EURASIP Journal on Information Security*, *2020*(1), 8. Advance online publication. DOI: 10.1186/s13635-020-00111-0

Karbassi, S., Levine, A., & Ortiz, J. (2022). Data Governance Frameworks for Smart Cities.

Katsikas, S. K. (2025). Towards a cybersecurity-oriented research agenda for digital sovereignty. *Procedia Computer Science*, *254*, 279–288. DOI: 10.1016/j.procs.2025.02.087

Kaur, G., Habibi Lashkari, Z., & Habibi Lashkari, A. (2021). Cybersecurity Threats in FinTech. In G. Kaur, Z. Habibi Lashkari, & A. Habibi Lashkari, *Understanding Cybersecurity Management in FinTech* (pp. 65–87). Springer International Publishing. DOI: 10.1007/978-3-030-79915-1_4

Kenneth, O. M., Bashir, S. A., Abisoye, O. A., & Mohammed, A. D. (2021). Face morphing attack detection in the presence of post-processed image sources using neighborhood component analysis and decision tree classifier. *Information and Communication Technology and Applications: Third International Conference, ICTA 2020, Minna, Nigeria, November 24–27, 2020, Revised Selected Papers 3*, 340–354.

Kerikmäe, T., & Pärn-Lee, E. (2020). Legal dilemmas of Estonian artificial intelligence strategy. *European Journal of Law and Technology*, *11*(1).

Kesan, J. P., & Hayes, C. M. (2014). *Creating a "Circle of Trust" to Further Digital Privacy and Cybersecurity Goals* (SSRN Scholarly Paper 2135618). Social Science Research Network. DOI: 10.2139/ssrn.2135618

Kessler, R., Raja, K., Tapia, J., & Busch, C. (2024). Towards minimizing efforts for Morphing Attacks—Deep embeddings for morphing pair selection and improved Morphing Attack Detection. *PLoS One*, *19*(5), e0304610. DOI: 10.1371/journal.pone.0304610 PMID: 38820451

Kethineni, K., & Gera, P. (2023). Iot-Based Privacy-Preserving Anomaly Detection Model for Smart Agriculture. *Systems*, *11*(6), 304. DOI: 10.3390/systems11060304

Khan, F. S., & Khan, S., Mohd, Mohd. N. H., Waseem, A., Khan, M. N. A., Ali, S., & Ahmed, R. (2022). Federated learning-based UAVs for the diagnosis of Plant Diseases. *2022 International Conference on Engineering and Emerging Technologies (ICEET)*, 1–6. DOI: 10.1109/ICEET56468.2022.10007133

Khanna, P., & Khanra, S. (2023). Citizen empowerment through smart surveillance: Evidence from Indian smart cities. Digital Policy. *Regulation & Governance, 25*(4), 385–401. DOI: 10.1108/DPRG-11-2022-0141

Khatri, V., & Brown, C. V. (2010). Designing data governance. *Communications of the ACM, 53*(1), 148–152. DOI: 10.1145/1629175.1629210

Kilincer, I. F., Ertam, F., Sengur, A., Tan, R.-S., & Acharya, U. R. (2023). Automated detection of cybersecurity attacks in healthcare systems with recursive feature elimination and multilayer perceptron optimization. *Biocybernetics and Biomedical Engineering, 43*(1), 30–41. DOI: 10.1016/j.bbe.2022.11.005

Killelea, P. (2002). *Web Performance Tuning: speeding up the web*. O'Reilly Media, Inc.

Kim, Y., Lee, J., & Park, H. (2020). Scalable and Real-Time Deep Learning-Based Anomaly Detection Systems. *IEEE Access : Practical Innovations, Open Solutions, 8*, 135550–135560.

Kim, Y., & Moon, J. (2021). Governing AI in South Korea: A participatory approach to algorithmic regulation. *Information Polity, 26*(4), 475–488.

Kindylidi, I. (2022). The Data Protection Implications of the EU AML Framework: A Critical Overview & the Case of AI. In A. Gryszczyńska, P. Polański, N. Gruschka, K. Rannenberg, & M. Adamczyk (Eds.), *Privacy Technologies and Policy. APF 2022. Lecture Notes in Computer Science, vol 13279: Vol. 13279 LNCS* (pp. 37–49). Springer Science and Business Media Deutschland GmbH. DOI: 10.1007/978-3-031-07315-1_3

Kitchenham, B. (2007). *Guidelines for performing systematic literature reviews in software engineering* (Vol. 5). Technical report, ver. 2.3 ebse technical report. ebse.

Klare, M., Hrestic, R., Stelter, A., & Lechner, U. (2025). Digital Sovereignty and Digital Transformation Practice Recommendation for the Software Life Cycle Process. *Procedia Computer Science, 254*, 221–229. DOI: 10.1016/j.procs.2025.02.081

Kocher, G., & Kumar, G. (2021). Machine learning and deep learning methods for intrusion detection systems: Recent developments and challenges. *Soft Computing, 25*(15), 9731–9763. DOI: 10.1007/s00500-021-05893-0

Kollu, V. N., Janarthanan, V., Karupusamy, M., & Ramachandran, M. (2023). Cloud-Based Smart Contract Analysis in FinTech Using IoT-Integrated Federated Learning in Intrusion Detection. *Data, 8*(5), 83. DOI: 10.3390/data8050083

Konkin, A., & Zapechnikov, S. (2023). Zero knowledge proof and ZK-SNARK for private blockchains. *Journal of Computer Virology and Hacking Techniques, 19*(3), 443–449. DOI: 10.1007/s11416-023-00466-1

Kularathne, Y., Janitha, P., Ambepitiya, S., Ahamed, T., Wijesundara, D., & Sothyrajah, P. (2024). SynthVision—Harnessing Minimal Input for Maximal Output in Computer Vision Models using Synthetic Image data. arXiv preprint arXiv:2402.02826.

Kumara, S., Singha, S. K., Kumarb, R., Subbac, C. K., Chuid, K. T., Brij, B., & Guptae, B. B. (2025). Neoteric Threat Intelligence Ensuring Digital Sovereignty and Trust through ML-Infused Proactive Defense Analytics for NEXT-G and Beyond Ecosystems. *International Conference on Digital Sovereignty (ICDS).* Elsevier ScienceDirect. *Procedia Computer Science, 254*, 39–47. DOI: 10.1016/j.procs.2025.02.062

Kuner, C. (2013). Transborder Data Flows and Data Privacy Law. In *Transborder Data Flows and Data Privacy Law*. Oxford University Press., DOI: 10.1093/acprof:oso/9780199674619.001.0001

Kuner, C. (2017). Reality and illusion in EU data transfer regulation post Schrems. *German Law Journal, 18*(4), 881–918. DOI: 10.1017/S2071832200022197

Kupferschmid, K. (2024, September 17). *Requiring AI Transparency Won't Destroy the Trade Secrets of AI Companies*. Copyright Alliance. https://copyrightalliance.org/ai-transparency/

Kusharki, M. B., Misra, S., Muhammad-Bello, B., Salihu, I. A., & Suri, B. (2022). Automatic Classification of Equivalent Mutants in Mutation Testing of Android Applications. *Symmetry, 14*(4), 820. Advance online publication. DOI: 10.3390/sym14040820

Kuzminykh, I., Ghita, B., Sokolov, V., & Bakhshi, T. (2021). Information Security Risk Assessment. *Encyclopedia, 1*(3), 602–617. DOI: 10.3390/encyclopedia1030050

Kwon, J., & Park, D. (2021). Toward Data-Adaptable TinyML using Model Partial Replacement for Resource Frugal Edge Device. *ACM International Conference Proceeding Series*, 133–135. DOI: 10.1145/3432261.3439865

Lauf, F., Scheider, S., Bartsch, J., Herrmann, P., Radic, M., Rebbert, M., ... & Meister, S. (2022). Linking data sovereignty and data economy: arising areas of tension.

Lenatti, M., Paglialonga, A., Orani, V., Ferretti, M., & Mongelli, M. (2023). Characterization of Synthetic Health Data Using Rule-Based Artificial Intelligence Models. *IEEE Journal of Biomedical and Health Informatics*, *27*(8), 3760–3769. DOI: 10.1109/JBHI.2023.3236722 PMID: 37018683

Leong, D., & Lee, W. (2021). The internet in Singapore: A study of its impact on society. *Asian Journal of Communication*, *31*(3), 210–225.

Li, A., Zhang, L., Tan, J., Qin, Y., Wang, J., & Li, X. (2021). Sample-Level Data Selection for Federated Learning. *IEEE INFOCOM 2021 - IEEE Conference on Computer Communications*, 1–10. https://consensus.app/papers/samplelevel-data-selection-federated-learning-li/8fcb7b02fb005d69a5b020ecf935b16a

Li, A., Zhang, L., Wang, J., Han, F., & Li, X.-Y. (2022). Privacy-Preserving Efficient Federated-Learning Model Debugging. *IEEE Transactions on Parallel and Distributed Systems*, *33*(10), 2291–2303. https://consensus.app/papers/privacypreserving-efficient-federatedlearning-model-li/65538867e75d549c92f8fa43330a3e38. DOI: 10.1109/TPDS.2021.3137321

Liamputtong, P. (2019). *Handbook of research methods in health social sciences*. DOI: 10.1007/978-981-10-5251-4

Liang, J., Pang, R., Li, C., & Wang, T. (2024). Model extraction attacks revisited. *Proceedings of the 19th ACM Asia Conference on Computer and Communications Security*, 1231–1245.

Lin, S., Xiu, Y., Kong, J., Yang, C., & Zhao, C. (2023). An Effective Pyramid Neural Network Based on Graph-Related Attentions Structure for Fine-Grained Disease and Pest Identification in Intelligent Agriculture. *Agriculture*, *13*(3), 567. DOI: 10.3390/agriculture13030567

Lin, W.-Y., Hu, Y.-H., & Tsai, C.-F. (2011). Machine learning in financial crisis prediction: A survey. *IEEE Transactions on Systems, Man, and Cybernetics. Part C, Applications and Reviews*, *42*(4), 421–436.

Li, S., & Huang, Y. (2021). The genesis, design and implications of China's central bank digital currency. *China Economic Journal*, *14*(1), 67–77. DOI: 10.1080/17538963.2020.1870273

Li, T., Sahu, A. K., Talwalkar, A. S., & Smith, V. (2019). Federated Learning: Challenges, Methods, and Future Directions. *IEEE Signal Processing Magazine*, *37*, 50–60. https://consensus.app/papers/federated-learning-challenges-methods-future-directions-li/dfd23c40c91d5511b4c14668a5f6cabc

Liu, T., Gu, X., Li, S., Bai, Y., Wang, T., & Yang, X. (2023). Static voltage stability margin prediction considering new energy uncertainty based on graph attention networks and long short-term memory networks. *IET Renewable Power Generation*, *17*(9), 2290–2301. DOI: 10.1049/rpg2.12731

Liu, Y., Dong, Z., Liu, B., Xu, Y., & Ding, Z. (2023). FedForecast: A federated learning framework for short-term probabilistic individual load forecasting in smart grid. *International Journal of Electrical Power & Energy Systems*, *152*, 109172. DOI: 10.1016/j.ijepes.2023.109172

Liu, Z. W., Wang, Z., Liu, X., Zeng, N., Liu, Y., & Alsaadi, F. E. (2017). A survey of deep neural network architectures and their application. *Neurocomputing*, *234*, 11–26. DOI: 10.1016/j.neucom.2016.12.038

Liu, Z., Yang, L., Fan, Z., Peng, H., & Yu, P. S. (2022). Federated Social Recommendation with Graph Neural Network. *ACM Transactions on Intelligent Systems and Technology*, *13*(4), 1–24. DOI: 10.1145/3501815

Li, Z., Bilal, M., Xu, X., Jiang, J., & Cui, Y. (2023). Federated Learning-Based Cross-Enterprise Recommendation With Graph Neural Networks. *IEEE Transactions on Industrial Informatics*, *19*(1), 673–682. DOI: 10.1109/TII.2022.3203395

Lokuliyana, S., Siriwardana, D., Kalupahanage, A. G. A., Bulathsinhala, D. N., Herath, H. M. S. D., & Herath, H. M. T. M. (2025). Enhancing IoT Resilience: Machine Learning Techniques for Autonomous Anomaly Detection and Threat Mitigation. *International Conference on Digital Sovereignty (ICDS)*. Elsevier ScienceDirect. *Procedia Computer Science*, *254*, 68–77. DOI: 10.1016/j.procs.2025.02.065

Long, M., Jia, C., & Peng, F. (2023). Face Morphing Detection Based on a Two-Stream Network with Channel Attention and Residual of Multiple Color Spaces. In Xu, Y., Yan, H., Teng, H., Cai, J., & Li, J. (Eds.), *Machine Learning for Cyber Security* (pp. 439–454). Springer Nature Switzerland. DOI: 10.1007/978-3-031-20102-8_34

Lopes, P. V., Silveira, L., Guimarães de Aquino, R. D., Ribeiro, C. H., Skoogh, A., & Filipe, A. N. V. (2024). Synthetic data generation for digital twins: Enabling production systems analysis in the absence of data. *International Journal of Computer Integrated Manufacturing*, *37*(10-11), 1252–1269. DOI: 10.1080/0951192X.2024.2322981

López-Martínez, A., Gil-Pérez, M., & Ruiz-Martínez, A. (2023). A comprehensive review of the state-of-the-art on security and privacy issues in healthcare. *ACM Computing Surveys*, *55*(12), 1–38. DOI: 10.1145/3571156

Lopez-Martin, M., Carro, B., Sanchez-Esguevillas, A., & Lloret, J. (2017). B. C.-E. (2017). Network traffic classifier with convolutional and recurrent neural networks for internet of things. *IEEE Access : Practical Innovations, Open Solutions, 5*, 18042–18050. DOI: 10.1109/ACCESS.2017.2747560

Losavio, M. M., Chow, K. P., Koltay, A., & James, J. (2018). The Internet of Things and the Smart City: Legal challenges with digital forensics, privacy, and security. *Security and Privacy, 1*(3), e23. DOI: 10.1002/spy2.23

Lu, L., & Chen, H. (2021). Digital Yuan: The Practice and Regulation of China's Central Bank Digital Currency (CBDC). *Butterworths Journal of International Banking and Financial Law, 36*(8), 601–603.

Mackey, T. K., Calac, A. J., Keshava, B. C., Yracheta, J., Tsosie, K. S., & Fox, K. (2022). Establishing a blockchain-enabled Indigenous data sovereignty framework for genomic data. *Cell, 185*(15), 2626–2631. DOI: 10.1016/j.cell.2022.06.030 PMID: 35868267

Madiega, T. (2020). *Digital sovereignty for Europe*. European Parliamentary Research Service.

Mahadeo, J., Hazari, Z., & Potvin, G. (2020). *Developing a computing identity framework: Understanding computer science and information technology career choice*. ACM Transactions on Computing Education., DOI: 10.1145/3365571

Mahmoud, A. A., Elkatatny, S., & Al Shehri, D. (2020). Application of machine learning in evaluation of the static young's modulus for sandstone formations. *Sustainability (Basel), 12*(5), 1880. DOI: 10.3390/su12051880

Mamba Kabala, D., Hafiane, A., Bobelin, L., & Canals, R. (2023). Image-based crop disease detection with federated learning. *Scientific Reports, 13*(1), 19220. Advance online publication. DOI: 10.1038/s41598-023-46218-5 PMID: 37932344

Manikandan, N. S., & Ganesan, K. (2022). Energy-aware vehicle/pedestrian detection and close movement alert at nighttime in dense slow traffic on Indian urban roads using a depth camera. *International Journal of Computational Vision and Robotics, 1*(1), 1. DOI: 10.1504/IJCVR.2022.10048790

Man, K., & Chahl, J. S. (2022). A Review of Synthetic Image Data and Its Use in Computer Vision. *Journal of Imaging, 8*(11), 8. DOI: 10.3390/jimaging8110310 PMID: 36422059

Manoury, M., Riedelsheimer, T., Hellmeier, M., & Meyer, T. (2025). Supporting Changes in Digital Ownership and Data Sovereignty Across the Automotive Value Chain with Catena-X. *Procedia Computer Science*, *253*, 374–383. DOI: 10.1016/j.procs.2025.01.099

Markevych, M., & Dawson, M. 2023. A review of enhancing intrusion detection systems for cybersecurity using artificial intelligence (ai), in: *International conference Knowledge-based Organization*, pp. 30–37. DOI: 10.2478/kbo-2023-0072

Martínez-Ramil, P., Bolaños-Frasquet, H., Hamuľák, O., & Kerikmäe, T. (2023). A Multidimensional Understanding of EU's Digital Sovereignty. In Troitiño, D. R., Kerikmäe, T., & Hamuľák, O. (Eds.), *Digital Development of the European Union: An Interdisciplinary Perspective* (pp. 235–247). Springer International Publishing., DOI: 10.1007/978-3-031-27312-4_15

Mattoo, A., & Meltzer, J. P. (2018). International Data Flows and Privacy: The Conflict and Its Resolution. *Journal of International Economic Law*, *21*(4), 769–789. DOI: 10.1093/jiel/jgy044

Mattsson, U. (2021). Privacy-Preserving Analytics and Secure Multiparty Computation. *ISACA Journal, 2*.

McKinney, S. M., Sieniek, M., Godbole, V., Godwin, J., Antropova, N., Ashrafian, H., & Darzi, A. (2020). International evaluation of an AI system for breast cancer screening. *Nature*, *577*(7788), 89–94. DOI: 10.1038/s41586-019-1799-6 PMID: 31894144

Mehta, S., Kukreja, V., & Gupta, R. (2023a). Empowering Precision Agriculture: Detecting Apple Leaf Diseases and Severity Levels with Federated Learning CNN. *2023 3rd International Conference on Intelligent Technologies (CONIT)*, 1–6. DOI: 10.1109/CONIT59222.2023.10205784

Mehta, S., Kukreja, V., & Vats, S. (2023). Empowering Farmers with AI: Federated Learning of CNNs for Wheat Diseases Multi-Classification. *2023 4th International Conference for Emerging Technology (INCET)*, 1–6. DOI: 10.1109/INCET57972.2023.10170091

Mishra,. (2019). A detailed investigation and analysis of using machine learning techniques for intrusion detection. *IEEE*, 686-728.

Misra, S., Barik, K., & Kvalvik, P. (2025). Digital Sovereignty in the Era of Industry 5.0: Challenges and Opportunities. *Procedia Computer Science*, *254*, 108–117. DOI: 10.1016/j.procs.2025.02.069

Mitrou, L. (2017). The General Data Protection Regulation: A Law for the Digital Age? In Synodinou, T.-E., Jougleux, P., Markou, C., & Prastitou, T. (Eds.), *EU Internet Law* (pp. 19–57). Springer International Publishing., DOI: 10.1007/978-3-319-64955-9_2

Moerel, L., & Timmers, P. (2021). Reflections on digital sovereignty. Brussels Privacy Hub Working Paper, 7(17).

Monteiro, A., Santos, S., & Gonçalves, P. H. (2021). Precision Agriculture for Crop and Livestock Farming—Brief Review. *Animals (Basel)*, *11*(8), 2345. https://consensus.app/papers/precision-agriculture-crop-livestock-farming—brief-monteiro/1eb-ba66706d655d390d22669be8bd500. DOI: 10.3390/ani11082345 PMID: 34438802

Mosa, M. J., Barhoom, A. M., Alhabbash, M. I., Harara, F. E., Abu-Nasser, B. S., & Abu-Naser, S. S. (2024). AI and Ethics in Surveillance: Balancing Security and Privacy in a Digital World.

Mpofu, P., Kembo, S. H., Chimbwanda, M., Jacques, S., Chitiyo, N., & Zvarevashe, K. (2023). A privacy-preserving federated learning architecture implementing data ownership and portability on edge end-points. *International Journal of Industrial Engineering and Operations Management*, *5*(2), 118–134. DOI: 10.1108/IJIEOM-02-2023-0020

Muhammed, D., Ahvar, E., Ahvar, S., Trocan, M., Montpetit, M.-J., & Ehsani, R. (2024a). Artificial Intelligence of Things (AIoT) for smart agriculture: A review of architectures, technologies and solutions. *Journal of Network and Computer Applications*, *228*, 103905. DOI: 10.1016/j.jnca.2024.103905

Mumuni, A., Mumuni, F., & Gerrar, N. K. (2024). A survey of synthetic data augmentation methods in computer vision. arXiv preprint arXiv:2403.10075.

Mustapha, A. M., Arogundade, O. T., Abayomi-Alli, A., Adesemowo, A. K., & Adeniran, O. J. (2024). An improved cloud-based business process compliance management system using a user-centered approach. *International Journal of System Assurance Engineering and Management*, *15*(11), 5111–5138. DOI: 10.1007/s13198-024-02494-6

Mustapha, A. M., Arogundade, O. T., Misra, S., Damasevicius, R., & Maskeliunas, R. (2020). A systematic literature review on compliance requirements management of business processes. *International Journal of System Assurance Engineering and Management*, *11*(3), 561–576. Advance online publication. DOI: 10.1007/s13198-020-00985-w

Mustapha, A. M., Arogundade, O. T., Vincent, O. R., & Adeniran, O. J. (2018). Towards a compliance requirement management for SMSEs: A model and architecture. *Information Systems and e-Business Management*, *16*(1), 155–185. Advance online publication. DOI: 10.1007/s10257-017-0354-y

Mustapha, A. M., Arogundade, O. T., Vincent, O. R., Adeniran, O. J., & Chen, X. (2017). A model-based business process compliance management architecture for SMSE towards effective adoption of cloud computing. *Proceedings of the IEEE International Conference on Computing, Networking and Informatics, ICCNI 2017, 2017-Janua.* DOI: 10.1109/ICCNI.2017.8123820

Nagel, L., Hierro, J. J., Perea, E., Lycklama, D., Mertens, C., Taillandier, A. S., . . . Grguric, A. (2021). *Design principles for data spaces: position paper* (No. RWTH-2022-09082). E. ON Energy Research Center.

Naik, N., & Jenkins, P. (2021). Sovrin Network for Decentralized Digital Identity: Analysing a Self-Sovereign Identity System Based on Distributed Ledger Technology. *2021 IEEE International Symposium on Systems Engineering (ISSE)*, 1–7. DOI: 10.1109/ISSE51541.2021.9582551

Nam, J., Jung, S., & Kim, J. (2024). The role of data hubs in South Korea's AI strategy. *Korean Journal of Information Policy*, *31*(1), 22–41.

Nandy, D. (2023). Human rights in the era of surveillance: Balancing security and privacy concerns. *Journal of Current Social and Political Issues*, *1*(1), 13–17. DOI: 10.15575/jcspi.v1i1.442

Nguyen, N.-B., Chandrasegaran, K., Abdollahzadeh, M., & Cheung, N.-M. (2023). Re-thinking model inversion attacks against deep neural networks. *Proceedings of the IEEE/CVF Conference on Computer Vision and Pattern Recognition*, 16384–16393. DOI: 10.1109/CVPR52729.2023.01572

Nnenna, U. J., Perpetua, U. I., Nchaga, A. M., Hadijah, T., & Mabonga, E. Accounting and Finance, Kampala International University, Uganda, & Nyamboga, T. O. (2024). Impact of Digital Governance on Public Service Delivery in East Africa. *IAA Journal of Arts and Humanities, 11*(1), 18–29. DOI: 10.59298/IAAJAH/2024/11.11829.11

Noor, Z., Hina, S., Hayat, F., & Shah, G. A. 2023. An intelligent context-aware threat detection and response model for smart cyber-physical systems. Internet of Things 23, 100843. NSL-KDD, K., accessed: 25.09.2024. nslkdd.https://www.kaggle.com/datasets/

Noor, U., Anwar, Z., Amjad, T., & Choo, K.-K. R. (2019). A machine learning-based FinTech cyber threat attribution framework using high-level indicators of compromise. *Future Generation Computer Systems*, *96*, 227–242. DOI: 10.1016/j.future.2019.02.013

Nyangaresi, V. O., Abduljabbar, Z. A., Mutlaq, K. A. A., Bulbul, S. S., Ma, J., Aldarwish, A. J., Honi, D. G., Al Sibahee, M. A., & Neamah, H. A. (2024). Smart city energy-efficient data privacy preservation protocol based on biometrics and fuzzy commitment scheme. *Scientific Reports*, *14*(1), 16223. DOI: 10.1038/s41598-024-67064-z PMID: 39003319

OASIS. (2013). extensible access control markup language (xacml) version 3.0. *A:(22 January 2013). URl:* http://docs. oasis-open. org/xacml/3.0/xacml-3.0-core-spec-os-en. html

Obermeyer, Z., Powers, B., Vogeli, C., & Mullainathan, S. (2019). Dissecting racial bias in an algorithm used to manage the health of populations. *Science*, *366*(6464), 447–453. DOI: 10.1126/science.aax2342 PMID: 31649194

Ogbonna Toochukwu, C., & Richards, D. and Y. H. (2024). Why Has Nigeria's Energy Deficit Persisted? A Literature Review on the Prevailing Factors Affecting Power Generation. In W. Hu Cungang and Cao (Ed.), *Conference Proceedings of the 2023 3rd International Joint Conference on Energy, Electrical and Power Engineering* (pp. 721–729). Springer Nature Singapore.

Olaye, E., Omafovbe, I., Aigbe, W. O., & Obuh, D. (2024). Personalized Governance Strategy for Patient Data in a Digital One Health Surveillance System. In S. Misra, P. Kvalvik, K. M. Kjølerbakken, & R. Damasevicius (Eds.), *International Conference on Digital Sovereignty (ICDS), Procedia Computer Science* (Vol. 254, pp. 20–29). Elsevier B.V. DOI: 10.1016/j.procs.2025.02.060

Oliveira, M. I. S., & Lóscio, B. F. (2018). What is a data ecosystem? In *Proceedings of the 19th Annual International Conference on Digital Government Research: Governance in the Data Age* (Article No. 74, pp. 1-9). Association for Computing Machinery.

Olson, R. S., & Moore, J. H. 2016. Tpot: A tree-based pipeline optimization tool for automating machine learning, in: Workshop on automatic machine learn- ing, PMLR. pp. 66-74.

Ortega-Delcampo, D., Conde, C., Palacios-Alonso, D., & Cabello, E. (2020). Border Control Morphing Attack Detection With a Convolutional Neural Network De-Morphing Approach. *IEEE Access : Practical Innovations, Open Solutions*, *8*, 92301–92313. DOI: 10.1109/ACCESS.2020.2994112

Osman, I. H., Anouze, A. L., Irani, Z., Al-Ayoubi, B., Lee, H., Balcı, A., Medeni, T. D., & Weerakkody, V. (2014). COBRA framework to evaluate e-government services: A citizen-centric perspective. *Government Information Quarterly*, *31*(2), 243–256. DOI: 10.1016/j.giq.2013.10.009

Otto, B. (2011). A morphology of the organisation of data governance.

Otto, B., Hompel, M. T., & Wrobel, S. (2019). International Data Spaces: Reference architecture for the digitization of industries. *Digital transformation*, 109-128.

Otto, B., Lohmann, S., Steinbuß, S., Teuscher, A., Auer, S., Boehmer, M., ... & Hierro, J. (2018). Ids reference architecture model. industrial data space. version 2.0.

Otto, B. (2019). Interview with Reinhold Achatz on "data sovereignty and data ecosystems". *Business & Information Systems Engineering*, *61*(5), 635–636. DOI: 10.1007/s12599-019-00609-z

Otto, B., Ten Hompel, M., & Wrobel, S. (2022). *Designing data spaces: The ecosystem approach to competitive advantage.* Springer Nature. DOI: 10.1007/978-3-030-93975-5

Ouahab, I. B. A., Elaachak, L., Bouhorma, M., Alluhaidan, Y. A., & Zafar, B. (2024, May). Voice Biometric Technology: Enhancing Public Safety and Security in Smart Cities. In *2024 Mediterranean Smart Cities Conference (MSCC)* (pp. 1-6). IEEE.

Palanisamy, V., & Verhaart, M. (2014). Compliance and Data Sovereignty Issues on Cloud Technology.

Palma, A., Acitelli, G., Marrella, A., Bonomi, S., & Angelini, M. (2024). A compliance assessment system for Incident Management process. *Computers & Security*, *146*, 104070. DOI: 10.1016/j.cose.2024.104070

Pampus, J., & Heisel, M. (2024). An Empirical Examination of the Technical Aspects of Data Sovereignty. In *Proceedings of the 19th International Conference on Software Technologies* (pp. 112-122). DOI: 10.5220/0012760600003753

Panwar, A., Khari, M., Misra, S., & Sugandh, U. (2023). Blockchain in Agriculture to Ensure Trust, Effectiveness, and Traceability from Farm Fields to Groceries. *Future Internet*, *15*(12), 404. DOI: 10.3390/fi15120404

Parker, L., Halter, V., Karliychuk, T., & Grundy, Q. (2019). How private is your mental health app data? An empirical study of mental health app privacy policies and practices. *International Journal of Law and Psychiatry*, *64*, 198–204. DOI: 10.1016/j.ijlp.2019.04.002 PMID: 31122630

Park, J., & Chang, H. (2022). Rethinking Korea's AI R&D ecosystem: From strategy to governance. *Asia-Pacific Journal of Innovation Policy, 7*(2), 144–160.

Patel, S., & Singh, D. (2019, July). Convolutional Neural Networks for Network Traffic Analysis. *IEEE Transactions on Information Forensics and Security, 14*(7), 1838–1847.

Patrick, H., van Niekerk, B., & Fields, Z. (2018). Developing Cybersecurity Resilience in the Provincial Government. In *Handbook of Research on Information and Cyber Security in the Fourth Industrial Revolution* (pp. 336–363). IGI Global. DOI: 10.4018/978-1-5225-4763-1.ch012

Pearson, S., & Benameur, A. (2010, November). Privacy, security and trust issues arising from cloud computing. In *2010 IEEE Second International Conference on Cloud Computing Technology and Science* (pp. 693-702). IEEE. DOI: 10.1109/CloudCom.2010.66

Pedreira, V., Barros, D., & Pinto, P. (2021). A review of attacks, vulnerabilities, and defenses in industry 4.0 with new challenges on data sovereignty ahead. *Sensors (Basel), 21*(15), 5189. DOI: 10.3390/s21155189 PMID: 34372425

Peng, L., Wang, N., Dvornek, N., Zhu, X., & Li, X. (2023). FedNI: Federated Graph Learning With Network Inpainting for Population-Based Disease Prediction. *IEEE Transactions on Medical Imaging, 42*(7), 2032–2043. DOI: 10.1109/TMI.2022.3188728 PMID: 35788451

Peterson, Z. N., Gondree, M., & Beverly, R. (2011). A position paper on data sovereignty: The importance of geolocating data in the cloud. In *3rd USENIX Workshop on Hot Topics in Cloud Computing (HotCloud 11).*

Pettenpohl, H., Spiekermann, M., & Both, J. R. (2022). International Data Spaces in a Nutshell.

Phillips, S. C., Taylor, S., Boniface, M., Modafferi, S., & Surridge, M. (2024). Automated Knowledge-Based Cybersecurity Risk Assessment of Cyber-Physical Systems. *IEEE Access : Practical Innovations, Open Solutions, 12*, 82482–82505. DOI: 10.1109/ACCESS.2024.3404264

Pocher, N., Zichichi, M., Merizzi, F., Shafiq, M. Z., & Ferretti, S. (2023). Detecting Anomalous Cryptocurrency Transactions: An AML/CFT Application of Machine Learning-based Forensics. *Electronic Markets, 33*(27), 1–17. https://doi.org/https://doi.org/10.1007/s12525-023-00654-3. DOI: 10.1007/s12525-023-00654-3

Pohle, J., & Thiel, T. (2020). Digital sovereignty. *Internet Policy Review, 9*(4). Advance online publication. DOI: 10.14763/2020.4.1532

Polatin-Reuben, D., & Wright, J. (2014). An internet with BRICS characteristics: Data sovereignty and the balkanisation of the internet. In *4th USENIX Workshop on Free and Open Communications on the Internet (FOCI 14).*

Pramanik, S., Pandey, D., Joardar, S., Niranjanamurthy, M., Pandey, B. K., & Kaur, J. (2023, October). An overview of IoT privacy and security in smart cities. In AIP Conference Proceedings (Vol. 2495, No. 1). AIP Publishing. DOI: 10.1063/5.0123511

Price, W. N.II, & Cohen, I. G. (2019). Privacy in the Age of Medical Big Data. *Nature Medicine*, *25*(1), 37–43. DOI: 10.1038/s41591-018-0272-7 PMID: 30617331

Qazi, E. U. H., Faheem, M. H., & Zia, T. (2023). Hdlnids: Hybrid deep-learning-based network intrusion detection system. *Applied Sciences (Basel, Switzerland)*, *13*(8), 4921. DOI: 10.3390/app13084921

Raghav, A., Singh, B., Raghav, R., & Edina, K. D. (2025). AI and Robotics in Smart City Governance: Ethical and Legal Pathways for Sustainable Urbanization. In Machine Learning and Robotics in Urban Planning and Management (pp. 1-24). IGI Global Scientific Publishing.

Raghavendra, R., Raja, K. B., & Busch, C. (2016). Detecting morphed face images. *2016 IEEE 8th International Conference on Biometrics Theory, Applications and Systems (BTAS)*, 1–7. DOI: 10.1109/BTAS.2016.7791169

Rahaman, M., Lin, C. Y., Pappachan, P., Gupta, B. B., & Hsu, C. H. (2024). Privacy-Centric AI and IoT Solutions for Smart Rural Farm Monitoring and Control. *Sensors (Basel)*, *24*(13), 4157. Advance online publication. DOI: 10.3390/s24134157 PMID: 39000936

Ramachandra, R., Venkatesh, S., Raja, K., & Busch, C. (2020). Detecting Face Morphing Attacks with Collaborative Representation of Steerable Features. In B. B. Chaudhuri, M. Nakagawa, P. Khanna, & S. Kumar (Eds.), *Proceedings of 3rd International Conference on Computer Vision and Image Processing* (pp. 255–265). Springer Singapore. DOI: 10.1007/978-981-32-9088-4_22

Ramesh, D., Santosh, T., Trivedi, M. C., & Le, C. H. (2024). Ensuring Digital Sovereignty in Cross-chain EHR Sharing: A Relay-as-a-Service Approach for Secure Healthcare Interoperability. In S. Misra, P. Kvalvik, K. M. Kjølerbakken, & R. Damasevicius (Eds.), *International Conference on Digital Sovereignty (ICDS) Procedia Computer Science* (Vol. 254, pp. 48–57). Elsevier B.V. DOI: 10.1016/j.procs.2025.02.063

Rao, P. M., & Deebak, B. D. (2023). Security and privacy issues in smart cities/industries: Technologies, applications, and challenges. *Journal of Ambient Intelligence and Humanized Computing*, *14*(8), 10517–10553. DOI: 10.1007/s12652-022-03707-1

Related Information Article 44. General Principle for Transfers, Pub. L. No. ISO 27701, GDPR training, consulting and DPO outsourcing 1 (2018).

Ren, H., Yue, Y., Zhou, C., Paffenroth, R. C., Li, Y., & Weiss, M. L. (2018). Robust variational autoencoders: generating noise-free images from corrupted images. Academic Press.

Rendón-Segador, F. J., Álvarez-García, J. A., & Varela-Vaca, A. J. (2023). Paying Attention to cyber-attacks: A multi-layer perceptron with self-attention mechanism. *Computers & Security*, *132*, 103318. DOI: 10.1016/j.cose.2023.103318

Rettore de Araujo Zanella, A., da Silva, E., & Pessoa Albini, L. C. (2020). Security challenges to smart agriculture: Current state, key issues, and future directions. *Array (New York, N.Y.)*, *8*, 100048. DOI: 10.1016/j.array.2020.100048

Rice, M. (2018). Estonia's digital embassies and the concept of sovereignty. *Journal of Baltic Studies*, *49*(4), 511–530.

Rivest, R. L., Adleman, L., & Dertouzos, M. L. (1978). On Data Banks and Privacy Homomorphisms. *Foundations on Secure Computation*, 169–179. https://people.csail.mit.edu/rivest/pubs/RAD78.pdf

Roberts, H., Cowls, J., Casolari, F., Morley, J., Taddeo, M., & Floridi, L. (2021). (Forthcoming). Safeguarding european values with digital sovereignty: An analysis of statements and policies. *Internet Policy Review*, *10*(3). Advance online publication. DOI: 10.14763/2021.3.1575

Roberts, H., Hine, E., & Floridi, L. (2021). Safeguarding European values with digital sovereignty. *Minds and Machines*, *31*(3), 405–417.

Rombach, R., Blattmann, A., Lorenz, D., Esser, P., & Ommer, B. (2022). High-resolution image synthesis with latent diffusion models. In *Proceedings of the IEEE/CVF conference on computer vision and pattern recognition* (pp. 10684-10695). IEEE.

Ross, A., Banerjee, S., & Chowdhury, A. (2020). Security in smart cities: A brief review of digital forensic schemes for biometric data. *Pattern Recognition Letters*, *138*, 346–354. DOI: 10.1016/j.patrec.2020.07.009

Sampson, F. (2021). Data Privacy and Security: Some Legal and Ethical Challenges. In Jahankhani, H., Kendzierskyj, S., & Akhgar, B. (Eds.), *Advanced Sciences and Technologies for Security Applications* (pp. 109–134). Springer., DOI: 10.1007/978-3-030-72120-6_4

Santhosh Kumar, S., Selvi, M., & Kannan, A. (2023). A comprehensive survey on machine learning-based intrusion detection systems for secure communication in internet of things. *Computational Intelligence and Neuroscience, 2023*(1), 8981988. DOI: 10.1155/2023/8981988

Sarabia-Jácome, D., Palau, C. E., Esteve, M., & Boronat, F. (2019). Seaport data space for improving logistic maritime operations. *IEEE Access : Practical Innovations, Open Solutions, 8*, 4372–4382. DOI: 10.1109/ACCESS.2019.2963283

Sarkar, E., Korshunov, P., Colbois, L., & Marcel, S. (2022). Are GAN-based morphs threatening face recognition? *ICASSP 2022-2022 IEEE International Conference on Acoustics, Speech and Signal Processing (ICASSP)*, 2959–2963.

Sarker, I. H. (2021). CyberLearning: Effectiveness analysis of machine learning security modeling to detect cyber-anomalies and multi-attacks. *Internet of Things : Engineering Cyber Physical Human Systems, 14*, 100393. DOI: 10.1016/j.iot.2021.100393

Saxena, D., & Cao, J. (2020). Generative Adversarial Networks (GANs). *ACM Computing Surveys, 54*(3), 1–42. DOI: 10.1145/3446374

Scardovi, C. (2017). Digital Transformation in Financial Services. In *Digital Transformation in Financial Services*. Springer International Publishing. DOI: 10.1007/978-3-319-66945-8

Schaberreiter, T., Wills, C., Quirchmayr, G., & Röning, J. (2017, September 10). Addressing complex problem situations in critical infrastructures using soft systems analysis: the CS-AWARE approach. *In* Westphall, C. M., Hof, H., Olmsted, A., Schauer, S., Latzenhofer, M., Abidin, A., & Yee, G. *(Eds.), SECURWARE 2017: The Eleventh International Conference on Emerging Security Information, Systems and Technologies (pp.* 99-105*). IARIA.*

Scheider, S., Lauf, F., & Geller, S. (2023a). Data sovereign humans and the information economy: towards design principles for human centric B2C data ecosystems.

Scheider, S., Lauf, F., Möller, F., & Otto, B. (2023). A reference system architecture with data sovereignty for human-centric data ecosystems. *Business & Information Systems Engineering, 65*(5), 577–595. DOI: 10.1007/s12599-023-00816-9

Scherhag, U., Kunze, J., Rathgeb, C., & Busch, C. (2020). Face morph detection for unknown morphing algorithms and image sources: A multi-scale block local binary pattern fusion approach. *IET Biometrics*, *9*(6), 278–289. DOI: 10.1049/iet-bmt.2019.0206

Scherhag, U., Rathgeb, C., & Busch, C. (2018a). Morph Deterction from Single Face Image: A Multi-Algorithm Fusion Approach. *Proceedings of the 2018 2nd International Conference on Biometric Engineering and Applications*, 6–12. DOI: 10.1145/3230820.3230822

Scherhag, U., Rathgeb, C., & Busch, C. (2018b). Performance variation of morphed face image detection algorithms across different datasets. *2018 International Workshop on Biometrics and Forensics (IWBF)*, 1–6. DOI: 10.1109/IWBF.2018.8401562

Schilling, L., & Uhlig, H. (2019). Some simple bitcoin economics. *Journal of Monetary Economics*, *106*, 16–26. DOI: 10.1016/j.jmoneco.2019.07.002

Schmidt, K., Munilla Garrido, G., Mühle, A., & Meinel, C. (2022, August). Mitigating sovereign data exchange challenges: A mapping to apply privacy-and authenticity-enhancing technologies. In *International Conference on Trust and Privacy in Digital Business* (pp. 50-65). Cham: Springer International Publishing. DOI: 10.1007/978-3-031-17926-6_4

Sedik, A., Tawalbeh, L. A., Hammad, M., Abd El-Latif, A. A., El-Banby, G. M., Khalaf, A. A., & Iliyasu, A. M. (2021). Deep learning modalities for biometric alteration detection in 5G networks-based secure smart cities. *IEEE Access : Practical Innovations, Open Solutions*, *9*, 94780–94788. DOI: 10.1109/ACCESS.2021.3088341

Seibold, C., Samek, W., Hilsmann, A., & Eisert, P. (2017). Detection of Face Morphing Attacks by Deep Learning. In Kraetzer, C., Shi, Y.-Q., Dittmann, J., & Kim, H. J. (Eds.), *Digital Forensics and Watermarking* (pp. 107–120). Springer International Publishing. DOI: 10.1007/978-3-319-64185-0_9

Seibold, C., Samek, W., Hilsmann, A., & Eisert, P. (2020). Accurate and robust neural networks for face morphing attack detection. *Journal of Information Security and Applications*, *53*, 102526. DOI: 10.1016/j.jisa.2020.102526

Senoo, E. E. K., Anggraini, L., Kumi, J. A., Karolina, L. B., Akansah, E., Sulyman, H. A., Mendonça, I., & Aritsugi, M. (2024). IoT Solutions with Artificial Intelligence Technologies for Precision Agriculture: Definitions, Applications, Challenges, and Opportunities. In *Electronics (Switzerland)* (Vol. 13, Issue 10). Multidisciplinary Digital Publishing Institute (MDPI). DOI: 10.3390/electronics13101894

Setianingsih, L. S., Pulungan, R., Putra, A. E., Wibowo, M. E., & Syarip, . (2021). Risk Assessment Methods for Cybersecurity in Nuclear Facilities: Compliance to Regulatory Requirements. *International Journal of Advanced Computer Science and Applications, 12*(9). Advance online publication. DOI: 10.14569/IJACSA.2021.0120979

Shafiullah, G. M., Oo, A. M. T., Ali, A. B. M. S., Wolfs, P., & Arif, M. T. (2013). *Renewable Energy Integration: Opportunities and Challenges* (pp. 45–76). DOI: 10.1007/978-1-4471-5210-1_3

Shanmugama, D., & Arumugamb, C. (2025). Effective Communication Compression Framework Using Federated Learning Privacy Model for Smart Grid. International Conference on Digital Sovereignty (ICDS). Elsevier ScienceDirect. *Procedia Computer Science, 254*, 164–170. DOI: 10.1016/j.procs.2025.02.075

Sharma, V., Mehta, S., Kukreja, V., & Aeri, M. (2023). Unravelling Peach Leaf Disease Severity: A Federated Learning CNN Perspective. *2023 2nd International Conference on Edge Computing and Applications (ICECAA)*, 976–982. DOI: 10.1109/ICECAA58104.2023.10212138

Sharma, K., & Shivandu, S. K. (2024). Integrating artificial intelligence and Internet of Things (IoT) for enhanced crop monitoring and management in precision agriculture. *Sensors International, 5*, 100292. DOI: 10.1016/j.sintl.2024.100292

Sheikh, H. (2021). European digital sovereignty. *Journal of European Integration, 43*(4), 495–510.

Shi, R., Wei, L., & Zhang, L. (2024). More Efficient and Verifiable Privacy-Preserving Aggregation Scheme for Internet of Things-Based Federated Learning. *Applied Sciences (Basel, Switzerland), 14*(13), 5361. DOI: 10.3390/app14135361

Shokri, R., & Shmatikov, V. (2015). Privacy-preserving deep learning. *Proceedings of the 22nd ACM SIGSAC Conference on Computer and Communications Security*, 1310–1321. https://doi.org/DOI: 10.1145/2810103.2813687

Shorten, C., & Khoshgoftaar, T. M. (2019). A survey on Image Data Augmentation for Deep Learning. *Journal of Big Data, 6*(1), 1–48. DOI: 10.1186/s40537-019-0197-0

Shorya, R., & Jagwani, P. (2024). Enhancing Digital Autonomy in Peer-to-Peer Energy Trading: A Blockchain and Predictive Analytics Approach. In S. Misra, P. Kvalvik, K. M. Kjølerbakken, & R. Damasevicius (Eds.), *International Conference on Digital Sovereignty, Procedia Computer Science* (Vol. 254, pp. 230–239). Elsevier B.V. DOI: 10.1016/j.procs.2025.02.082

Shuqin, D. (2020). A deep feature learning-based method for network traffic Outlier hunting. *Journal of Electronic and Information*, 695-703.

Silva De Freitas, E. (2020). Cryptocurrency Regulation in the EU AML Regime: the path towards effective harmonization? *2nd Crypto Asset Lab Conference - CAL2020*, 1–5. https://ssrn.com/abstract=4175341

Simpson, S. S., & Evens, J. (2024). Corporate environmental non-compliance and the effects of internal systems and sanctions. In *Research Handbook on Environmental Crimes and Criminal Enforcement* (pp. 36–67). Edward Elgar Publishing., DOI: 10.4337/9781035309511.00011

Singh, T. (2023, October). AI-Driven Surveillance Technologies and Human Rights: Balancing Security and Privacy. In International Conference on Smart Systems: Innovations in Computing (pp. 703-717). Singapore: Springer Nature Singapore.

Singh, P., Masud, M., Hossain, M. S., Kaur, A., Muhammad, G., & Ghoneim, A. (2022). Privacy-Preserving Serverless Computing Using Federated Learning for Smart Grids. *IEEE Transactions on Industrial Informatics*, *18*(11), 7843–7852. DOI: 10.1109/TII.2021.3126883

Soleymani, S., Chaudhary, B., Dabouei, A., Dawson, J., & Nasrabadi, N. M. (2021). Differential Morphed Face Detection Using Deep Siamese Networks. In Del Bimbo, A., Cucchiara, R., Sclaroff, S., Farinella, G. M., Mei, T., Bertini, M., Escalante, H. J., & Vezzani, R. (Eds.), *Pattern Recognition. ICPR International Workshops and Challenges* (pp. 560–572). Springer International Publishing., DOI: 10.1007/978-3-030-68780-9_44

Song, C., Ristenpart, T., & Shmatikov, V. (2017). Machine learning models that remember too much. *Proceedings of the 2017 ACM SIGSAC Conference on Computer and Communications Security*, 587–601. DOI: 10.1145/3133956.3134077

Song, J., Zhong, Q., Wang, W., Su, C., Tan, Z., & Liu, Y. (2021). FPDP: Flexible Privacy-Preserving Data Publishing Scheme for Smart Agriculture. *IEEE Sensors Journal*, *21*(16), 17430–17438. DOI: 10.1109/JSEN.2020.3017695

Soon, C. B., Rui, Y. T., & Chan, W. L. (2023). Digital trust and AI use in Singapore's public services. *Journal of Asian Public Policy*, *16*(1), 98–115.

Sowmya, T., & Anita, E. M. (2023). A comprehensive review of ai based intrusion detection system. *Measurement. Sensors*, *28*, 100827. DOI: 10.1016/j.measen.2023.100827

Spelman, F. (2022). *Predictive Analytics for Malware Detection in FinTech using Machine Learning Classification* [PhD Thesis, Dublin Business School]. https://esource.dbs.ie/bitstreams/87a6224b-fbea-4e25-9027-e39e0b4b1025/download

Stojanović, B., Božić, J., Hofer-Schmitz, K., Nahrgang, K., Weber, A., Badii, A., Sundaram, M., Jordan, E., & Runevic, J. (2021). Follow the trail: Machine learning for fraud detection in Fintech applications. *Sensors (Basel), 21*(5), 1594. DOI: 10.3390/s21051594 PMID: 33668773

Subbagari, S. (2024). Counter Measures to Combat Money Laundering in the New Digital Age. *Digital Threats : Research and Practice*, *5*(2), 1–13. DOI: 10.1145/3626826

Subeesh, A., & Mehta, C. R. (2021). Automation and digitization of agriculture using artificial intelligence and internet of things. *Artificial Intelligence in Agriculture, 5*, 278–291. https://doi.org/https://doi.org/10.1016/j.aiia.2021.11.004

Sun, Y., Zhang, J., Xiong, Y., & Zhu, G. (2014). Data security and privacy in cloud computing. *International Journal of Distributed Sensor Networks*, *10*(7), 190903. DOI: 10.1155/2014/190903

Su, Z., Wang, Y., Luan, T. H., Zhang, N., Li, F., Chen, T., & Cao, H. (2022). Secure and Efficient Federated Learning for Smart Grid With Edge-Cloud Collaboration. *IEEE Transactions on Industrial Informatics*, *18*(2), 1333–1344. DOI: 10.1109/TII.2021.3095506

Talukdar, J., Singh, T. P., & Barman, B. (2023). Supervised Learning. In *Artificial Intelligence in Healthcare Industry. Advanced Technologies and Societal Change* (pp. 51–86). Springer. DOI: 10.1007/978-981-99-3157-6_4

Tan, A., Yu, H., Cui, L., & Yang, Q. (2021b). Towards Personalized Federated Learning. *IEEE Transactions on Neural Networks and Learning Systems*. https://consensus.app/papers/towards-personalized-federated-learning-tan/8c8c3f64c7fc5a8e8a36e90e343b11e3

Tan, A., Yu, H., Cui, L., & Yang, Q. (2021a). Towards Personalized Federated Learning. *IEEE Transactions on Neural Networks and Learning Systems*, •••, 1–11. https://consensus.app/papers/towards-personalized-federated-learning-tan/8c8c3f64c7fc5a8e8a36e90e343b11e3 PMID: 35344498

Tan, C. (2020). Citizens go digital: Singapore's Smart Nation initiative. *Journal of Southeast Asian Studies*, *51*(2), 234–250.

Tan, C., Chi, M., & Lam, W. (2021). Analysis of digital sovereignty and identity. *Journal of Information Technology & Politics*, *18*(2), 123–138.

Tang, D., Qin, B., & Liu, T. (2015). *Document Modeling with Gated Recurrent Neural Network for Sentiment Classification*. Association for Computational Linguistics. http://ir.hit.edu.cn/

Tang, Y., Jia, R., Zhou, X., Li, Z., Jin, H., & Zhao, C. (2021). Federated Learning of User Mobility Anomaly Based on Graph Attention Networks. *2021 7th International Conference on Computer and Communications (ICCC)*, 1652–1658. DOI: 10.1109/ICCC54389.2021.9674388

Tan, K. L., Chi, C. H., & Lam, K. Y. (2023). Survey on digital sovereignty and identity: From digitization to digitalization. *ACM Computing Surveys*, *56*(3), 1–36. DOI: 10.1145/3616400

Taqafi, I., Maleh, Y., & Ouazzane, K. (2023). A Maturity Capability Framework for Security Operation Center. *EDPACS*, *67*(3), 21–38. DOI: 10.1080/07366981.2023.2159047

Taylor, S., Surridge, M., & Pickering, B. (2020). Regulatory Compliance Modelling Using Risk Management Techniques. SSRN *Electronic Journal*. DOI: 10.2139/ssrn.3716778

Technical Committee, I. J. 1/SC 27. (2022). ISO - ISO/IEC 27001:2022 - Information security, cybersecurity and privacy protection — Information security management systems — Requirements. *Iso/Iec*.

Teoh, T. T., Chiew, G., Franco, E. J., Ng, P. C., Benjamin, M. P., & Goh, Y. J. (2018). Anomaly detection in cyber security attacks on networks using MLP deep learning. *2018 International Conference on Smart Computing and Electronic Enterprise (ICSCEE)*, 1–5. https://ieeexplore.ieee.org/abstract/document/8538395/

Teoh, T. T., Zhang, Y., Nguwi, Y. Y., Elovici, Y., & Ng, W. L. (2017). Analyst intuition inspired high velocity big data analysis using PCA ranked fuzzy k-means clustering with multi-layer perceptron (MLP) to obviate cyber security risk. *2017 13th International Conference on Natural Computation, Fuzzy Systems and Knowledge Discovery (ICNC-FSKD)*, 1790–1793. https://ieeexplore.ieee.org/abstract/document/8393038/

Thakkar, A., & Lohiya, R. (2020). A review of the advancement in intrusion detection datasets. *Procedia Computer Science*, *167*, 636–645. DOI: 10.1016/j.procs.2020.03.330

Thakkar, A., & Lohiya, R. (2021). A review on machine learning and deep learning perspectives of ids for iot: Recent updates, security issues, and challenges. *Archives of Computational Methods in Engineering*, *28*(4), 3211–3243. DOI: 10.1007/s11831-020-09496-0

Thakkar, A., & Lohiya, R. (2023). A review on challenges and future research directions for machine learning-based intrusion detection system. *Archives of Computational Methods in Engineering*, *30*(7), 4245–4269. DOI: 10.1007/s11831-023-09943-8

Thomas, M., & Garcia, R. (2020, December). Comprehensive Evaluation Metrics for Anomaly Detection Systems. *IEEE Transactions on Network and Service Management*, *17*(4), 2232–2245.

Timmers, P. (2021). Ethics of AI and cybersecurity when sovereignty is at stake. *Minds and Machines*, *31*(3), 397–404.

TITH., D., & COLIN, J.-N. (2024). A Trust Policy Meta-Model for Trustworthy and Interoperability of Digital Identity Systems. In S. Misra, P. Kvalvik, K. M. Kjølerbakken, & R. Damasevicius (Eds.), *International Conference on Digital Sovereignty (ICDS), Procedia Computer Science* (Vol. 254, pp. 88–97). Elsevier B.V. DOI: 10.1016/j.procs.2025.02.067

Topol, E. J. (2019). *Deep Medicine: How Artificial Intelligence Can Make Healthcare Human Again*. Basic Books, March.

Tramèr, F., Zhang, F., Juels, A., Reiter, M. K., & Ristenpart, T. (2016). Stealing Machine Learning Models via Prediction APIs. *25th USENIX Security Symposium (USENIX Security 16)*, 601–618. https://www.usenix.org/conference/usenixsecurity16/technical-sessions/presentation/tramer

Treasury, H. M. (2019). *Economic crime plan 2019 to 2022*. Crown copyright. https://www.gov.uk/government/publications/economic-crime-plan-2019-to-2022

Truong, T. T. H., Tran, T. K., Nguyen, C. T., Phan, T. H. H., Nguyen, A. T., & Nguyen, N. S. (2024, August). An approach of generating synthetic data in military camouflaged object detection. In *2024 International Conference on Multimedia Analysis and Pattern Recognition (MAPR)* (pp. 1-6). IEEE.

Tseng, S.-P., Yeh, L.-Y., Wu, L.-C., & Tsai, P.-Y. (2022). Analyzing Federated Learning with Enhanced Privacy Preservation. *2022 23rd IEEE International Conference on Mobile Data Management (MDM)*, 446–451. DOI: 10.1109/MDM55031.2022.00097

Ueda, D., Kakinuma, T., Fujita, S., Kamagata, K., Fushimi, Y., Ito, R., Matsui, Y., Nozaki, T., Nakaura, T., Fujima, N., Tatsugami, F., Yanagawa, M., Hirata, K., Yamada, A., Tsuboyama, T., Kawamura, M., Fujioka, T., & Naganawa, S. (2023). Fairness of Artificial Intelligence in healthcare: Review and Recommendations. *Japanese Journal of Radiology*, *42*(1), 3–15. Advance online publication. DOI: 10.1007/s11604-023-01474-3 PMID: 37540463

Van Efferen, L., & Ali-Eldin, A. M. (2017). A multi-layer perceptron approach for flow-based anomaly detection. *2017 International Symposium on Networks, Computers and Communications (ISNCC)*, 1–6. https://ieeexplore.ieee.org/abstract/document/8072036/

Veličković, P., Cucurull, G., Casanova, A., Romero, A., Liò, P., & Bengio, Y. (2018). Graph Attention Networks. In International Conference on Learning Representations. In *International Conference on Learning Representations*. ICLR.

Velickovic, P., Cucurull, G., Casanova, A., Romero, A., Lio', P., & Bengio, Y. (2017). Graph Attention Networks. *ArXiv, abs/1710.10903*. DOI: 10.17863/CAM.48429

Venkatesh, S., Ramachandra, R., Raja, K., & Busch, C. (2020). Single Image Face Morphing Attack Detection Using Ensemble of Features. *2020 IEEE 23rd International Conference on Information Fusion (FUSION)*, 1–6. DOI: 10.23919/FUSION45008.2020.9190629

Vogel, B. (2022). Potentials and Limits of Public-Private Partnerships against Money Laundering and Terrorism Financing. *Eucrim*, *1/2022*, 52–60. DOI: 10.30709/eucrim-2022-002

Voigt, P., & von dem Bussche, A. (2024). *The EU General Data Protection Regulation (GDPR): A Practical Guide* (2nd ed.). Springer Nature Switzerland., DOI: 10.1007/978-3-031-62328-8

W3C (2018). ODRL vocabulary & expression 2.2. https://www.w3.org/TR/odrl-vocab/

Walskaar, I., Tran, M. C., & Catak, F. O. (2023). A Practical Implementation of Medical Privacy-Preserving Federated Learning Using Multi-Key Homomorphic Encryption and Flower Framework. *Cryptography*, *7*(4), 48. DOI: 10.3390/cryptography7040048

Walters, J. (2022). AI adoption in government and the risk of digital inequality. *Government Information Quarterly*, *39*(3), 101664.

Wandzik, L., Kaeding, G., & Garcia, R. V. (2018). Morphing Detection Using a General- Purpose Face Recognition System. *2018 26th European Signal Processing Conference (EUSIPCO)*, 1012–1016. DOI: 10.23919/EUSIPCO.2018.8553375

Wang, L., Cheng, Y., Xiang, A., Zhang, J., & Yang, H. (2024). Application of Natural Language Processing in Financial Risk Detection. *Financial Engineering and Risk Management, 7*(4), 1–10. https://doi.org/http://dx.doi.org/10.23977/ferm.2024.070401

Wang, C., Zhou, J., Zhang, Y., Wu, H., Zhao, C., Teng, G., & Li, J. (2022). A Plant Disease Recognition Method Based on Fusion of Images and Graph Structure Text. *Frontiers in Plant Science, 12*, 731688. Advance online publication. DOI: 10.3389/fpls.2021.731688 PMID: 35095941

Wang, H. (2023). How to understand China's approach to central bank digital currency? *Computer Law & Security Review, 50*, 1–7. DOI: 10.1016/j.clsr.2022.105788

Wang, H., Wang, Q., Ding, Y., Tang, S., & Wang, Y. (2024). Privacy-preserving federated learning based on partial low-quality data. *Journal of Cloud Computing (Heidelberg, Germany), 13*(1), 62. Advance online publication. DOI: 10.1186/s13677-024-00618-8

Wang, Q., Niu, H., & Xu, N. (2024). Where do data sovereignty security risks come from?-production perspective based on social reproduction. *Advances in Education. Humanities and Social Science Research, 11*, 133–133.

Wang, X., Wu, Y. C., Zhou, M., & Fu, H. (2024). Beyond surveillance: Privacy, ethics, and regulations in face recognition technology. *Frontiers in Big Data, 7*, 1337465. DOI: 10.3389/fdata.2024.1337465 PMID: 39027377

Weixiong Y., Kon L., Zahra S. S. T. and Zahra F. T. (2023). "Security and Privacy Concerns in Wireless Networks - A Survey". *communication, networking and broadcast technologies.* October 30, 2023

Wing, J. M. (2019). The Data Life Cycle. *Harvard Data Science Review, 1*(1). Advance online publication. DOI: 10.1162/99608f92.e26845b4

Wohlin, C., Mendes, E., Felizardo, K. R., & Kalinowski, M. (2020). Guidelines for the search strategy to update systematic literature reviews in software engineering. *Information and Software Technology, 127*, 106366. DOI: 10.1016/j.infsof.2020.106366

Wong, J., Henderson, T., & Ball, K. (2022). Data protection for the common good: Developing a framework for a data protection-focused data commons. *Data & Policy, 4*, e3. DOI: 10.1017/dap.2021.40

Woubie, A., Solomon, E., & Attieh, J. (2024). Maintaining Privacy in Face Recognition using Federated Learning Method. *IEEE Access : Practical Innovations, Open Solutions*, *12*, 39603–39613. DOI: 10.1109/ACCESS.2024.3373691

Wu, C., Wu, F., Cao, Y., Huang, Y., & Xie, X. (2021). *FedGNN: Federated Graph Neural Network for Privacy-Preserving Recommendation*. ArXiv., DOI: 10.1038/s41467-022-30714-9

Wuyts, K., Scandariato, R., & Joosen, W. (2014). *LIND (D) UN privacy threat tree catalog*. CW Reports.

Xiao, Y., Li, X., Li, T., Wang, R., Pang, Y., & Wang, G. (2024). A Distributed Generative Adversarial Network for Data Augmentation under Vertical Federated Learning. *IEEE Transactions on Big Data*, 1–12. DOI: 10.1109/TBDATA.2024.3375150

Yan, A., Hou, R., Yan, H., & Liu, X. (2023). Explanation-based data-free model extraction attacks. *World Wide Web (Bussum)*, *26*(5), 3081–3092. DOI: 10.1007/s11280-023-01150-6

Yang, Z., Shao, B., Xuan, B., Chang, E.-C., & Zhang, F. (2020). Defending model inversion and membership inference attacks via prediction purification. *arXiv Preprint arXiv:2005.03915.*

Yang, L., Elisa, N., & Eliot, N. (2019). Privacy and security aspects of E-government in smart cities. In *Smart Cities Cybersecurity and Privacy* (pp. 89–102). Elsevier. DOI: 10.1016/B978-0-12-815032-0.00007-X

Yoon, S. (2024). AI and ethical infrastructure in South Korea: Policy, practice, and promise. *Ethics and Society*, *10*(1), 55–72.

Žalik, K. R., & Žalik, M. (2023). A Review of Federated Learning in Agriculture. In *Sensors* (Vol. 23, Issue 23). Multidisciplinary Digital Publishing Institute (MDPI). DOI: 10.3390/s23239566

Zatarain, J. M. N. (2019). Smart cities and personal data: balancing innovation, technology and the law. Revista Direito, Estado e Sociedade, (54).

Zeng, G., Wei, H.-N., Lu, K.-D., Geng, G., & Weng, J. (2024). DACO-BD: Data Augmentation Combinatorial Optimization-Based Backdoor Defense in Deep Neural Networks for SAR Image Classification. *IEEE Transactions on Instrumentation and Measurement*, *73*, 1–13. DOI: 10.1109/TIM.2024.3436130

Zhang, X., Yang, F., Hu, Y., Tian, Z., Liu, W., Li, Y., & She, W. (2022). "RANet: Network intrusion detection with group-gating convolutional neural network". *Journal of Network and Computer Applications*, Volume 198-213, 2022, 103266. ISSN 1084-8045. Available online at: DOI: 10.1016/j.jnca.2021.103266

Zhang, H., Ramachandra, R., Raja, K., & Busch, C. (2024). Generalized Single-Image-Based Morphing Attack Detection Using Deep Representations from Vision Transformer. *2024 IEEE/CVF Conference on Computer Vision and Pattern Recognition Workshops (CVPRW)*, 1510–1518. DOI: 10.1109/CVPRW63382.2024.00158

Zhang, J., Li, C., Ye, J., & Qu, G. (2020). Privacy threats and protection in machine learning. *Proceedings of the 2020 on Great Lakes Symposium on VLSI*, 531–536. DOI: 10.1145/3386263.3407599

Zhang, K., Liu, Y., & Wang, S. (2019, May). LSTM Networks for Anomaly Detection in Network Traffic. *IEEE Journal on Selected Areas in Communications*, *37*(5), 1202–1212.

Zhang, K.-Y., Huang, A.-J., Tu, K., Li, M.-H., Zhang, C., Qi, W., Wu, Y.-D., & Yu, Y. (2024). Experimental Secure Multiparty Computation from Quantum Oblivious Transfer with Bit Commitment. *Quantum Physics*, 1–19. http://arxiv.org/abs/2411.04558

Zhang, X., Hu, M., Xia, J., Wei, T., Chen, M., & Hu, S. (2020). Efficient Federated Learning for Cloud-Based AIoT Applications. *IEEE Transactions on Computer-Aided Design of Integrated Circuits and Systems*, *40*(10), 2211–2223. https://consensus.app/papers/efficient-federated-learning-cloudbased-aiot-zhang/4d4a67d77d0b5407acff2ceff30da900

Zhang, Y., Jia, R., Pei, H., Wang, W., Li, B., & Song, D. (2020). The secret revealer: Generative model-inversion attacks against deep neural networks. *Proceedings of the IEEE/CVF Conference on Computer Vision and Pattern Recognition*, 253–261. DOI: 10.1109/CVPR42600.2020.00033

Zhou, J., Su, Z., Wang, Y., Pan, Y., Pan, Q., Liu, L., & Wu, J. (2024). Toward Privacy-Aware Efficient Federated Graph Attention Network in Smart Cloud. *2024 9th IEEE International Conference on Smart Cloud (SmartCloud)*, 19–24. DOI: 10.1109/SmartCloud62736.2024.00011

Zhou, M., Zheng, Y., Guan, Y., Peng, L., & Lu, R. (2021). Efficient and privacy-preserving range-max query in fog-based agricultural IoT. *Peer-to-Peer Networking and Applications*, *14*(4), 2156–2170. DOI: 10.1007/s12083-021-01179-2

Zhou, W., Xia, Z., Dou, P., Su, T., & Hu, H. (2023). Double Attention Based on Graph Attention Network for Image Multi-Label Classification. *ACM Transactions on Multimedia Computing Communications and Applications*, *19*(1), 1–23. DOI: 10.1145/3519030

Zhu, M., & Shang, J. (2022). Remote Monitoring and Management System of Intelligent Agriculture under the Internet of Things and Deep Learning. *Wireless Communications and Mobile Computing*, *2022*, 1–13. DOI: 10.1155/2022/1206677

Zieglmeier, V., & Pretschner, A. (2021). Trustworthy transparency by design. *arXiv preprint arXiv:2103.10769.*

Zinovieva, E., & Shitkov, S. (2023). Sovereignty as practice in digital age. In *Digital International Relations* (pp. 75–90). Springer. DOI: 10.1007/978-981-99-3467-6_5

Zrenner, J., Möller, F. O., Jung, C., Eitel, A., & Otto, B. (2019). Usage control architecture options for data sovereignty in business ecosystems. *Journal of Enterprise Information Management*, *32*(3), 477–495. DOI: 10.1108/JEIM-03-2018-0058

Zyskind, G., Nathan, O., & Pentland, A. S. (2015). Decentralizing Privacy: Using Blockchain to Protect Personal Data. *2015 IEEE Security and Privacy Workshops, (SPW)*, 180–184. DOI: 10.1109/SPW.2015.27

About the Contributors

Sanjay Misra, a distinguished Senior Member of IEEE and ACM Distinguished Lecturer(21-24), currently serves as a Senior Scientist at the Institute for Energy Technology (IFE) in Halden, Norway. Previously, he held positions within the Computer Science and Communication department at Østfold University College, also in Halden. Dr Misra holds a Ph.D. in Information and Knowledge Engineering (Software Engineering) from the University of Alcala, Spain, and an M.Tech. in Software Engineering from MLN National Institute of Technology, India. His expertise spans Applied Informatics, encompassing Software Engineering Applications, Cyber Security, Health Informatics, and Intelligent Systems utilizing AI and computational techniques. With an impressive publication record, including around 150 JCR/SCIE articles in prestigious journals such as Computers & Security and Engineering Applications of Artificial Intelligence, Dr. Misra consistently ranks among the top 2% of scientists globally, as recognized by Stanford University and 6th in the whole Norway(2024). He has received numerous awards for his outstanding contributions, including the 2014 IET Software Premium Award (UK). Dr Misra serves as Editor-in-chief and editor of multiple international journals, including the International Journal of Human Capital & Information Technology Professionals(EIC, IF. 1.9), Nature: Scientific Report((Impact Factor: 4.996), Elsevier: Alex. Engineering((Impact Factor: 6.8, Q1)), General chairs of several IEEE and Springer conferences and has edited numerous special issues and authored over 100 books and conference proceedings. A sought-after speaker, he has delivered over 100 keynotes and invited talks at prestigious conferences and institutes across more than 60 countries.

Petter Kvalvik is Head of Business Development and a senior scientist at the Institute for Energy Technology (IFE). He is responsible for the strategic research area on Digital Sovereignty at IFE, the My Digital City program, the test-before-invest services in the European AI Hub Nemonoor and the Norwegian FIWARE iHub. Petter has a background in security and safety critical systems, strategy and program management and applied computer science. He started his career at IFE in 1996 and has held various research, pharmaceutical operations, ICT and management positions.

Morgan Kjølerbakken is a physicist, computer scientist, and entrepreneur, with a passion for research, technology, and innovation. He is currently a department lead at Institute for Energy Technology where leads a team focused on data science and AI. In addition, Kjølerbakken is a dedicated educator and serves as an Associate Professor at the Department of Physics, University of Oslo. Dr. Kjølerbakken's research interests lie in various fields, including sensor technology, computational physics, audio, electronics, signal processing, and AI. He is fostering interdisciplinary collaborations and contributing to the development of innovative theories and methodologies. Beyond his academic pursuits, Dr. Kjølerbakken brings valuable experience from the industry, having funded and contributed to several successful startups, including; Squarehead Technology Elliptic labs, and Airmont.

Per-Arne JÃ¸rgensen is a senior researcher and cybersecurity specialist with more than two decades of experience in ICT, critical infrastructure protection, and cyber-physical systems. He holds a Masterâ€™s degree in Applied Computer Science with specialisations in Cyber-Physical Systems, Security Operations (SecOps), and IoT from Ã˜stfold University College. Throughout his career, Per-Arne has held a range of leadership and technical positions, including Head of the ICT Department, Head of the Security Operations Center (SOC), and Head of the Risk and Security Research Department. He has spearheaded the development of IFEâ€™s IT/OT SOC, designed and implemented secure database and data lake solutions for the OECD Halden Reactor Project, and the establishment of IFEs Cybersecurity Laboratory. His work sits at the crossroads of industrial control system security, advanced data management, and applied cyber resilience. Combining deep technical expertise with strategic leadership and an extensive collaborative network, Per-Arne is actively driving innovation in cybersecurity for critical infrastructures, with a particular focus on the convergence of IT/OT, FIWARE, and Data Spaces technologies.

***

Abereowo O. O. is a Lecturer in the Department of Information Systems at the Federal University of Technology, Akure where he mentors students by utilising his experience and knowledge. He is also currently undergoing his PhD in Computer Science in the Federal University of Technology, Akure with his research interest in machine learning, cybersecurity and data science.

Olawale Surajudeen Adebayo is a Computer and Cyber Security Consultant and enthusiastic. He Lecture Computer Science and Cyber Security at the Department of Cyber Security Science, School of Information and Communication Technology, Federal University of Technology Minna, Niger State, Nigeria and many other places. Presently an Associate Professor of Cyber Security at the of Cybersecurity, National Open University of Nigeria. Before then, he has been a teacher of Mathematics in some secondary schools. He earned his PhD in Computer Science from International Islamic University Malaysia in 2017. He also earned Bachelor of Technology in Mathematics and Computer science from Federal University of Technology, Minna, Nigeria in 2004 and was conferred with his MSc in Computer Science by the University of Ilorin, Kwara State, Nigeria in 2009. His current research themes include malware detection, information security, cryptology, and data mining security. He has published many academic papers in these research themes. He is a fellow of Classical Entrepreneur and member of Computer Professional Registration Council of Nigeria (CPN), Nigeria Computer Society (NCS), IEEE, Cyber Security Expert Association of Nigeria (CSEAN), Global Development Network, and International Association of Engineers (IAENG) among others. He is a reviewer of many local and international journals. He was an academic volunteer of Nigeria to Islamic University in Uganda between 2022 and 2024.

Oluwasefunmi Arogundade is a professor of software theory and a reviewer for journals and conferences. She is an experienced reviewer and researcher.

Ambrose Azeta is a Professor in the Department of Software Engineering, Faculty of Computing and Informatics, Namibia University of Science and Technology (NUST). He has Bachelor of Science (BSc), Master of Science (MSc) and PhD in Computer Science from University of Benin, University of Lagos and Covenant University Nigeria, respectively. His current research interests include Applied Software Engineering, Artificial Intelligence and Machine Learning. Prof. Azeta has several articles in Conferences, Journals and Books that are indexed in Google Scholar, Scopus and Web of Science. He has received several awards and supervised several postgraduates students at Masters and PhD.

Temitayo Elijah Balogun is a lecturer in the Information Systems Department at the Federal University of Technology, Akure. He holds a B.Tech, M.Tech, and is currently rounding up his PhD. in Computer Science from the same institution.

He is machine learning expert and web developer with a proven track record in developing effective web solutions. His research interests span across Data Science, Information Management, Open Computer Vision, And Web Development. Temitayo is passionate about research and currently serves as a co-researcher on a TETFUND NRF grant. He has received several scholarships and grants and has authored and co-authored numerous high-indexed publications. Temitayo is also committed to community impact volunteering with organizations such as DaVoicce and the Carrington Youth Fellowship Initiative. He has been involved with the Data Science Network, where he trained people in the fundamentals of machine learning. Temitayo is a dedicated professional with a strong desire to improve and positively impact lives.

Kimia Ghasemi has over a decade of experience in Urban Planning, I have built a strong foundation in diverse areas such as Urban Planning, Social Justice, Spatial equity and inequity, and Geographic Information Systems. I am currently involved in multiple ongoing research projects, addressing topics such as urban livability, spatial inequalities, and the correlation between urban sprawl factors and city spatial structure. My commitment to contributing valuable insights to the field of Urban Planning remains steadfast, driven by a passion for creating sustainable and equitable urban environments.

Maritta Heisel is a full professor for software engineering at the University of Duisburg-Essen, Germany. Her research interests include the development of dependable software, pattern- and component-based software development, software architecture, and software evolution. She is particularly interested in incorporating security considerations into software development processes and in integrating the development of safe and secure software. She co-authored more than 80 refereed publications, including monographs, book chapters, journals and conference papers. She is member of various program committees and served as reviewer for a number of journals and conferences. Morevover, she is a member of the European Workshop on Industrial Computer Systems Reliability, Safety and Security (EWICS).

Abhishek Kumar possess a master's degree in political science with grade 'O' and a first class graduation degree in B.A with political science, history and sociology as the core subject, apart from these he has completed his Bachelor's degree in Law (3 year course) from RTM Nagpur University and Master's degree in Constitutional and Administrative Law from RTM Nagpur University. He is currently pursuing PhD in international relations from Symbiosis Centre for Research and Innovation (SCRI) Symbiosis International (Deemed) University, Pune. Apart from Academics Abhishek Kumar Also has a teaching experience of 9 years.

Muhammad Bello Kusharki is a seasoned researcher specializing in artificial intelligence, data science, and software development, with a focus on advancing sustainable agricultural practices through innovative AI techniques. Currently, he is a Computer Science PhD student at Federal University of Lafia and he serves as Assistant Chief Programme Analyst at the National Defence College Nigeria, where he leads initiatives in data quality, software development, and technical leadership. He holds an MSc in Computer Science from Nile University of Nigeria, with published work addressing challenges in federated learning and mutation testing for Android applications. His PhD research on "FEDERATED AIoT FRAMEWORK FOR PRIVACY-PRESERVING AND SUSTAINABLE CROP DISEASE MANAGEMENT IN PRECISION AGRICULTURE" exemplifies his commitment to leveraging AI for sustainable solutions in agriculture. Muhammad is an active contributor to community projects and youth leadership as a member of Junior Chamber International (JCI) Nigeria, where he has held key roles in advancing the UN Sustainable Development Goals.

Mohamad Molaei Qelichi is an Assistant Professor at the Institute for Humanities and Cultural Studies. His research focuses on smart cities and land use planning using geospatial decision support systems.

Niloofar Moradhasel is an Assistant Professor at the Research Institute for Information and Communication Technology. Her research focuses on the digital economy, econometrics, and public-private partnerships.

Bilkisu Larai Muhammad-Bello is a distinguished Computer Scientist specializing in cloud computing, federated learning, and AI-driven applications in agriculture. Currently a Senior Lecturer and Postgraduate Program Coordinator at Nile University of Nigeria, she holds a PhD in Computer Science and Electrical Engineering from Kumamoto University, Japan. Her academic journey includes a Master's with Distinction from the University of Manchester and a First Class Bachelor's in Computer Science and Mathematics from Federal University of Technology Minna. With numerous peer-reviewed publications, Dr. Muhammad-Bello's work is widely recognized for advancing privacy-preserving technologies and sustainable digital solutions.

Abiodun Mustapha is a lecturer and researcher at Anchor University with vast experience in software engineering, artificial intelligence, and information systems. He has published in several journals and conference proceedings.

Mary Ogbuka is a PhD candidate at Imperial College London focused on Multimodal AI, Natural language process and Computer Vision

Nwaocha, Vivian Ogochukwu is an Associate Professor at National Open University of Nigeria (NOUN), my area of research interest includes Cybersecurity and artificial intelligence. Dr Nwaocha has several articles in Conferences, Journals and Books that are indexed in Google Scholar, Scopus and Web of Science. He has received several awards and supervised several postgraduates students at Masters and PhD.

Temitope Ogunbiyi holds a PhD in computer science with vast knowledge in software engineering. She is a researcher and academic lecturer in Nigeria.

P. K. Olotu is a lecturer and researcher whose research interest spans across Intelligent Information Systems, Deep Learning in AGriculture, eCommerce Systems and Blockchain technology

Patric Omote, a IT professional from the Department of CSIS, Covenant University, Ota Nigeria. My research interest are in Artificial Intelligence, Machine Learning, Cybersecurity

Karun Sanjaya is an Assistant Professor at Symbiosis Law School, Nagpur and a Research Scholar at VIT School of Law, Vellore Institute of Technology, Chennai, India. He specialises in the area of Intellectual Property Laws. He is a recipient of many awards, including the prestigious Justice V.R. Krishna Iyer Memorial Merit Awards in the years 2019 and 2022. He has published over sixty research items and is a keen researcher in diverse areas of law, including intellectual property law.

Klaudia Szabelka is a dual PhD researcher in International Law and Cybersecurity at the University of Glasgow, and in Water Justice and Political Ecology at Glasgow Caledonian University. With a multidisciplinary background as a lawyer, political scientist, and economist, Klaudia has studied and conducted research in seven countries. Their work focuses on global governance, justice, and the complex challenges emerging at the intersections of law, environment, and technology.

Index

A

B

C

D

E

F

G

H

I

L

T

U

V

www.ingramcontent.com/pod-product-compliance
Lightning Source LLC
LaVergne TN
LVHW062329300926
849161LV00007B/1625